blues with a feeling

the Little Walter story

Tony Glover,
Scott Dirks,
& Ward Gaines

ROUTLEDGE
NEW YORK AND LONDON

Published in 2002 by
Routledge
29 West 35th Street
New York, NY 10001

Published in Great Britain by
Routledge
11 New Fetter Lane
London EC4P 4EE

Routledge is an imprint of Taylor & Francis Group.

Printed on acid-free, 250-year-life paper.
Manufactured in the United States of America.
Design and typography: Jack Donner
10 9 8 7 6 5 4 3 2 1

Cataloging-in-Publication Data is available from the Library of the Congress.

ISBN 0–415–93710–8 (hb)
ISBN 0–415–93711–6 (pb)

contents

acknowledgments

This book has been the result of many people's contributions and efforts. The following gave generously of their time and memories to help paint a picture of the elusive subject: Joyce DeShay Anderson, Billy Boy Arnold, Latelle Barton, Carey Bell, Elvin Bishop, John Broven, Rosa (Jacobs) Brown, Joe Lee Bush, Marshall Chess, Francis Clay, Norman Dayron, James DeShay, Marion (Jacobs) Diaz Reacco, Gary Duncan, Honeyboy Edwards, David Freiberg, Fred Glaser, John Goddard, Nick Gravenites, Henry Gray, Bob Hall, Bernie Hayes, Gabriel Hearns, Waver (Glascock) Humphries, Mark Kazinoff, Bob Koester, Sam Lay (who graciously did it again when the tape machine failed), Sam Leviege, Jim Lombardi, Lillian (Jacobs) Marshall, Pops McFarlane, Charlie Musslewhite, Dave Myers, Bobby Parker, Ron Polte, Mark Power, Jimmie Lee Robinson, Mattie Rollins, Jessie Mae (Leviege) Sampson, Paul Shapiro, Hugh Smith, Walter "Guitar Red" Smith, Abu Talib (Freddie Robinson), Marguerite (Glascock) Wallace, Bill Warren, Frank Weston, Sylvia (Glascock) Williams, Armilee Williams, Jody Williams, and Val Wilmer.

Several researchers and authors kindly shared unpublished interviews from their files: Bob Corritore (Henry Gray, Luther Tucker); Steve Cushing, excerpts from his radio interviews (Uncle Johnny Williams, Robert Jr. Lockwood, Willie Smith, John Brim); Robert Gordon (check out his biography, "Can't Be Satisfied: The Life and Times of Muddy Waters"); Paul Oliver, (Dave Myers, James Cotton); Bill Greensmith (Dave Myers); and Karen Hanson (Bobby Rush).

Over the years, a number of people furnished xeroxes, provided research assistance, shared photos, tapes, and contact information, and did translations. This work would not have been as complete without their valuable aid. Special thanks to: Mary Katherine Aldin, Alan Balfour, Tom Ball, Scott Baretta, Anthony J. "Tony C" Cabanellas, Randy Chortkoff, Nadine Cohodas, Dennis and Michelle DeShay, Rick Estrin, Bruce Ewan, Les Fancourt, Kim Field, Joe Filisko, Ray Flerlage, Walter Glenn, Bill Greensmith, Steve Guyger, Steve Jacobs, Lex Janssen, Breton Littlehales, Bill McCormick, Andy McKaie, Bob Margolin, Lillian Marshall, Mark Naftalin, Justin O'Brien, Paul Oscher, Jim O'Neal, Bert Van Oortmarssen, Eric Peltonimi, Robert Palinic, Victor Perlin, Jerry Portnoy, Tom Principato, Robert Pruter, Mattie Rollins, Jay B. Ross and Associates, director of Little Walter rights of publicity, Mike Rowe, Dick Shurman, Willie Smith, William Strauss, Dave Waldman, Charles Walton, Dave Williams, and Winslow Yerka.

Lastly, thanks to Richard Carlin, our editor at Routledge for his dogged determination to keep the primary focus on Little Walter. His sharp eye and sharper pencils helped lash our thoughts into their final form. It was a pleasure debating the worth of words with him.

—The Authors

Personal appreciations

Thanks to Kevin Loucks for supplying functional PCs when previous machines crashed and burned; Pete Lee, of KFAI-FM Minneapolis-St. Paul for tracking down Walter's jazz and root influences and sources, loaning tapes and vinyl, as well as offering suggestions on the ms; Peter Guralnick for his wise and detailed business counsel and connections to sources; and most of all to my wife Cyd Nadler, for suggesting the project in the first place, then nurturing it, reading and editing the preliminary drafts, and general patience above and beyond the wildest hopes a writer could muster.

—Tony Glover

Thanks to my wife Michelle and daughter Katie, for unwavering encouragement, understanding and patience, and to everyone who offered help and direction along the way.

—Scott Dirks

Thanks to Alicia Grimes, who willingly put up with almost four continuous years of my research and writing about Little Walter—for constant inspiration, companionship and good counsel. Thanks to Nadine Cohodas, Jan Mark Wolkin, and Tom Ellis III, who as writers and as friends have continually supported and aided my research efforts. Thanks to Breton Littlehales for innumerable services to this project, and to William Strauss, Charlie Sayles, Bruce Ewan, Pierre Beauregard, and Anthony Cabanellas for their moral support, advice, and assistance.

—Ward Gaines

Thanks to the following book publishers:

Billboard Books, an imprint of Watson-Guptill Publications, New York for excerpt from "All The Rage" by Ian McLagan. © Ian MacLagan, 2000. Used by permission.

Chicago Review Press for excerpts from "The World Don't Owe Me Nothing" by David Honeyboy Edwards © 1997 by David Edwards, Janis Martinson and Michael Robert Frank. Used by permission of Chicago Review Press Incorporated.

Thanks to the following music publishers for allowing us to quote from the following songs:

"Black Gal" by John Lee Williamson © Berwick Music Corp. Used by permission.

"Can't Hold Out Much Longer" by Walter Jacobs © 1970 Arc Music Corporation. Used By Permission. All Rights Reserved. International Copyright Secured.

"You're So Fine" by Walter Jacobs © 1953 (Renewed) Arc Music Corporation. Used By Permission. All Rights Reserved. International Copyright Secured.

"Come Back Baby" by Walter Jacobs © 1995 Arc Music Corporation. Used By Permission. All Rights Reserved. International Copyright Secured.

"Last Night" by Walter Jacobs © 1954 (Renewed) Arc Music Corporation. Used By Permission. All Rights Reserved. International Copyright Secured.

"You Better Watch Yourself" by Walter Jacobs © 1959 (Renewed) Arc Music Corporation. Used By Permission. All Rights Reserved. International Copyright Secured.

"Can't Stop Lovin' You" by Walter Jacobs © 1995 Arc Music Corporation. Used By Permission. All Rights Reserved. International Copyright Secured.

"Just A Feeling" by Walter Jacobs © 1956 (Renewed) Arc Music Corporation. Used By Permission. All Rights Reserved. International Copyright Secured.

"One of these Mornings" by Walter Jacobs © 1995 Arc Music Corporation. Used By Permission. All Rights Reserved. International Copyright Secured.

"Blue and Lonesome" by Walter Jacobs © 1969 Arc Music Corporation. Used By Permission. All Rights Reserved. International Copyright Secured.

"Break It Up" by Walter Jacobs © 1995 Arc Music Corporation. Used By Permission. All Rights Reserved. International Copyright Secured.

"Everything Gonnna Be Alright" by Walter Jacobs © 1959 Arc Music Corporation. Used By Permission. All Rights Reserved. International Copyright Secured.

"I Love You So (Oh Baby)" by Walter Jacobs and Willie Dixon © 1965 (Renewed) Arc Music Corporation. Used By Permission. All Rights Reserved. International Copyright Secured.

"Boom Boom Out Go the Lights" by Stanley Lewis © 1957 (Renewed) Arc Music Corporation. Used By Permission. All Rights Reserved. International Copyright Secured.

"What Have I Done" by James Lane © 1997 Arc Music Corporation Used By Permission. All Rights Reserved. International Copyright Secured.

"It's Too Late Brother" by Al Duncan © 1956 (Renewed) Arc Music Corporation. Used By Permission. All Rights Reserved. International Copyright Secured.

"Be Careful What You Do a/k/a Be Careful" by John Brim © 1968 Arc Music Corporation. Used By Permission. All Rights Reserved. International Copyright Secured.

"Who" by Bernard Roth © 1957 (Renewed) Sunflower Music, Inc. Used By Permission. All Rights Reserved. International Copyright Secured.

"Good Evening Everybody" by Willie Williamson © 1976 Sunflower Music, Inc. Used By Permission. All Rights Reserved. International Copyright Secured.

"Too Late" © 1955, ® 1983.

"I'm Ready" © 1954, ® 1982.

To say that Little Walter Jacobs was to harmonica blues what Charlie Parker was to jazz saxophone, what Jimi Hendrix was to rock guitar, or what Frank Sinatra was to pop vocals is no exaggeration—in fact, it could actually be an understatement. Not only did he set the standard by which all who followed would be measured, he was responsible for creating much of the musical language that would be used by those who chose to take up the instrument in his wake. Almost a half-century after his greatest achievements, it's difficult at times to gauge his influence: not because you can't find it, but because it's hard to find anything related to both blues and harmonica that *isn't* influenced by him. It's so pervasive that it simply seems like it was always there.

But it wasn't always there. Whenever you hear a wailing, bluesy harmonica in a McDonald's commercial, a movie soundtrack, on a concert stage, or at your local blues joint, you're hearing a direct link to Little Walter's legacy. There are schools of post-Walter harp players who have added shading to the picture, but scratch any part of the surface of modern blues harmonica, and you'll see pieces of Little Walter's musical palette directly underneath. It's no secret that those who are thought of as the greatest living blues harmonica players today all point directly to Little Walter as the wellspring of their instrument. The only route out from under the blanket of his influence is to go back and study the players and the styles that existed before Walter revolutionized the instrument. Little Walter Jacobs is inarguably the single most influential artist in the history of blues harmonica.

What made his music so special? Many point to his pioneering use of amplification, coupling his small 10-hole Hohner Marine Band harmonicas with the cheap microphones and easily overloaded public address amplifiers common in blues clubs when he began playing professionally in the 1940s. This combination opened an entirely new spectrum of sounds that could be coaxed from the harmonica, allowing everything from sweetly resonating tones to razor sharp howls to explosive, thundering chords: sounds that had quite literally never existed before, and were certainly not associated with a cheap instrument often thought of as a child's toy. On one level, the comparison to Hendrix fits especially well here. Both men not only incorporated into their music the distortion and harsh tones produced when pushing their amplifiers beyond their intended limits, they did so intentionally, in ways that were new, different, and most importantly, musical. But Little Walter was not the first harmonica player to amplify his instrument. And even if he'd never done so, his musical genius would still have shone through, as his many unamplified recordings amply prove. His true genius was not tied to a *technical* advance, it was in the way he ignored, and ultimately erased, the *musical* limitations that his humble instrument was thought to possess.

The harmonica was a relatively new invention, less than a hundred years old when he first picked it up. It was designed as an inexpensive (and many thought inexpressive) portable mouth organ, and was used mainly to provide basic background accompaniments in folk music in Europe and the U.S. beginning in the mid-19th century. In the early years of blues, there were certainly players who were capable of producing virtuoso performances, but the essential use of the instrument was locked into a rather small range of styles. Limited by its volume and tonal range, it was commonly used as a background instrument. Most of the best players in the blues field either specialized in solo pieces that used the instrument to imitate sounds commonly heard in the country—trains, barnyard animals, etc.—or used it to echo the melody or vocal line of the song being performed. Even among the very best players, a shared trait was the reliance on playing and repeating seldom-changing one- or two-bar patterns, which were established as themes at the beginning of a song and played with little variation throughout the piece. This, at the time, was the language of blues harmonica.

Influenced as much by horn players as by other harmonica players, and as much by jazz as he was by blues, Little Walter freed the harmonica of these customary, if self-imposed, restrictions for the first time. Where other harp blowers played "on the beat," Walter's music possessed an unmistakable "behind the beat" phrasing that made the harp swing like never before. Where other harpmen created phrases that began and ended in neat, compact, one- or two-bar phrases, each beginning and ending on the beat and tied tightly to the basic twelve-bar blues structure, Walter's phrases often began off the beat, where they'd have maximum musical impact. Freed from the strictures of playing the harmonica as a rhythm instrument, he would reel off melodies and figures of irregular lengths and accents, then bring them back home for unpredictable yet perfect resolutions that sounded as if they'd been worked out months in advance. He'd change time signatures or the accent of the beat in the middle of a solo, in the middle of a phrase, or even in the middle of a note, toying with the beat, seeming to sabotage his own improvisations with a musical left turn down an apparently dead-end alley, then at the end of the phrase break through the wall and into the sunlight again in a way that made it clear that the entire run was part of his plan from the beginning. Other harp players would be left wondering, "How in the HELL did he do that?"; casual listeners just grooved on the undeniable swing of it all, and everyone knew they'd never heard anyone play the harp that way before. Little Walter set the harmonica free, granting it equal footing with every blues guitarist, horn player, or pianist in the land. He did it with brash confidence, unfettered creativity, and groundbreaking style. And, once he'd opened the door, he led the way for a slew of other great players who'd go on to stake their own claims in blues history. Of those influenced by him firsthand, only a few remain today, but Junior Wells, James Cotton, George "Harmonica" Smith, Carey Bell, and countless others all acknowledged his preeminence.

Walter accomplished all of this by the time he'd reached his mid-20s. His relentless creativity and tireless drive propelled him to the top of the national R&B music charts, with 14 Top-10 hits, including two that reached #1, a feat never accomplished by Muddy Waters, Howlin' Wolf, or Sonny Boy Williamson, his successful blues label mates at Chess and Checker Records. He was the first Chicago blues artist to play New York's famed Apollo Theater. He toured the country as part of Alan Freed's legendary Rock & Roll package tours, and toured Europe twice. B. B. King and Ray Charles would come out and sit in with his band in Chicago. He was one of the primary architects of the classic Chicago Blues band sound. His talents as a session player were used to enhance dozens of records by other blues artists over the course of his career.

So why, nearly a quarter-century after his tragic death at the age of 37, did he still lay in an unmarked grave in the "budget" section of a Chicago-area cemetery? Why are only the most basic facts of his life known, even to the most curious blues fans? The answers, if there are any to be found, are in the way that he lived his life. The counterbalance to his audacious creativity and ambition was an essentially rootless existence permeated with trouble and violence. These themes, of course, were not uncommon among black musicians of his generation, but the degrees to which they marked Walter's life were. The highs may have been higher, but the lows—which so often are the price paid for the peaks—were deeper and more profound. His struggle to escape from his deep personal valleys and leave them behind was undoubtedly a prime driving force behind his creative genius. In Walter's case, the freedom of having nothing to lose not only swung open the door to his creativity, it ripped it off the hinges. At the same time, his success was inexorably bound to the difficulties of his life; he would not have striven so hard for success had he not known its absence so intimately, yet knowing his own weaknesses and failures so well meant that he could never completely let them go. The result was a complex man who could be warm and giving at one moment, mean and distrustful the next, outrageously outgoing in his music yet intensely private with everything else (even family members and those closest to him echo the sentiment that "he wasn't much for small talk"). He openly praised some of his musical elders but jealously berated and discouraged anyone who he considered even a distant competitor. In his youth he was older than his years; in his adulthood he sometimes acted like a spoiled child; and in the last decade of his life, he often presented a tired, bitter, and angry front, rather than wearing the mantle of elder statesman that he'd earned.

These many faces and facets of his personality have kept any clear, complete pictures of Little Walter, the man, from emerging. Many of those closest to him sought to protect the positive aspects of his legacy by concealing the distasteful, which has meant that many details of his difficult early years and life outside of his music never came to light. At the same time, the years have taken away many of those who were with him when he enjoyed his greatest successes, so in-depth accounts of the good times have become even scarcer. Consequently, much of what has been known about his life has come from those who first encountered him only after his long final decline had already commenced, and the result is that we have been left with a sad, one-dimensional picture that ends with the cheap, unmarked grave.

But the notion that Little Walter was simply a gifted loser who enjoyed a brief shining moment of glory couldn't be further from the truth. The Little Walter story may be marked by tragedy as it moves towards its inevitable ending, but it is also the story of towering triumph over seemingly incredible odds, and of the joy of pure, unrestrained genius flowering to its fullest potential. It's the story of an unlikely individual finding a freedom in his music that he may never have found in his life. Ultimately, Little Walter's music, although he may never have taken the time to think about it this way, was a finely honed wedge that he used to successfully crack open the barriers of race, culture, and even time. This is his story.

1 *night train*

Louisiana 1920–43

The true circumstances of Little Walter's early life—of his birth, his family, and his upbringing—are cloaked in deep layers of myth and thick mists of time, more than for any other blues musician who reached his level of fame and prominence in the second half of the 20th century. Details and hard facts seem slippery shape-shifters that vary with each telling—and teller—and pervasive auras of southern-gothic darkness and secrets untold underlie all.

Still, some unassailable facts have been established. He was born in Marksville, Louisiana, some 140 miles north and west of New Orleans in east central Louisiana, in Avoyelles Parish, along the northern edge of an area known as "Cajun country." Marksville is about 30 miles from the Mississippi River, and within easy driving distance, even in the early days, of the delta area that spawned so many blues greats. There's very little to differentiate this part of the countryside from that of Mississippi to the east, other than the Cajun and Creole influence most evident in the French names borne by so many streets, rivers, lakes, and other geographic features. The town itself marks the approximate northern apex of a triangle that extends south to encompass the Louisiana Gulf-Coast and everything in between, thus defining the boundaries of Cajun influence in Louisiana.

The nearest "big city" is Alexandria, about 30 miles to the north, in an area now touted by the local tourist board as "The Crossroads," and also advertised as a part of the state where "you'll find the hills and bayous, the prairie and the rich Red River Delta, each with its own history and traditions," as well as "opportunities for fishing, hunting and camping." Conspicuously absent from the tourist board literature—at least from the perspective of the music fan—is any reference to Little Walter, the area's most famous blues son, or to the area's Cajun and Creole musical traditions.

The area is also mentioned as the locale for an early traditional "devil at the crossroads" story—the legendary pact wherein a musician reputedly gains his musical prowess by making a deal with the devil. Writer Michael Tisserand quotes Mary Thomas, who grew up around Lake Charles:

There was a four corner road out there in Marksville, and a man told my daddy, if you come here and you wait for twelve o'clock with a black cat, it was selling your soul to the devil. . .He went and there at twelve o'clock stood the tallest man he had ever seen in his life, with red, red eyes—and every time his mouth opened all he could see was red. And he didn't ask him anything—he just told him "Play a waltz." Five minutes later, he was gone, and that cat had disappeared . . . And the next morning when he started up, he played the accordion, the violin, the harmonica, guitar, bass guitar. Anything he put his hands on[,] he could play . . .

Although today it's a small city with a population nearing 6000, in the 1920s Marksville was a "one horse town," consisting of a center square and a small five- or six-block downtown area that catered mostly to the needs of the surrounding farms and the people who worked them. As in many rural towns in this part of Louisiana, white "Cajuns" (descendants of the Acadians who migrated south from Nova Scotia in the early 1800s) have lived side-by-side with mixed-race "Creoles" (descendants of Black slaves, many from the West Indies) for generations. They've shared the same French-based Creole patois, the same Roman Catholic religion, the same food, the same music, and they have celebrated the same holidays. It wasn't uncommon for them to sometimes even share the same lineage, if one looks back past the layers of southern respectability to the heritage of the original Louisiana Creole culture of the 18th century. There was a long-observed (although seldom spoken-of-in-polite-company tradition) of the white man with his secretive "left-handed marriage" to a black or mixed race mistress, which often lasted throughout his lifetime. This came originally out of a cultural acceptance and even respect given a white man of a higher social status keeping and supporting an "octoroon" mistress in "French" Louisiana despite the legal strictures of the day. Mulattos became part of an "elite" freeman class among other blacks, called "gens libre de couleur." Out of this heritage, some of their descendants today still retain a bit of this Creole "snobbery." Author Nick Spitzer points out that both Creoles and Cajuns spoke a mixed and broad French Creole, "using French words within a Creole grammar that came from a variety of African tongues, which probably arose in the plantations of the West Indies." Spitzer writes, "To be of mixed blood or mulatto carried greater social status than pure African ancestry. The term Creole may have come from persons claiming their European ancestry, and from an attempt to distinguish descendants of French culture from the English-speaking Americans." However, in the mid-19th century, the term "Creole" commonly meant "a person of French or Spanish ancestry, who may or may not be of mixed blood."

Early in 1920, census takers made the rounds down the lanes of Marksville, and on January 30th of that year, they visited the farm of Louis Leviege on Duprines Road. Among those the officials registered there that day were the parents-to-be of the man who would change forever the role of the harmonica in blues music. At the time, Little Walter's grandparents, Louis, 42, and his 36-year-old, blue-eyed wife Canelia, had eight children living on the farm that he was still working to pay off. Both of Louis's parents had been born in Louisiana; his father was said to be "negro and Indian, came from New Orleans," according to Walter's older sister Lillian, while his mother was white. Canelia's mother "came from France and was all French." Both were listed as being

English speakers, able to read and write, although Louis report communicating in Creole, speaking English only when visitors can.

In 1920, the eight Leviege children ranged in age from 2 1/2 to 1, daughters and three sons (see chapter appendix). Also enumerated in that day was a boarder, 22-year-old Adam (better known as Bruce) Jacobs, erate, and a "farm laborer." Adam was darker but shared some of the same fac. atures his future son would inherit: high cheekbones and narrow chin, but with a thinner face that matched his rather slight build.

It probably came as a surprise to no one that Adam would kindle a romantic connection with one of his boss's daughters. At any rate, it's unlikely that Adam Jacobs was there because he couldn't find anywhere else to stay in Marksville: he had family throughout the area. In reality, in those days Marksville could almost have been called "Jacobsville": the 1920 census shows some 24 separate Jacobs households, mostly "farmers" or "laborers," but also including a Reverend Wallace Jacobs, and his seven sons. Many of the Jacobs were loosely related (some referring to themselves using the Creole pronunciation "Yocko"), but there was also another group that also bore the name "Jacobs" that claimed ancestral roots in Jamaica.

A couple of days after visiting the Louis Leviege household, the census takers recorded Adam's parents living in one of the two main sections where Jacobs congregated along Island Road, not far from Choctaw Bayou and about 5 miles west of town. Like the Levieges, 59-year-old Joseph Jacobs and his 25-year-old second wife Elizabeth also worked a mortgaged farm, and lived there with six children (see chapter appendix). There were also at least three other brothers and sisters of Adam Jacobs living in the vicinity in their own homes, all listed as being in their early to mid-20s.

But there were a couple of things the census takers definitely weren't informed about. According to records found on file in Avoyelles Parish, on February 22, 1919, patriarch Louis and his boarder Adam had gone to the courthouse and applied for a marriage license between Adam and Louis's second oldest daughter, Cecille. The men filled out the regular forms including one that bonded Adam (as principal) and Louis (as security) to pay $100 to the governor of Louisiana. This was apparently a form of breech-of-promise insurance, because the form continued: " . . . the condition of the above obligation is such that if there should be no legal impediments to this alliance then said obligation to be null and void." A license was duly issued for the marriage of the 22-year-old Adam and 16-year-old Cecille. Five days later the wedding took place, officiated over by a Catholic priest and attended by a couple of Louis's nephews and two other witnesses.

But clearly Adam had a roving eye; the second item omitted in the census report was that about nine months after the wedding, in November of 1919, a daughter, Lillian, was born to Adam—and his wife's older sister, Beatrice. Beatrice was a slender but busty young woman with thick wavy hair, coffee-with-cream complexion, and high, wide cheekbones that tapered down to a narrow chin, all of which evidenced her French Creole roots. It's easy to imagine that she might have been considered quite a catch for any young suitor—and just as easy to see where Walter got his fine-featured good looks.

Was the marriage of Adam and Cecille already over when the census takers came around a couple of months after Lillian's birth? Or was it just that the family considered the tangled relationships private family business, and not the government's affair? It's hard to say, but as one of the younger relatives later put it, "I knew something happened; they kept great secrets as well as they could." Lillian was the first of three children Adam and Beatrice would have together over the next decade, despite an apparently continuing, on-and-off relationship between Adam and Cecille. A few years later, on Christmas Eve (c. 1926) along came John; "He looked like my mother, brown-skinned, had curly hair like her," Lillian said. Sometime around the turn of the decade, Adam and Beatrice had a final falling out, probably a result of the infidelities in which he reportedly engaged throughout his life. (It was whispered that he had eyes for the mother-in-law as well, and some suggested that he was "trying to go through the whole family.") Whatever the reasons for the split, daughter Beatrice was again pregnant and on her own. The rather strict Levieges considered her a compromised woman.

Louis Leviege and his wife eventually had three more children; Samuel was born a month after the enumerators came through, then younger sister Rita, and finally Carlton, born around 1930. Sam remembered his father as " . . . a beautiful dad, maybe has a first grade education, but [he] was a family man, loved his family and was a good provider." Under his hard work, the farm grew to some 40 or 50 acres, including some 25 acres of swamp land. The main crop was cotton. "As far as you could see was cotton, nothing else to raise but cotton," Sam said. "And we had a great big garden with everything else that was our survival, corn, peas, you name it . . . I learned how to eat meat, possum and coon." There were also chickens, cattle, and hogs that were slaughtered for food. The kids were expected to do chores, Sam remembered: "They didn't stop you from going to school, but when you got out of school, you went and picked cotton, chopped cotton, and everything else." Like many of the local creole families, the Levieges were Catholic, and Sam recalled a long walk to the church and the nearby school. "I had relatives living out in the country, they'd come to school in a buggy, black couldn't ride no bus." Sam remembered his sister Theresa singing in the choir; "She had a voice like Aretha Franklin." Sam's oldest brother Rimsey was quite a baseball player: "If Negroes could've been playing in the major leagues—he was a shortstop, made Jackie Robinson look like a rookie." Unfortunately Rimsey was never able to capitalize on his talent; he was hit and killed by a train after wandering too close to the tracks following a night of hard drinking.

On May 1st, 1930, Beatrice gave birth to her second son, whom she named Marion after his grandmother's father. According to Lillian, he was 10 or 12 years younger than her and wasn't known as Walter then, and wouldn't be till later years. (No birth certificates have been found for any of the Jacobs children, and it's likely that none were issued at the time, a common occurrence with the many home births in the rural south in those days.) Years later while on tour with Walter through the south, Jimmie Lee Robinson, his guitarist and friend from early Chicago days said Walter's grandfather, introduced as "Papoou," showed him the place where Walter was born, under a tree outside the family's house. He was told that Beatrice wasn't allowed by the family to have the baby in the house because she was "out of wedlock"; she'd permanently separated from Adam at some point during the pregnancy. Walter's older sister Lillian flatly denies this account, and shows a faded photograph of the cabin where she was born and the one nearby where she says Walter was born. The small one- or two-room "shotgun-shack" style dwellings are made from boards of weathered and fading pine, each with a tin roof and a small front porch. The dirt road connecting the two adjacent houses winds past fields bordered by split-rail fences, and they appear to be in a relatively secluded area: there are no other structures visible in the photo.

Whether he was born in the house or outside of it, Walter's birth was a harbinger of a difficult life to come, with Beatrice hemorrhaging and sick following her delivery. Hearing reports of Walter's arrival (and possibly the "under the tree" story), and perhaps fearing for the survival of the mother, Adam showed up three days later, seeking to take both John and the new baby with him over to relatives near Alexandria, some 30 miles away. "My grandfather and them didn't like my mother, and they told her she couldn't stay over there with his baby," Lillian admits. "Even though she had two other kids, people was just crazy. When you separated like that, they didn't allow you to be back with your husband or nothing . . . But my mother didn't want to stay, she wanted to be where *her* mother was at." Adam wound up leaving his older son John in Marksville with the Levieges but taking newborn Marion. Lillian wouldn't see him again until he was 11 years old. Adam carried the baby over to the home of his uncle Samuel Jacobs where the boy would spend most of those years, raised by Samuel and his Aunt Dawn. Samuel may have actually been a blood relative, but it would have mattered little even if he wasn't. During those times, kinship was a fairly flexible connection; any older person who cared for any child could be considered an uncle or aunt, any abandoned child living with another family might be referred to as a cousin, and so on. Possibly seeking to disguise the boy's identity from any Levieges who might come looking for him—or maybe just in an effort to completely distance him from that side of his family—Adam and his family dispensed with the name "Marion." It was at this point that the boy became known as "Walter."

Adam/Bruce had a reputation as a gifted musician, and undoubtedly there was a fair amount of music around his house. "The man could make that violin cry!" Lillian recalled. Lillian's younger stepsister Sylvia recalled, "I heard many people say he could play just about anything you put before him—accordion, guitar, harp." He also played piano, and there was a sort of informal Jacobs family band. "All his brothers would play music," his niece Rosa remembers. Her father Shelby played guitar, another brother violin, a sister played organ; "He came from a musical family." There was also the influence of the radio, which broadcasted a rich variety of regional music, including country music like the popular "Grand Old Opry" show, which could be heard beaming from Nashville throughout the south. Harmonica soloist Deford Bailey, one of the first black musicians to be heard on radio, was a regular on the "Grand Old Opry" from 1926–41. He recorded several sides in 1927, and his train imitation pieces set an early standard for what harp players had to do to be taken seriously. It is unknown whether Walter ever heard him, but Bailey's playing was so influential and widely imitated that Walter could hardly have escaped hearing someone who had come under Bailey's spell at some point.

Sometime later, younger brother Sam Leviege left his father's house. "My sister Cecille didn't have any children," Sam recalled, "so she took me. I was just a youngster, she was just like a mother to me. She worked for the rich people; when their kids outgrew their clothes, they give 'em to her and she brought 'em home to me. What they didn't eat, she brought the cold plate to me." It seems her estranged husband Adam/Bruce was still coming around. "I remember the night he killed this guy," Sam recounted:

> My sister Cecille and I had left my dad's house, had to go about a quarter mile to her little country home. This guy, a mechanic named Milton, was visiting my dad. He left, cut across the cotton fields and cornfields, coming to my sister's house. Well, Bruce was supposed to have been gone, but he came back and was standing right side the chimney. And he shot—this guy was supposed to be Cecille's boyfriend. I witnessed to the killing. Bruce shot and killed him right there.

Adam ended up in Angola prison, where, according to Sam, he eventually became a guard/trustee. From 1917–92, Angola had no hired guards, using instead trustees picked from those in prison for murdering friends or relatives—usually one-time crimes of passion rather than for profit—as a cost-cutting move. The armed guards were told to shoot to wound only—but that was hard with a shotgun. Jacobs again demonstrated his affinity for firearms when he shot a couple of escaped prisoners during a manhunt that ended in woods near Marksville. Sam left town in 1936 to go to work for the CCC (Civilian Conservation Corps, a Depression-era employment program) and moved on to Shreveport.

Beatrice found consolation over the loss of both her unfaithful lover Adam and baby Marion with a young light-skinned man named Roosevelt Glascock, the son of a black African woman and "a man buried in the white part of the cemetery," as one daughter put it. According to another daughter, "His daddy was Irish." Roosevelt's mixed-white blood didn't protect him from the violent and organized racism that was prevalent at the time, however. There is a family legend passed down about Roosevelt and his mother having to hide in a mattress because the Klan was after them. Glascock was an educated man—"These mulatto kids was all educated"—in fact his eleventh-grade schooling qualified him to teach public school had he chosen to do so (completing eighth grade was the teaching requirement then). But Glascock had other business on his mind; his biracial background would come in handy as he ran "Dubeau's Corner" a "black and tan" gambling club, "white on one side, black on the other," in downtown Marksville right across from the courthouse and the town lock up. Beatrice and Roosevelt soon hooked up, and around 1934 she gave birth to Lula, the first of three daughters they would have together.

Walter later said he started blowing harmonica when he was eight years old, which would have him first picking up the instrument around 1938 while living in Alexandria. A Sears mail-order catalog from that time shows the Hohner "Marine Band" model harmonica—the harmonica of choice for many professional blues players even today—retailing for 59 cents, but the entry level "Regimental Band" was going for 23 cents each. The feisty streak that would bless his music but curse his personal life was evident from the very start:

> I just liked the sound of it, but what really made me choose it was that most of the kids, my mother too, tried to dissuade me from playing it. Of course that made me more inter-

ested and the more they tried to disgust me with it, the more I caught on. If you give up you lose the fight you know, so eventually I got good at it. The first harp player I heard was a white feller, Lonnie Glosson, who yodeled and played a lot of hillbilly stuff.

It turned out that Glosson was a fitting role model for footloose Walter. An inveterate rambler, Glosson spread his influence far and wide, and saw much of the country while hitching rides on freight trains, carrying a brakeman's hat and gloves so he could pass himself off as an employee in freight yards. He was one of the few white harp players who played "cross-position," a technique until then favored mainly by bluesmen who liked the chords and note-bending possibilities that could be obtained by playing harps in a key a fourth above the pitch for which they were tuned. In the 1930s and '40s, Glosson had quite a career playing on southern radio stations, which is probably where Walter first heard him, and he made a good living selling mail-order "talking harmonicas."

On April 1, 1939, Beatrice and Roosevelt had a second daughter, Marguerite. Like her sister Lula, she favored her light-skinned father. But tragedy struck the Glascock family near the turn of the decade. Beatrice's son John, around 14 years old at the time, was hit by a car while riding his bicycle at night; he lingered a few days with a severe head injury before dying. There are other veiled recollections of this incident that cast it in a somewhat more sinister light: suggestions that Glascock might have attempted an assault on his stepdaughter Lillian, with young John coming to her defense, and his "accident" occurring suspiciously soon thereafter. Mother Beatrice had often cried with guilt and loneliness for the missing Walter before this incident, but after John's death emotions ran rampant. "That's all she talked about, she said 'my oldest son is dead, I don't know where my baby boy is at, I sure wish I could find him,'" Lillian says.

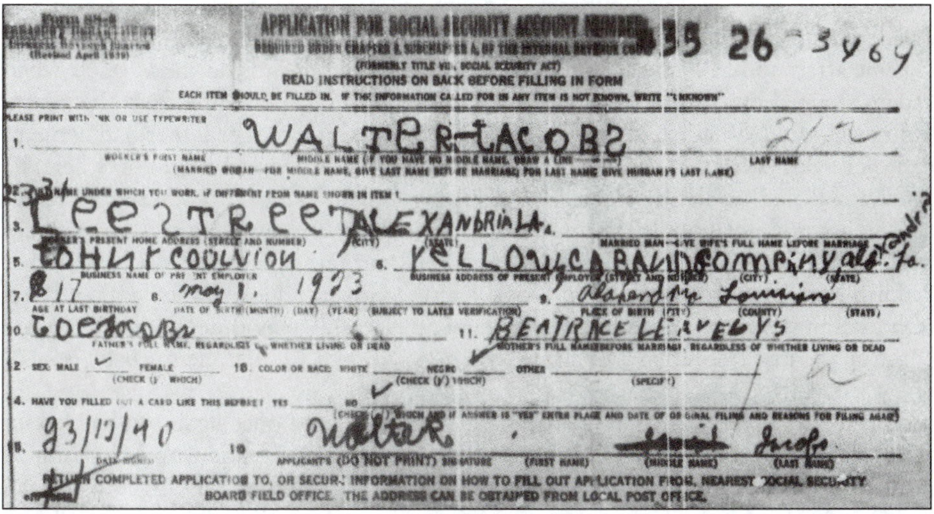

Figure 1.1 Little Walter's Social Security Application.

In the absence of a birth certificate, the earliest known documentation of Walter's "official" existence came on March 12, 1940. While living in Alexandria, he'd apparently found employment that necessitated his obtaining a Social Security card. He filled out the application, giving his name as "Walter Jacobs," mixing block letters and script, and upper and lower cases—and reversing the "s," "j," and "n" as well. He gave his address as Lee Street (someone else later entered the address "2331"), Alexandria, LA, and listed "Yellow Cab And Company, Alexandria" as the business address of his present employer, and "Johny Coolvion" as the business name. He gave his father's name as Joe (which was actually his paternal grandfather's name; perhaps Adam was still in prison, and he thought of his grandfather as the next best thing). He listed his mother as "Beatrice Leavegys"—a phonetic spelling—with place of birth entered (in someone else's handwriting) as Alexandria. His age is filled in as what looks like an "8," but on closer inspection might well be a backwards "9," close to his true age then, since he was born in 1930. This was then crossed out and replaced—again in someone else's handwriting—by "17." His birth date is given as May 1, 1923. Over the years the May 1st date would remain constant, but on practically every document Walter filled out he gave a different year of birth. The most logical reason for adding the extra years here would be that having a card was necessary for his employment. Whether he was 9 or 17, he would still have been too young to work as a cab driver; maybe he washed cabs, or ran errands. Whatever the case, it would have looked better on the books to have a young man employed instead of an underaged kid.

It wasn't until the early years of World War II that Beatrice was finally reunited with her lost son. "My father had kept him [Walter] hid all that time," Lillian recalls. "He made out like he didn't know where [Walter] was at, he said my uncle had moved . . . but what had happened, a white guy came over to my uncle's to ask him for something, and his dog came by the man, and the man shot the dog, and then my uncle shot *him*. So he went to the penitentiary and we didn't see him no more. People didn't talk in them days, especially if you kill somebody white, just a hush-hush . . . my father had [also] went to prison, and when he got out in 1942 he looked up his son."

One afternoon Lillian was in the living room playing records on the Victrola when Adam stopped by the Glascock household and called out her name from the porch. Roosevelt said "What's *he* doing over here?" Lillian, thinking her father had come to visit her, said, "What do you mean, what's he doing over here? His kid's over here, he come to see me!" Lillian continues, "Then Adam called 'Tell your mother to come out on the porch, I got something to give her,' he said. I went out—me and my dad and brother Walter looked just alike, you can tell he's our father. Me and Walter had that reddish skin like our father. When I looked at the kid and I looked at my father, I said 'Oh that must be my brother!,'" and sure enough it was! My mother had lost her other son 2 or 3 years before then. When she saw him she said, 'Ohh, there my baby is . . . ,'" she was real happy to see him."

But it had to be rather wrenching for Walter, uprooted once again, to be back in Marksville with people that he'd virtually never seen or known, and who called him by a different name, one he hadn't heard before. "Him and mother got on good," Lillian says, but "it was a hard thing to take a kid away from where all he known was, all he'd learned. That's all he'd ever known coming up from a baby, he didn't know nothing but Alexandria. So he come on back home [to Marksville] but he would never stay too long." There was a college in Alexandria, and Walter would help himself to an unlocked bicycle there and ride it the 35 miles down to Marksville and stay for a month or so. Then he'd get restless, find another bike and ride it back, and spend another month back in Alexandria. "We never could rid him of the habit," Lillian recalls wryly.

While in Marksville, Walter (still known there as Marion) briefly attended Holy Ghost, a Catholic school built right next to the church. His cousin Rosa remembers him not being very interested in the baseball or basketball games that went on at recess; "He was always in the music line," she recalls. "He always loved that little harmonica, he'd take his lunch money and buy him one." Although Rosa didn't recall street musicians around town, there were clubs and house parties, with music drifting out in the warm night air. Walter apparently didn't adapt well to the discipline and regimentation of academic life, and wasn't much interested in school. "My mother didn't push him," Lillian explains. "She was so glad for him to come back home. My mother's cousin, his wife Mary Leviege, was a schoolteacher. My mother would give her 75 cents a week to teach Walter, he'd go over there across the field to school in the afternoon for two hours. She was licensed, he'd go there four days a week. He went to school when he was little but nobody pushed him to do nothing. He was his own man all his life. He didn't allow nobody to tell him what to do."

Walter was small and slightly built, and an outsider as well, but he made up for it with a self-sufficiency that was unusual, even in a time when kids grew up fast. This self-sufficient attitude may have been fueled by feelings of abandonment or estrangement, as evidenced by Lillian's recollections. "Him and my stepfather, they loved one another. But his father, after he got out of prison, I don't think he liked him much no more. I don't know why, maybe because somebody told him his father was the cause of his leaving. He would come and ask me, 'How come mama gave me away?' I'd say 'She didn't give you away, she couldn't find you—but I think dad knew where you was all the time, 'cause he brought you back.'"

But Walter wasn't always a loner. Lillian remembers him hanging out with his uncle and lifelong friend Carlton, who was about the same age. She also recalls them together " . . . making old tire swings on a tree, throw a baseball every now and then . . . in the country, what'd you have to do? Nothing . . . My grandfather had so much land, had a big old tractor, he'd cut the land and have it all smooth. We'd go back there and play, boys and girls, make our own band, all that stuff."

Jessie Sampson, a younger cousin of Walter's, remembers that the Glascock home was entered via the back porch and through the kitchen, into a larger living room. She recalled Beatrice, her "Aunt Zoot," as a neat, meticulous person, a woman with long straight hair, and a spotless housekeeper. "You knew to take your shoes off at the back door before going in," she recounted. Walter found music at Mama's home, including a wind-up phonograph. "All we had over there was Blind Lemon [Jefferson]," Lillian says, "Walter would play with guitar, might have imitated from him—then he'd blow the harmonica, juice harp. We didn't have blues, there was nobody making records in those years, nobody in the '40s. Louis Jordan and them was just coming along then."

Walter's determination impressed Lillian:

He was all the time grown, he was never a child, he never thought like a kid. He always thought big. He'd say "Hey mama." I said, "What?" He said, "I want a dime." I said "What you wanna do with that?" He'd say, "Wanna get a harmonica." Thing would be broken before he'd get back to the house, because he was learning how to play, a lotta spit would get in it, and he'd hit it on his hand. Then he learned how to dry 'em out, the sun be so hot down here. He'd wash 'em, tear 'em all loose to find out what make 'em blow and all that. Then he said, "Lemme have 20 cents." I said "My piggy bank done started getting small now." He said, "One of these days I'll make you a lot of money"— so I said, "Okay, go on boy, get you another dime." So he got a juice harp and a harmonica, started that "bwing bwing bwing bwing" 'til he'd break out that little piece in the middle [the metal tongue of the Jew's harp]. He'd play from one to the other. He'd say, "Oh, that one sound—," he'd always try to get it to sound different from anybody else. He was self-learning. For a kid of his age 11 or 12, that was really young to be doing that. He played by ear. . . .

Walter's younger stepsister Marguerite recalled growing up in the Glascock house: "Grandfather Leviege, he had a farm, we didn't farm at all, we lived in the French Quarter. My uncle Hamilton always wanted my brother to go there and do something, and my father [Roosevelt] said he didn't have to go. I remember once my uncle gave Walter a severe whipping. I ran all the way downtown, to my father's club." She also commented on the social strata as it applied to Cajun and Creole culture: "Cajuns weren't popular like they are now; the white people didn't want them, no part. Cajun was white trash. Like if you called a black person a nigger, in those days you called a Cajun a Cajun, that was a fight. They lived in the quarter with us."

One of the more well-known Cajuns on the scene was Delma Lachney, a fiddler whose family had moved to Marksville from Quebec in the early 1800s. A member of a family band active in Louisiana in the first decades of this century, in 1929 Lachney traveled north to Chicago with guitar player Blind Uncle Gaspard, and cut several 78s marked by a country waltz feel and sung in French. Between 1939 and 1943, his band frequently played dances at Marksville's Black Cat Club. Whether Walter ever heard Lachney play is unknown, but anyone possessing even a passing interest in music could not have avoided exposure to the sounds of the French-influenced Cajun and Creole musicians in and around town in those years. As his long-time friend and early traveling companion David "Honeyboy" Edwards later noted, Walter in the early days had "that Cajunly" sound on harmonica, "like a pushbox (accordion)."

Marguerite also recalled musical influences from Louis. "My grandfather would listen every Saturday to that hillbilly music that came on the Nashville station [WSM, home of the 'Grand Ole Opry'], the violin music, he'd say 'Ooo-Wee!'" She remembers Walter's first amateur band at home:

It was with a guy called Toopsie and another named Bebe. They used to jam in the backyard with the rub-board, and the tub that people used to scrub clothes in, they'd have that for drums. We had some records, my mother and them considered 'em dirty records. Children had to go outside where they couldn't hear 'em be played. But we could hear them, and we could recite the lyrics. Louis Jordan was top honcho those days, what was that song? Something like "Night Train"—[Walter]'d play that on his harmonica, "duh-duh duh-duh duh-duh duh-duh," then take it away from his mouth and go "boom-boom." Then there was the drums, and the spoons hitting on the tub, and the rub-board was another sound . . .

Around 1943, Lillian married her first husband, Floyd Owens, and they moved out of the Glascock home and into their own place. Walter would sometimes stay with Lillian as well as continuing to move back and forth between his mom in Marksville and his uncle in Alexandria. At the tender age of 13, he had already established the essentially rootless lifestyle that would carry him through the rest of his life, for better or worse. He may have had a lot of places to lay down, but it's unlikely any of them really felt like "home."

He entered his teen years undisciplined, precocious, and headstrong, and trouble couldn't stay far away for long. When it first reared its head, it was in the form of a fire that burned down a barn and part of the gambling club that Glascock ran. A local man called Toot-Toot accused Walter of setting the barn on fire. "Which was a blatant lie," Marguerite states indignantly, and laughingly goes on to provide his alibi: "My brother was with a grown woman having sex! Her name was Moonu, can you imagine? Her face favored 'moonu' too, and she had a heinie you could set a hat on the back of." In spite of this alibi (or perhaps as a result of it), it was decided that Walter needed to be uprooted and shipped away once again. Marguerite continues, "My grandfather knew everybody in town, he was so well-liked—all they would have had to do was tell the sheriff that this was Louis Leviege's grandson and they would've cleared it. But my dad sent him to New Orleans, to stay with distant relatives." These relatives included a young woman named Waver Humphries whom Roosevelt had fathered with another woman, Ruth Ward Denis. Although Walter's time in New Orleans would be brief, Waver would play a part in Walter's life in years to come.

On his way to New Orleans, Walter stopped by Lillian and Floyd's, told them "something" had happened, and said he wanted to leave town. Floyd gave him some traveling money, and with that the young exile embarked on the biggest trip of his life. Lillian wouldn't see him again for another 7 years; by the time she did, he'd be well on the way to becoming one of the brightest stars on the booming Chicago Blues scene.

Appendix: 1920 Census Data for Avoyelles Parish, Marksville, Louisiana

LOUIS LEVIEGE Household 500 Duprines Road January 30, 1920

Louis Leviege, husband, 42, home owned/mortgaged, married, able to read/write, both parents & self born in LA, able to speak English; Canelia, wife, 36, married, able to read/write, both parents & self born LA, able to speak English; Beatrice daughter, 18, able to read/write, born LA, cook for private family; Cecille daughter, 16, not able to read/write, born LA, helper-farm; Theresa daughter, 13, able to read/write, born LA, attended school; Rimsey son, 10, able to read/write, born LA, attended school; Hamilton son, 7, born LA, attended school; Raymond son, 5, born LA; Bernice daughter, 3½, born LA; Mildred daughter, 2½, born LA

ADAM JACOBS boarder, 22, single, able to read/write, both parents and self born LA, able to speak English, laborer-farm

JOSEPH JACOBS Household 551 Island Road February 2, 1920

Joseph Jacobs husband, 59, home owned/mortgaged, married, able to read/write, both parents & self born LA, able to speak English, farmer; Elizabeth wife 25, able to read/write, both parents & self born LA, able to speak English; Mary daughter, 24, married, able to read/write, born LA, helper-farm; George son, 20, able to read/write, born LA, laborer; Eola daughter, 5, born LA; Landey son, 3 months, born LA

Other Children of Joseph Jacobs Found Elsewhere:

LEONDRY JACOB Household 885–945 Chaucton Road

Leondy Jacobs husband, 23, born LA; Florence wife, 23, born LA; Thelma Japprion orphan, 2¾, born LA

SHELBY JACOBS Household 586 Island Road February 3, 1920

Shelby Jacobs husband, 24, able to read/write, born LA, laborer-farm; Lou Ella wife, 18, born LA; Semonia sister(?) 30, divorced, able to read/write, born LA, laundress at home; Julia niece (?) 3½, born LA

AMUS JACOBS Household 708–753 Hickory Hill Road Amus Jacobs husband 26; Clara wife, 22, born LA (Clara named as sister to Adam by Rosa?)

2 *good evenin'*
everybody

New Orleans/Helena, Arkansas: 1943–44

The streets of New Orleans were busy, moving at a pace faster than any place Walter had seen before. The city was bigger, taller, wider, full of people bustling everywhere, moving in every direction all at once—on foot, in cars, and in streetcars that let out a guttural blue moan when they slowed to a stop. The air was thick with good smells too: crawfish and gumbo wafting on the breeze, from pushstands and restaurants spicing up the humid air. Almost anything you might want could be found on the streets, from groceries to knife-sharpening. And music: Walter had never heard so many musicians playing so many different styles before. There were the street peddlers with their carts, attracting customers by blowing horns as they passed, or singing chants to sell their flavored ices, "red hots," or seafood. Walking down the busy sections of Canal, Rampart, or Basin Streets, one could hear gospel, blues, popular tunes, jazzmen blowing trumpets, drummers beating out polyrhythmic Afro-Caribbean beats, and almost every other kind of music imaginable, usually behind an open instrument case or someone passing the hat for donations.

Then there were the clubs; in some parts of town they ran almost all night. The old-timers could still be heard playing traditional Dixieland in some places, but the real heart and soul of the music scene was in places where a younger generation was swinging and dancing to a bigger, newer, more insistent beat. Those like Walter who were too young to get into the clubs could still hear the music by standing out front, next to a side window, or at the backdoor in the alley. Sometimes before the band hit the stage or during a break, a young or particularly brash hustler might try to ply the crowd outside for some spare change by performing a dance routine with bottle caps on his shoes for taps, or maybe blow a version of one of the recent big-band hits on a harmonica or beat-up trumpet, until the doorman shooed him away.

Walter's harmonica talents sometimes actually got him past the doormen and into the clubs, if only to play during the breaks. Years later, in describing when he first played professionally, he told an interviewer, "Oh, I was about fourteen . . . I had been playing a lot of them big shows, you know, would have bands, you know? The band would come off; I'd go up and blow my harp, they'd throw tips up on the bandstand. I'd get pennies and nickels. But I had never got no group together." Walter probably played solo on the streets at first, playing instrumental pieces (he would later tell those who asked that he only took up singing in order to give himself a breather from his harp playing), imitating the sounds of the squeezebox-driven Zydeco and Cajun tunes around Marksville, in addition to mimicking other popular blues and country harmonica players.

But playing on the streets of New Orleans required a wide repertoire, and the ability to quickly assimilate the latest musical trends. If a street musician couldn't or wouldn't play any request he might receive, he limited his chances of making money. Many of the musicians who worked the streets (and who were recorded as "bluesmen" on record company field trips to the south in the 1920s and '30s) featured blues as only a part of their repertoire; many played reels, dance numbers, pop ballads, and vaudeville pieces as well. And in New Orleans, it didn't hurt to include a few waltz-time numbers to help open the change purses of the Cajuns and Creoles in the crowd.

Walter was also listening to jukeboxes and the radio, and assimilating riffs from popular artists like Louis Jordan and Cab Calloway. He liked the sound of horn bands, and saw how impressive a saxman looked under bar lights, fingering a gleaming horn, coaxing showers of bluesy tones out of metal and reed. And he almost certainly took note of how the ladies looked at a star soloist, and he could see then that "front and center" was where the action was! Walter would hang around the doorways of clubs and listen to horn-players sometimes, but if he got inside it wouldn't be long before a waitress or the doorman would run him out on the street again. But by then Walter already had a new riff or two ringing in his head, and he'd quickly figure out how to play them on his harp. He was a proverbial musical sponge, soaking up and incorporating anything that sounded good or helped to grab a crowd's attention, and pulling it out the next time he was playing on the streets.

Even the most rudimentary street musician might attract a passerby's attention for a fleeting second by making enough noise, but it took a special talent to get them to actually stop and listen for a moment or two. And getting them to pause for that moment was the key to unlocking wallets for a few coins, or if he was really good, then maybe even a little folding money. And what a performer lacked in musical virtuosity, he could sometimes make up for with a bit of flash, a charismatic bit of show business to catch and hold the eye: like dropping to his knees or rocking spasmodically in the grip of the music whenever it got especially intense; clowning with his instrument, maybe flipping around his guitar à la Charlie Patton, or beating out a syncopated rhythm on it; or the old "look ma, no hands" trick of playing a harmonica while it was stuck halfway into his mouth like a big cigar. Street musicians were plentiful in New Orleans, and you needed something special to stand out from the competition. Later described as "quite a dancer" by his fellow Chicago musicians, perhaps Walter threw down some fancy footwork between or during his tunes, but his main gimmick on the streets was probably simply that he was a skinny little kid who had the musical powers of a man.

At any rate, details about his time in New Orleans are scarce. Walter's half-sister

Marguerite thought he was only there for "maybe three months," and spoke disparagingly of the people with whom he'd been sent to stay in New Orleans. They were the family of his stepfather Roosevelt Glascock's "outside" daughter from an earlier relationship; Marguerite emphatically states "they were no kin to him, they were related to us, distant. I don't think they treated him right. I'm sure he was abused in New Orleans ... when I met with those people in Los Angeles they were cruel. [To support himself] he used to go to Bourbon Street and try to play for nickels and quarters."

Exciting as New Orleans was, the city's overall carefree mood had tightened up with the outbreak of war in December 1941. The day of the Pearl Harbor attack, army troops were moved into the vulnerable port city to protect highways, water purification plants, and other vital facilities. In days to come, German subs would be patrolling just south in the Gulf of Mexico, and in one hectic month, May 1942, twelve allied ships were sunk. The 1942 Mardi Gras was canceled (only the third time this had occurred in one hundred and fifteen years), and food and gas rationing, war work, and air raid drills became part of daily life. But the war also brought prosperity back to New Orleans. The local shipyards began to run full tilt with several shifts, producing PT Boats and landing craft for the U.S. Navy.

Seeing the big, fast, exciting world that existed beyond rural Louisiana must have added fuel to Walter's wanderlust, because after a short time in New Orleans, he began rambling in earnest. He returned briefly to Marksville, and from there his uncle Sam Leviege brought him to Shreveport for a short time. Sam's first wife recalled a very quiet young man, who stayed with them maybe a week or so: "He played his music all the time. That's all I can say about him." Sam bought him a 35-cent harmonica and Walter left, working his way north. "He rode the train with the hobos," Marguerite says. One of his stops was Monroe, Louisiana, a town some 40 miles south of the Arkansas border, where his mother had family; he later told British blues historian Paul Oliver that he picked up some club work there, "play[ing at] the Liberty Inn for a spell." But given his age at the time, it seems more likely that he played on the sidewalk in front of that club. Eventually he reached Stephens, Arkansas, 75 miles northwest of Monroe. It seems that he did find some way of exploiting the commercial potential of his music there. "We used to receive boxes from him with no [return] address," Marguerite recalls, "because he didn't want my mother to know where he was living. We knew where it was from by the label on the box. He'd send little fur coats, very expensive coats, he'd send to Lula and I. He had to be making money playing to send us boxes."

Eventually, Walter worked his way north to Helena, Arkansas, a bustling, "wideopen" port town along the Mississippi river, some 50 miles downstream from Memphis. The town had been settled two centuries earlier atop a gravel ridge, the only high ground in that part of the country, an area full of malarial swamps that was also subject to spring flooding by the Mississippi. In the early '40s, Helena was just beginning to lift itself out of the Depression. Due to a thriving farm economy, it served as a center of commercial activity and as a ready source of jobs. The main street, Cherry Street, was parallel to the levee, and it boasted dozens of saloons for white patrons, while Elm Street, running just behind, was dotted with black saloons. Bluesmen knew they could get work in Helena. Pianists Roosevelt Sykes and Sunnyland Slim were among those who worked the clubs, and here Sykes composed his "West Helena Blues." Memphis Minnie used to sing about "Reachin' Pete," an unpopular cop on Cherry Street.

Bluesman and Helena native Cedell Davis describes the scene:

> There was more [musicians] in Helena and West Helena than there was in other places in Arkansas . . . They had an opportunity to be on the air, on radio, you know what I mean, and [there] was a lot of joints. You see, Helena was wide open at this time. Wide open gamblin' and just about everything. Most anything that you wanted to throw away some money, and it was there . . . No, there wasn't nothin' like that in Mississippi. You see, now most of the things like that in Mississippi was happenin' was on the farms, see, it wasn't too much happen in towns—not for black peoples anyway. They wasn't allowed. They could go to town and stay there till maybe 9 o'clock or 12 o'clock; they'd get out, you see. But now Helena, you didn't have to worry about no time, see wasn't no time—all night, see, because the joints stayed open all night, all day, you know, what I mean like that. Well, anything that you wanted to spend some money on or buy, it was there. Well, all them sawmills was open then, all them joints was open. Used to have a joint there I used to play at called The Hole In The Wall. Well, that joint would open on a Saturday, oh, about 12 o'clock. That's when the people be comin' off the farms and comin' into town, and peo-ple'd be gettin' out, you know. And they had a live band there.

Another native of Helena, Hank Harvey, remembered Saturdays in town: "It seems that there was music everywhere. Musicians played on streetcorners, at the Missouri Pacific depot, and down on Walnut Street, in the section of town where most blacks lived. There were men and boys with guitars, washboards, harmonicas, and drums, mostly; they played a brand of music that no one could quite define. The radio stations called it 'race' music, and it wasn't heard much because there were so few records around." As he ventured deeper into this musically fertile region, Walter was exposed to more blues harp players than he'd heard before, both firsthand and through the juke-boxes in the local joints. He'd derived much of his early inspiration from the records of John Lee "Sonny Boy" Williamson, who was hugely popular and influential both in Chicago and throughout the blues-rich southern states from the time of his first record-ings in 1937. The Tennessee-born Williamson had migrated to Chicago in the late '30s, after establishing himself on the then-thriving St. Louis scene. He began his 10-year recording career just about the time Walter was first picking up a harp. More than any musician before him, Williamson brought the harmonica to the fore and popularized it as a featured "lead" instrument in the blues. His earliest recordings of string-band blues with musicians like guitarist Big Joe Williams and mandolinist Yank Rachell led to a partnership in Chicago with guitarist/vocalist Big Bill Broonzy starting around 1939. He eventually led piano-guitar-drums backup groups, assembling the necessary ingredients for what later became the basic Chicago Blues band sound. The magnitude of his recorded output serves as proof of his widespread popularity. Over the course of his career, he cut some 120 titles for the widely distributed RCA and Bluebird labels, and a number of his originals have become oft-recorded blues standards.

Williamson almost single-handedly took the harp from being a novelty device used either in jug bands or to imitate train or animal sounds and raised it to the level of a "real" instrument, fitting accompaniment for blues vocals. His records generated lots of plays on the "Seabird" (a common nickname for the popular Seeburg-brand) jukeboxes, and consequently were widely imitated by almost every aspiring harp player between the Delta and Chicago. Any harp player worth his salt would have to be able to cover some Sonny Boy numbers in order to be taken seriously; no doubt Walter put in his time with an ear to the speaker, soaking in the sounds, and trying to master the techniques.

But in Helena, Walter began hearing about another harp man who also called himself Sonny Boy Williamson. This "new" Sonny Boy hadn't yet recorded, but had developed substantial local fame by performing live on a popular noon-hour program on radio station KFFA five days a week. Thanks in part to the popularity of this radio program, Helena became something of a magnet for blues musicians, and boasted a jumping little blues scene in and around the town. Walter recognized that this Sonny Boy was not the same person whose records he'd heard, but he was drawn to him nonetheless, and soon came to know him as "Rice" Miller.

Miller was a man of considerable talents and charisma who had by then been musically active in the Delta region for at least a decade. At some point in the early 1940s—accounts differ as to how and when, although certainly not why—Miller had assumed the performing name "Sonny Boy Williamson." It has been suggested that Max Moore, the proprietor of the Interstate Grocery Company that sponsored Miller's radio program, might have instigated this deceit; others claim Miller himself was the culprit. At any rate, clearly the intent was to capitalize on the considerable fame of the established jukebox favorite. The assumption might have been that the program wouldn't be heard in Chicago, where the real Williamson was headquartered, and because Williamson seldom traveled through this part of the south, what difference did it make?

By the time Walter encountered him in the early 1940s, Miller was already a larger-than-life character, a charming scoundrel and veteran bluesman who must have seemed to young Walter to have been around forever. Miller had started on the radio as "Little Boy Blue," and at various times gave his name as Willie, Alex, or Rice Miller, among several other aliases. In his earlier travels, he played occasionally with Robert Johnson, Johnson's "stepson" Robert Lockwood, and other notables, and Howlin' Wolf later said he learned harp from him while Miller was courting Wolf's sister. Tales, some undoubtedly apocryphal, abound of him stealing mules, playing his way out of jail, and otherwise eluding the law or staying one step ahead of trouble. He was known as a two-fisted drinker, and was usually seen carrying a small satchel in which he kept his harps, a microphone, and a pint of liquor.

Not long after KFFA got its license in December 1941, Miller began appearing on a daily live broadcast advertising King Biscuit Flower for the Interstate Grocery Company, answering mail-in requests and plugging his gigs at local juke joints. He started out playing solo, then was joined by his old running partner Robert Lockwood on guitar. Within a year there was a regular but flexible "King Biscuit Boys" band that included Joe Willie Wilkins on guitar, Dudlow Taylor on piano, and Peck Curtis on drums backing Miller's harmonica and vocals. Later on Willie Love and Joe Willie "Pinetop" Perkins occasionally took over the piano stool, and Houston Stackhouse would come in on guitar. The group made regular Saturday afternoon public appearances plugging King Biscuit Flour, playing on the back of a flatbed truck in various small towns around the listening area, and drawing large crowds. They became so popular the company soon put out a brand called Sonny Boy Corn Meal, featuring Miller's likeness on the bag.

Hank Harvey remembers as a teenager riding bikes with his friends:

> . . . down to Helena Crossing, a black community where the highway crossed the railroad as it curved west around Crowley's ridge; Sonny Boy in action was worth the trip. Even with the thermometer on the side of the grocery store pushing 100, he stood there in knee boots with slits cut in the sides. He wore a thick belt with loops for his harmonicas. When he played, he flapped his arms sometimes and did a dance step. He could make the harmonica cry or yell, or make it moan like a steamboat whistle if he wanted to. He got up right next to the microphone and played, then sang and sometimes seemed to play and sing at the same time. He sometimes put the harmonica completely in his mouth and played it that way. The black people would dance and clap hands and raised a cloud of dust. I wanted to be more reserved, but my feet kept wanting to move around. Some people thought he knew only blues, but if he ran out of something to play, people would yell out requests and he played hillbilly tunes, spirituals, or any kind of song.

Hugh Smith was a staff announcer at KFFA from 1942 to 1951, and over that time appeared on some 3,100 King Biscuit Time broadcasts. He was a combination announcer-engineer; not only did he make the station IDs and introduce the shows, he also ran the control board, and switched the various mike, turntable, and network lines, as well as setting mikes up in the studio. The combined population of Helena, West Helena, and outlying areas made for a community of approximately 20,000 people, and KFFA was the clear voice of the area. "The studio was just the bare necessities," Smith explained. "Transmitter, control console, three or four mikes, and one studio, that was about it." As part of his daily duties, Smith announced for the King Biscuit Flour show, which took over the studio for fifteen minutes during the lunch hour, and ran a half-hour on the weekends, shows that were done as live free concerts from the Plaza Theater. "The station had a fairly limited range, it was 250 watts," Smith recalls. "However at that time, in the '40s, the AM band was not as crowded as it is now, so each station didn't require as much power to reach out a considerable distance. I'd say we had a radius of 75 miles or so." Smith figured the audience for the show was mostly black. "At the time this was looked on as 'race' music. The Mississippi-Arkansas delta areas were predominantly black at the time. Phillips County, where Helena is located was, I believe, about 67 percent black, the delta even more, perhaps running to 80–85 percent." The station carried a gamut of music, including country-and-western shows. "We showcased a great deal of everything," Smith recalled, "[We] played a lot of records by big bands. At that time we were in the big band era—the big band idiom or country-western was the white type music," with blues considered to be black music, although certainly there was some crosspollination going on.

Smith worked from a script the sponsor provided, carried over from the Interstate Grocery office by Sonny Boy, detailing which products were to be pushed. The show opened with Sonny Boy and the group singing the King Biscuit Boys theme song:

Good evenin' everybody, tell me how do you do
Good evenin' everybody, tell me how do you do
These King Biscuit Boys has come out to welcome you.

Every morning for breakfast, King Biscuit on my table
Every mornin' for breakfast, King Biscuit on my table
Invite my friends and all my next door neighbors.

But if the commercials were tightly scripted, the rest of the show was loose, with the studio often full of onlookers at air time. "There were any number who would come visiting into the studio," Smith explained, " . . . I have no doubt there were many would-be or just beginning musicians that came to sit and watch. Sometimes, if Sonny Boy or the band thought someone was good enough, they'd let them do a number." Odds are that Walter was among those attending the broadcast, harps in his pockets, hoping to be called on to show his stuff. It's certain that he watched Miller closely as he played, the older man's hands dancing over the harp, shaping the tones so that it sounded as if it was talking and singing. Miller's huge hands engulfed the harmonica completely, and he seemed to be able to change the sound of the instrument dramatically with just a small movement of one of his fingers or a turn of his hand. When Miller advertised the location of his upcoming appearances at the local clubs or juke joints out away from town, Walter took note and began frequenting Miller's gigs. He listened and learned, pulled out his harp and showed off what he knew when the opportunity arose, and occasionally sat in when Miller took a break to drink, gamble, or go off with a woman during an intermission.

In Helena, Walter first encountered three guitar players who all would play roles in his musical life to come. The first, David "Honeyboy" Edwards, was a guitar-playing rambler and gambler from Mississippi who'd traveled with Big Joe Williams, played with Robert Johnson, and been recorded by a Library of Congress team a couple of years earlier, in 1941. Sonny Payne, another announcer for the King Biscuit show from its earliest days, remembers Honeyboy's appearance on the scene:

Honeyboy Edwards used to come up here to Helena when we were doing the King Bis-cuit show live on York Street, every damned day of the week. He'd ask me, "Sonny, when you goin' to let me play some on the radio?" I'd tell him I wasn't the one he had to talk to. He'd go back there and ask four or five days in a row. One time I asked the boss, "Would you let that sombitch play his guitar and sing?" So he starts singing "The West Helena Blues!" I could barely get him off! Hell, I used to see him coming into town all the time but I never heard him play. So there he was playing and I said, "Well I'll be damned! He's better than [W.C.] Clay was." Clay had replaced [guitarist] Robert Junior [Lockwood] on the show at that time [1943].

Honeyboy recalled meeting Walter in Helena, although he's given contradictory dates for their first encounter. In his autobiography, Edwards says it was the summer of 1943, but in earlier interviews he's said either 1945 or '46. The earlier date for a first meeting seems more likely, because Edwards stresses Walter's youth:

He was a little boy, he heard about all the news that was happening around Helena, all the musicians—so he run off from Louisiana, come up through McKeough to Baldress. When he first came to Helena, you could hear he WAS a harp player. He had that Cajunly sound, that Louisiana thing. He come from Marksville; a lot of Frenchmen live there—he was a Frenchman himself, Creole, talked that funny talk I couldn't understand. What I mean by Cajun style, [the] French would play the push-box [accordion], he played the harmonica with the style of that, that chromatic [harmonica] sound. On account of he's a Frenchman, he blow like that. But blues was the only style he liked, so that gave him a push off the other harp [style]. He was playing straight notes, mixing the shit quite a bit.

Guitarist Jimmy Rogers was in his late teens when he first encountered Walter in Helena around 1943. Rogers resided in the area then, but previously had heard Rice Miller on the radio beaming from Helena, down in Mississippi, up in Tennessee, and through large portions of Arkansas and Missouri as well. Rogers had grown up in Mississippi, listening to recordings of musicians such as Big Bill Broonzy and Tampa Red. At the time he was playing harmonica, like so many others, in a close approximation of John Lee "Sonny Boy" Williamson's style. He also doubled on guitar, and was in his mid-teens when he first met Rice Miller, arriving one day before the radio show went on the air. Miller wanted to hear what the youngster could do, *and* take a break, so he put Rogers onstage while he was in the backroom gambling.

Rogers was playing for small change in those days: "All the whiskey I could drink, and maybe a dollar and a half cash money." Rogers had made his way to Helena from Minter City, drawn by the hopes of getting gigs around the broadcast area. "That's where the whole bunch were, right there in Helena, broadcasting on KFFA. That's where I met Willie Love, Elmore James, all them." Echoing Honeyboy, Rogers said, "[Walter] was a little boy then. He was kinda on the same route I was. He'd go around these musicians and sit in and look around. They didn't want to recognize him, but he was learning something. He'd get up to one of the guys, say Rice Miller would let him take the harp, he'd be gambling, go over to the craps house, and Walter would be with the band like that." According to one legend, one night a woman came at Walter with a knife in a juke joint and Sonny Boy stepped in and saved his life. Years later, Walter would admit to blues researcher Mike Ledbitter that he'd learned a lot about blues harmonica from Miller, a seemingly rare moment of generosity that may have been motivated by this memory. At any rate, Rogers only spent a short time around Walter then, but several years later in Chicago they'd team up again, for some of the most important years in their careers.

The third important connection Walter made in Helena was with Miller's sometime guitarist and traveling partner Robert "Junior" Lockwood, who had been introduced to Miller in 1936 by his "stepfather" (actually his mother's boyfriend), the fabled bluesman Robert Johnson. Miller had taken the 20-year-old Lockwood on the road with him, playing streetcorners in Mississippi, Arkansas, Tennessee, and Missouri, averaging $35–40 per performance, a very good payday at the time. Lockwood also wound up in Helena, where he also remembered how young Walter was when they met. "Just a kid," Lockwood recalled. "He didn't really have a home . . . he'd come down to my house, I'd be eating, the old lady be fixing dinner, I'd give him mine." Walter would also secretly hide himself on Lockwood's car, in order to get him to include him in his out-of-town gigs:

> I used to go play plantations in the fall. They'd be picking cotton out there, I'd come home with as much money as the farmer had made. I'd go to the country to play, start playing by myself. Walter had got on the spare tire [of my car], and just before the turn-off to the house, he'd get off, brush the dust off and stay outta sight till the house get full of people. Then he's in the house! I can't take him back home to Marianna, cause I done started to work. So I let him play harp, and I'd end up making the man give him some money.

Guitarist Luther Tucker, who worked extensively with both Lockwood and Jacobs in the 1950s, related stories that he heard about Walter's early encounters with Lockwood, and another musician whose story would intertwine with Walter's over the years in the south and in Chicago, veteran piano player Sunnyland Slim:

> [Walter] left home when he was about nine years old, he ran away and followed Robert Junior and Sonny Boy Williams [sic] and Sunnyland Slim. They was playing together, all down south, Mississippi, Louisiana, Memphis. So Walter had run away from home and every place that Robert Junior and Sunnyland Slim would play, Little Walter would show up, and say, "I wanna be a harmonica blower, I wanna be like Sonny Boy." Robert Junior said, "Hey, you're too young to be out here by yourself, why don't you go on home?" He say, "I ain't going back home, I'm gonna go with you all." Robert Junior say, "Naw, you can't do that." They put him out of the house, said, "You go back home!" Little Walter'd say, "Naw, I ain't going home!" So they was playing in Louisiana, and they had another job in Memphis, Tennessee. Robert Junior sneaked away from Little Walter and went to Memphis, Tennessee. They was sitting up there playing, they looked around and there was Little Walter again. He say, "I'm not going no place, I'm gonna follow you all." So Robert Junior says, "Well we can't get rid of him, we tried that." [Walter]'d just started blowing harmonica and he sounded pretty good.

So, the older men's resolve to ditch the youngster was finally worn down, and Walter began playing with them regularly.

According to Tucker, Walter also endeared himself to the older musicians by offering other services to them: "[Walter] started cooking for Robert Junior, Sunnyland Slim and Sonny Boy Williamson. They'd go out and work, when they come back, Little Walter would have dinner ready for them, at that age—so young." Tucker says of Walter's indentured servitude to the older blues masters: "It taken him about a year, he started playing with Robert Junior and Sunnyland, all the old blues players. They'd taken him in, he just started working with the band. He had been around the fellers to learn their numbers, what they was doing."

But it was Honeyboy Edwards who had the closest ties with Walter during these early years. Honeyboy wanted to get something going with him right then; he related in his autobiography that around 1944 or so, "I went looking for Little Walter, I wanted somebody to play harp with me. I knew he was a good player, and wanted to hook up with him." Honeyboy was impressed with Walter's abilities to deal with bad harps. "During the wartime, they [harps] were rationed, you couldn't get them. Walter would play a harp with nothing but two basses [notes] and make it sound good." Despite

Honeyboy's approval, "Sonny Boy and them didn't pay him any attention cause he was so young, but the boy grew. He was so good people looked at him," Edwards said:

> He left and went on up to Marianna, Arkansas, near Memphis, he told me where he was going. I said, "Well, I'll be up there to get you next week," so I went and picked him up. He was staying there with an older woman name Pearl, she was up there with her mama. He done shared with her, got pretty clothes on. I got there that day, he was laying up in bed, a quart of milk beside the bed. Lazy son of a bitch, too! I say "Get up man, lets go! You gonna live with this woman?" He says to her "Well, I'll be back *much* later mama—." And she ain't seen him no more.

Edwards writes, "For the next few years we was together almost all the time. Me and Walter hoboed around. We'd do anything and didn't want to stay nowhere. We didn't really care where we was going or when we get there—we just felt lucky to be going."

With rambling on both their minds, they left Helena together bound for Memphis, "in the summer of '45" according to Edwards. Walter's older sister Lillian recalls:

> I had a picture of him leaving [which she'd apparently gotten from Walter years later]. A man passed by and took a picture. Him and another guy, older than him, two of 'em on the picture, I don't know who he was. [Presumably the second man in the picture was Edwards.] They had their thumbs stuck out, I asked him [Walter] "What is this picture, you're doing like that?" He said "That's me and this guy hitch-hiking . . . two is better than one."

Walter wasn't all that familiar with Memphis yet, but the older Honeyboy knew the city well, and knew where they could earn some money. They soon arrived on Beale Street, the black musical and cultural hub of the entire Delta region. They headed for W. C. Handy Park, where musicians congregated. It was here that Walter first encountered Big Walter Horton, a harpman who was already a veteran of the Memphis scene, and considered to be one of the best in the region.

"His mama told me Horton had been playing harp since he was five years old," Edwards says. "He played with Son Brimmer, Will Shade, all them, and he HAD the music. He was a hell of a harp player." Horton was influenced by both of the Sonny Boys; the first record released under his own name several years later bore an obvious similarity to Miller's just-released Trumpet recordings. The older, more experienced Horton had the edge over Walter then, and Walter soaked up stylistic flavors like a sponge. The trio played in the park, sometimes hooking up with Little Buddy Doyle as well. They stayed there for two or three weeks.

But once again, Walter got restless and took off on his own for St. Louis . . .

3 wonder harmonica king

St. Louis/Points South/Chicago:
Summer 1943–46

It could have been just a young man's urge to ramble, to see what's over the horizon. To the young, footloose, and unencumbered Walter, it must have seemed the whole world was laid out in front of him, and all he had to do was choose a direction and stick out his thumb. It was summer time, the warm winds were blowing, and hitching a ride on a sunny day must have seemed like the natural thing to do—and if he had to walk a bit, or sleep under the stars, no big deal. Over the next three years, Walter logged some serious miles traveling up and down the Mississippi River and beyond, on a well-traveled circuit that included Helena, Cairo, Illinois, St. Louis, and Chicago. Each new town provided a way station with a large black population for the southern migrants headed to the industrial north, and each was bustling with activity in the war years. And, they all offered country-boy Walter new lures, new experiences, and—just as important to a rapidly maturing and more worldly young man—more women to impress with his prodigious musical skills.

Perhaps he'd heard some of the older musicians talk of the long-established music scene in St. Louis. As the first, large urban stop up the Mississippi from Memphis, it had become the final destination for many of the southern musicians who'd migrated north, but who didn't want to endure the harsh winters of Chicago or Detroit. For a time in the 1930s, it was a bigger blues Mecca than Chicago. Southern railroads ran excursion fares with cheap overnight round trips to St. Louis, because it was only a short trip north of Tennessee, Mississippi, and Arkansas, putting the city within easy reach of any southerner who aspired to see any bright lights and big city beyond Memphis. John Lee Williamson, a/k/a Sonny Boy I, had established himself there before moving on to Chicago, and all his early recording groups featured men he had worked with in St. Louis. The city was home base to such players as Robert Nighthawk, Peetie Wheatstraw, Henry Townsend, and Big Joe Williams, as well as pianists Roosevelt Sykes, Walter Davis, and Sunnyland Slim for a time, along with countless lesser-known players.

Or maybe it was pride that gave Walter the urge to ramble. By this time he'd no doubt acquired a taste for being the focus of attention, and he'd gotten used to being noticed, even among fellow musicians. His energy and youthful appearance made his musical talents appear more special, helping him to stand out from the older men who were then his musical associates and mentors. But in Memphis he was somewhat in the shadow of Walter Horton. Though thirteen years older, Horton was also known as a former child prodigy, and his years of experience had provided him with both the "chops" and a musical focus that were still beyond Walter's grasp. This must have been painful for the younger man to admit; he wasn't particularly gracious about taking tips from his elders. Jimmy Rogers, who was on the scene at that time, recalled, "Big Walter [Horton] would tell him this and that, and Little Walter just throw his hat off. [He'd go off], practice it by himself, then come back and it'd work. Big Walter showed Little Walter lots of cuts but he wouldn't admit it." So, maybe Walter wanted to go somewhere where he stood a better chance of being the alpha wolf in the pack.

Whatever the reasons, Walter made his way to St. Louis. Honeyboy Edwards arrived there several weeks later, and as usual, was soon playing on the streets. Edwards writes that, one day while playing out on Jefferson Street, a listener told him, "I heard a harp player, a little boy, I wish you could meet him. That sonofabitch can play harp, and you'd sound so good together. He works at the lounge right up the street." Edwards headed there and hung around, and soon Walter came striding down the street, swinging his arms. "That was the harp player!" Edwards said. Walter spied Honeyboy and exclaimed, "Mother-fucker, where'd you come from?" Reunited, they were soon playing as a duo once more. According to Edwards, Walter kept them supplied with decent clothes; besides working at the lounge, he also had a day job at a laundry. Every day at work he'd take a shirt from a pile at the laundry, put it on underneath his own, "and come home with something new every night. We didn't have no clothes and all those nice shirts was there." For his part, Honeyboy was handy with dice, so utilizing their various musical and other skills, they were able to survive, but before long, inevitably, the time came to roll on again.

They headed back down south, some 300 miles into Mississippi. With fall crops in and colder weather coming on, the small town weekend activities were slowing down and the spare change earned playing on the streets was getting harder to come by. The two hoboed over to Ruleville, about 60 miles south of Helena, and signed on as share-croppers on a plantation. They were paid a $100 advance against their share of the crop they were hired to plant, till, and harvest in the coming season, and used it to buy groceries. But, "First time the weather broke, when it quit raining and snowing we got away from there," Edwards writes. "They farm in March, but me and Walter, we marched in March! Nobody going to hook us up all summer in that hot sun, no Lordy."

They soon found themselves in New Orleans, where Edwards was again reminded that Walter marched to a different drummer. They'd played outside the Union Hall on Rampart St., and afterwards Edwards took off walking, while Walter stayed behind talking with a listener. A police squad car passing by turned its spotlight on Edwards and called him over. "Come here boy; what's your name? Where you from?" As Edwards was replying, Walter came running up. "[Walter] said, 'What's going on man?' Police say, 'Who wants to know?' He say 'Me, that's my partner!' Police said, 'Both of you get in the car!'" Apparently hoping to put a good scare in them, the officer drove them around for several blocks, but when he couldn't come up with a good reason to arrest them, he pulled over and told them to get the hell out. "He [Walter] was a crazy old boy," Edwards muses, "fractious." It wasn't the last time the rambunctious Walter's mouth would raise the ire of an officer.

Working their way back north, by mid-1944 the pair were in Carruthersville, Missouri, a town north of Memphis, nestled in the corner of the state near northeast Arkansas. The pianist Sunnyland Slim had established himself quite comfortably there, with two houses, one in the city and another out in the country. A half-white patron who went by the name "Juke" had set the enterprising Sunnyland up with a whiskey and gambling joint. Sunnyland also had a woman named Enid, "a good looking dark gal," Edwards writes. "Tall and heavy, built like a stallion, hair all puffed up on her head." Honeyboy and Walter were playing on the street when Sunnyland happened along, spotted them, and invited them to sit in that night on his gig at the seawall down by the levee. Enid came in later, "and damn if she didn't fall for Walter . . . Walter starts slipping around with her. Sunnyland gets mad, but hell, ain't no man going to turn down no woman. Sunnyland got mad, me and Walter had to go back to playing on street corners." A few weeks later, the duo were playing a little club in town when Sunnyland turned up in the audience, and spent a long time staring at them without saying a word. Having apparently weighed the relative merits of hooking up with them versus rejecting them in favor of Enid, Sunnyland finally approached them. "Hey man, come on out to where I'm playing at," he said, Edwards writes. "I'm not gonna fall out with you over no goddam woman. If that woman wants you, she wants you. She ain't nothing to me, nothing but a goddamed whore anyway." The trio was back in business, and Walter was with Enid, Honeyboy remembers, "clean until we left town. We wouldn't carry nobody with us when we left, though!" And of course, the leaving was inevitable.

Once again Walter found himself in St. Louis. Downtown, he wandered into Hackie's, a beer joint at 21st and Market Streets, and saw another recent arrival from the south playing there. James DeShay had come from Mississippi, and found work at the large Monsanto Chemical plant. Although music was more of a sideline than a career choice for him, DeShay was a talented musician who had learned guitar from his older brothers and from Charlie Patton records. He'd been awed by the sight of Howlin' Wolf playing on the streets of Pace, Mississippi. Walter showed up several times at DeShay's gigs, and they began to talk. When DeShay discovered Walter had no place to stay, he took him in, and they developed a friendship that soon flowered into a musical alliance as well.

Besides taverns and house parties, when DeShay wasn't working his day job on Saturdays they'd set up their amps and a tip bucket, and play on the streets downtown, around Jefferson and on Clark and Chouteau. They could pull in "somewhere between 25-to-30 dollars by playing couple hours, two, three, four," an amount equal to half a weeks wages or more according to DeShay. They played the popular tunes of the day, and got frequent requests for Sonny Boy I's numbers: "'Good Morning Little School Girl' was a favorite of people, they used to ask us to play it all the time." They also played on streetcars, working the captive audience for tips. The friendship that was forged then would last a lifetime, and over the next couple of years Walter would room with and play music with DeShay whenever his wandering took him back to St. Louis. DeShay's daughter Joyce recalls her father laughingly telling a story "going back a ways" of how he'd caught Walter urinating in the sink downstairs in the kitchen, instead of going upstairs to use the bathroom. "When I look back at the way our house was made downtown . . . we only had one bathroom in this two family flat," she explains. "They were both just ordinary people from the south, used to going to the outhouse. They figured out he did not want to go upstairs to the bathroom." James had gotten suspicious, and sought to prevent future incidents. "My father laid up and watched for him [and caught him in the act], and told him 'Hey!'—they didn't fall out, but Walter left not too long after that."

Having extensively worked the route from New Orleans to St. Louis, the next logical stop for Walter was Chicago. He and Honeyboy had heard about Maxwell Street, Chicago's bustling weekend outdoor market neighborhood. The scene had been immortalized in 1925 by one of the big blues stars of the day, "Papa" Charlie Jackson, in his record "Maxwell Street Blues"; whether or not Walter and Honeyboy had heard Jackson's record, they certainly would have been aware of the allure of Maxwell Street throughout the south, well attested to in Papa Jackson's song. It sounded tailor-made for itinerant musicians like themselves:

> Lord I'm talkin about the wagon, talking 'bout the push cart too,
> 'Cause Maxwell Street's so crowded, on a Sunday you can hardly pass through.
> There's Maxwell Street, South Water Street, Market, too,
> If you ain't got no money, the womens got nothing for you to do.

A talented musician could earn the equivalent of a day job's weekly salary just playing weekends on the streets in the Maxwell Street shopping district, thereby leaving the rest of the week free to pursue other musical opportunities or just "lay up" waiting for the next weekend. So with Maxwell Street beckoning, they set out for Chicago.

Honeyboy has given varying accounts of their first trip to Chicago, around May or June of 1945, probably because it's a route he eventually would travel with Walter a number of times. The first version, recounted in his book, has them leaving St. Louis, and hitchhiking to Decatur, Illinois. "We only had a few dollars, so we hit the streets, and found a little whiskey house, played a while there," he writes. "Then we walked to the train station, set up there and played . . . people coming in to the depot stopped to listen. And we made enough at that station to buy tickets to ride to Chicago."

A second account comes from a 1999 interview. In this version, the pair departed Memphis, traveled through Missouri to Charleston, then over to Cairo, Illinois, a wide-open river town in the southernmost tip of the state, bordering on Kentucky. They went to the freight yards and found a friendly brakeman who told them what time the train for Chicago was scheduled to leave. They laid up in the bushes, watching while the train was made up, avoiding the railroad yard "dicks," who'd turn up just before departure time to foil the plans of potential freeloaders. When they saw the brakeman at the caboose wave his lantern signaling time to go, they ran down the hill and jumped on the already-moving freight. They rode to a switching yard at Effingham, Illinois, where the line branches out east towards Indianapolis, and north to Chicago. There they found a hobo jungle, "built out of pasteboard boxes, with tarps pulled over them," Honeyboy said. "Had a place to wash the skillets out, hang 'em up. I think it was June when we come, hot. Right out from the railroad was a lake . . . we got to the lake and washed our pants out with soap, cause we didn't want to come to Chicago dirty and nasty. We washed our khakis out in the lake, wrung 'em out, stretched 'em and hung 'em in a tree . . . in about an hour and a half them things was dry." Walter went into downtown Effingham and hit a bakery, asking for a handout. The man told him he had some day-old cakes, but he'd have to wash out the cake pans. Walter did, and stopped at a local market for some other provisions as well. Honeyboy recalled, "That boy came back with a bag of cinnamon rolls, cakes and bread. We had a big five-gallon can and a brick fire. Pour our water in there, put our pig foot and pig ears in there, started to boil it, added our salt and pepper." After dinner they played some cards before going to sleep. Before they left the next morning, they heeded a sign posted nearby; "Effingham Jungle, leave it clean," and washed their dishes and hung them up, for the next travelers' use.

Honeyboy's accounts converge midstate, at Decatur, Illinois: "We thought we could make a little money there. But there wasn't no black people there much. Walter was funny . . . he says, 'Man I ain't seen ne'er a boot walking the streets!'—he called us boots, you know. 'I ain't seen but white people around here . . . we ain't gonna make no money here.'" But when they got to the station, the ticket agent spotted Honeyboy's guitar and the harps around Walter's waist. "'You play guitar? Hit me a tune,' he says, and that's what we wanted . . . started playing blues in the depot, and the white folks started gathering in there. We made enough money to come to Chicago and had some change in our pockets."

"We rode the cushions," the inveterate boxcar rider boasted. They hit Union Station in Chicago near midnight, and headed down Halsted, over to Maxwell Street. Even at that hour the streets were bustling. The town was wide open then, "Steel mills, slaughter houses, packing plants, Armour, all them—we had two or three stockyards then. Everybody had a job," Edwards recalled, "They didn't never sleep!" The plants were running two or three shifts and the laborers came from all over, a mixed lot—Jews, Mexicans, blacks, and whites. "They'd come to Jewtown, listen to the blues all day long, on a Monday. Guys go to work at four o'clock, get off at twelve. Or come to work at eight o'clock in the morning, get off at eight, make it to Jewtown—somebody'd probably be sitting around playing. Boy it'd be something!" Edwards fondly reminisced. They met a steelworker there who recognized them as musicians, and offered them a place to stay. Edwards took him up on the kind offer, but the younger man declined. "Walter was like a flea, he was hopping."

Next morning, Walter was shaking Honeyboy awake by 7:00 AM: "Hey man, get up, let's make us some money. These sonsabitches out there playing the blues, get up! Get up!" Edwards protested that he had nothing to wear but the old dirty shirt he been traveling in. Walter took some of his change, went out on Maxwell Street and quickly picked up a cheap, second-hand shirt and some underwear for Edwards. Now suitably attired for their Maxwell Street debut, the pair hit the street.

On weekends, the Maxwell Street market area resembled an open-air, eastern-European style bazaar, the biggest flea market in the world, covering dozens of city blocks. Pushcart peddlers competed with storefront shops offering "special bargain prices," and hawkers tugged your arm, offering "a good deal, for you only." Anything that had ever been sold as new could be found there used—clothes, auto parts, dishes, musical instruments, old magazines—with stands selling hot food cooked outdoors over coals to the shoppers who browsed the shopping stalls that lined the streets and sidewalks. Additionally, the main streets of Halsted and Maxwell were lined with tailor shops, carpet and appliance stores, and small shops selling cheap or used versions of anything that might be needed by a new arrival to Chicago from the south—or from anywhere else in the world. Willard Motley, an African-American novelist living in the Maxwell Street neighborhood in the mid-'40s, remembered the scene on Sundays, as the Maxwell Street Market, "stretched . . . extending between low, weather-grimed buildings that knelt to the sidewalk on their sagging foundations. On the sidewalk were long rows of stands set one next to the other," as far as one could see:

> On the stands were dumped anything you wanted to buy: overalls, dresses, trinkets, old clocks, ties, gloves—anything . . . men and women shouting their wares in hoarse, rasping voices, Jewish words, Italian words, Polish and Russian words, Spanish, mixed-up English . . . The smells were hot dog, garlic, fish, steam table, cheese, pickle, garbage can, mold, and urine . . . The people were crowded in thick, shoulder to shoulder, tripping over each other, pushing down the street in a noisy, bargain hunting crowd. The pavement had no rest from the shuffle of their feet. They even took up every bit of room in the middle of the street as they wove around their pushcarts. The vendors gestured and lifted their wares for the people to see.

Bluesman "Hound Dog" Taylor, a funky slide guitarist who would be paired up with Walter on a European tour in the late '60s, described coming to Maxwell Street from the south, in the early '40s:

> I'd heard about Jewtown and went to see it for the shoppin.' You meet all your friends there from the south. You go over there when it's warm and just stand around on the corner. And you'll see 'em walkin' by. I used to say, "Hey, how you doin' man? I know you from so and so place." "Yeah, yeah, yeah, man." You know, have a conversation. And then me and him be standin' there talkin' and here come somebody else he knowed. I know 'em too. "Man, lookee there so and so." Yeah, ain't nobody down south I know now. All them cats is split.

And there was music: storefront churches offered gospel songs, live and on record; and musicians of every color and kind spread out along the avenue wherever there was a crowd to play to and a space to set up, all hoping to pick up a share of the money that exchanged hands so freely here. Edwards recalls Floyd Jones, Earl Hooker, John Henry Barbee, and Snooky Pryor as all being regulars. "We went out in the street and made more money than we ever made before," Edwards writes, "made about $20 apiece, emptied out our cigar box four or five times. We had the biggest crowd around us, people chucking quarters and dollars at us. Money was floating then," and of course a 1940s dollar went a long way. "Take that hamburger stand on Maxwell and Halsted, sitting in the same spot now, open everyday. You get a polish sausage there for a dime, porkchop sandwich, get that for 20 cents, stacked all up with meat and onions. Get one, feed two people. We was making money then."

Walter picked up where he'd left off with his romantic pursuits. He soon hooked up with another older woman (a habit that would continue throughout his life). While they were playing on the street, a woman walked up, wrote her name and address on a tablet, and dropped it in the kitty. "The note said come and visit me," Edwards writes. "She was a church woman too, about forty, and good looking. She had a sanctified Jesus Christ church up on North Avenue somewhere . . . Walter looked at that letter and said, 'Man, I'm gonna see what this old broad is talking about.'" He was gone for a couple days, and when he returned to Maxwell Street before the next weekend he was decked out in a blue suit with cable stitching and a dark fedora "crimped up on his head. I saw him, said, 'Man, who is you?'"

Another of Walter's romantic adventures had more dramatic consequences. Several weeks after arriving in Chicago, Walter began seeing a woman called Marie, who lived on Newberry Street in the Maxwell Street neighborhood. One morning, Edwards and Walter went to her house, and another of the woman's boyfriends also happened to show up. Angry, jealous words were exchanged. "Walter was mean," Honeyboy said. "And he never got mean for no reason, but he was quick tempered if somebody started something." Walter had what Honeyboy described as "an old hawk billed knife," and he cut the man in the mouth. Figuring it might be best to blow town a while, the pair went downtown and immediately caught a commuter train to Milwaukee, 90 miles north of Chicago. There, they found a club near 6th and Juneau with a house band. They spent several weeks playing there, backed by a rhythm section of drums and standup bass. After they felt that enough time had passed for things in Chicago to cool down, they returned to Maxwell Street, and took up playing again in their old spot. Walter meanwhile had bought a .25-calibre automatic pistol and had it stashed in the back of his amp. One Sunday morning, the old boyfriend turned up, glowering. Walter jumped up, pulled his gun, and said, "What the hell you looking at me like that? Get on now!" Walter took a shot, which—luckily for both men—missed. The man ran off and got the cops, but when they were confronted, the musicians protested they had no weapon—and the crowd backed them up. "Walter was crazy," Honeyboy muses once again.

Near the end of August, Honeyboy felt the chill coming in the air and decided to head back to the warmer climates of the south. Having apparently developed a taste for big-city life, Walter opted to stay on in Chicago. "Honey, I ain't going back down there," he said to his old traveling companion. "I'm sticking around to freeze with these niggers here." But it wasn't easy. With the cold weather, the crowds around Maxwell Street thinned out. The resourceful Walter discovered that the Salvation Army clothes collection boxes found on some street corners and in some parking lots were big enough for a man to sleep in. They provided shelter from the arctic Lake Michigan winds that could produce wind chills down to 30 degrees below zero in winter, and warmth beneath the mounds of cast-off clothing. "He suffered a lot in Jewtown," his sister Marguerite later said. "He was cold, hungry." With no regular income, Walter subsisted on a diet of cheap junk food, she says. "He used to drink RC Cola, and he told me he used to eat Stage Plank cake, which is sorta like ginger cake, has an icing on it." She sobs at the memory. "He used to have to put tape on his jacket to keep out the cold, and had to stay with a woman old enough to be his mother," although Walter himself may not have seen this last aspect in the same negative light as Marguerite did. By December, with locals telling him the worst weather was yet to come, he decided he'd had it with fighting off frostbite, and worked his way back down to Helena, Arkansas.

The musical scene in Helena, while still going strong, had changed somewhat in his absence. Rice Miller had left the area, but the King Biscuit show still aired on KFFA, with a group still known as the King Biscuit Boys. The band was fronted by drummer and sometime tap dancer Peck Curtis, and included another transplant from Louisiana and veteran of Rabbit Foot Minstrel Shows, Dudlow "Mr. Five by Five" Taylor on piano. Joe Willie "Pinetop" Perkins was on the scene as well, and sometimes filled in for Taylor. Joe Willie Wilkins was on guitar, and they were eventually joined by Mississippian Houston Stackhouse.

Stackhouse had previously played violin and mandolin with a stringband styled after the Mississippi Sheiks, and had learned guitar from bluesman Tommy Johnson. He retired his violin and mandolin when he came to town to play guitar on his cousin Robert Nighthawk's daily 3:30 PM Bright Star Flour radio show. Before long, the sponsorship for the radio show dried up, and although Nighthawk continued for a while, paying for the air time himself, he eventually was forced to give up his slot. Stackhouse and Nighthawk continued working together in a band that played regular dances in Mississippi and Arkansas, but their partnership dissolved after a money dispute. Stackhouse eventually joined the King Biscuit Boys, earning a weekly salary as a sideman of $5 for the five fifteen-minute shows. There were also the Saturday flatbed truck shows, where the band traveled to the surrounding small towns, setting up in front of the local grocery and playing for fifteen minutes or so advertising King Biscuit Flour, then packing up and heading on to the next town—sometimes hitting as many as nine stores a day. Pinetop Perkins would be on the truck with his piano, while the rest of the band set up on the ground at the rear of the truck, wearing their blue, hand-stitched Sonny Boy Corn Meal shirts.

Not long after Walter returned to Helena, he wrangled himself a KFFA radio spot too, teaming up with Dudlow Taylor for a daily program, probably taking over the 11:15 AM spot with Mother's Best Flour as a sponsor. People would send in cards requesting songs for them to perform, and Stackhouse reported that Walter's program got more mail than the King Biscuit show. "They'd have a stack of cards in there . . . a stack of letters," he recalled. "More than me and Pinetop and Peck and all of 'em, we'd have two or three letters maybe. That Little Walter was blowing that harp, boy." Over the next couple of years, Stackhouse and Walter played some gigs together, "down there at Lyon, Mississippi near Clarksdale, and over at Henry Hill's. Then Walter would play with me at Helena Crossing," Stackhouse continued. "There be so many people you couldn't get in there hardly, they's all out in the streets. That fella selled a lot of whiskey at the store there. Little Walter be blowing that harp and everybody get to feeling good and dancing—it'd be more whiskey bought, yeah. [Walter] carried a bigger crowd down there than Sonny Boy did, I think."

Walter soon heard that Honeyboy was in nearby Belzoni, Mississippi, and he called him to come to Helena. Honeyboy frequently joined in with Walter and Dudlow Taylor for the radio show, and their area gigs included the Hole In The Wall Club, where

Edwards met his future wife. Honeyboy had acquired an electric guitar by then, after his steel-bodied National guitar was stolen in Coahoma. "I didn't have no money, couldn't do nothing, so I went out and pulled a mugging," he confesses. "Made enough to buy me an electric, then went back with Walter." Sometimes Walter would plug a microphone for his harmonica into Edwards's amp as well, but before long he got an amp of his own. "It was a little one, at the time there weren't too many heavy amps like we got now. It sounded good singled out, 'cause there wouldn't be but one instrument on the line. Get too loud, you cut it down or it carry feedback at you." In contrast to his previous experiences playing primarily on the streets or for tips, Walter was now picking up plenty of "professional" experience playing real gigs at the juke joints and country dances, and before long he felt he was ready for another trip north.

By the summer of 1946, Walter had found his way back to Chicago, and was again on Maxwell Street, playing gigs with Sunnyland Slim, who had by then settled in Chicago, and with Floyd Jones. Jones lived near Maxwell Street, having gravitated to Chicago after spending time in Helena and West Memphis with people like Howlin' Wolf and Robert "Junior" Lockwood. Jones was soon playing Chicago joints like the 21 Club and working with Little Walter, who Floyd believed had only recently arrived in Chicago for the first time from St. Louis. "[We'd] take a streetcar and go from one tavern to another, come back, maybe, nine, ten dollars apiece," Jones said of their casual appearances playing for tips in local taverns. But they'd have to quit early, because Floyd didn't want to jeopardize his day job at the American Coin Foundry, out in the Blue Island neighborhood:

> At night we'd have to lay down around twelve or one o'clock. I worked five days, nine hours, and five hours on Saturday, making $44.75 pouring iron. Walter says "Man, you're crazy, I wouldn't pour that hot iron. You making eight or nine dollars a night, then Sundays we was making $20–$35 on the street. Why work? If you get laid off you can draw unemployment compensation, you always have something to fall back on." He said, "Man I'm gonna take this harp and make my living." And he did, too—he throwed it away, but he made some money in his life.

Another regular on Maxwell Street was a kinsman to Little Walter: guitarist "Uncle" Johnny Williams, also from Alexandria, Louisiana. After travelling back and forth several times, he finally settled in Chicago in 1938. Williams worked day labor for Armour Meat Packing, then took a defense job at Chrysler when the war broke out, a good job which also had the fringe benefit of saving him from military service. In the early '40s his musical career consisted mostly of playing house-rent parties, and Maxwell Street on Sundays from around noon until 4:00 or 5:00 PM. "You worked with different guys, there'd be maybe seven, eight bunches." Williams explained:

> Maybe this Sunday I'd work with Floyd [Jones] and Snooky [Pryor], next Sunday I'd work with Little Walter and somebody else. Wasn't too many that had set places, just whatever group got there and set up, well, there they were. Somebody's gonna let you play with them—if you could play, you could play with somebody. They wasn't snooty . . . It used to be a barbershop along Newberry Street too—round about Peoria—where me and Floyd and Little Walter would get our juice [electricity] from. We'd have that long extension

cord run up through the window, and we'd get our juice from those people that had homes there. That's how we run our guitars and microphones. We'd pay 'em about a dollar, dollar and a half . . .

Walter also sometimes worked with Lazy Bill Lucas, a guitarist/pianist who'd come from St. Louis in the early '40s, and who was a musical cohort of Sonny Boy I. Walter gave Lucas the nickname "Lazy" because later, when they worked at the Purple Cat Club, Bill would forget to turn the amplifiers on, to warm them up. Lucas had first met Sonny Boy on Maxwell Street, and before long was playing guitar behind him on local gigs. He and Williamson played "suburban places around the city, like Battle Creek, [Michigan] and South Bend, Indiana, one-nighters in taverns and at parties. Sonny Boy, he would book himself," Lucas said. "He wouldn't go through no booking agency." Lucas backed Williamson on and off for about a year before Williamson's death in June 1948. He and Walter met when Walter was rooming in a building owned by Lucas's father, and they began a loose Maxwell Street association. "Johnny Young, he was playing with us too," Lucas remembered, "mandolin."

One of Walter's most auspicious meetings during this time occurred when he reconnected with a fellow he'd met back in his earliest days in Helena, guitarist Jimmy Rogers. Rogers had settled in Chicago, and Honeyboy recalled seeing him there after he'd just got out of the army, wearing a suit and high straw top hat, with his girl who had a little baby. Rogers, like so many others, was casting around here and there and picking up whatever musical gigs he could, including doing fill-in gigs for Sunnyland Slim, sitting in when somebody didn't show up. Shortly after his arrival around the end of 1945, Rogers had met and began playing with another recent southern arrival named

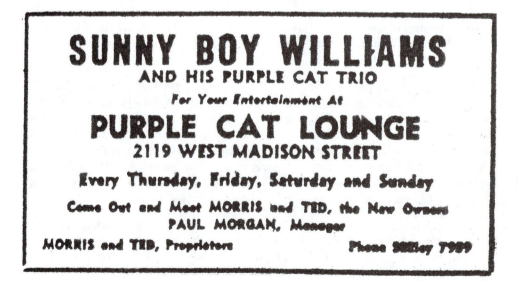

Figure 3.1 "Sunny Boy" at the Purple Cat Lounge; *Chicago Defender* advertisement, July 20, 1946.

McKinley Morganfield, a quiet man who at the time was still playing acoustic guitar, and was yet to be known as Muddy Waters. Neither Muddy nor Rogers had heard Walter play yet, but that was about to change.

At the time, Walter was following one of his heroes, John Lee "Sonny Boy" Williamson I, who was appearing frequently in area clubs. One of Sonny Boy's regular gigs was at a club on the west side of the city, in the shadow of the old Chicago Stadium; the July 20, 1946 *Chicago Defender* advertised "Sunny Boy Willams [sic] and his Purple Cat Trio, for your entertainment at Purple Cat Lounge, 2119 West Madison, every Thursday, Friday, Saturday and Sunday." Walter almost certainly spent some time there watching and listening to Sonny Boy. Harp player Snooky Pryor had encountered Sonny Boy there the previous year, after being discharged from the army at Fort Sheridan north of the city. "Sonny Boy, he was playing at this place called The Purple Cat on Madison," Pryor said. "They had the bandstand up in the ceiling, you had to climb a ladder to get in up to the bandstand . . . This bartender, he used to get Sonny Boy to let me do a few numbers." Snooky quickly made his mark. "I could play better than he could . . . people started to give me more calls than Sonny Boy. He come up there, snatched me down off his bandstand. All the way down the ladder, he told me 'Goddam, Junior, you ain't getting up there no more.'"

Pryor also remembered when Walter first began showing up on Maxwell Street: "He didn't hardly fool with anybody too much. Walter was half crazy man," he states, echoing Honeyboy's assessment. "He used to come up around March of every year, play out on the streets until about September, then start hoboing back." Pryor wasn't too impressed with the young man's prowess. "Kind of sloppy," he chuckled. "He couldn't sing at all—he had one song he could really sing and play a bit, 'Just Keep Loving Her'; But nobody could ever play with him hardly but John Henry Barbee, because Walter's time was bad. . . . [Later on] he changed style, after Louis Jordan started putting out records, then Walter picked up Louis Jordan's swing." Honeyboy recalls Walter sitting around listening to the radio and records, "trying to steal sounds outta different things . . . He'd hear Bullmoose Jackson play the horn, he used to try and follow him. Says 'I'm gonna play my harp, make it sound just like this man playing the horn.' And he could near about make it sound like that!" But for now it seems he was doing his best to cover the popular Mr. Williamson.

Evidence that Walter made his presence known at The Purple Cat during Sonny Boy's stay comes from a display ad that appeared in the *Defender* the following week, on July 27th, 1946, when he was hired to replace Sonny Boy as one of the attractions at the club. The boldface type at the top of the ad went to recent RCA recording artist "Memphis Jimmy," and Johnny Temple, who had records out on Decca, but right in the middle was listed: "The Wonder Harmonica King 'Little Walter,'" his first known published billing (although it's likely that he'd had enough renown in Helena to merit at least some hand-lettered placards in tavern windows). It must have felt like quite a milestone for the young man; he'd managed to earn a place on the same stage as his idol, and it's not too difficult to imagine that he'd even felt some pride at "stealing his gig."

This gig provided Walter's first small toehold into an entertainment scene that was thriving in black Chicago at the time, as is evidenced by other ads on the same page of

Figure 3.2 Purple Cat Lounge advertisement, July 27, 1946, Walter's first advertised gig.

the *Defender*: Roosevelt Sykes playing The Flame; Memphis Slim (with "Merle Costello, queen of the shake dance") at the Timber Tap Lounge; "King Coles double" Robert "Prince" Cooper, fronting a jazz trio at Jacks Club Showboat —and a "gala Joe Louis Jubilee, featuring the heavyweight champion of the world IN PERSON" at the Rhumboogie. Walter's "debut" gigs at The Purple Cat must have gone well, because a couple of weeks later the ads were still running, with the same line-up handling the Thursday through Sunday night stretch. Mr. Williamson dropped in on at least one gig and spent some time checking out the young "Wonder Harmonica King." Six or seven years later, Walter would tell then-fledgling harpist Billy Boy Arnold that Sonny Boy had advised him then that he "played too fast."

Walter's engagement at The Purple Cat also connected to an interesting and note-worthy coincidence. Some six weeks later on September 27th, 1946, the pianist with whom Walter had been recently sharing The Purple Cat stage, "Memphis Jimmy" Clark, was in a recording studio for Columbia cutting some tracks for fabled blues businessman Lester Melrose. Jimmy recorded under the name James "Beale Street" Clark, and split the eight-song session with vocalist Homer Harris and a still unknown guitar player making his second anonymous appearance in the recording studio. Clark did a couple, Harris three, then the guitarist stepped up to the mike for three tunes, all done in producer Melrose's trademark "sweet-blues" style. None of his tracks cut that day would be issued at the time, so the unknown guitarist, Muddy Waters, would have to wait a while before he'd see his name on a record release. It wasn't until after he hooked up with the Chess brothers and their fledgling Aristocrat label the following year that his first "real" recording would come out. There's no evidence that Little Walter and Muddy Waters met then, but if James Clark bothered to mention either to the other, the possibility exists that the first seeds of their musical partnership were already planted.

Around this time, Rogers had a place on Peoria St., a block off Maxwell Street. One Sunday he heard a harp sound that caught his ear. He threw on some clothes and headed over and found an "amazing" youngster blowing. "He knew how to execute the harmonica, but he didn't know how to place it, his time was bad," Rogers opined. "He was just running wild with it, but he had some good action." Rogers may not have realized that Walter's timing was possibly rooted in the Creole sounds he grew up with. Also, as Sonny Boy Williamson had pointed out, the energetic youngster was already bucking the harmonic trends of the time, playing faster and busily executing virtually non-stop rhythm riffs. The two started talking, and from what Rogers gathered, Walter had come recently from St. Louis with Sunnyland Slim. The two talked for a while, until a quick, heavy rain came up and they decided to head back to Rogers's place. By the time they arrived they were soaked to the skin, so Rogers let Walter have a dry change of clothes and the two talked for several hours, about the places and people they knew. Rogers discovered that Walter lived close by, and after that every two or three days Walter would call up, or stop in. The two soon began playing together, initially opting for the quick and easy money to be had on the street circuit. Rogers then mentioned Walter to another musician friend. "I was talking to Muddy about [Walter]," Rogers said. "I told him I'd met a boy down in Jewtown who could really blow." And, with that, the stage was set for a partnership that would have an incalculable and permanent impact on the shape and sound of the blues.

4 *i just keep loving her*

Chicago/Points South and/or
St. Louis/Chicago: c. 1946–48

Although it was commonly known as "Jewtown," Maxwell Street was not an exclusively Jewish marketplace or neighborhood; the district was also home to many black businesses and residences. In 1893, the first wave of Jewish immigrants from Poland and Russia began settling in the Maxwell Street neighborhood. As time passed and these Jewish immigrants became more economically secure, they moved out of the area to more prosperous neighborhoods. In their wake came newly arrived southern blacks. By 1910, the area was still 90 percent Jewish; in the '20s the neighborhood jumped from 0 to 60 percent black. And, by 1930, the strip between Maxwell Street and 14th Street became "solidly black."

Chicago restauranteur Daniel Medlevine, one of the immigrants to America, who lived with his family on Maxwell Street from 1922 to 1935, was a part of the tail end of the primarily Jewish presence in the area. Medlevine was bootlegging liquor at a young age during the Al Capone era in Chicago, and recalled the area as "a rough street." During this time, his parents ran a dry goods store on the first floor of 912 Maxwell; their living quarters were above. Medlevine described the residences: "I slept in a little bedroom on Maxwell Street that was so hot. A hot, hot room. No window. Too small even for a dresser. Just a bed. I scored enough money to buy an oscillating fan. I pulled up a chair and put the oscillator on the chair. And that fan would hit me . . . That was the biggest thrill of my life." Medlevine remembers moving from the building in 1935 because, "We didn't have no steam heat. As soon as a Jew could make a little money, he moved into a steam-heated building . . ." Medlevine later ran the Chez Paree, a Chicago nightclub noted for bringing in national acts.

Jimmie Lee Robinson was part of the next wave to settle in the neighborhood. Born in nearby Cook County hospital in 1930, he was in his early teens when he first met Walter on Maxwell Street. Robinson had been playing guitar on the street for a couple of years by then, and was living nearby at 1405 Washburne. Jimmie had a cousin named Della who lived in the same building at 912 Maxwell Street that the Medlevines had occupied a decade earlier, across from Jerry's Cozy Corner, notorious as a "bucket of blood" club. Della's house had a long flight of stairs going up, as Jimmie remembered, and, "she lived on the first floor." She was a "churchwoman," a Mason, and an occasional blues singer, who also supplemented her income by renting out her spare bedrooms to recent arrivals from the south who'd found their way to Maxwell Street. Della's boyfriend was a "policy maker," a numbers runner in the well-organized but illegal lotteries that flourished in the black communities of Chicago and in other cities.

Whether it was individuals looking to play the numbers, or someone searching for a room to rent, Della's roominghouse saw a flurry of people coming and going, and Della and her boyfriend were well-known to the neighborhood. Floyd Jones had roomed at Della's, and so did the "recently arrived" Little Walter, along with ". . . his skinny girlfriend, the girl who bought Walter his first amp," according to Robinson. "There was a music store right next to Della's, a lot of people were getting their first amps around this time." Robinson, who a decade later would become a member of Walter's touring band, recalls seeing Walter a lot when he was young, ". . . on Maxwell more on the weekends—he was like a cousin to me, by him living with Della." Although Walter was actually little more than 16 or 17 at the time, he seemed older to Robinson, carrying himself with the assurance that comes with being self-sufficient and independent. Walter never seemed to have a permanent residence for long; Robinson recalled him "bumming around," staying a few days here and there with different people in the area. Walter was also seen regularly in the company of ". . . a whore on Maxwell Street named Billy, everyone knew her. She was really built!" Jimmie says. This association probably further enhanced Walter's reputation as a fast-living playboy, but he nevertheless struggled to survive.

Years later, Walter told blues historian Paul Oliver that he spent his first three years in Chicago playing mainly on the street, and that he came under the wing of Bluebird recording artists and Chicago blues legends Tampa Red and Big Bill Broonzy. They had been among the founders of the popular "Bluebird beat" sound that dominated the Chicago blues scene for at least a decade before Walter's arrival, leading jukebox-friendly recording-session combos, and also backing a number of other recording vocalists, producing an almost interchangeable group sound. Tampa Red had a large house in Chicago, which had been a popular hangout with both the older and younger generations of blues musicians. Both blues veterans quickly recognized Walter's talent, and extended their generosity to him. The two had been recording prolifically since the 1920s, and Big Bill may have developed an affinity for harp players, because he had worked regularly both on records and in clubs with Sonny Boy I. Widely known as a good-hearted, helpful man, Broonzy wouldn't hesitate to give encouragement to younger musicians. Though his recording career had slowed down during the '40s, he was a much beloved patriarch in the blues community whose influence touched many. Guitarist Floyd Jones, a newcomer to Maxwell Street, told of Bill's watchful advice about being careless with his own new song, "Stockyard Blues," which would become his signature piece. Floyd recalled, "After I start singing it on the street, this fellow Big Bill Broonzy said, 'You'd better play with me or somebody's going to take it.'" By wrapping his mantle around him, Bill effectively warned off those who might take advantage of the rookie. Broonzy was also the first musician Muddy Waters ever saw playing electric guitar. Walter sent his little sister Marguerite one of Bill's records, letting the family know the kind of esteemed company he was beginning to keep. As Walter told interviewer Max Jones later, "There's one man I can give credit to—a friend and a good musician: Big Bill Broonzy, he could play, and not just blues."

Henry Townsend was another frequent weekend player on the streets. A guitarist and pianist from St. Louis, Townsend had driven Sonny Boy I from St. Louis to Chicago for his first recording session. In his autobiography, Henry recalled Walter and his idol Sonny Boy competing for listeners on Maxwell Street:

> Jewtown was Sonny Boy's hangout over on the West Side. We used to have music duels, Otha Brown and Little Walter, [guitar player] Eddie El and myself. We used to get together and do what they call "battle royals." I would work with Sonny Boy and Otha would work with Little Walter, Eddie was working with another fellow, his name was Pinkie or something. We'd get on street corners and it was a very good hustle . . . we'd get together and just jam it on out. We'd be on the same corner and we'd switch off; they'd do a session, we'd do a session. We'd get to doing a battle royal and the street would get blocked; sooner or later the police would come by and tell us to scatter . . . Now this was also a scam to put you in any of them clubs—see, club owners would come out and see these guys. You could be beneficial to his place, so you'd get a job right away. I always knew I didn't have to worry about being hungry nowhere . . . that was a meal ticket at any time and I knew that.

Jimmy Rogers and other non-union, newcomer musicians found another way of hustling (without having actual jobs with the clubs) by just dropping in. Jimmy explained, "We'd call it scabbin', y'know. You hit here, you set up with asking this guy that owns the club if he wouldn't mind you playing a few numbers—quite naturally it was good for his business, he would say okay. You'd play a number or two, they'd like it—you'd pick up a buck here, a buck there, y'know." When Jimmy ran into Little Walter again on Maxwell Street, the two began to do the same thing:

> We'd go from one club to the other, we were playing for the kitty. And we started doin' that. We were out by 8:00 at night, and different taverns started around 9:00, so by the time the taverns closed at 2:00 we maybe done hit four or five, maybe six different taverns, and we had a pocket of money apiece, maybe $15, $20 apiece. That's pretty good money back durin' that time. Extra good for a musician, and we started doin' that, [but] not because I really liked it that way. I wanted a steady job someplace, steady gig.

One of the businesses on the street was Maxwell Radio and Records at 823 Maxwell St., owned by Bernard Abrams. He stocked the Top 10 hits of the day, but in a hustle of his own, he'd acquired an inexpensive acetate disc recorder, with an eye towards making a few extra dollars recording some of the neighborhood talent that he saw attracting crowds on the weekends. He often cut one-off records for neighborhood singers, either to use as demos, or as gifts for their girlfriends.

It was here that Little Walter made his first recordings. Guitarist Floyd Jones recalled of Abrams, "He had a record shop. And we'd go in there and I'd see him cuttin' little dubs. He come down the street to see us playin'. He says, 'Whyn't y'all come on. I want to make a dub of y'all.' So we went in there and made a dub. A lot of people went there, and he sold some of them dubs. He dubbed and dubbed and dubbed, and he was sellin' them dubs for a dollar." It was on one of these one-shot "vanity" discs that Walter made his recording debut, probably playing second guitar with Floyd on a version of the song "Ora Nelle Blues," which he would soon come back to recut—on harp this time—backing singer/guitarist Othum Brown. Jones acknowledged that it was Brown who sang and played on Walter's first issued record, but proudly stipulated that ". . . me and Walter made the first one Little Walter had on wax."

He may not have appreciated it at the time, but in later years Abrams was justly proud of having opened doors for some of the locals. "Little Walter and Johnny Young were the first to cut records here," he said. "These fellas that were down here, they used to come into my store. I used to have a little disc recorder and a mike, they'd sit on a box or something and sing. Well one day I thought this might sell. I took it to a pressing plant and had records made, a thousand or so." These records were pressed under the "Ora-Nelle" label.

The sides were the first release for the label, with the disc optimistically bearing the release number 711, from crapshooter's parlance for winning throws of the dice; the label credits went to "Little Walter J., harmonica and Othum Brown, guitar." Not much is known about Brown; he reportedly came from Richland, Mississippi, and was on the Chicago scene till the early '50s when he disappeared. (Jimmy Rogers later stated that Brown died not long after returning to the south.) Walter took the vocals on "Just Keep Loving Her," while Brown sang "Ora Nelle," and each received composer-credit for their respective numbers.

There are two surviving takes of each tune. The originally unissued first take of "Ora Nelle Blues" is a bit faster than the issued version; Little Walter's harmonica is a little more prominent on take two. Brown sings with feeling and plays a solid "chopping" rhythm guitar behind the lead guitar work, which was probably supplied by Jimmy Rogers, who later recorded the same tune himself as "That's All Right." Both Rogers and Brown had probably first heard the song from Robert Lockwood, who was performing it years earlier in Helena, Arkansas. Muddy Waters said, "'That's All Right,' that Robert Jr.'s song." Brown sings a different second verse on take two, leaving out a few words in order to fit the tempo better. As he closes out the second chorus with the refrain, "I wonder who loving Ora Nelle tonight?" an enthusiastic Walter jumps in, interjecting "I wonder that too, boy—you sang the blues for me, now?" Brown responds, "Play it for me, boy," and Walter responds with a harp solo drawn directly from the Sonny Boy I bag of tricks. He begins with sustained chords, adds intensity with hand wah-wah effects, and ends with single notes, all shaped with the familiar John Lee Williamson vocal tone. Brown tosses in encouraging comments over Walter's solo, and the resulting 2 minute, 45 second side is quite a respectable blues recording debut.

Walter's B-side number, "Just Keep Loving Her," has a strong resemblance to "Keep What You Got," a walking boogie number recorded by Floyd Jones around the same time. It was the kind of piece that undoubtedly got toes tapping on Maxwell Street. Walter begins with a solo harp introduction, joined after a few beats by a driving up-tempo guitar figure. He sings three relatively generic, wellspring blues verses ("Woke up this morning feeling bad, thinking about the girl I once have had," etc.) in a youthful but confidently open voice, answering his vocal lines with little harp interjections. Then he jumps into a quick loping harp break with his chords keeping pace with the running bass line. As with "Ora Nelle," an enthusiastic but slightly sloppy first take was followed by a clearly more focused second attempt, which was the issued version. The guitar and harp now work together better on the intro, and get the tune off with a solid kick. Again the tune ends with a flourish of chords up the neck of the guitar.

The only other single to be issued on the Ora Nelle label was by Uncle Johnny Williams and Johnny Young, a duo with whom Little Walter worked at The Purple Cat club. A few other sessions went unissued; one featured Sleepy John Estes. Another acetate that went unissued at the time—and which is further evidence of the musical crosspollination going on—featured Jimmy Rogers backed up by Little Walter, reworking another Sleepy John Estes' song, "Liquor Store Blues." Rogers called his version "Little Store," and matches Estes original brisk pace. Walter's harp locks into the quick tempo, as he takes the opportunity to really work out and strut his stuff, playing virtually non-stop phrases, slowing down to breathe only when he shouts encouragement or answer Rogers's vocals with exclamations such as "What her name, man?" Again, there are two takes, both solidly cooking. On the second version, Walter plays with increasing confidence, as he stretches out with more single-notes riffs and phrases instead of the chugging rhythms that marked the first attempt. Walter acquits himself admirably, playing with gusto and some well-defined if slightly derivative chops. Perhaps the reason the track went unreleased then had more to do with Abrams's limited finances than the quality of the recordings, which hold up well today.

Abrams's shiny, brittle acetate discs had a homemade look about them; the label was handwritten, and usually wound up slightly off-center. They didn't have much durability, either; worn needles and a few plays would soon obscure the music in a wash of hiss and surface noise. So it was a real pleasure for Walter to hold his own manufactured record, with its own shine and smell, and a heft that the thinner acetates didn't have— and there was his name, imprinted under the song title. It must have also been a kind of cocky vindication; among the many talented men plying the blues trade, he'd been singled out, recognized and given his due: his own recording. Anyone who wanted a copy could buy it in the store, and it was likely to be heard on area jukeboxes as well. And having a record out put a bluesman in a different league when it came to getting a gig in the local bars; he now had a "hit" to perform, even if it was on a strictly local scale. It also helped solidify Walter's image as primarily a bluesman; in the past he'd been proud of his ability to play all kinds of music to please the passersby on the street.

Saleswise, the record didn't do much. Of the thousand or so copies Abrams pressed, there were still some in stock at his store at a dollar each shortly before he closed for good almost 30 years later. And Walter said he never saw any money from it at all. But it certainly must have helped his image on the street, not to mention with the women.

Walter played with his "label mates," Uncle Johnny Williams and Johnny Young, as a trio at The Purple Cat club. Williams had almost given up the guitar after losing a finger in an accident while working at a meat packing plant, until one day when he saw the musician Blind Arvella Gray playing on the street. Gray was playing guitar with even fewer fingers, the result of a shotgun-blast that had also robbed him of his sight. Williams reevaluated his own situation, and spent some time woodshedding, learning new ways to finger his guitar. Perhaps concerned about losing any more digits, he took a big step towards changing careers and pursuing music full-time when he joined the musicians union in 1947, which meant he now was sanctioned to play in the union-controlled nightclubs earning a relatively respectable union scale—but he was also prohibited from playing for tips on Maxwell Street. Gigs done there, or anywhere else without official union contracts, were considered "scabbing," and offenders could be fined, or kicked out of the union.

Williams landed a job at The Purple Cat club, backed by Little Walter, and in a later interview the older man had nothing but praise for his young harp player. "Just overall [he] was good. I ain't ever heard anybody who could do more with a harmonica than Walter," Williams said. Jimmy Rogers later made some disparaging remarks about what he perceived as Walter's erratic timing, to which Williams responds, "Jimmy Rogers wasn't even playing nowhere! He'd come around where we was playing and sit down and play a number with us, that was it. Little Walter was going about his business and Jimmy Rogers didn't even have a job. Any key you got in, Walter had a harp for it. I'm not gonna lie on it, 'cause if he hadn't o' had good time Muddy wouldn't have wanted him."

Usually, on a Saturday night, Williams's cousin Johnny Young would stop by to sit in at The Purple Cat, almost becoming an ad hoc third member of the group. The Purple Cat job kept them busy. "Generally the gigs we had was three nights a week, some places would go four. Very few places went every night—but The Purple Cat did, every night except Monday," Williams explained. "I was working at Oscar Mayer's [meat packing plant]. I'd go to work at four in the morning, I'm off at twelve noon. Come home and go to sleep. Get to the Purple Cat and the music starts at nine in the evening, going from nine 'til two in the morning. Sometimes I'd get back home in time to catch a little nod, then I'd go back to work again. I did that for about two months."

One night, another regular patron turned up with his saxophone, wanting to sit in, but Walter nixed the idea. Sit-in guests were sometimes a welcome relief for a tired bandleader, but inviting an unknown on stage to jam opened up the risk of sending the gig into a tailspin if the guest lacked the talent. There was also the ever-present potential for friction between harp and horn players; they both worked in the same tonal range, often trying to weave their instruments into the same areas of the musical tapestry, and, of course, even an unamplified sax could easily drown out a harp. At any rate, Walter felt they had a good balance going as things were, and he objected strongly to rocking the boat by allowing the sax player to join them onstage. "That's when him and Johnny Young got to arguing . . . got into a fight up there on the bandstand," Williams recalled. "Big as Johnny was, he would have tore him in two pieces. Johnny was a screwball anyway when he started to drinking." The upshot was that "the Jewish owner, a guy named Ed, he laid Little Walter off," and Williams and Young continued on at The Purple Cat as a duo.

In retrospect, this appeared to Williams to be a turning point for the young harp player, because Walter's next alliance in Chicago was the one that would catapult him to national prominence. Williams later remarked about the event, "That's when Little Walter went with Muddy Waters." But in fact Walter didn't immediately hook up with Waters. Rogers, who'd been jamming regularly with Walter and playing occasional house parties, recalled it was about this time that "Walter vanished off the scene. He left

Chicago and went someplace else. Eventually he did come back, maybe some six months later."

Some thought he might have gone back to Helena, but more than likely Walter was in St. Louis during at least a few of these months, visiting his friend James DeShay. The two played frequent gigs, hitting smaller taverns and house parties, when they could fit them in around DeShay's day job schedule. After a few months, Walter was talking about returning to Chicago, but DeShay didn't pay it too much mind. Then one day after they'd done a gig, Walter ". . . got his little bag and stuff together and just left," DeShay said. But there was a problem: Along with his little bag, he also left wearing one of DeShay's brother's suits. "He couldn't fit mine," DeShay noted. That put a bit of a chill on the friendship, and for a long time after that, when Walter hit St. Louis, he would find somewhere else to stay, and did not contact his old friend. DeShay bumped into Little Walter again, completely by accident, on a tourist trip to Chicago a few years later, and the two reaffirmed their friendship.

Around the time of Walter's initial recording attempts for Ora Nelle in 1947, another fledgling record company had opened its doors in Chicago. Aristocrat Records was founded in April of that year by Charles and Evelyn Aron (along with three other financial backers), with offices in Aron's painting shop in one of the white business districts on Chicago's South Side. The label's direction was a bit schizophrenic at the outset; the first two sessions involved the Sherman Hayes Band (a white hotel band with steel guitar and a syrupy sax section) and the Five Blazes, a black harmony group. By September, Aristocrat had another investor, Leonard Chess, an ambitious, hustling young Jewish entrepreneur, whose family had emigrated from Poland to Chicago's South Side while Leonard was a boy. With his younger brother Phil, Leonard was running a bar and after-hours joint called The Macomba Lounge, catering to black clientele, featuring mostly jazz and jump-blues acts. Leonard became involved in the record company to promote a singer at the club, Andrew Tibbs. Leonard thought Tibbs was worth recording and sought out information about the business, then ran into the Arons. *Billboard* magazine soon reported that Chess had been named as a new addition to the sales staff of Aristocrat. Chess started out wholesaling 78s out of the trunk of his Buick, but before long he bought out the silent backers, and increased his share of the firm. With the connections he'd made booking black musical acts into The Macomba Lounge, Aristocrat soon evolved into a major player in the local black record-buying market. During 1947, the company recorded or acquired some 136 sides, and although most of the artists were black, only ten titles could really be called blues numbers; the rest were jazz, piano-boogie, pop-styled R&B, lounge ballads, and even some gospel. Although Leonard may not have known it yet at the time, a change in this ratio would ultimately pay big dividends, and Little Walter was going to play a major role in the company's growth.

Jimmy Rogers was another artist whose involvement with Leonard Chess would eventually lead to much bigger things. While Leonard was still learning the ins and outs of the record business, Jimmy was gigging around the area with different pickup bands, including a quartet with guitarist Claude "Blue Smitty" Smith, a pianist recalled only as "King," and "Porkchop" (possibly Eddie "Porkchop" Hines, another Maxwell

Street regular) on drums. Jimmy also did gigs with Sonny Boy I in a combo that included Muddy Waters, who'd been hired probably as much for his wheels as his musical ability. Waters was the only one in this group to own a car at the time, a rust-colored '40 Chevrolet two-door he'd bought, according to Rogers, with an inheritance from his grandmother. "That's what really started him going around," Rogers said. "Whenever they had to go out of town, someplace where they couldn't ride a bus or get a cab reasonable, then they'd call Muddy—like Gary, [Indiana] or some place like that." Frequently the group played in the bars there for $10 or $15 apiece, and Williamson's hard-drinking habits ultimately benefited both Waters and Rogers. Sonny Boy was a carouser of note; he liked his booze, and would frequently drink to the point of belligerence, or until he simply passed out. Both Muddy and Jimmy told stories of taking the stage and leading the band when Williamson was a bit too far gone to continue; on those nights, Rogers would cover in the reed department. "We'd go on over there and John Lee, Sonny Boy'd get high and I'd play the harp, and Muddy was bumping the bass on the guitar, Sunnyland Slim would bring in the piano and we'd make the gig," Rogers explained.

Rogers was also playing harp now and then in a group with Muddy, and often with Blue Smitty on guitar. Smith was a 9 to 5 electrician who played music on weekends. A cousin of Muddy's introduced the two when Muddy had a problem with the pickup that he'd attached to amplify his guitar, and Smith soldered and repaired it for him. Smith noted that Waters was still playing in the "country" manner, with his guitar tuned to an open chord, and playing almost exclusively with a slide on his finger. The two got to talking, and Smith started to show him some "single note picking" in standard tuning. The two soon were getting together several times a week at Muddy's, after Smith got off work. One night, on his way back home, Smith had his guitar and Gibson amp with him when he stopped in a barbershop for a haircut. He got talked into playing a couple of numbers there, and one of the other patrons was impressed enough to offer him a job at his joint, The Chicken Shack—if he could put a three-piece band together. Smith called Muddy, Muddy got Rogers, and they went into the club, Friday through Sundays, at $5 a man per night. "We started playing for him and that place stayed jam packed," Smith recalled. "Then he wanted us on Thursday nights [too] . . . Jimmy Rogers was blowing harmonica then, I was playing first guitar and Muddy was playing second. And this one boy was playing, had a bass string hooked to this washtub . . . We played there for him, oh I guess all that year." But Smith's day job apparently began taking its toll on his attendance at the gigs. On the increasingly frequent nights when Smitty failed to show up or disappeared at intermission, Rogers himself ". . . had to play guitar—if [Smitty] was [there] I'd play harmonica."

According to Smitty, it was pianist Eddie Boyd who got them into the union so they could play a gig at a slightly more upscale club, The Flame; ". . . I know a guy wants some blues players, but you gotta be union—you can be making $63 a week a piece, and be off on Tuesdays," Boyd promised. Sure enough, he got them their membership cards, and Rogers and Muddy worked there backing Boyd until Boyd quit and went off to Gary, Indiana. Boyd, who thought of himself as a higher-class musician, came to regret his decision to sponsor the men. He didn't really appreciate Muddy's "gut-bucket" style, and he had even less patience when Little Walter showed up to try and sit in on harp.

Saying that "A harmonica degrades a musician," he'd tell Walter not to get up on his stage. After Boyd moved on, Sunnyland Slim, who'd by then settled permanently in Chicago, came in for several weeks. When that gig ended, he promoted another, over at the Cotton Club.

Jimmy Rogers, who was by then playing more guitar than harmonica, remembered the young harpman from Maxwell Street and mentioned him once more to Muddy, prior to their working with Boyd. At the time Muddy said, "Bring him by." So Rogers carried Walter over and the three started jamming together in Muddy's living room. Waters was impressed; "Yeah, he's real good," he told Rogers. Then began a period of intense rehearsing. Rogers would later claim that it was he and Muddy who made Walter the player he became. "In about six or eight months we had him pretty well lined up," Rogers recounted:

> The only problem we had with that unit was getting Walter down, bringing him down. He was just wild man, he'd get to executing and go on. He'd been used to playing by himself or with musicians who didn't know much. His timing was real bad . . . he was just following around, whatever we were playing he would try to play it on the harp. But after he got with us, he listened to what we were doing and I learned him his count pretty good.

Rogers suggests that, either by design or by mistake, Walter was straying outside the standard twelve-bar, three-chord blues pattern. Of course, so was Muddy, who liked to lag behind the beat vocally, and altered the chord changes to make them fit his sometimes longer lyric lines.

It wasn't long before Walter was a regular on the Chicken Shack gig. Recognizing Walter's superior skills on harp, Rogers switched to guitar full time. Some nights, three guitars would be lacing together, probably with Muddy taking the bass lines, Jimmy playing chords, and Smitty taking the leads. After a bit, the group moved over to The Purple Cat. Smitty recalled that around this time he and Walter would cram into phono-booths where they would cut one-off records for a quarter, trying out different sounds. But Smitty, with other interests and a good day job, eventually dropped out and moved out of the city to the south suburbs, away from the burgeoning urban blues scene.

The whole scene was quite fluid, with most musicians, even those who led their own bands, picking up work when and wherever they could, and playing as sidemen on nights off from their regular gigs. Even though it seemed that his main chance to make it was with Muddy, Rogers did one-nighters with Floyd Jones, Eddie Taylor, and others. Muddy jobbed with Sunnyland Slim and Sonny Boy, and in fact on a few occasions, was even hired by Walter as a sideman. "Little Walter was a good little hustler," Muddy chuckled. "He'd play with you or get him a gig by himself, get him a guitar player and go on and do it. I played a gig with him one night. Sideman, before I got going. Yeah, I played a couple gigs with him." Walter also worked around town with various people. In general, there was a lot of back and forth and mix-and-match scuffling to make a buck.

Around November 1947, Waters got another chance to record, this time for Leonard Chess's Aristocrat Label, with pianist Sunnyland Slim. "Sunnyland Slim is the one who put us all in the record business," Rogers explained. "He was going strong and he had good connections in the field, he boost us on over." The Sunnyland session produced four songs; Muddy backed Sunnyland's vocals on two numbers, then moved up to the mike himself for two. He sang "Gypsy Woman," a blues ballad with Slim and Muddy taking a mellow instrumental break, backed by Big Crawford's booming standup bass, followed by "Little Anna Lee" in the same vein. Muddy's voice already was completely recognizable, but the feel is more smooth and urbane than the hair-raising down-home funk that was to come a couple of years later. The record was put on the shelf for a few months, possibly due to internal turmoil at the label, finally seeing release around March 1948. By then, Chess's partners at the label, the Arons, had separated; Charles Aron had no interest in the label, leaving Evelyn Aron and Leonard Chess in complete control.

Sunnyland then made it clear that he held no grudge against Walter for his previous woman-poaching back in Missouri when he landed a session with Tempo-Tone, and brought Walter aboard for the date. Tempo-Tone was another of the short-lived blues labels sprouting up in the city to take advantage of the blossoming scene, this one started by the enterprising owner of a tavern not far from The Purple Cat. Sunnyland also brought along Muddy and Floyd Jones on guitars, and another of their local running partners, "Babyface" Leroy Foster, on drums. Foster, born in Alabama and raised in the Mississippi delta, was also a guitarist and singer, and had been following Muddy's group on gigs. This session produced the first-ever recordings of Muddy Waters and Little Walter together. On the "A" side, "Blue Baby," Walter takes the vocal on a number still cast solidly in the Sonny Boy tradition. "It's the blues baby, keep on worrying me," Walter sang. "If I don't find my baby somebody gonna bury me," borrowing closely from Williamson's record "TB Blues" from a decade earlier. Going into the middle instrumental chorus he even quotes Sonny Boy's frequent "I got it myself" spoken interjection, as he called for his own solo.

The "B" side, "I Want My Baby," is a jump-blues with Muddy thumping out walking-bass lines behind Walter's harp once again showing John Lee's influence. Walter sings the playful lyrics "Two old maids, lying in the bed, one turned to the other and said—I wants my baby," with Muddy and Sunnyland joining in on the refrain, "I wants my baby right here beside o' me." The number is a lightweight romp, and both Walter and Slim get off solid instrumental sections, while Muddy mostly handles the rhythm. If the overall sound was derivative, it was nonetheless well executed, and Walter's playing was improving; his harp phrases are better-articulated than on his Ora Nelle recordings of just a few months earlier.

Around March of 1948, Chess called Muddy and Sunnyland back to the studio. According to Rogers, Chess was inspired by recent hits by down-home styled, unaccompanied bluesmen Lightning Hopkins and John Lee Hooker (whose "Boogie Chillen" was then hot on the charts), and he wanted to get his own deep blues artist going. Slim suggested that his guitar-playing partner might fill the bill. Despite some reservations about recording solo, "old-time" pieces—in contrast to the smoother style that had won him some moderate success in the Chicago clubs—Muddy reached back and pulled out a couple of suitable numbers. Like his first foray into the studio for Chess, it was again a split session. On the first couple of numbers, backed by Sunnyland's piano and a droning sax background, Muddy again sang in his more current, laid-back, "sweet" blues style. Then everybody sat out except for Ernest "Big" Crawford on bass, and Muddy went back down home. He retuned his guitar to an open chord that Smitty had weaned him from, pulled out his slide, and recut two deep blues that he'd originally done for a Library of Congress field recording session in Mississippi some six years earlier. "I Can't Be Satisfied" is an ironically jaunty lament, propulsively fueled by Crawford's jumping bass. "I Feel Like Going Home" sounds like Muddy's early influence, Robert Johnson—but plugged in, turned up, and ready to kick the ass of anyone who doesn't feel like going home with him. Waters hits some heavily tremoloed sustained chords with his slide, his amp contributing an edge of growling distortion. His vocals jump off the record with a compelling urgency and sexual undercurrent to them. In retrospect, it's obvious that a corner had been turned.

Aristocrat issued the first two, more generic, numbers in May, and nothing much happened. Chess was reportedly not completely convinced of Muddy's potential; "I can't understand the lyrics," he said after listening to one take. But when the label released the down-home tracks a month or two later, Muddy became practically an overnight star. Within a couple of days, the initial pressing of 3,000 copies was almost sold out, bought mostly at the barbershops, beauty parlors, and corner stores that doubled as record outlets in the black community. At 33, Muddy had his first bona-fide hit, a tune that would soon begin climbing the charts. By September it was #11 in the *Billboard* listings. Thanks in part to Muddy's success, Aristocrat had by then moved to bigger offices at 52nd St. and Cottage Grove, closer to the heart of Chicago's black community.

For the time being, the core trio of Waters, Rogers, and Walter continued playing clubs, often augmented by "Babyface" Leroy Foster on guitar or drums. The music was a blend of current hot numbers and some of Muddy's original down-home tunes. The mix of the rhythmically intertwining guitar riffs, Walter's dynamic harp, Muddy's whining amplified slide playing and passionate vocals, and Foster's raucous drums, was just what the bar patrons wanted. For the many southerners who'd come north looking for jobs, it was a sound familiar from down home, now cast in a newer, big-city mold. "We kept that Mississippi sound," Waters told an interviewer. "We didn't do it exactly like the older fellows, with no beat to it. We put the beat with it. . . . We learned the beat, we learned what people's moving off of. Even if it's the blues we still had to drive behind it."

The group played most of the area's blues hot spots: The 708 Club at 708 E. 47th; Docie's Lounge on 51st and Prairie; the Du Drop Inn at 36th and Wentworth; on the near West Side in clubs like the Zanzibar at 13th and Ashland, and the Boogie Woogie Inn; and on special Sunday Matinees at Silvio's on West Lake Street. Matinees ran from 2:00 to 8:00 PM; often the band would also have a regular gig that night, starting at 9:00 PM, going till 2:00 AM, a grueling schedule that tapped into their reserves of stamina and drive. But Muddy's band was hot and they knew it; when they weren't booked, they'd go out looking for blood. The trio came to be known informally around town as The Headcutters or The Headhunters; whichever, their intent was clear. They went to places where other blues bands were playing, looking to "cut heads" musically, stealing gigs from other bands. "If we get a chance, we were gonna burn 'em," Muddy recalled. Rogers adds, "We'd get an amp from the car, quick bring it in and set up and play a few numbers. And when we'd leave, the crowd would leave too [laughs]." Rogers recalled that bands usually sat down in chairs while performing in those days, a custom probably based at least in part on seeing that big bands and other "professional" musicians always performed that way. One of the fringe benefits of sitting for a small blues combo was that if they didn't have drums, they could keep time with tapping (or stomping) feet. "Babyface, oh man, he'd click 'em both!" Rogers said.

The biggest influence on Walter remained Chicago's reigning king of the blues harmonica, Sonny Boy I. Walter was later to say, in a rare public display of respect for a fellow harp player, "On the harp, well, I heard them all, and I give Sonny Boy Williamson the credit as a creator. I was crazy about his records. He had a true balance. He was the only man I really admired, but I didn't model myself on him. Know him? Yes I did—used to be with him all the time." Williamson held a longtime regular gig at the Club Georgia at 4547 S. State. When he first started there, the club had a jazzy band fronted by fleet-fingered guitarist Lonnie Johnson, and Sonny Boy was only a featured guest. The club owner must have recognized the harpman's popularity with the crowd. He eventually staged a "Battle Of The Blues" contest between Johnson and Williamson. Sonny Boy apparently prevailed, because he was soon the only headliner, backed by piano and guitar. "Sonny Boy was a carouser," harpman Billy Boy Arnold later said. "He liked people, he was a gregarious guy. He liked to gamble and go around—Memphis Slim said that everywhere he went he had four or five people following him around, they was getting free drinks."

Sunnyland Slim kept an illegal gambling den and after-hours drinking club in his residence for his musician friends, paying off the police for protection. Years later, Sunnyland boasted of having "a big bull-moose" white patrolman standing guard out front, and that he would pay the cops off for each shift, afternoon and evening. Snooky Pryor recalled:

> Sonny Boy used to go by Sunnyland's basement hangout for musicians on 26th and Prairie. Floyd Jones and Moody Jones, too. But I never did used to go by there unless'n I went by to take Floyd or Moody, one or the other. I didn't gamble, that kind of mess. It was kind of rough in that neighborhood. If you won any money, you couldn't walk out of there with it. If you was kind of strange over there, you went in and come out of there, somebody'd be out there to stick you up man, and take your money.

Sonny Boy had another regular gig at the Plantation Club at 31st St. and Giles Ave., which was just five-minute walk up Giles Avenue from Sonny Boy's apartment. He must have felt relatively at ease in his own neighborhood, which proved to be his downfall. Billy Boy Arnold later recounted what happened:

> Sonny Boy, when he got paid that night [June 1, 1948], he liked to hang out and gamble. That's a bad sign, fooling around in those gambling joints, dangerous places. You go there, win all the money, then they want something back—"Hey man, give me $50, motherfuck, give me something, you won all my money!"—and then they wanna fight. Well, Sonny Boy had probably been drinking, there was more than one [of them], somebody picked up a piece of concrete and hit him in the head.

Sonny Boy somehow made his way home and up onto his front porch. His suit was full of dust, and he was propped against the door when his wife Lacey Belle answered the ringing doorbell. (According to Eddie Boyd, she was annoyed that, once again, he'd come home late, and had obviously been drinking, so she let him wait at the door half an hour before finally going downstairs and letting him in.) When she opened the door he said, "They got me, they got me, I won more money tonight than I ever won." Lacey helped him out of his clothes, thinking he was just drunk again. But when he began to groan, "I'm dying, I'm dying," she called the authorities. It was too late; he was transported to nearby Michael Reese Hospital, but was dead on arrival. He was 34, and his senseless beating death was a foreshadowing, a dark omen for his protégé, who would die under almost exactly the same conditions, almost exactly twenty years later.

Within a few months, the Aristocrat label moved to capitalize on Williamson's passing by issuing a record called "Memory Of Sonny Boy" by one of the most accurate of his many imitators, "Forrest City Joe" Pugh. His untimely death marked an end of an era, but unbeknownst to the many fans and friends who were mourning his passing, it marked the beginning of a distinctly new era in Chicago blues. For many, Sonny Boy's style was becoming a bit too familiar, old hat to the blues-buying public. People were hungry for sounds that kept up with the pace of the rocking and screeching "L" trains, the flash of the blast furnaces at the steel mills, and the hard reality of the killing floor at the slaughterhouses. Muddy Waters, Jimmy Rogers, and Little Walter thought they had something the people wanted. As it turns out, they were right: they had the foundation, the very bedrock, for the new sound of Chicago Blues.

5 *ebony boogie*

Chicago/Helena/Mississippi/Chicago:
September 1948–Fall 1951

On September 9, 1948, Walter walked into the Selective Service office at 22 West Jackson Blvd. in the heart of the downtown "Loop" area, and filled out a registration card for the military draft, which all 18-year-old males were then required to do. But it was not just an act of good citizenship. Walter considered himself a full-grown man as he became a regular in the south side "sawdust clubs," but he still had occasional problems with bouncers and bartenders who thought he might be under the legal drinking age of twenty-one. Any place that served liquor could be closed down if the cops caught a minor on the premises, and most bar managers were diligent about making sure everyone was legal. So as many young men have done, before and since, Walter set out to get a fake ID, a draft card stating that he was over the age of twenty-one.

Unlike his Social Security registration from a few years earlier, this time he supplied both names his parents had given him, and identified himself as Marion Walter Jacobs of 910 Maxwell Street. He gave his occupation as "junk man," working at 1362 S. Sangamon, right around the corner from his residence. In the box labeled "firm or individual by whom employed," the clerk who filled out the form wrote "does not know."

The most interesting entry is in the date-of-birth section, where Walter offered the date May 1, 1925, in Alexander [sic], Louisiana—padding his age by five years to make him a ripe old twenty-three. Possibly in an attempt to add further credence to his claimed age, he indicated his martial status as "married" and "separated." On the back of the card, he gave his description as: brown eyes, black hair, dark complexion, height 5' 8½", weight 145, and his race as Negro. Under "other obvious physical characteristics which will aid in identification," the clerk filled in "scar on right forehead." On the signature line Walter again printed his name in block letters, using all capitals, and reversing the "N" in Marion as he had on his Social Security application. He now had a government-issued ID that would prove he was old enough to enter any club or tavern he wanted. Although it's not indicated on the registration form, he must have also informed the Selective

SELECTIVE SERVICE SYSTEM
REGISTRATION CARD

SELECTIVE SERVICE NUMBER
., 18 25 23 0

[Registrar will not enter Selective Service number]

1. Name   *JACOBS   MARION   WALTER.*
   (Last)   (First)   (Middle)

2. Place of residence *910 W. MAXWELL ST.*
   CHICAGO   ILL.
   (City, town, village, or county)   (State)
   [The place of residence given on the line above will determine Local Board jurisdiction]

3. Mailing address *910 W. MAXWELL ST.*
   CHICAGO, ILL.

4. Name and address of person who will always know your address
   LESLIE GIZEMS   910 W. MAXWELL ST. CHICGO, ILL.
   (Name)   (Address)

5. Date of birth *MAY   1   1925*
   (Month)   (Day)   (Year)

6. Place of birth *ALEXANDER   LA.*
   (City, town, village,   (State or country)
   or county)

7. Occupation   *JUNK MAN*

8. Firm or individual by whom employed   *DOES NIT KNOW*

9. Nature of business, service rendered, or chief product   *JUNK SALVAGE*

10. Place of employment or business
    1362 S. SANGAMON   CHI.   COOK   ILL.
    (Number and street or R. F. D. number)   (Town)   (County)   (State)

11. Local board with which registered under Selective Training and Service Act of 1940, as amended
    LEE COUNTY, ARK.

12. Were you ever rejected for service in the armed forces? Yes ☒ No ☐ When? *1944 & 1945*

13. Marital status: Single ☐   Married ☒ [Living with wife ☐   Separated ☒   Father ☐   (Over)
                                             [Divorced ☐   Widower ☐

---

14. Active duty in the armed forces of the United States or a cobelligerent nation since Sept. 16, 1940:
    NONE
    (Branch of Armed Forces)
    (Name of last organization)
    (Service or serial number)   (Date of entry)
    (Date of separation)

15. Present membership in a reserve component of the armed forces:
    NONE
    (Branch of Armed Forces)   (Service or serial number)
    (Grade and organization)   (Date of entry)

I affirm that I have verified the foregoing answers and that they are true:
MARION WALTER JACOBS
(Signature of registrant)

DESCRIPTION OF REGISTRANT

16. Color of eyes *BR.* Color of hair *BLK* Complexion *DARK.*
    Height (approx.) *5 ft. 8 2 in.* Weight (approx.) *145* Race *N*
    Other obvious physical characteristics that will aid in identification:
    SCAR IN RIGHT FORE HEAD.

I certify that my answers are true; that the person registered has read or has had read to him his own answers; that I have witnessed his signature or mark and that all of his answers of which I have knowledge are true, except as follows:
NONE TO MY KNOWLEDGE

SEPT 8 1941   *Robert E. McL*
(Date of registration)   (Signature of registrar)

Registrar for local board *14*   *CHICAGO   ILL.*
(Number)   (City or county)   (State)

LOCAL BOARD NO. 18
CHICAGO AREA OFFICE NO. 1

226 W. Jackson Blvd.

(Stamp of the Local Board having jurisdiction as determined by item 2, front of card)

U. S. GOVERNMENT PRINTING OFFICE: 1940—O-790018

Figure 5.1 Little Walter draft registration.

SELECTIVE SERVICE SYSTEM

EXTRACT OF REGISTRANT CLASSIFICATION RECORD

The following information concerning the Selective Service registrant named has been extracted from the Classification Record (SSS Form 102). Unless otherwise noted, all entries on this record are included. See reverse side for brief explanation of classification descriptions.

Name of registrant: _JACOBS MARION WALTER_

Selective Service No.: _11 - 18 - 25 - 230_   Date of Birth: _MAY 1, 1925_

Classification Questionnaire: Date Mailed _11-12-48_   Date Returned _____

Classification and Date of Mailing Notice:

	Class		Date			Class		Date
1. Class	3A	Date	12-8-48		5. Class		Date	
2. Class	5A	Date	8-16-51		6. Class		Date	
3. Class		Date			7. Class		Date	
4. Class		Date			8. Class		Date	

Armed Forces Physical Examination: Date(s): _____   Results: _____

(Qual - Qualified; Acc - Accepted; NQ - Not Qualified; Rej - Rejected)

Entry on Active Duty or Civilian Work: Date: _____

Branch of Service (if indicated): _____

Mode of Entry: ☐ Inducted (IND)   ☐ Enlisted (ENL)
☐ Commissioned (COMM)   ☐ Ordered

Date of Separation from Active Duty or Civilian Work: _____

Entries from Remarks Column: _____

OTHER ENTRIES: Entered below are any entries (with the appropriate column headings) which appear on the original classification record and for which there is no fill-in space above:

FRC USE ONLY

Date Prepared: _12/16/92_

Prepared By: _J Roland_

FRC Stamp: _CHICAGO FRC_

TO:

SSS FORM 708
JUL 77

Service that he was the head of a household; three months later his draft eligibility status would be officially classified 3A, "registrant with a child or children; or registrant deferred by reason of extreme hardship to dependents." Not only was Walter now covered in the taverns, but he didn't have to worry about the draft, either.

Walter may have been one of the youngest working musicians on the blues scene then, but before long there would be other young harpists following closely on his heels. Down in Arkansas, there was James Cotton, then a 13-year-old runaway who'd claimed to be an orphan in order to get close to the other Sonny Boy, Rice Miller, and was learning his style by following him around on gigs. In Chicago, John Lee "Sonny Boy" Williamson's disciple, 12-year-old Billy Boy Arnold, was beginning to study the harp in earnest as he mourned the death of his idol. The loss was particularly personal for Billy, who had received an impromptu music lesson from Sonny Boy just a week before his murder, and had gladly lent the older man one of his new harps. Billy never saw the man, or the harp for that matter, again. (Williamson's widow Lacey Belle offered to repay the youngster for the lost harp. Arnold declined, "No, I don't want you to pay, he was my friend.") Amos Blackmore, a 13-year-old from Memphis, was driving his family nuts by tying up the bathroom as he practiced his harp there, enamored of the echo that the tile and tub produced. Soon to be known as Junior Wells, the youngster had an early encounter with Walter and Muddy's band around this time.

Junior's older sister had a boyfriend who was a police officer, and the two took the 13-year-old to an afternoon matinee at popular WGES radio DJ Sam Evans's Ebony Lounge. The show started at 3:30 PM, and featured the four-piece Muddy Waters group. Although they were stopped at the door, the officer's badge gained entry for the youngster. They listened to a set, Wells's ears locked on Walter. On a band break, Junior's escort approached Muddy and asked if the boy could sit in. Muddy asked Junior if he "knew his timing." When he replied, "I think so," Muddy said, "Well if you think you can do it, it's all right with me. But first you have to ask Little Walter, because that's his amplifier and microphone and I can't give you permission to use his stuff, but I'll ask him and if he say it's okay, it's all right." Muddy went over to Walter, pointed to the lad and explained the deal to him. Wells heard Walter say, "That little old pipsqueak? Well, if he thinks he can do it, let him do it."

After the break the band came back and played a few, and then Muddy started working the crowd, mentioning that there was a kid in the house who was supposed to be a blues singer, and did they want to hear him? Amidst good-natured clapping, Wells took the stage, "Got on one of Muddy's tunes and went to walking the floor and all that—after a while money started coming up to the stage." At the time union scale per sideman on a live gig was $12.50, and the leader got $15; Wells said he did considerably better, pulling in about $75 in tips. The novelty of the 13-year-old harp player with Muddy's band proved popular enough that Junior was welcomed to stick around so he could be brought up during the next set as well.

Once Junior was off stage, Walter pulled him aside, asking him if he drank. Wells replied no. Walter said, "Give me five dollars for me to go get some gin." Wells said no, he didn't drink and he wasn't going to give Walter any money after he'd called him a pipsqueak. Wells's sister's boyfriend reminded him that he'd used Walter's amp, so Wells finally spotted Walter the cash to go around the corner and buy a pint. After Walter came back with the gin he took Wells out the back door of the club. "You and I can take a taste," he said. Wells again demurred, but Walter said "You saying no now, but if you stay in this business that you want to get in now, you're gonna take a drink sooner or later, you can believe that." Wells finally took a sip, and it was "the worst thing" he'd ever tasted. When it was time to go back on for the next set, Wells set up his harps on top of the amp. He turned around to face the clapping and hollering crowd, and he began shaking, overcome with nervous anxiety. Walter said, "You want that drink now?" Wells replied "Give me some!" Wells said:

> I went out there and started playing and then, wow! it kind of quiet my nerves. I found out if the people in the audience be drinking and you not drinking, they have a tendency when they get high, they get on your nerves and you can't socialize. Muddy told me, "You can't disrespect the people because they're drinking . . . if they're drinking and you ain't drinking, they'll piss you off." I had to do that too."

And so too did Walter, who'd obviously progressed quite a bit from the "kid drinking nothing but Pepsi Cola" that Muddy had met not long before. Over the years, drinking would become a serious problem for Walter, but for now it was a badge of manhood, and a way to deal with the pressures of the rough-and-tumble life of playing the bars.

The exposure and acclaim whetted Junior's appetite, and soon he was regularly playing with a young group then known as The Three Deuces, which featured Louis and Dave Myers on guitars. The two Myers brothers from the Mississippi hills just below Memphis came from a musical family, and at the time were still too young to play in the bars and clubs. They worked regularly playing at house parties around their south side neighborhood in Chicago, and were backing old-time bluesman Big Boy Spires when they first met Junior. The two had learned to play guitar at a very young age and developed a near-telepathic musical rapport, each perfectly supporting and complementing the other. Their burgeoning local reputations had already brought them to the attention of Big Bill Broonzy, who called them the "Little Rascals" out of respect for their musicianship combined with amusement over their young ages.

The Myers first applied their talents to the down-home styles they'd learned from their father's peers while living in Mississippi. When the family migrated to Chicago in 1941, the teenage brothers were soon taken with the more modern sounds of the swinging big bands they were hearing on the radio and record players in the city, and they sought to emulate these sounds with their guitars. Louis generally took the lead/rhythm chores while Dave tuned his strings down low and played bass patterns, sometimes clicking his strings against the fretboard for rhythm effects like a stand up bass player, occasionally switching to chords to accent and provide counterpoint to Louis's leads. The youngsters were learning jazz tunes like "Castle Rock" and "Lester Leaps In," and began rehearsing every other day. They concentrated particularly on more up-tempo shuffle beats, having noticed dancers responding favorably to this material when they were playing at house parties and sitting in on Sunday-matinee blues battles. Louis and Dave were both close to legal age, and hoped it wouldn't be too long before they found themselves work in the clubs.

Muddy's band continued getting regular club work in Chicago into 1949, and crowds mobbed the clubs that the band played. As Jimmy Rogers told a radio interviewer years later:

> Memphis Minnie, Tampa Red and Memphis Slim and fellows of that nature, they had been real hot with the blues—but they were dying off. They got real common—that type of blues at that time. And we came in right at that time and grabbed the blues again and put fire behind them and started livenin' it back up again. Because all those people were playin' man, they were famous when I was a little boy, some before I was born. And they'd come around to hear us play, to see what we were doin' and every one of them gave us a good compliment. "You're doin' something for the blues. I'm glad somebody's bringin' 'em back alive." And we livened the blues back up again, and more people decided they wanted to try to play the blues.

In those days, the American Federation of Musicians was a union with some real clout. If union agents found a bar or club was hiring non-union "scab" musicians, or paying musicians less than the standard union scale, they could virtually close the place down. All they had to do was call a strike, set up a picket line, and the Teamsters union would honor it and not cross it to make deliveries of beer and liquor; it wouldn't take long for stubborn club owners to change their minds and toe the union line. Union members were obligated to file contracts on their engagements, and pay a percentage of their income to the union. Failure to do so could result in fines and penalties costing more than the gig would pay. The union had recording sessions covered as well. Record companies were required to file reports with them listing all sessions, and to use only union musicians, then make the appropriate payments to the union, who then deducted their fees before paying the established union scale to the session participants.

The union may have overlooked some of the smaller or part-time music venues in the black community, and missed some of the one-off, hit-and-run recording sessions for small labels, but membership was a necessity for anyone who intended to make a living playing or recording professionally. And since the union scale was a step up from the payday offered by non-union gigs, it was in the best interest of most musicians to become members. So, on March 17, 1949, Walter went to the union hall, paid his dues, and joined up as a harmonica player with local 208, Chicago's "Black local" unit of the American Federation of Musicians. Again, he listed himself as Marion Walter Jacobs from Alexander, [sic] Lousiana—but this time he gave the same birthdate as on his Social Security records, May 1, 1923. One of the perks of union membership was a small life insurance policy that the union referred to as the "death benefit"; as beneficiary, Walter listed his mother, Beatrice.

Despite the success the band was demonstrating with Chicago blues audiences, Aristocrat didn't see any reason to rock the boat by recording Muddy with his full group, preferring to stick with the winning sound that had produced his first hit. Leonard's reluctance to allow any change may also have been a product of his own superstitious beliefs stemming back to his early childhood in a Jewish village in Poland. Malcolm Chisholm, a recording engineer at Universal in the '50s who later went on to work in the Chess studios, distinctly remembers this aspect of Chess's personality. "There was a tremendous amount of superstition involved," Chisolm says:

You would find him acting irrationally in odd ways. He didn't like to record on Fridays, and he'd never record on the thirteenth [of the month], but the seventh and eleventh were nice. I've been told that. . .on Muddy's first successful session, the bass player wore a red shirt. The record sold. The next session Leonard said, "Get that bass man. And have him wear a red shirt."

In late 1949, Muddy finally recorded for Aristocrat with a full group backing: still not quite his regular working line-up, but getting closer. It was another split session, starting out with pianist Johnny Jones as featured vocalist on two numbers, backed by Waters and Jimmy Rogers on guitars, and Leroy Foster on drums. When Muddy stepped up to the mike, he led off with "Screaming and Crying," an intense mid-tempo number, with some deep echo effect on the vocals. The other two sides sung by Waters that day were more run-of-the-mill, although "Last Time I Fool Around With You," a throwback to an earlier decade in style, was reputed to feature the venerable Tampa Red on guitar.

Muddy's band got another shot at recording, this time for Regal, a New Jersey-based label that did some recording in the Chicago area, featuring musicians like Memphis Minnie, Sunnyland Slim, and St. Louis Jimmy. Rogers was up front on vocals, backed by Walter on harp, either Johnnie Jones or Sunnyland on a distant piano, Crawford on bass, an unknown drummer, and possibly Muddy on guitar. The tune was Rogers's "Ludella," and though unissued at the time, it is the earliest known recording of Muddy's core band from this era. Walter still shows the Sonny Boy influence on his "wah-wah," vocal-toned bends, but he's right there playing his own rhythm and melody lines, and claiming his own space. It's only two verses and a guitar-based break chorus; still, the track is a tantalizing foretaste of things to come.

With all the club work, Walter's stock was rising a bit along the avenue and he bought a used car. Around this time, he proudly posed for a photo standing in front of his newly acquired 1939 Buick, leaning on the large hood, a foot propped jauntily on the solid metal bumper. The picture gives an idea of the Maxwell Street neighborhood at the time: behind Walter is a large, two-story, wood-frame residence, with a painted wooden sign advertising that there is also a business within: "Watches, Jewelry Repaired." Beside it stands a newer brick building with a neon sign overhanging the sidewalk. Walter is wearing a late '40s style high-crowned, wide-brimmed Stetson hat, a dark sport coat with a light shirt, white socks, and rather worn shoes. The hat makes Walter look older, and his expression is hardened and hungry. If his intent was to give a sign of prosperity, it was obviously hard-won, newly found, and not easy to maintain.

Walter took another step towards stability when he began what would be a long-term, live-in relationship with Ella Mae Taylor, a "very nice looking woman with nice complexion and nice hair." Taylor worked at the American Laundry, a few blocks down from their apartment. Walter's sister Marguerite considered Ella his common-law wife, and said that when they first hooked up, Walter was still scuffling. "She struggled with him through thick and thin, when he was just playing a little bit," Marguerite recalled.

Muddy put in a call down to radio station KFFA in Helena, and lined up a spot for a daily show. He was hoping to expand his opportunities a bit, and get out of town to escape the oncoming northern winter weather for a while. The pay was still only a dollar a day for a sideman, but the real payoff was the free advertising for the band's public appearances in the area. In December, Muddy traveled down south with his current four-piece group, Walter, Rogers, and Foster. They packed their gear and headed to Helena in two cars, Muddy's new convertible and Walter's Buick Special. When the group got to Helena, they found that they had secured their radio spot all right, the only problem was that it was from 6:00 to 7:00 AM! Following their blues program the station reverted to hillbilly and big-band records, until the noon hour when the King Biscuit Time show came on. Muddy's program was sponsored by Katz Clothing, one of the station's heavy advertisers.

Despite the show's early hour, Waters's decision to make the Helena station his base of operations was a good one. Calls began coming in from neighboring towns, where people wanted to hire the group they heard on the radio. There wasn't much work in Helena itself outside of the Owl Cafe, but they heard from a lot of little towns across the river in Mississippi: places like Clarksdale, Shelby, Cleveland, and Boyle. Soon the band was working frequently, often taking the ferry across to Mississippi, playing until 1:00 AM, then catching the last ferry from Friar's Point, crossing back to Helena to get a few hours sleep before airtime. One morning, Rogers and Walter, who were staying separately from Muddy, overslept. The radio was on at their hotel, and they heard only Foster beating away on his drums behind Muddy's slide. The announcer came on: "Well, Jimmy Rogers and Little Walter is somewhere sleeping it off. If they hear us, come on in." Rogers woke Walter and the pair raced to the studio, located upstairs in the Floyd Truck Lines building on York Street, arriving 20 minutes late. Muddy gave them a stern eye, but they quickly set up and, by the time the commercial break was finished, they were ready to get down to business. "That was a lot of fun. We didn't have no beef about it," Rogers recalled. While in Helena, the men connected with various old running partners, and Houston Stackhouse recalled a "right smart" of drinking around that town, with Rogers, Walter, Robert Jr., and himself out having a few while Muddy slept. They ended up staying there and playing around the neighboring area for about six weeks according to Waters, though it seemed more like three or four months, from October to January, according to Rogers.

Eventually the party ended and the group made their way back to Chicago. In December 1949, Evelyn Aron, part owner of Aristocrat, had remarried and left to form a record distribution company. The Chess Brothers would soon buy her out, becoming sole owners of the label, and brother Phil was now getting involved with Leonard in company operations. But their policy of keeping Muddy a solo artist remained in place.

Leonard must have felt that tampering with Muddy's winning formula might kill the goose that laid the golden egg. If Muddy was getting frustrated by Chess's refusal to record the band, it's easy to imagine that Walter and Rogers were feeling equally disappointed. They'd proven in the clubs that together the three of them were an unbeatable front line, and that the music they were playing was something new and vital. The band was a hot attraction around town, drawing a hard-drinking, appreciative crowd; but on the jukebox, the records were labeled only "Muddy Waters & his guitar." Nonetheless, the men were garnering a widening reputation in blues circles, as evidenced by a display ad the 708 Club ran in the *Chicago Defender* advertising a contest between Memphis Minnie and Big Bill Broonzy on Sunday afternoon, November 6th: "Sunnyland Slim, Muddy Waters and Jimmy Rogers" were prominently listed in the ad as the judges of this rematch. The contest ran from 3:00–8:00 AM, and following it, "entertainment rest of nite till closing by Memphis Minnie and Little Son Joe."

Leonard and Muddy had a handshake deal which retained him as an exclusive Aristocrat artist, but Muddy was obviously chafing at the musical restrictions, and seized an opportunity to do something about it. In mid-January 1950, shortly after the band's return from Helena, Muddy accompanied the band (minus Rogers) into the studio for yet another company, the newly formed Parkway Records. Independent distributor Monroe Passis announced that the label would be devoted exclusively to "Blues & Rhythm" offerings. The free-wheeling and high-spirited Parkway session produced eight titles, with two singles apiece issued by The Baby Face Leroy Trio and The Little Walter Trio. Walter recut the tune he'd first waxed for Ora Nelle a couple of years previously, now retitled "Just Keep A Loving Her." This time, he set the tempo just a bit slower, but the piece swings even more, with a confident authority that the previous version lacked. Foster keeps up a solid bass-drum kick marking the bottom, while Muddy plays both chords and single-note runs. Walter opens with three verses from the earlier cut, then takes a couple of solid harp choruses, once again chording in the familiar Sonny Boy style. A final verse harks back to an earlier era as Walter sings: "Tell me now baby where you stayed last night, your shoes ain't buttoned and your hair ain't right."

Next up at the vocal mike was Foster, who led off with "Boll Weevil," an ironic number making use of stop-time verses. If there was any hope of Muddy keeping a low profile and not having his cover blown, it flew out the window when Foster called for an instrumental chorus: "Well all right Little Walter, come here Muddy Waters!" The two instrumentalists weave tightly together, Walter playing strong single tones, Muddy chunking out solid chords. Although he took no lead vocals and his name didn't appear on the record labels (thus remaining technically faithful to his Aristocrat agreement), Muddy is very much in evidence. His slide guitar is a driving force on the two-part "Rolling & Tumbling," a song based on a traditional delta theme popularized on a 1929 record by Hambone Willie Newbern. The tone is set by an insistent instrumental lead-in, guitar and harp together playing the sinuous, hypnotically droning riff. Foster sings with passion as Muddy moans wordlessly behind Foster's vocals, and Foster even quotes the "Baby's going to jump and shout, when the train come wheeling up, and I come walking out" verse that Muddy had used on his hit "I Can't Be Satisfied" a year and a half earlier. Walter plays with fire, sometimes echoing, sometimes answering Muddy's biting lead lines. The take was so hot that they immediately continued on with another take, this one with wordless vocals, Foster and Waters moaning in unison lines, Foster taking the high end. Walter carries the lead melody on a few choruses, his harp tone fat and funky. The result is a compelling two-sided release, with an insistent groove that just won't quit. All of the elements are in place: a driving urbanized rhythm, keening slide guitar, superlative harmonica playing, and almost other-worldly moaning vocals on the B side. It is now rightly considered by many to be one of the pinnacles of postwar Chicago blues. Foster's "Red Headed Woman" is more ordinary; Muddy plays walking boogie figures while Foster's vocal phrasing echoes the tongue-tied hesitations that characterized Sonny Boy's singing. Again Walter takes the lead on the multiple instrumental choruses, with playful and now increasingly inventive single-note lines.

Walter's fondness for the guitar showed on his other vocal tracks when he put down his harp to pick up the six string. Moody Jones was one of several players who claimed to have taught Walter guitar, and he recalled the days encountering him on Maxwell street: "I'd be out there playing—I'd be way up the street, he'd hear my electric guitar you know. He'd holler up there, 'Do that again. You better not do that again or else I'll do it!'" In a recent interview, early Maxwell Street buddy and later touring band-member Jimmie Lee Robinson said that Walter always wanted to play guitar on stage but, among full-time guitarists, he wasn't considered a "real player, couldn't play more than two or three keys without a clamp [capo], and used only three-chord patterns." Still, his abilities were effective enough to keep the coins coming in on Maxwell Street, and in later years he was photographed there with a solid body National electric guitar, which he played as much as he did harp on the street then. His continuing presence on Maxwell St. on weekends was in direct violation of union rules; Muddy later commented, "I had a heck of a time getting Walter off the corner. That boy, I had to chase him out of Jewtown regular. He'd see me coming, and grab his mike and gone! [Laughs]. He done made a lot of money down there, sometimes Walter'd take in $35 or $40. That was good money then, more'n a club was paying us."

Jimmy Rogers recalled similar experiences with Walter on Maxwell Street:

> . . . we had to try to break Little Walter up from playing over there, man . . . Got in that union and stuff. He would sneak off down there on Sunday morning. [Laughs] We played Saturday night, man, and somebody, would come to us, said, "Hey man," said, "Get your boy down there. Go get him, man." We'd go get him, he'd get mad when he see you comin' 'cause he knows you don't want him down there, man. He's makin' more money than on the gig, but I knew about it. After you joined the union they had so many rules, at that time, and we was new in the field, we was tryin to, y'know, abide by the rules, because they fine you and all that stuff . . .

Walter recorded three songs accompanied by his guitar and the rest of the band at the Parkway session. On "Moonshine," Walter exhibits a basic country guitar sound, with a nasty-edged distortion on the amp. Walter borrows the melody from Sonny Boy's 1938 Bluebird side "Whiskey Headed Blues." But where Sonny Boy's song is a lament about the harmful effect drinking had on the singer, in Walter's version it's his woman with the problem: "My baby loves moonshine, she drinks it all the time, if she don't stop drinking, Muddy Waters, she got to lose her worried mind." Walter gives the instrumental chorus to Muddy, playing a walking-boogie line behind Muddy's picking, while hooting encouragement.

"Muskadine" is borrowed from another mentor of Walter's. Robert Junior Lockwood had cut the tune as "Take A Little Walk With Me" in 1941, and no doubt played it on gigs with Walter sitting in with him back around Helena. (The tune has been reputed to be an unrecorded number written by Lockwood's stepfather, Robert Johnson.) Here Walter uses Lockwood's melody, chorus, and one of the verses, but turns it to a lost-love lament-cum-travelogue. He alters Lockwood's chorus, "Please take a walk with me sometime," adding "Way down south, must be Muskadine bound." The lyric refers to the town of Muscadine, Alabama, some 50 miles west of Atlanta, Georgia, just across the Alabama state line. Although it's unlikely Walter had ever been to Muscadine, the intent is clear. Like so many blues songs of the era, it plays to the homesick feelings felt by many recent southern transplants, as reinforced by both Muddy and Foster as they shout out town names like "Clarksdale," "Stovall, Mississippi," and "Memphis, Tennessee" in the background. The cut closes with Walter taking a two-chorus guitar ride, displaying his funky if rudimentary chops.

Walter's final vocal that day was on "Bad Acting Woman," a medium blues that opens with the same turnaround guitar pattern as "Muskadine," and throws together some generic verses from the blues stockpile. Walter's guitar break again is functional if not particularly noteworthy, and his vocal is about the same, making for what amounts to a journeyman side. If nothing else, the session makes it obvious where his real talent lies.

Parkway announced their debut in February with the release of Foster's "Rolling And Tumbling." As it started selling rapidly, Leonard Chess at Aristocrat hit the roof. Jimmy Rogers said, "Muddy got himself in pretty big trouble with Chess. I laughed myself sick about it. Leonard didn't want Muddy to use that slide on any other label." Chess called Muddy into the studio right away and insisted he recut the number for Aristocrat, but, again, they used only Crawford on bass as accompaniment; the record was rushed out in an effort to draw attention away from the Parkway record. Muddy borrowed verses from Robert Johnson's "Kind Hearted Woman" to fill out side two. Although Muddy plays with the same intensity and Crawford's bass snaps along briskly, musically the number suffers from the absence of Walter's harp and Foster's drums, and it just doesn't match the power of the Parkway release. Nevertheless it had the effect Chess desired, and stole sales away from the other version. Soon Foster decided to take his shot and left Muddy to pursue a career leading his own group, and the drum chair in Muddy's band was next occupied by Elga Edmonds (also known as Elgin Evans, among several other names).

By March, Monroe Passis of the now-faltering Parkway label saw the writing on the wall, and embarked on a new business venture, teaming with J. Mayo Williams to form a personal management firm. Announced as "under contract" were Memphis Minnie, Muddy Waters, Sunnyland Slim, Jimmy Rogers, Little Walter, Baby Face Leroy, and St. Louis Jimmy. On June 3, 1950, having completed their negotiations to buy out their partners in Aristocrat, the Chess brothers became sole owners of the label, and announced that it would henceforth be known as Chess Records. Leonard's superstitious nature was evident; the Chess brothers launched the label bearing their name by christening their first release #1425, after a childhood address of the Chess family. Their first two releases under the new imprint came in July with "My Foolish Heart" by saxman Gene Ammons as Chess #1425, and Muddy's "Rolling Stone," a raw, guitar-only track from the "Rolling & Tumbling" session, as Chess #1426. The Ammons tune became one of his only chart hits, reaching #9 on the *Billboard* charts; although Muddy's release didn't chart nationally, it did well locally, and things were looking very good for the new label.

By July, Muddy and his full band were being featured every Tuesday night at the former Docie's Lounge, now known as Ada's Lounge & Chicken Shack. Possibly following the lead from the way Chess was marketing his records, the *Defender* ad for this gig mentioned only "Muddy Water." Waters and company were also booked for an occasional matinee "Battle Of The Blues," like the one they participated in at Evan's Ebony Lounge on the 30th, from 4:00 to 8:00 PM. There were also regular "Celebrity Matinees" at the Dew Drop Inn with drop-in guests like Tampa Red, Muddy, Walter, Eddie Boyd, John and Grace Brim, and others.

Clearly Walter's place among the elite of the Chicago blues scene was becoming undeniable, and he was starting to develop his own following, with younger women as attracted to him as their older sisters were to the smoldering sexuality that the more mature Muddy exuded. Walter was also learning the tricks of the trade; he might show up late after an intermission, waiting just outside the door and listening until the band was already onstage jamming. Then when he came in, his presence was much more noticeable and appreciated, by the audience if not by his band mates. Walter's harp was as much the focal point of the band's sound as Muddy's guitar, and his tone and phrasing were taking on more horn-like qualities as he intertwined with Muddy's vocals. This, and the recent Parkway recordings under his name that made it obvious that Walter had drawing power on his own, did not escape the attention of Leonard Chess, and he finally relented and okayed bringing Walter in on the next Muddy session.

It took place probably on Tuesday, August 15th. On the first tune of four Muddy cut at that session, "You're Gonna Need My Help," Walter's harp is immediately in the foreground, on equal footing with Muddy's slashing slide. Even though it's played unamplified into the vocal mike, Walter more than holds his own with Muddy's amplified guitar and Crawford's throbbing bass. One of the striking elements that may not be so obvious to today's ears but was quite groundbreaking at the time was that, throughout the session, Walter broke with the established tradition that relegated the harp to simply responding to the vocal line, but holding back during the actual singing. Instead, he plays throughout the vocal verses, sometimes in unison, sometimes in counterpoint—but always in service to the song, enhancing the vocals rather than distracting from them. He's not showboating: On the contrary, all of his talents are directed towards enriching Muddy's performance, adding previously unheard color and contrast.

"Sad Letter" was a remake of Muddy's previously unissued cut "Burying Ground" from the year before. Walter is a bit more restrained here, in volume if not intensity. "Early Morning Blues" continues the delta mood, harp and guitar meshing seamlessly. "Appealing Blues" reused the same basic melody and backing. It was clear by now that Muddy and Walter shared something deeper than just their mutual drive to succeed in the blues world. They'd developed a musical empathy that allowed their musical parts to fit together like the tightest-fitting jigsaw puzzle, while at the same time maintaining a looseness and swing that made it clear that at least part of what they were playing was improvised on the spot. Walter's harp plays into and around the guitar lines, as well as responding to the vocals; Muddy's guitar perfectly complements Walter's passages. The total effect is some very powerful, surprisingly complex music. If they'd never recorded again after this day, they still would have left a legacy that placed them among the all-time masters of their craft. But this was in many ways only the very beginning.

Guitarist Jimmy Rogers wasn't used on those tracks, but he was in the studio waiting for his chance. Rogers said, ". . . you had to come in and rush the shit out. Box it up quick as you can man, and get outta there on time, 'cause he's clocking him." Chess was paying about $75 per session for the studio; by union reckoning a session was three hours, the quota was four tunes. Add leader scale of $82.50 with sidemen getting half that, and for Chess, time was money. After Muddy and Walter nailed their numbers, he got his shot. Backed by Walter and Crawford, Rogers cut another version of the tune he'd been playing now for several years, "That's Alright." Walter alternates between chords and intensely fluttered "wah-wah" single tones on his break. Although Rogers's singing doesn't have Muddy's primal power, his more laid-back delivery and the irony of the lyric give the cut an urbane edge, echoing the sound of the band in the bars. The flip side "Ludella" is another remake for Rogers, this time from his unissued 1949 Regal session. Walter leads in with some high-end single notes before settling into a counterpoint accompaniment to Rogers rolling guitar riff. Again he's right up there in the mix, playing horn-like lines, and taking the lead on the instrumental break chorus. With their underlying rock-solid swing, it's easy to forget that these quintessential Chicago blues cuts were made without drums.

Billy Boy Arnold remembers the impact when the records by both Rogers and Waters were released in October: "Both were hits at the same time, in fact, Jimmy's was the biggest hit. I heard this harmonica player, I said goddam! This wasn't no ordinary harmonica player, the harp was at least 75 percent of the success of the records . . . the harmonica player was blasting!" Putting things into the perspective of the time, Arnold says, "Sonny Boy was the pacesetter, Walter took his place, Sonny Boy was dead and off the scene," Arnold continued. "In fact, Walter was playing so much harmonica that the record-buying public thought it was Muddy Waters. That's when Chess started putting on the labels 'Muddy Waters and his guitar,' to let people know that Muddy wasn't the harp player."

Keeping this new fire stoked, Chess called Muddy and company back into the studio for a Monday session on October 23rd. Muddy cut two titles that day, "Louisiana Blues" and "Evans Shuffle," again backed by only Crawford and Walter. (Some discographers have listed this session as Elgin Evans' first trip into the studio with Muddy, but if he was there he left no aural evidence. The strong clicking pulse heard on these sides is provided by Crawford slapping the bass strings as he plays [in a style later adapted by rockabilly bassmen like Bill Black with Elvis], and none of the idiosyncratic Evans' trademarks—the syncopation, bass drum "bombs" or cymbal splash accents—are heard.) The first cut starts with solo slide guitar then moves into an easy lope. "I'm going down to New Orleans, get me a mojo hand," Muddy sings, to which a presumably homesick Walter replies off-mike, "Aww, take me with you man when you go!" The break belongs to Walter, as he hits strong single-tone lines, moving yet another step away from the shadow of his mentor Sonny Boy.

The next track was one of the very few instrumentals Muddy cut. It's based on the riff for "The Honey Dripper," first recorded by pianist Roosevelt Sykes in 1936, and covered more recently and with great success by Joe Liggins in 1945. Muddy holds down the steady two-note vamp on his guitar and Crawford snaps the bass strings while Walter takes off on a series of exciting variations on the sax melody lines from Liggins's record. After employing the same false ending that Liggins had used, Walter comes back with some piercing high notes to wrap up an instrumental tour de force. Although released as a Muddy Waters tune, this one is all Walter. The tune was eventually titled "Evans Shuffle" after the popular radio DJ Sam Evans, theoretically insuring that it would get some air play on Evans's late-evening radio program, which had become widely popular, an institution to black Chicagoans. Just to make sure that no one accidentally overlooked the significance of the title's point of reference, "Evans Shuffle" was subtitled "(Ebony Boogie)," after Evans's popular blues club the Ebony Lounge.

The session wrapped up with Rogers stepping up to the mike to cut the mid-tempo blues "Going Away Baby." Walter wasn't the only one mining the Sonny Boy songbook; Rogers reworks Williamson's "Lord, Oh Lord Blues," using the same first verse and riff, in this song. Again, there's a repeating guitar figure that Walter twines with, although there's no instrumental chorus. Rogers followed with "Today Today Blues," a slower lament, with Walter taking a chorus featuring generous use of his hand vibrato in the style of Sonny Boy. On both tracks, his harp is the standout instrument, with the guitar playing mostly background chords.

Next, Chess utilized Muddy, Walter, and Jimmy as a backing trio behind Johnny Shines, a contemporary of Muddy's who came up in Arkansas, learned guitar from Howlin' Wolf, and ran with Robert Johnson in the 1930s. He'd moved to Chicago in 1941, and cut an unreleased session in 1946 for Lester Melrose. Shines was a powerful singer with a trademark heavy tremolo in his voice. The two sides recorded by Shines are fine examples of the transitional period between Mississippi and Chicago blues; Shines sings movingly, supported by the interlocking guitars of Muddy and Jimmy and Walter's relaxed and superb harp blowing. Ultimately, however, they were held back from release, presumably because their stylistic similarity to Muddy's records would have stolen sales from the up-and-coming hitmaker in whom Chess had already heavily invested.

Muddy's sides were released in December, while the band was still working a regular gig at Ada's on a twin bill with Bali Beach & Combo. "Blues guitar King Muddy Waters" was also being featured every Sunday at the Dew Drop Inn, which also had the "piano stylings" of the Eddie Boyd Trio, and a special holiday show headlined by Hersolene Roberts and her all-star female impersonator revue.

Somewhere around this time, Walter got word that his mother Beatrice had died down in Marksville of cancer after a short illness. According to his older sister Lillian, Walter's younger sister Marguerite sent a telegram to a Chicago radio station, asking that an announcement be made on the air in an effort to locate him (not an uncommon practice in those days). Leonard Chess heard the announcement, and notified Walter. Despite a lifelong bitterness about what he considered his parents' abandonment, he went home for the funeral. It was a sad reunion for the family, the first time they'd all seen each other since he left home some seven years earlier. Beatrice was buried in the Catholic cemetery in Marksville, in a grave facing the highway, according to a family friend. Walter remained in Marksville for a bit before returning to Chicago, while sister Lillian returned to California where she'd settled with her husband a few years earlier.

Chess wasn't about to let the market cool down, so Muddy, Walter, and Crawford were called back to Universal Studios, on Tuesday, January 23, 1951. Of the four tunes Muddy cut that day, two would become blues classics: "Long Distance Call" and

"Honey Bee." On "Long Distance Call," Muddy's slide guitar work and Walter's harp playing dance around each other, in a tandem cause, finally overlapping each other on the line "Hear my phone a-ringing, sounds like a long distance call," when both come together to simultaneously imitate a ringing telephone. Years later, while listening to the recording, Muddy would scowl and remark that Walter was playing all over his singing. But then he smiled and added that "Walter was so great he could break the rules and make it work." "Too Young To Know" was the flip side; it's a plaintive lament, harp and guitar dueling and driving during the middle instrumental break. On "Honey Bee," Walter switches to guitar, playing a single-note walking bass line behind Muddy's slide work. The tune sprang from "Sail On Little Girl," a 1938 Jazz Gillum Bluebird recording. Although his lead guitar skills may have been rudimentary, here Walter's backing guitar provides the perfect solid support for Muddy's stinging tones. The last track "Howling Wolf" went unissued until years later; it uses the "prowling predator" sexual metaphor in the same vein as John Lee Hooker's 1949 hit "Crawling King Snake," among many other blues.

Jimmy Rogers was next up to record, backed by a four-piece band that included pianist Eddie Ware, saxman Ernest Cotton, and drummer Elga Edmonds/Evans, but with Walter sitting out this time. Billy Boy Arnold later speculated that Jimmy may have been somewhat jealous of all the attention Walter was getting, and insisted on using a sax instead of Walter's harp to prove the point that he could make successful records without the help of the harp player. The sound was easygoing R&B, with the sax or piano most prominent, but these attempts lack the drive and excitement present on his earlier sessions featuring Walter's backing.

Following Rogers's session, pianist Eddie Ware took over as leader. Evans stayed, Walter and Crawford came back, and Eddie Chamblee on tenor sax was added; however, Walter only played guitar. The session produced five cuts, three of which were issued at the time. Walter's guitar is in the forefront on "Jealous Woman," adding a down-home funk to the rather doomy slow blues. Walter also acquits himself well on the instrumental "Rumba Dust," taking a couple of solid choruses, and overall playing in a jazzier, more sophisticated vein than he'd displayed on any of his other guitar appearances. It looks like Chess was trying to diversify, and get as much mileage out of the various band members as the market would bear.

Chess was convinced he was on the right marketing track when "Long Distance Call," released in March, jumped to #8 by April, giving Muddy his highest-charting record to date. The pattern continued when "Honey Bee" hit #10 in late June. Another session was called for—and although it couldn't have been known by any of the participants at the time, this one would write blues history.

In July 1951, several parallel events marked musical turning points. After years of playing and recording in urban blues combos, Big Bill Broonzy took a step backwards in time in an attempt to rekindle his fortunes. He reinvented himself in the mold of a country blues artist, and flew to Europe to perform some solo concerts in Paris. After a dramatic decline in the market for the music he'd recently been playing, Bill had spent the previous months working as a janitor at Iowa State College in Ames, where he'd performed as part of a folk troupe, playing for white audiences. In Europe he followed the trail Lead Belly had blazed in 1948 and presented himself as one of the "last living blues singers," playing solo acoustic concerts, and talked to his audiences about plowing the fields with his mule.

At almost exactly the same time, on Wednesday, July 11, Leonard Chess took a step forward in time when he finally allowed Walter to record with Muddy using the amplifier he'd been playing on club gigs for several years now. Ironically, the tune that would change the sound of Chicago blues forever by "urbanizing" the final rural element, the harmonica, was named "Country Boy." It features only Waters and Walter, playing with their amplified instruments turned right up to the ragged edge of distortion. In their club work, Walter had discovered that the amp could shape and color the tones of the harmonica in ways that made it sound almost like an entirely new and different instrument than the wheezing, reedy-sounding harmonicas of his predecessors. He hits long, fat, sustained tones, alternating between mellow warmth and intense, keening cries. This recording gives ample evidence of why the amplified blues harp would come to be known as the "Mississippi saxophone"; here it serves the same function as a horn, and for the first time, is able to cut through the sound of whatever is accompanying it. Again the guitar and harp interlace almost telepathically, winding and weaving their way through the throbbing number.

There were problems with the next tune cut. Muddy recalls:

> My drummer couldn't get that beat on "She Moves Me." The verse was too long . . . my drummer [probably Elgin Evans] wanted to play a turnaround there, and there wasn't no turnaround [a syncopated drum lick signaling the end of one verse and beginning of another] there. I had to go another 6 or 8 bars to get it turned around . . . my drummer couldn't hold it there to save his damn life. So Leonard [Chess] told him, "Get the fuck out of the way, I'll do that."

And Chess took over, whomping out the downbeat using only the bass drum, giving an ominous (and at times, slightly awkward) pulse to the tale of a woman who could "make the dead jump up and run." Walter's harp again alternates between fat, sax-like tones and resonant, organ-rich chords.

On "My Own Fault," Walter toys with the beat, sprinkling eighth-note figures behind Muddy's vocals. If Muddy's singing is a bit prosaic, Walter's harp is fresh and inventive. On "Still A Fool," Muddy reworks the delta standard "Catfish Blues," with its insistent and inexorable riff. During performances in clubs, the band would "double-time" the number at the end as Muddy chanted over and over "She's all right, she's all right," while prowling from one edge of the stage to the other, working the crowd. This was more effective when he was unfettered by a guitar. In the studio, Muddy handed off his instrument to Walter, and the backup was handled by Rogers and Walter's snaky-sounding guitars. They provide a funky, rolling support that is hypnotic.

As usual, Jimmy Rogers had his own session immediately following Muddy. Again, Rogers used a somewhat different outfit, adding Eddie Ware on piano, Willie Dixon on bass, and Evans on drums. On the first couple of slow blues numbers, Walter continued on guitar, filling in with walking bass figures. On "Chance To Love" Walter returned to his amplified harp, filling out the instrumentation into what would become known as the classic Chicago blues five-piece of guitar, harp, piano, bass, and drums.

During the verses, Walter fills diffidently in the background, but on the break he takes the lead, his tone burning, on some long sustained notes that sound almost like plaintive screams. "My Little Machine" works off the "my car won't start" euphemism. Throughout, Walter adds long, hot fills, and is again placed way up front in the mix. Why the cut wasn't issued at the time remains a mystery.

At the end of the day, Walter must have felt vindicated. At long last he was being heard on record the way he ought to be, on equal footing with the guitar, sometimes even in front of it. No longer were his subtleties of tone and inflection and his tricky phrasing being buried in the mix; no longer was he drowned out by an over-enthusiastic drummer. Walter was riding the tiger at last, and he knew it.

A little over a year earlier, President Truman had first ordered U.S. ground forces into Korea and authorized the bombing of North Korea by the U.S. Air Force; since that time, U.S. military involvement in Korea had regularly been on the front pages. But if Walter had ever been concerned about the draft that he'd registered for, on August 16 he got some good news; his status was reclassified "5A," meaning that the registration he'd falsified now put him over the age limit for eligibility. The following month, Muddy's "Still A Fool"/"My Fault" single was released. An advertisement for it in one of the trade papers mistakenly called it "Still A Wolf." Maybe Wolf was on Chess' mind, because that same month they signed an exclusive contract with another delta bluesman, Chester Burnett, better known Howlin' Wolf, winning him away from the west coast Modern label who'd also issued some of his earliest sides. By November, Muddy's single was up to #9 in the *Billboard* charts. Early that month an ad in the *Chicago Defender* plugged a special Midnight Show on Saturday, November 3rd, featuring "King Of Blues Muddy Waters & his Blue Boys" at the Indiana Theater. Also on the bill were vocalist Erline Harris, Father Howard (a dancing drummer novelty act), and exotic dancer Kaye Du Conge. The Indiana Theatre represented an earlier vaudeville tradition, for an older audience of black patrons. The "Midnight Ramble" held every Saturday "was where comedians, singers, and dancers put on their 'bluest' jokes, their 'special material' songs and their most revealing dance routines for the midnight audience."

On a Sunday afternoon in 1951, a few up-and-coming musicians decided to drop by Sam & Gussie's Lounge to check out a 2:00 PM "Cocktail Party" jam. The party consisted of the Myers brothers, Louis and Dave, and their harp-playing frontman in the three Deuces, Junior Wells. They met up with Billy Boy Arnold and headed on to the club. It was the first time Billy Boy actually entered a club and recalled it as "really a beautiful time," seeing "all the great bluesmen." Among others in the crowd that day were pianist Johnnie Jones, J. B. Lenoir, Jimmy Rogers, and Little Walter. Onstage, Sunnyland Slim and Robert Jr. Lockwood were working out. Arnold wound up sitting in a booth with Louis, Wells, Walter, and Jimmy Rogers. "So I told Jimmy Rogers, 'I'm a harmonica player.' He pointed to Little Walter and said, 'Well, this is my harmonica player,'" Arnold said. But when Rogers and Walter later took the stage, Billy was a bit let down that Walter played only guitar and no harp.

Arnold thought that Walter was the bigger star then, and felt that Muddy and Rogers didn't appreciate him. "They thought Walter was a great harp player, and they knew he was packing them in," Arnold opined:

They knew that Leonard Chess [now] didn't want them to make a record without Walter—but they felt, well, he was just a harp player. Jimmy had made his record, "Ludella" and "That's Alright," so Jimmy felt he was over Walter. You listen to the record, Walter stole the show—if it wasn't for Walter it wouldn't have been as popular as it was. But they had Walter categorized . . . they would readily say he can't sing, so he was no threat. Most musicians jealously competing with each other you know. For the blues crowd, you had to be able to sing, cause it was music about storytelling. The singer always got the recognition—unless he was [an] oustanding [player] like Walter.

On the last Saturday of the year, December 29, Chess called for another session. Muddy's "She Moves Me" was beginning to climb the charts, and Leonard wanted to stock the larder. Muddy was putting pressure on Chess to include Rogers and Evans on the sessions, to get the full band sound they were presenting live in the clubs. It was even said that Muddy had been shopping around, looking for a label that would be more accommodating to his musical wishes. Not wanting to lose his brightest blues star, Leonard finally agreed; this session was the first to feature the quartet that was knocking them dead in clubs. However, on the first number up, "They Call Me Muddy Waters," Chess hedged his bets, taking Walter off his amp and putting him back on acoustic harp. Rogers's guitar adds a rhythmic foundation behind Muddy's slide, and Evans plays simple but effective drums, keeping the beat throbbing. Again, guitar and harp duet beautifully on the instrumental break. The track went unissued, probably due to a slightly flubbed intro.

Muddy then tried out "All Night Long," an early version of a song he'd later redo with great success as "Rock Me." (This version was inspired by a year-old side by Texan Lil' Son Jackson, "Rockin' And Rollin.") The first take features Walter playing a constant and insistent harp throughout, in a heavily echoed setting with drums prominent. It's a great track, but again Chess hedged his bets, pulled Evans off the drums, and had the rest of the band do a few takes at a slower pace with a sparser, drumless arrangement that more closely matched Muddy's earlier successes. This time, Walter's harp concentrates more on answering the vocals than improvising. It appears that Leonard Chess's instinct was right; the result is a sinuous, slow-burn number heavy with unconcealed eroticism. The shorter of the two drumless versions was the one that was ultimately chosen as the master and issued as Muddy's next single.

In retrospect, listening to the three takes of "All Night Long" reveals a point about Muddy's philosophy of music making, a philosophy that would prove troublesome to Little Walter over time. Most likely Muddy had been playing this number on stage for some time, and had worked out an arrangement that pleased him, because his part varies little on all three takes, either with or without drums. But equally telling is that Walter's harp backing is almost exactly the same on all three takes, including his solos. Given his choice, Walter rarely played the same song the same way twice, and in fact had been confiding with friends outside of the band that he was feeling constrained working within the relatively rigid musical confines of Muddy's band. Muddy had his songs, and he had his way of doing them, and that's the way they were done, night after night. Once Walter had created a harp part that Muddy liked, he was expected to play it that way from then on. This play-by-the-numbers approach was to become a sticking point with Walter, who (as would be revealed amply in his own recordings later) preferred an improvisational, fly-by-the-seat-of-the-pants approach to playing, experimenting with something new every time he put the harp to his lips. But Muddy was older, more successful, and after all, he was the "star" of this band, so for now, Walter deferred to his way of doing things. And that meant that on Muddy's sessions, he'd play it Muddy's way, at least for the time being.

After nailing down a satisfactory take of "All Night Long," the whole ensemble returned for "Stuff You Gotta Watch," an up-tempo number adapted from a Buddy Johnson Band 1945 jump-blues ballad. Rogers and Walter provided a counterpoint to Muddy's vocal line, "The girl you love stays out all night long" with the repeated chant, "Should be mine, should be mine." Walter takes an effective two-chorus harp break, recalling the solo on his very first Maxwell Street recording from four years earlier, while at the same time imbuing the piece with a jazzy swing. It's unlike anything Muddy had recorded before—which may be why it wasn't issued at the time. The next track recorded, "Lonesome Day," returns to the slide guitar, slow blues formula. Evans throws in a few more drum fills here, adding some rhythmic interest. On the break, Walter's high-end harp squalls don't quite blend with Muddy's slide work. This cut wasn't issued, either.

Muddy and Evans packed up and moved on, but Walter and Rogers stayed behind to work on a session with guitarist Floyd Jones, and mystery drummer Willie Coven. Jones had worked with Bill Broonzy and Lonnie Johnson, and was a regular at Vi's Lounge and the 708 Club. Earlier that year, Jones had cut his classic numbers "Dark Road" and "Big World" for Joe Brown's J.O.B. label, backed by Sunnyland Slim, Moody Jones, and Elga Edmonds.

The Chess session began with two new numbers, "Overseas" and "Playhouse." Then, Leonard had Jones record the two songs he had released on J.O.B. Jones felt Chess was simply trying to squash the competition by recutting these songs; "All he [Chess] wanted to do was just get something out there. He was so strong he killed the good one." Jones's recording of "Dark Road" was based on delta bluesman Tommy Johnson's 1928 hit "Big Road Blues," and included eerie, falsetto vocal jumps. Jones vocal doesn't have quite the edge or confidence of his earlier version, but Walter's harp, similar in style to the "All Night Long" track with Muddy, adds a haunting quality to the track. The flipside, "Big World," features a guitar break by Rogers, but Walter outshines him, even while ostensibly holding back.

The fact that Walter was an outstanding player wasn't lost on the record-buying public or the hard-drinking music lovers on the South Side. Walter was quickly becoming recognized as not only Chicago's premier harp player, but also the pioneer of a brand new sound that was making people throughout the music world sit up and take notice. A few may still have considered him just "somebody's harp player," but that was about to change.

6 *"juke"*

Chicago Blues Turns a Corner:
Winter 1951–52

Blues music was flourishing again both in the south and in the northern urban centers by early 1951. While harmonica blues was still being played by anyone interested enough to come up with the $2 price of an instrument, there was currently no blues harmonica "star." The prolific and hugely influential John Lee "Sonny Boy" Williamson had been the dominant figure in blues harmonica from the late 1930s until his murder in 1948. But since his demise, no other harmonica player had yet stepped forward from the crowd of disciples, or presented any significant new sounds or stylistic advances, to claim the crown of king of the blues harp players. The time was right for another harpman to emerge out front with a band.

1952 was a pivotal year for Little Walter and the sound of Chicago blues as a whole. If Williamson made people take the harp seriously, Walter moved it into position as the primary focus of the band. In jazz, instrumental stars were common; skilled soloists were widely celebrated for their virtuoso ability. In the blues field, by contrast, the attention was usually on the singer, not the band—but Walter was about to change that. Using his own amplifier like the guitarists did, and cupping the harp in his hands with his hand-held mike, Walter not only added a power and volume to the sound of the tiny reeds, he put the harmonica on equal footing with the loudest electric guitars. Until then, harp players had always been at the mercy of the guitar players and drummers, and could be easily drowned out by overenthusiastic sidemen. If the harp was amplified at all, it was usually nothing more than the player blowing as he always had while standing in front of a vocal microphone; not much changed except the volume.

While it may have started as a lucky accident in an attempt to be heard in the clubs, Walter had discovered that there were other ways to play harp that utilized the amplifier itself to help color tonal shadings and add punch and power that had previously been missing. Walter had clearly been exploring and exploiting some of the electric possibilities of this new combination for some time, including when he first recorded his amplified harmonica with Muddy a year earlier. He was learning to play it like a new instrument, creating and utilizing different playing techniques, playing fresh licks that were especially suited to this new aural palette. Not only did the tonal range of the harp change when amplified, Walter utilized amplification to provide a dynamic range in his harmonica playing that had never been explored in a full band; it simply wasn't possible previously. Now, instead of blowing full blast like most acoustic players had to in order to be heard, Walter could lay back, and, while tightly cupping the harp and mike together, play very softly, turning up the amp to provide the necessary volume. This softer attack on the harmonica's reeds produced a smoother, mellower, "rounder" sound that could be subtly manipulated to create an entire new spectrum of expressiveness and emotional range. Then, when he wanted to really make an impact with note or phrase, he could punch it full blast and pierce through with a deep, searing wail, a match for the sinuous moan of the electric slide guitar that Muddy played. Chords now had impact, richness, and depth; octaves were full and resonant; and single notes soared and swooped above the rest of the ensemble. In Walter's hands, a $2, 10-hole harmonica had all the color, punch, and authority of a jazzman's horn.

On May 12, 1952, five months after the groundbreaking first session featuring Muddy's full band, Leonard Chess called another session at Universal Studios on Chicago's near North Side. Chess had no doubt taken note of the fact that Walter was emerging as a star attraction in his own right. Not only was he a driven and inventive player, he was also young and good looking, flashy in a way that the darker, older, and more aloof Muddy wasn't. Chess must have also considered his sales figures on Jimmy Rogers's first hit "That's Alright" from a year-and-a-half earlier; the more singles he could get out of already signed and established artists, the better. Walter's harp sound had obviously been a driving force behind several of Rogers's and Waters's best-selling records over the last two years. Because he was not himself signed as a Chess artist, Walter was free to cut a few singles on his own. Although the Chess label was already emerging as the premiere Chicago blues label, Walter's moonlighting projects surely must have been seen as competition for record sales by Chess. It made sense to give the young man his own shot.

Guitarist Jimmy Rogers recalled the first tracks that Walter cut for Chess as being organized the same way his own were, at the end of a Muddy session. And of course it *was* Muddy's complete band in the studio backing Walter. But the session log kept that day proves that the primary purpose of this session was to record a couple of songs from the fiery young harp virtuoso to be released as a single. According to the sequence of the master numbers assigned to the tracks as they were recorded, the first order of business was recording an instrumental showcase for Little Walter's harp.

As with many working bands of the day, Muddy's band had a standard instrumental theme that they used to begin and end their live sets, in this case, a slightly jazzy, jump-blues styled number in deliberate contrast to the heavier, slower, delta-based vocal pieces. This gave the featured instrumentalists the opportunity to show off a few hot licks, and then the band would vamp while the bandleader introduced the individual band members or rapped to the audience about "taking a pause for the cause." Of course, the break time not only gave the musicians a breather, but more importantly to the club owner, gave the dancing patrons a chance to knock back a few from the bar and make the cash register ring. Per the musician's union rules of the day, bands were allowed a 15-minute break after every 45-minute set, so these instrumental themes got a lot of play. The band members would not only know their parts as well as any other piece in their repertoire, they would be comfortable improvising any new twists on the arrangement "on the fly." Although the intermission theme Muddy's band was using didn't officially have a name yet, it went over well enough with crowds that they felt it was worth recording. And so it was that Little Walter's breakthrough harmonica instrumental "Juke," the song that would become the "national anthem of blues harmonica," was recorded that day.

Universal was the top recording studio in Chicago at the time, and charged accordingly, which meant Chess was paying about $25 per hour recording time for the studio, big money in those days. Factor in the musician's fees and that meant there wasn't time for much fooling around. The band might have run down the tune a couple of times while engineer and Universal proprietor Bill Putnam balanced the mikes for the right mix and adjusted the reverb and added echo via his homemade tape echo to make the frisky tempo kick a bit.

Major labels always recorded on fresh reels; Chess was thriftier, and reused their tapes. They'd cut tracks until a usable take occurred, then rewind and reuse the tape up to that point again. Earlier takes from the session—as well as brief ghosts from an even earlier recording of a local radio program—can be heard bleeding through between the

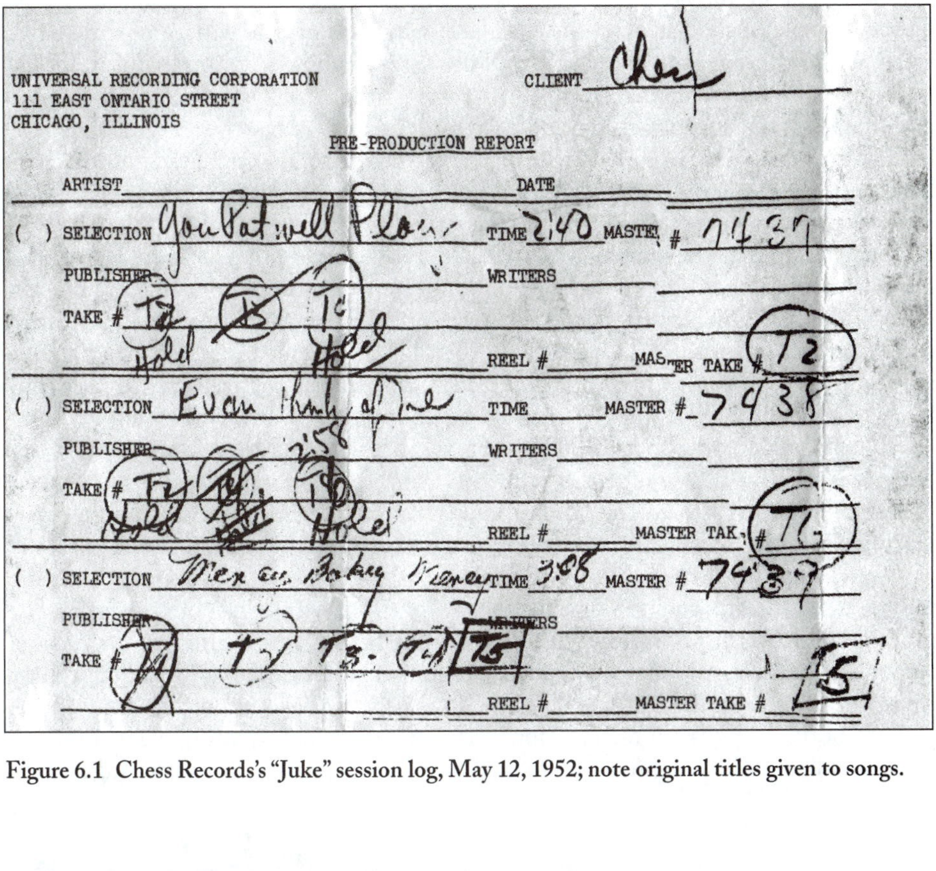

UNIVERSAL RECORDING CORPORATION
111 EAST ONTARIO STREET
CHICAGO, ILLINOIS

CLIENT Chess

PRE-PRODUCTION REPORT

ARTIST DATE

( ) SELECTION TIME 2:40 MASTER # 7437
PUBLISHER WRITERS
TAKE #
REEL # MASTER TAKE # T2

( ) SELECTION TIME MASTER # 7438
PUBLISHER WRITERS
TAKE #
REEL # MASTER TAKE # T6

( ) SELECTION TIME 3:08 MASTER # 7439
PUBLISHER WRITERS
TAKE # T4 T3 T5
REEL # MASTER TAKE # 5

Figure 6.1 Chess Records's "Juke" session log, May 12, 1952; note original titles given to songs.

music tracks. The session commenced with the band's instrumental theme song, initially titled "Your Pat Will Play" on the session logs. There's no "Take 1" on the existing tape reel from this session, suggesting that the first take attempted was incomplete, and as was the custom, the tape had been rewound. Take 2—the first complete take—is a fully formed little masterpiece, and was ultimately chosen as the master. It's a focused and driving piece that starts with a distinctive opening theme, explores melodic and dynamic variations on it, and finishes with a punch that makes this one a surefire jukebox coin-grabber. The tune opens with a catchy, repeated ascending run up the harp, with accent chords on the guitar for emphasis, the rhythm section firmly locked into place. Then the guitars establish a loping and infectious boogie riff while Elga Edmonds taps out steady time on the echo-laden high-hat, with occasional punctuation on the snare. On the second chorus, Walter uses a repeating single-note idea, followed by alternate choruses focusing on either long sustained tones or lilting chords and melodic figures. An effective stop-time verse adds some excitement in the middle of the tune, with a nice tension/release marked by a cymbal splash. Walter provides more sustained tones and a repeat of the single note stabs, then into the final chorus, pulling things back to the main motif of the tune, building to a swinging climax borrowed from big-band arrangements of a generation earlier.

Although to modern ears it's obvious that this cut is a gem just as is, it was apparently decided that the number might benefit from a little spicing up. After some discussion among the band about how they might change the arrangement, they took another couple of shots at it. It was decided to try a faster take with a more dynamic intro, with just Walter's harp and Elga's drums pounding out a powerful, stabbing opening that built to a climactic "stop" after the first four bars, at which point Muddy and Jimmy's guitars would launch the band into the body of the tune. As the tape rolls on Take 3, Jimmy reminds Walter, "I'll give you that boogie" on guitar, and then the band tries out the new arrangement for the first time. It starts promisingly, but Evans loses his place, and instead of hitting the musical climax at the end of the first four bars, he continues to play the opening beat. Walter and the band follow him for a few bars, but when it becomes apparent that he's not going to hit the "stop," they falter and everyone stops playing. Evans confesses, "I was off"; Walter calmly explains to Leonard and the band, "You see, if he'd a kicked it off right, we coulda made it, and I coulda given you the 'bop bop bop bop bop bop BOP!'" that leads into the "stop." Muddy confers with Walter, "When you give me that bop bop bop BOP . . . ," as Evans explains, "Well, I'm watchin' your foot when you start. Well, I'm gonna start with you this time, when you start . . ."

Putnam interrupts the discussion by calling out to the band, "Take 4," and they start playing almost instantly. This time Walter leads everyone into the "stop" perfectly, and the band locks into place for a flawless take. Even though it's taken at a somewhat faster tempo, it's 15 seconds longer than the released version, with two more choruses. The guitars interlock into a sprightly walking boogie figure, and Walter leads the band through a wild ride, reeling out a cavalcade of musical ideas, some of which might have been worked out on the bandstand, some obviously improvised on the spot. On the second chorus, he pulls out the jazz horn-man's trick of briefly quoting the melody line of the child's ditty "It's raining, it's pouring," then improvises his own answering riff. He plays around with some soft sweet notes, followed by harsher, biting tones and chords, with each phrase locking into the easy swing of the band. Over the course of the song, he explores various combinations of quick staccato riffing, long swooping phrases, variations on the opening theme, changes in the dynamics, and repeats of the stop-time punches. At 2:55, the tune winds down to the end without much special flourish; it's likely that Walter was signaled from the booth to "take it home" and he did so without taking the opportunity to embellish with any particular musical climax.

Take 4 is a very respectable take, and nobody screws up, but it's not as completely focused or composed as Take 2, either. There's almost too much going on, with so many varied ideas being tossed in, that it's not all completely connected. Ultimately, the first complete version, Take 2—which was probably closest to the version they were playing on the bandstand, and therefore the best rehearsed—was chosen for release, and given a new, catchier title: "Juke."

The tune itself has been claimed by several other harp players, and it is possible that Walter could have heard other versions before recording his own. Dave Myers, who soon would become a part of Little Walter's musical inner circle, recalls the memorable opening riff as coming from an early big-band arrangement. He's probably referring to "Leap Frog," the theme song of the Les Brown swing band. In the mid-'40s, Brown performed regular, weekly radio broadcasts, and the familiar rising cascade of notes was the recurring musical theme that opened every show. This simple figure was widely imitated by other swing bands, to the point that it became almost a cliche among horn players: It found its way into countless recordings from the late '40s onward.

The first harp player to exploit this signature riff on record was Snooky Pryor, on his 1948 Planet Records release with Moody Jones called "Boogie," a mostly instrumental number with spoken comments echoing John Lee Hooker's then-current hit out of Detroit, "Boogie Chillen." Pryor claims that Walter stole "Juke" from his record. A side-by-side comparison with "Juke" shows that the opening verse on both tunes is virtually identical, as is the walking boogie guitar line, but the similarities end there. Jimmy Rogers recalls;

> Snooky had this thing that went on kind of the kick of "Juke" was on now, "Snooky and Moody's Boogie." And we heard this thing, and Little Walter ran through the phrases of the harmonica part, and Sunnyland Slim used to have a little thing he'd play when he's going on, "Get Up The Stairs Mademoiselle." He'd do it on the piano. So we put the two together and kept jamming around with it. We used it, we built that for our theme song.

Later on Junior Wells would also lay claim to the song that became Little Walter's calling card. Wells said that it was a number used by his group, The Three Aces, as *their* theme tune. Wells said, ". . . it was a good thing for ending a show, and the people would dance off it and stuff like that. I was just playing a harp and Louis and Dave started fillin' in with it. We was doing it before [drummer] Freddie Below got with us." (Below joined the group circa mid-1951, shortly after release from his second stint in the army. A schooled jazz drummer, he'd been recommended to the Myers' by Muddy's drummer, Evans.)

"It was a place on 40th between Michigan and Indiana," Wells continued. "It was that big hotel [The Brookmont] . . . Walter heard me playing it and me and him got on it one day and was doing it at a Blue Monday party. We was doing it as a duet, every-body was getting into it and dancin' everywhere . . . Chess needed something else to put on the other side of a tune. So Walter blew our theme song. And there it was, wasn't nothing we could do about it."

In fact, Walter *had* sat in previously with the Myers brother's band several times. Guitarist Louis Myers talked about Walter wanting to play with them because they were playing faster music than Muddy's, and "People liked to dance with a little speed," which was now amply provided by Below's swinging jazz-based drumming. One night, The Aces went to hear Walter with Muddy's band, on the West side. According to Myers, "Little Walter said, 'Muddy, let them sit in and play a set with me.' So we played a set with Little Walter and I never heard nobody in the world sounding like that man playing that harmonica. He got up there and played, and every way he go we could cover him, because this was the type of stuff we was doin' anyway. Man I never heard nobody play harp like that day."

From wherever Little Walter borrowed the opening twelve bars of "Juke," the rest of the song was clearly his own invention, with very little in common with anything that had come before it. For all the haggling over who played it first, the signature opening figure used on the issued take isn't even utilized in the later takes of the tune, suggesting that this part of the song wasn't considered by Walter to be its key element. But regard-less of the influences, the fact remains that no other harp player ever released anything that grabbed the attention of the record-buying public or other aspiring harp players the way "Juke" did.

After recording the satisfactory take of "Juke," of course Chess also needed a vocal number to put on the other side. According to Jimmy Rogers, Walter got a bit nervous, since in his role as Muddy's harp player he hadn't been singing a lot lately, and hadn't recorded a vocal since his Parkway session two years earlier. Rogers later recounted taking Walter into the bathroom, and running through some songs that Rogers thought Walter could remember. One of them was "Black Gal," a 1937 recording from Sonny Boy's second Bluebird session. Rogers recalled:

> Walter knew about two, three verses of it, 'cause he would try to sing it sometimes over the night when everybody was high. We went back out, and when he first started singing, the introduction was fine. But when he got to singing about "Crazy 'bout you black gal," Leonard shut him off. Said "No, we don't want that 'Black Gal.'" The song is all right, but you got to change 'Black Gal' . . . .I said maybe "Wild about you baby." So we were sit-ting together and when he would sing "Wild about you . . . ," I would touch his knee and he'd say "baby." Every time he'd get to that part I'd tap him so he'd remember, "wild about you baby!" Three, four takes, we got it.

Actually, "Can't Hold On Much Longer" was stitched together from several sources. It follows Sonny Boy's structure by opening with a harp intro, but only the guitar lines and chorus, "Crazy about you baby, you don't care nothing in the world for me,"—come from the Sonny Boy tune. It's used as the opening, then repeated twice more. In between, Walter sings a verse he recalled from "I Need My Baby," a 1946 Victor recording by Doctor Clayton: "Can't sleep at night, just catch naps through the day." After a slow and snaky harp break with some nice guitar/harp interplay, Walter returns with a standard blues verse that had been used memorably in Robert Johnson's 1936 recording of "Kindhearted Woman": "Ain't but one thing baby, that makes your daddy drink." Walter's version has an urgency and power that sets it apart from Sonny Boy's track; it's unmistakably of its time and place. The country-sounding forerunner had been given an updated urban edge. Walter needn't have worried about his vocals, which by the time they recorded the master take, were passionate, heartfelt, and completely appropriate.

Leonard's input on this number extended beyond adjusting the "black gal" lyrics to the musical arrangement. As the tape starts for Take 1 of the song logged that day as "Ever Think of Me," Leonard can be heard instructing the band, ". . . 'Crazy 'bout you baby,' then, WHAM!" The first take starts, then is immediately stopped by Leonard, who is annoyed by the feedback on Walter's harp intro. Leonard tells Walter, "Turn your volume down." It's Walter's first session as a leader for Chess, and he doesn't make waves or argue the point; he answers quietly, "It's turned down, Leonard." Putnam then calls, "Take two," and Walter starts immediately, and plays a solid, complete take with a nice harp solo, but he seems a little bit nervous about his vocals, focusing more on his harp playing than his singing.

Chess apparently felt Walter could do better, so another take was attempted. Putnam is still concerned that Walter's amp will feedback, and tells him so, then calls off Take 4. An apparently eager-to-please Walter forgoes his amp altogether on this take, playing acoustically directly into the vocal mic, and at a faster tempo than the earlier takes; however Putnam stops him again, worrying about feedback. After a few more audio problems, the band finally plays the version that would be released as "Can't Hold On Much Longer" on the flip side of "Juke."

To complete this session, Muddy took Walter's place at the vocal mike to sing "Please Have Mercy," another slow, insistent piece. Muddy's pleas for forgiveness are emphasized by some spoken and overdubbed asides, and by Walter's plaintive harp playing throughout. The fact that only one Muddy tune was recorded that day is a further indication that the session was scheduled primarily to record Walter.

At first, Leonard was unsure about the commercial potential of "Juke." However, he was convinced after an incident that occurred while he was playing an acetate of the track. Chess's son Marshall later explained:

> Blues has always been a woman's market. "Juke," what prompted my father to put it out, it was a rainy day, we had a canopy over the place and the door was open, 'cause it gets very hot here in the summer. [The Chess offices were then at 4858 South Cottage Grove.] He was playing "Juke," it had been recorded a few days before. Well, he was listening to the record, and there was this old lady, an old colored lady, standing under the canopy to keep out of the rain, and he saw her digging it, dancing. So he played it again, and then they rushed it into release, and it was one of our biggest hits ever.

Underscoring Walter's growing status with blues fans was the fact that the Chance label reissued his five-year-old Ora Nelle sides, featuring the singing of "Little Walter J" on "Just Keep Loving Her."

On July 11th, Walter was back in the studio, cutting as a sideman on a Memphis Minnie session. Minnie was an extremely popular and talented singer and guitarist who had been on the recording and club scene since 1929, and was universally recognized as the equal of any man on guitar. Her first big hit, "Bumble Bee," was cut in 1930, the same year Walter was born. Minnie had gone through several guitar-playing husbands/accompanists. On this session, she was backed by Little Son Joe (Lawlers), and a drummer; the guitars were amplified as she reached for a harder, more contemporary Chicago sound.

The first track of four that day featured piano, then Walter joined in on unamplified harmonica on the other three titles. This was probably at Chess's suggestion. It would be smart to pair an older artist with one of the hot young hit-makers in an attempt to introduce Minnie to a new audience (and in fact Chess was beginning to use Walter liberally in this capacity). Walter's playing throughout recalled his old mentor, Sonny Boy Williamson I, particularly in the use of hand wah-wah effects. Throughout the session Walter plays with a confidence, and even playfulness, that suggests that, even at the tender age of 22, he wasn't intimidated by recording with a bona fide living legend whose records he must certainly have listened to in his formative years.

Walter also sessioned with another artist, the enigmatic Louisiana Red (born Iverson Minter). A talented singer and guitarist from Alabama who primarily performed solo, Minter did a session for Chess under the pseudonym Rocky Fuller that probably took place around this same time, but went unissued. One tune saw the light of day years later: the strong, doomful slow blues piece called "Funeral Hearse At My Door" featured powerful harp accompaniment by Walter, his unamplified playing giving the song a distinctly Muddy-esque feel.

Checker Records was the new Chess subsidiary label started with an eye towards reaching beyond just the down-home blues fans. In July, the new label released their hot new number "Juke." In August, a large trade magazine ad for Checker appeared, with a picture of a swami looking into a crystal ball, and the caption, "Operators! Dealers! Even if you gaze into your crystal ball—you will find Dollars of profits when you buy 'Juke' featuring Little Walter." Chess told the press that they were selling 1,000 copies a day.

Despite all the outside activity, Walter was still working as a band member with Waters. Muddy and the group were back on the road in Louisiana on a tour featuring John Lee Hooker and promoted by the DJ "Groove Boy" when "Juke" hit the jukeboxes down South. While in Shreveport, they hit a club and noticed that a familiar tune kept getting played and replayed on the jukebox. When they took a look to check it out they discovered that it was labeled as performed by "Little Walter and the Night Cats." Walter was knocked out; he was out front at last, and it was *his* name on the tune getting all the play.

The band went to downtown Shreveport to be fitted for some lightweight stage clothes suitable to the sweltering late-summer, Louisiana climate: drip-dry uniforms with short-sleeve, eggshell-colored shirts, and beige seersucker suits. They needed some alterations; Walter was too thin for the off-the-rack slacks. Muddy and Rogers went back to the tailor to pick up their new stage clothes later that afternoon, and when they returned to the hotel they were told by the desk clerk that Walter had departed in their absence: "That little guy with the checkered hat on? He said for you to take care of his amplifier, he's sick. He had a terrific nosebleed. He's going back to Chicago. He got a cab and left as soon as y'all did." Jimmy Rogers later suggested the real story was that Walter called Leonard, complained that everybody but him was making money, and left. The band filled out the dates with a sax player replacement, and when they returned to Chicago, Walter turned up, expecting his full payment for the tour. He asked Muddy, "Wh-wh-where's my money?" Replied Muddy sardonically, "I thought you brought it witcha."

Despite being somewhat rankled by the money situation, Walter rejoined Muddy until, as legend has it, one night at the popular Zanzibar Club on Chicago's West Side at 13th and Ashland, where Muddy had a regular "home base" gig when not on the road. A customer wanted to hear the tune that was a #1 hit in Chicago, Memphis, Dallas, and Cincinnati. He approached the low bandstand where the band sat playing, and exclaimed, "Okay, y'all play me that 'Juke' piece you got." As an incentive, he put a quarter on Muddy's knee, a quarter on Rogers's knee, and for Walter—a dime! That was the last straw for the hot-blooded Walter's young ego; the time had come for him to strike out on his own.

What transpired next varies depending on who's telling the story. The bottom line is that Walter took over The Aces, the band that had been recently featuring teenage harp player Junior Wells, consisting of brothers Dave and Louis Myers on guitars, and Fred Below on drums. He then took them out on tour billed as "The Jukes" to capitalize on his still-popular hit. At about the same time, Wells joined Muddy's band on the road and on their next recording session. In Wells's version, Walter telephoned him after abandoning Muddy and said, "Junior, me and you are all right with each other and the band [The Aces] sounds good. What you and me need to do now is to get our heads together and team up here. Me and you gonna run the rest of these so-called Mississippi saxophone players out of town. Me and you gonna start doing these duet things." While Wells was mulling that one over, Muddy also called and offered him the position Walter had recently vacated. Wells said he figured that Walter's offer was an attempt to show Muddy up by keeping Wells from playing with him. Despite Walter's alleged "begging," Wells chose to join forces with the established hit-maker Muddy.

According to Dave Myers, who thought of The Aces as *his* band and Wells as the hired harmonica player, the first he knew of the change was when Junior failed to show up for a gig. The band was at The Flame Club, and with people lined up in the streets waiting for the music to start inside, they had started playing without Wells. After the harp-less first set, Dave spotted Walter in the bar. Myers knew Muddy was out on tour but thought Walter was still with him, so he asked:

"Hey Walter, what you doing back in town? Y'all come back already?" Walter said, "No, I left Muddy and them out there. I just left 'em, man. They got somebody [on harp]." I say, "Who they got?" He say, "They got Junior Wells." I said, no wonder he's not at the show! He didn't even tell me he was leaving. Walter say, "He didn't have time, Muddy sent for him."

Louis Myers recalled a different version:

Walter called me up and told me Junior was gonna split. Said, "Your boy done split on you." Junior hadn't told me nothing about it. The union was strict, you have to give the proper notice. I asked him, "Junior, when is you leavin' to join Muddy?" That was a surprise to him, that I knew. He said, "Well, I'm supposed to leave Friday." I hired Walter because we needed a harp player with Junior gone, and Walter wanted to be on his own.

Dave felt that the split with Muddy was inevitable:

When Walter and Muddy made "Juke" they went on the road. Two stars together like that, people started to call for different things, they start to calling on Walter for that harp. I think Walter was kinda knocking Muddy with that harp, 'cause that harp began to pick up a lot of weight real fast. Muddy would just sing that old slower type blues; that harp was fast, gave more of a fast sense of conception of music, more to the dance type activity. It was unusual, it took off. It hurt Muddy a little bit. Walter started to get ahead of Muddy, it got where it didn't work out.

Walter needed a younger, more swinging band, and The Aces, who up until that point were strictly a local band, fit the bill. So according to Dave: "We made a deal. Walter needed us, the agents had been coming after him for traveling music, they wanted him to chase his record." Of course, "traveling music" meant that The Aces would have to take the plunge and become fulltime musicians, and for Dave this meant giving up his day job with the Campbell's Soup company: "That ended that . . . Walter had to make a decision, we decided to help him, I knew we could make a little more, get a little more exposure by moving around a little bit . . . he could fit with us real good, we could handle him, he could handle us."

Walter played with The Aces for a few weeks at Chicago's Hollywood Rendezvous club, and then had to leave for a two-week package tour that the Shaw Agency had booked, featuring an all-girl band. The Aces filled in during the interim with a couple of other harp players, including the sophisticated Rhythm Willie Hood, and John Lee Williamson disciple Forrest City Joe Pugh.

On the heels of his tour, another one of those magical street meetings occurred in Alexandria, Louisiana. Walter was driving down the road, when he came across his old running partner, Honeyboy Edwards, who was hustling his way around the area, driving tractors on a farm as well as playing in a club. "Walter drove up and said 'God damn man, what the hell are you doing here?'—he got out of his car and we talked," Honeyboy later wrote. Walter was heading on to Marksville, his hometown, "Driving home to his people in a black 1951 Cadillac, his record was swinging then, keeping the juke boxes hot as fire. He said: 'I'm going to Marksville, my home. I'm gonna put on a dance, you come work with me.'" Walter drove over, met up with a club owner, and set up a Friday night gig. He:

Drove around and put placards up all up and down Louisiana . . . by being Little Walter he packed that joint. His record was playing on the jukeboxes, people come to see him from fifty, sixty miles away. He got a local drummer and me, and we packed that house—I made $100 that night. He left back to Chicago after that and I had enough money to hit the road.

On his way back north, Walter also made a triumphant stopover in West Helena. His former guitar buddy Houston Stackhouse recalled, "He sure enough got famous when he made them records, he'd go back through there then, he was driving his big new Cadillac." It was quite a contrast with Walter's earlier days in the area:

> He was sleeping on crap tables down there, and an old boy, his name was Fraction, bought him some dinner one day, bought him a pack of cigarettes and told him "Boy, you're too good a harp blower to be fooling round here, sleeping on these crap tables at night." Little Walter taken him at his word, said that sunk in his head. He went on to Chicago, got lucky and made that money and everything. Got him a big old Cadillac and went back down there, looked him up and found him, said "Boy you were right! You taught me right. Say, here's $50 for you, boy. You put me on my foot." Walter say he taken it and thanked him. Walter had plenty money then, he was flying high.

In mid-September, Muddy was back in the Chess studios with Junior Wells in Walter's place, the first time Muddy had recorded with a harp man other than Walter. Twenty-eight years later Muddy recalled how Walter's leaving shook him: "When Little Walter quit me in '52, it was like somebody cutting off my oxygen—I didn't know how I was going to play without him. But soon I realized I had to put the slide back on my finger and go out and be Muddy Waters." But Muddy needn't have worried. Little Walter was quickly developing a cadre of emulators who would readily come forward to try and fill his shoes in Muddy's band. When asked about finding a new harp player, Muddy later noted, "Well, after Little Walter started, you didn't have to look, because everybody trying to play the harp. You didn't have to look 'cause they was out there, you know. So you didn't have no problem. You could find a harp player." Muddy's subsequent harp players were directed to emulate Walter's style when performing songs that had originally featured Walter as a sideman; when recording new material, they followed the template that Walter had established for the way a harp should sound with Muddy's music. (This would cause considerable confusion among discographers who later tried to sort out which harp player was present on which Muddy sessions.) About harp players, and the loss of Little Walter, Muddy remarked:

> . . . After Little Walter left I would try to get them to put in some things that was going on. But there was a lot of things that they couldn't exactly put in there, you know. But you can't stop because one member drops out. You must keep going. Old saying, "One monkey don't stop no show, slows it down."

Wells was a precocious and prodigiously talented young harp player, just 18 years old when he joined the 37-year-old Muddy. Four songs were cut at that session, three of them basically the same slow-burn tune with different words; the second track, "Standing Around Crying," was the killer. Wells more than adequately filled Walter's big shoes; he was blowing full out, heavily amplified and with an "in your face" audacity that Little Walter himself would have been proud of. It's a hair-raising performance, and one hell of a recording debut for Junior.

By October, "Juke" was number one in half of the *Cashbox* city-by-city charts, hitting the Top 10 in all but Los Angeles and NYC. From the standpoint of modern ears, it's hard to fathom the impact that this record had. *The Chicago Defender* on Oct. 11 wrote that Little Walter was "leading the nation at present with his disc smash of 'Juke' . . . Walter skyrocketed to fame when the nation took his 'Juke' to heart . . ." "Juke" introduced a soaring, chilling new harmonica sound to the public's ear. The song was remarkable for Walter's inexhaustible range of tone, his varied attack, and the way he built a solo. The harmonica had never sounded that way before; an "electric harmonica" was how the 1950s press described Walter's new "instrument." Today, the components first heard in "Juke" are an integral part of virtually every Chicago-style blues harp player's repertoire; as Jimmy Rogers succinctly put it, after the song's release "If a harmonica player couldn't play 'Juke,' he couldn't play harmonica." These days, the elements that make up "Juke" are just part of the basic language, and a common reference point. But at the time Little Walter was exploring uncharted territory. Nobody ever heard harp played with that kind of zest, style, and power before.

The Shaw Agency (a major booker of black jazz and R&B acts) opened up a Chicago office in the early '50s. They soon signed Little Walter to a five-year booking contract, at the same time inking a deal with Walter's label-mate Eddie Boyd, the veteran pianist with several Chess hit singles under his belt. Billy Shaw, owner of the agency, was no dilettante. He'd started out as personal manager of crooner Billy Eckstine, launched his own agency in New York in 1949, and went on to sponsor the great jazz saxman Charlie Parker. He was instrumental in getting Parker's cabaret license reinstated, giving the drug-addicted Parker a chance to again earn money playing on the crucial New York City jazz scene.

With "Juke" riding high on the charts, in October 1952 Walter was back at Universal Studios, for the first time leading his own band, soon to be known on record as The Jukes. Three of the four tunes cut that day were instrumentals, and all were in the key of E. Walter was recorded with a lot of reverb, still a relatively new studio novelty, and all the pieces have a distant echoey sound. Where Walter's debt to John Lee Williamson had been obvious on his early solo recordings, now his interest in jump-horn bands and players like Louis Jordan, Gene Ammons, and Illinois Jacquet was coming to the fore. Not only was his tone deep and organlike, he was beginning to phrase his lines more like a jazz player, his harp phrases dancing around the beat and across bars as well, with an unerring sense of swing throughout.

The first two tunes recorded went unreleased at the time. There are two existing takes of the first tune, "Blue Midnight." A slow, late-night blues, it's a showcase for Walter's skill at using dynamics to evoke a mood and feeling in the listener. Solo harp takes it in with a long, swooping note, soon joined by an easy loping walking bass line by Dave, with Louis adding some arpeggio chords up high on the guitar neck. Walter sets the mood with the use of sustained fat tones and easy warbles for the first couple of choruses, then hits some harsher, darker licks to drive up the intensity before returning to the mellow flow. The track was held on the shelf until 1960. The next, untitled tune is a driving instrumental once again in a horn-band mode. It's easy to imagine this as a piece a honking tenor man like Red Prysock or Illinois Jacquet could have cut. Walter is all over the harp, hitting fat, squalling, sax-like tones with a percussive attack, barely pausing to breathe. It builds to an abrupt and flashy stop at the end. Maybe Chess thought it was too busy; whatever the reason, it was shelved at the time.

The next two tracks became Walter's new single. "Mean Old World" was based on a 1945 Rhumboogie label single by T-Bone Walker. Walter uses Walker's first verse virtually intact, then improvises, singing a plaintive vocal over a simple "lumpty-lump" bass line on the guitar. Filling in between the vocals and during the harp break in the middle of the song, Walter shows off a sound rarely heard before on amplified harp: he hits a chord, then adds a warble by rapidly moving the harp back and forth over his lips, hitting the neighboring notes briefly. The effect is a powerful, plaintive trill that adds greatly to the intensity level. Guitarist Dave Myers spoke about this particular technique, recalling that Walter had been voicing dissatisfaction over playing behind Muddy, how he was bored with so many slow blues. Myers suggested he try to find some other way to play the tunes. Not long after that Walter showed up "ready to shout, he was so happy," according to Myers. "I found out the other night," Walter said. "Man I felt that shit that I been thinking about a long time back a bit, I put that shit together and came up with that quiver. I don't worry about nothing now!" Myers felt that the "quiver" was one of the elements that made Walter so unique.

"Sad Hours" was a medium-slow instrumental, utilizing a loping bass line and atmospheric chording, which The Aces had been featuring at their regular Hollywood Rendezvous gigs. Based on "Blues After Hours," first made popular in a 1940 recording by The Erskine Hawkins Band, The Aces most likely borrowed it from west coast guitarist Pee Wee Crayton's 1948 R&B hit version. "We played that for one particular man, the proprietor," Dave recalled. "Every night we had to play it two or three times. When Walter came in after Junior cut out, he could fit the harp in with it . . ." When the band started messing around with the riff in the studio, Chess said, "Hey, let's cut it," but Walter balked. "That's as honest as a man could be," Dave admitted. "He said 'Look, that's one of the men's ideas, I've got my own numbers I've already made.'" But Chess was insistent, and finally convinced Dave that he'd get credit for the number, so they rolled tape. (After later hearing the tune on the jukebox, Dave discovered that the label credit listed only Jacobs as composer. When they returned to Chicago, he went down to see Chess, "hot as a potato." Chess had a secretary write Myers a check for $400, but Myers wasn't happy—he'd hoped to record it on his own.)

The recording begins with guitars and drums setting the mood for the entire first chorus. Then Walter comes in high and full, alternating warbling chords with solid sustained tones. Louis's guitar steps forward for a verse, then Walter comes back hard, stressing some bent tones. The intensity builds with Walter repeating some rhythmic chords, then eases a bit before sailing into the final chords. Altogether a winning and evocative piece, and evidence that the band was already a potent unit.

Louis Myers talked about the preparations—or lack thereof—for recording with the band: "We never did rehearse, we just walked into the studio; because we were playing with one another, I know what he's gonna do." Walter commented on the speed at which they worked: "We cut four numbers in about 20 minutes. When you know what you're going to do, we played together so long we know all our turnarounds . . ." Nonetheless, the results of the entire session sound focused and well structured.

That same month, Walter was booked as a headliner at the famed Apollo Theater in New York, brought in to capitalize on his hit number. Harlem's black newspaper, *The Amsterdam News*, ran an ad for the show: "Harlems High Spot/World's Greatest Colored Shows—One Week Only, beginning Friday Oct 24; New Recording Star . . . 'Juke'/Little Walter and his Night Cats/by demand, Duke Hampton Boy & Girl Band/New King of the blues H-Bomb Ferguson/Tokayer Troupe/Crackshot &

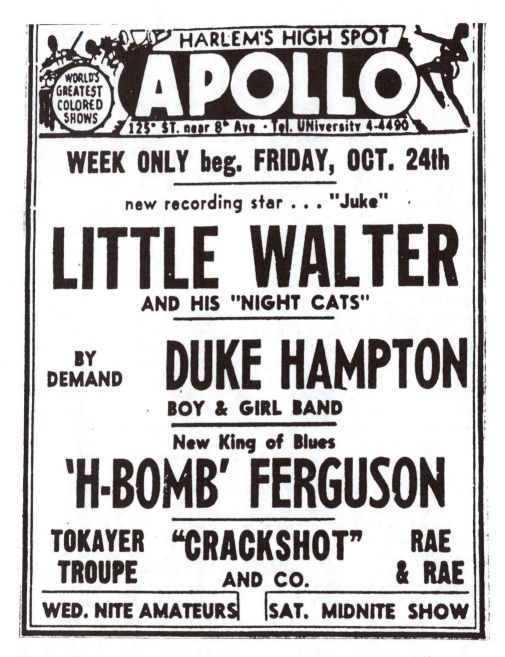

Figure 6.2 Apollo Theater advertisement, *Amsterdam News*, October 25, 1952.

Co./Rae & Rae." Little Walter and The Jukes were the first Chicago Blues band ever to play the venue, which was famed for tough crowds, who booed loud and long when they didn't care for an act. Walter called his little sister Marguerite to share in his triumph; he said, "Hey momma, guess where I'm playing tonight?" When she asked where, he replied "The Apollo Theater—and guess what, Muddy's not playing there, I'm the first one!"

The Amsterdam News previewed the show:

NEWCOMERS HEAD BILL ON APOLLO'S BOARDS—Some of the most unique young talents to come along in months will be making their first appearance at the 125th street APOLLO THEATER. . . . Among them will be LITTLE WALTER and his "Night Cats". . . When one listens to "Juke" he is struck by the unique sound, for never before has such an expert harmonica been blended with more standard instruments, reeds, horns, rhythm . . . and never before has this particular combination of tones been heard. One next wonders why no one has ever tried it before, because the combination is "right". . . the effect is most pleasing to the ear. However the unique often seems obvious only after someone has had the courage to try it out . . . and this is just what "Little Walter" has done. This is a driving, fast-moving, exciting combination . . .

On this first big trip out of town, Walter brought along a female companion, 22-year-old Armilee Thompson, whom he'd met while he was still playing with Muddy. The two hooked up again later at the Hollywood Lounge after Walter had begun playing with his own band, and began an off-and-on affair for the next four or five years, during which time she was one of Walter's "road women." Meanwhile at home, Ella Mae continued her day job at the laundry, and she kept the house. Always quiet about his personal life and affairs, Walter wouldn't share much about his business, even to those he was intimate with. "Walter didn't do too much talking about his family life," Armilee says, ". . . he was the type of person that never did a lot of talking or bragging about anything, he was just Walter." He went to great lengths to compartmentalize the various facets of his life, juggling his various girlfriends and other relationships—although not always successfully, and not without its costs. There were several people around town who considered him a "best friend" or a "main squeeze," but who knew nothing of each other's existence. Walter was not alone in this lifestyle; many of his fellow musicians were well-known to have regular women in almost every town they visited, but Walter seemed to have his women in closer proximity to one another, in Chicago. Consequently he needed to keep a tighter lid on his personal life in order to avoid potential trouble.

Having a hit single made a big difference in Walter's lifestyle, and his fortunes were rising fast, Armilee recalled. He'd been living in a six-flat tenement in Chicago. In New York City, the agency had booked them rooms at the famed Hotel Theresa. On 125th Street and 7th Avenue, the place was just a few minutes walk to the Apollo Theater, and at the time was considered the hub of Harlem's social life. "Just as the Waldorf is home for the white elite," *Ebony* magazine wrote in a 1946 feature article, "The Theresa is social headquarters for Negro America." The 13-story, 300-room building's regular guests included Lena Horne, Count Basie and Eddie Anderson—"Rochester" on the

Jack Benny radio show. Rooms were booked months in advance by big shots, band-leaders, society folks, and "upper-class people." Walter was getting a first taste of high life in the Big Apple—and liking it.

At the theater, as The Jukes were setting up their equipment before the performance, a stagehand asked "When does the band get here?", to which they replied "We *are* the band." Dave Myers recalls it as a killer show; nobody in New York City had ever heard such a huge sound coming from such a small band before. This was the first time a Chicago blues band had played the legendary East Coast theater, and according to Myers, the emcee tried to pave the way with his introduction:

> He said, "Ladies and gentlemen, we know you've heard all the other shows and you're enjoying yourself, because you peoples are very lively. Now we come to this situation—I don't know how to explain it to you—but it's two guitars, a harp and a drum. They're introducing a *new* style of music to the music scene. We'd like for you to hear them so you can have an opinion of how they play. We'd like for you to sit back and relax, let's see what to make of these people." So we came on.

As they were preparing to launch into the first number, drummer Fred Below fell backwards off his drum riser reaching for a cymbal. The audience applauded, thinking it part of the show. "That Professor got a-loose back there," Walter wryly joked to the crowd. Myers continues:

> We came on, couldn't do but one tune. Walter figured out the best tune to play was "Tommy Dorsey's Boogie," he tried to do exactly what he thought would please the people. [The tune, a big-band remake of "Pinetops Boogie Woogie," had been a massive hit for Dorsey in 1938.] But Walter said, "I can't remember all that . . . ." I said, "You just listen to me, you'll do it, I already know you can do it. Just play it in sections—one part, one part, one part . . ." See, Walter was nervous and scared, that's what made him blow so hard. We took off on that tune, you never saw people go so crazy. We played through about three choruses, next thing we know, the whole Hampton big band got back up there with them goddamned trumpets. Boy you talk about sounding good! Walter was *playing* that tune, and we was whipping them guitars on his ass! One of the people in charge, he came down and stopped us, got on the mike and said, "Ladies and gentlemen, we are not relaxing here, we're all over the place, we're loud, I have to stop the music to settle you down . . . ." We couldn't continue, they went berserk. He said, "Tomorrow night they'll be here, we hope that everybody will be back, they'll be here all week long."

According to Myers, the audiences continued to grow throughout the weeklong engagement:

> Boy, they was all up and down the street, we'd see 'em lined up when we was coming in to work. Get inside, the damn place was full. A lot of entertainers was there, Alvino Ray, [West Coast jazz pianist] Carl Perkins, and the big booking agent Billy Shaw and his staff. He's the one that told us if we got past the Apollo, we didn't have to worry about where else we go, because we'd be able to go everywhere . . . So that introduced us to the world and from then on we didn't have a day's rest . . . couldn't come back to Chicago for four or five months . . .

On the next-to-last night of Walter's engagement, there was some early morning excitement at the hotel. Fire trucks arrived to rescue by ladder a 4th floor permanent resident trapped in his burning room around 4:00 AM.

Following the Apollo success, according to a story told by drummer Below (which, while sounding somewhat incredible, was nonetheless confirmed by Myers), Walter was offered a thirty-nine day gig at the Palladium in London, but he turned it down. "Fresh out, he did not know what was going on," Below later opined, and also speculated that Walter's fear of flying kept him from accepting a tour that might have changed the course of music history.

Meanwhile, in Chicago, Walter continued to develop a group of devoted proteges. "Sleepy" Otis Hunt came to Chicago from Arkansas in 1945, tap danced in taverns for tips, and eventually began learning harp, hoping to win back his wife who'd left him for a flirtation with Howlin' Wolf. He said it was Walter who got him started playing, while Hunt was tending bar at the Stadium Sports Club, where Walter was playing on Mondays and Tuesdays:

> He come over there in the daytime, set down and say, "Come on boy, take this harp." Then he grabbed it back, said, "Nah, you ain't gonna learn." I said, "Yes I is too." He said, "I'm gonna give you this one, and you better learn how to blow it too." I took that harp and I messed with it a good long while, kept on till I got the right tone.

Later on, Walter was playing at Ricky's on 39th and Indiana and Hunt showed up. Walter was mid-set when he spotted Hunt, stepped off the stage and handed him his harp and mike while he went to the washroom. When he came back Hunt was onstage, blowing with the band. Walter said, "Well you big son of a bitch!" "I told you I was gonna learn," Hunt replied.

Hunt said that Walter was going with his sister. One night, they both dropped by to hear Walter play at the Zanzibar. Hunt's wife turned up, they got to arguing about their kids, and Hunt told her to go home and take care of them. Instead she sat down beside Howlin' Wolf on a stool. When Hunt came over and told her to go on and beat it, Wolf stood up and pulled out his pistol, which he held off to the side hidden from Hunt's view, and said, "She ain't got to go nowhere, little old boy." Words were exchanged, and unaware that Wolf had a gun in his hand, Hunt was about to make a move on him.

Hunt continues:

> Walter was playing a long time up on the bandstand. He seen what was happening and jumped down there on the floor between me and Wolf. He told Wolf, "You shoot that boy and you'll have to shoot him right through me." I said, "Shoot?" I looked around Walter then and saw the pistol in his hand. Here I was gonna hit him if I got close enough on him—and he mighta shot me! I went home, got my shotgun and came back. Walter told Wolf, "You better get your big black butt outta here. That young boy gonna blow your head off, man. That's that boy's wife."

When Hunt got back, Wolf was gone.

Much later, Walter took Hunt over to see Wolf's band playing a gig at Silvio's. "I want you and Wolf to meet and make friends," he said. During intermission, Wolf came to the two men's table. Walter said, "Wolf, you probably don't remember this guy . . . this is the boy you drawed a pistol on that night. He just wanna make friends." Wolf said "I apologize." To Hunt he seemed like his father, and the two got on well enough that Wolf would call him up to sit in with his band. Hunt's wife did come back for a few weeks—but after all that Hunt decided he was better off without her, and he took the kids and left. Hunt claimed that he and Walter were "like that, like brothers," and when the band left town Hunt would do fill-in gigs at the Zanzibar. He recalled Walter "drinking that green stuff and clowning." Hunt said, "He'd get up on the counter and walk the counter and then go out the door. His cord would reach way out there in the street. He was as good as he wanna be. He was blowing 30 years ahead of hisself . . ."

On Nov 15th, a boyishly handsome Walter made the cover of *Cashbox*, the music business trade magazine. Walter posed holding harps in hand, jaunty and dapper, flanked by Leonard Chess and powerful WGES disc jockey Al Benson. The caption read: "One of the biggest disks in the R&B field is currently 'Juke' . . . which has gone into the smash category." The same month, Chess released Muddy's "Standing Around Crying," and Walter's new single. Muddy's working band lost another member that month when Jimmy Rogers pulled out to set up his own group, hoping to capitalize on the success of the songs he'd been cutting at the end of Muddy's sessions. But as always, Chess was reluctant to tamper with a winning formula in the studio, and Jimmy would continue to be brought in to appear on Muddy's recordings for several more years. (Walter would find himself in a similar situation. After his departure, Muddy used Junior Wells and then Big Walter Horton in Walter's place on his next two sessions. One single came out of each session, but some magic must have been noticeably absent to Chess, because Walter then rejoined Muddy's studio line-up for virtually every session for the next four years.)

Young harpist Billy Boy Arnold was 17 the first time he saw Walter playing with The Aces in Chicago, at the Hollywood Rendezvous at 39th and Indiana, "Right on the alley." Arnold explained, "He had just went to the Apollo, and played 'Juke' . . . whenever he was in town, he was there [The Rendezvous] five–six nights a week." It became Walter's home base over the next few months. Arnold stated, "If he came in [town] today, this afternoon, he could play there tonight. If the man knew he was here, whoever was gonna play there didn't have no job. Walter would stay there till he gotta leave, which was frequent. He come in town, be there a couple days, then gone again, maybe a month or two." The club was filling fast when Arnold arrived that night during the first set, the booths and tables mostly taken. "People came out dressed up, it was like an event. Walter was real hot, people were coming in to hear him. He had two records out. 'Mean Old World' had just come out, and 'Juke' was still burning the airwaves up—it was on every jukebox. . . ." The bar sold set-ups; "a half pint of whiskey and a coke and some ice, some cherries, glasses for as many as were in your party." People were mostly sitting down and listening—and drinking. When Arnold arrived, the band was already playing, everybody sitting down: Walter in the center, Louis Myers on one side, Dave Myers on the other, and Below behind, towards the right of Dave.

Besides playing his current releases, Arnold remembers hearing a lot of instrumentals. According to Arnold, "everything had an uptempo beat," including an early version of the yet-to-be-recorded "Off The Wall." "He did a version of 'Rock Me Baby' like Muddy, but faster, uptempo," Arnold continued, "... a girl told me once that 'Little Walter sound like a hipped-up Muddy Waters,' meaning the same music, just hipped up some—and she described it right. He was just wailing, he was a swinger; a lot of beautiful solos."

When Arnold passed the bandstand on his way to the bathroom, he heard Louis, who he knew, say to Walter, "That's one of them counterfeit harp players"—and Walter's eyes followed Billy as he crossed the room. Next set, after a few numbers, Walter gets on the mike, "We gonna call a boy up here, he gonna blow the sides off a harp." He turned to ask Louis, "What's his name, what's his name?" then announced "Lets gets Billy up here." Arnold blew a couple, Sonny Boy Williamson style. Afterwards he asked Walter if he knew Sonny Boy. Walter replied, "Yeah, I knew him. He was really good man, he was the best. He used to tell me 'you play too fast, you play too fast.'" Arnold stayed at the club until closing time, soaking in the excitement.

The evening ended with Walter being rushed to the back by a couple of the other non-musician Myers brothers. When Arnold asked what happened, he was told "Walter got high, Walter's drunk." But it wasn't apparent to Arnold at the time; "It was at the last, when the joint was getting ready to close, after he was done playing." Arnold heard Walter with Muddy's band later, on a Sunday afternoon matinee at the Dew Drop Inn. "He sat in and blowed 'Going Away Baby' with Jimmy Rogers, made Jimmy sound just like the record."

If there was any doubt that Walter was becoming a full-fledged star, his burgeoning fame was confirmed when an impostor played a gig under Walter's name at the Dew Drop Inn in New Orleans. Over the years, there's been a long history of "Muddy Waters Jr.," "Little B.B. King," "Howling Wolf Jr.," and of course the two famous Sonny Boy Williamsons. Local blues players seeking to gain some attention would capitalize on the name recognition of an established star. Some of these were true tributes, others were wannabe artists playing one night hit-and-run shows in out-of-the-way venues. Guitarist Earl Hooker toured for a while in the south with a harpist named "Little Walker"; the name was often deliberately misspelled as Walter on posters. Another pretender was Papa Lightfoot, a talented harpman in his own right out of Natchez, Mississippi, who cut some instrumental sides for Alladin Records in November; he sometimes billed himself as "Little Papa Walter." The resulting brouhaha with lawyers, booking agents, and record companies weighing in was tsk-tsked over by a trade mag columnist. Walter would find himself in similar positions again several more times over the course of his career.

The real Walter was riding high. The new single climbed to #2 and spent 16 weeks on the charts. The Shaw Agency had lined up a long southern tour, starting with a month's worth of one-nighters around Texas beginning in January. His records were ruling jukeboxes across the land. Walter soon purchased a cream-and-blue station wagon with pictures of his records and "Little Walter & His Jukes" lettered on the door (for the band gear), and a black Cadillac (for himself). He was ready to roll.

7 *diamonds and cadillac cars*

Chicago/East and West Coasts/Southern States:
January 1953–February 1954

The December release of the followup to "Juke" was marked by a display advertisement in the national record trade magazines. It featured a drawing of Walter, emblazoned "Seasons Greetings from Little Walter, Sensational 'Juke' artist." The ad plugged the new single as "R&B Bomb of '53 with 'Mean Old World' backed by 'Sad Hours.'" Elsewhere, a column item noted ". . . the weird and spine tingling sounds that emerge from the mouth organ of Little Walter assure the youngster of another big etching in his 'Sad Hours' on the Checker label. This hunk of wax should outsell 'Juke' the side which introduced the harmonica specialist to the country." The *Billboard* R&B charts listed both "Juke" and "Sad Hours" in the Top-10 "most played in juke boxes" category, and "Sad Hours" was in the Top-10 chart listings from St. Louis, Washington, DC, and at home in Chicago. On the December 29th charts, both tunes were on the Top-10 national bestsellers list. It made sense for Chess to get some more product ready in order to capitalize on Little Walter's growing momentum.

Leonard called for another session for the hottest-selling artist on his label. Again, the engineer at Universal was Bill Putnam; he ran the board on a three-and-a-half hour session dated only as "January" on the log sheet. Although none of the tunes cut this day would be issued at the time, some solid groundwork for future releases was laid. The first tune up was an instrumental, an early version of a song Walter was no doubt playing on the bandstand at the time, and which would eventually be reworked and issued as "Off The Wall"; here it's marked "no title" on the log sheet. Thirteen takes were attempted that day; the resulting three completed versions and various starts, stops, and verse fragments on the reel offer a fascinating look at an inventive musician at work. The opening "head" and some phrases carry over from one take to the next, but each take explores new variations on the theme, with unique ideas and execution. With "Juke" as Walter's big hit number, he probably wasn't using it as a set opener and intermission theme anymore; it's likely that this new instrumental was something he'd been playing with and using in the same role that "Juke" had earlier served

Figure 7.1 Chess advertisement, December 1952.

with Muddy's band. The tune has a brisk, solid-rocking pace, and the earlier takes feature a steady walking boogie figure laying down a bed for Walter's fat horn tones and insistent warbles. Later takes feature a slightly jazzier backing, with Louis using more 9th chord accents on the guitar, and cymbal splashing punctuations from Fred Below, as well as dynamic variations in volume and tighter ensemble playing from the band, which was augmented that day by the talented bass player Ernest "Big" Crawford.

Next up was another instrumental, also logged at the time as "no title." Another sprightly paced piece, this one is driven by a clip-clop "country shuffle" rhythm pattern by Below and Crawford. It features some rapidfire, well-conceived riffing by Walter, which he'd been working on in-between takes of the other tunes he recorded that day. Only one take was recorded. It's unlikely that this was because they felt they'd perfected it on the first take; the band seems a little tentative at the start, and Louis fumbles awkwardly through his guitar break in the middle of the song. More likely Chess realized that the clock was ticking, they'd been at it for a good while now, and what they really needed was a strong vocal number for the "A" side of Walter's next single, not another instrumental "B" side. (It was finally issued many years later titled "Don't Need No Horse," the name assigned then by a Chess producer because the tune reminded him of a later Junior Wells-Earl Hooker piece called "Galloping Horse And A Lazy Mule.")

The last tune Walter attempted at this session was a cover version of the breakthrough 1945 Charles Brown hit "Drifting Blues." Take 1 follows Brown's lyrics closely, but in the middle Walter inserts a break, borrowing the distinctive stop-time bridge from tenor sax player Jimmy Forrest's huge number-one hit from just a few months earlier, "Night Train." After the first tentative run-through, Walter decides to switch to a key that better suits his vocal range, and at Leonard's suggestion, changes the final verse. Understanding the importance of radio air play, he changes the final line of the song to "I'm gonna get some disc jockey, to play my blues to you." In between takes Walter can be heard singing the line for himself, then satisfiedly saying, "That's just what I'm gonna do Mama, Get some disc jockey to play my blues to you!" Take 2 is a bit slower and more soulful, and although it's marked on the session log as the master, like the first version, it's marred by a sloppy break in the middle as the band falters its way through the "Night Train" quote. It appears that all the tracks cut that day were held back because Chess was looking for numbers that made harder-hitting first impressions, and which could match the impact of Walter's other efforts for the label.

A few days later Muddy was also in the studio, this time with Big Walter Horton as his harp player, filling in for Junior Wells who'd been drafted into the army, and then gone AWOL and disappeared. Horton was playing at his peak these days, although due to his unreliability, this would be his only session with Muddy for Chess.

There was a new president, Dwight D. Eisenhower, now in office on a peace platform, the Korean Conflict was slowing down, and the public was beginning to worry about the possibility of another economic depression, but there was still plenty of work for a hot band like Little Walter's. He and the men hit the road headed for Houston, and a midweek gig starting on January 21st. Life on the road with the band was quite a bit different from the usual club engagements around town. On local gigs all they had to do is show up far enough ahead of starting time to set up their amps and tune their instruments. If it was one of the regularly scheduled weekly gigs like at the 708 Club or The Hollywood Rendezvous, they'd often just leave the equipment there afterwards rather than lugging it back and forth each night. Then it was easy to follow up on whatever the night had brought to them—maybe a rendezvous with a sweet young thing met on a band break, or perhaps a craps game, or maybe just a solitary night with a bottle—and they probably wouldn't see their bandmates again until starting time the following night.

Out on the road it was a different situation. First, they'd spend many hours, if not all day, jammed together into a station wagon. All the available room was taken up by amps, guitars, and a drum kit, with the overflow lashed on top of the car. Close quarters can lead to a real camaraderie—or to intense friction. They might start out joking, pointing out sights along the road, reading the maps, enjoying the hum of the highway. But before long it's too hot, or too cold, the radio's too loud or not loud enough, or someone needs a stop to "water the bushes" but the driver's in a groove and wants to keep moving. Everyone is walking on eggshells in order to avoid conflict, and as frustrating as it might be, it's wiser to watch what's said, because they were all going to be crammed together for some time: the Shaw Agency lined up a month's worth of bookings in Texas alone. It was 1,100 pre-interstate highway miles south from Chicago before they pulled into the parking lot for the first gig. So although you might be tempted to tell the loudmouth in the back seat to hold it down so you can catch up on your sleep for a bit, it was better to keep the peace. They'd be sharing the wagon, hotel rooms, and stages with each other for the foreseeable future. Each knew that they had to try and get along if they didn't want to end up standing by the side of the highway with a garment bag and guitar in hand, watching the station wagon disappear over the horizon.

First off there were the Myers brothers, who got along with each other the same way most brothers do; they were allies one minute, in each other's faces the next. Then there was Below; they called him ". . . Fess, the professor. Below was what you'd call more educated than what we were," Louis Myers said. "When you don't have the appropriate education on some things that's said, Below was always there, he would always speak, put it right." And finally there was Walter, still just a kid in many ways; they called him "Little Goola," because of the way he acted sometimes. But even though he was the youngest in the group at 22, he *was* the boss. It was his name painted in big letters on the door of the station wagon.

From the beginning, Louis wasn't too happy about that:

> Before we left town, going out on an engagement, he used to change the name, to The Jukes, and we were already The Aces. I told the man we should let it be "Little Walter featuring the Aces," so we wouldn't get lost out there . . . We was in the car talking, Walter wasn't saying nothing because he'd got them together on me, Dave and Below had left me, I was just one, so the majority won. I said, "You already a star Walter. You should let us remain The Aces," but he couldn't hear that and Dave and Below agreed with him, so that was the end of that.

Sharing the bill with Walter on the tour, at Leonard Chess's suggestion, was pianist Eddie Boyd. Boyd was not too enthusiastic about playing the South since he'd left it for Chicago in the early '40s. He was proud to say he'd only played two gigs in Mississippi in his whole career, and he hated the place. Texas, though, was a more pleasant scene in his opinion. "They have a different mentality about musicians and things, nobody harassed you down there," Boyd said. " Little Walter and me [played] for thirty-one days and went from one side of the state to the other. Thirty-one gigs man, in one month. Every day, and never got out of that state. And never was harassed one time by no cops or nothing."

Walter and The Jukes played all over in a variety of venues, from auditoriums and night clubs to dance halls and road houses. This was their first time out of Chicago on a road trip and they had a conquering mentality; they'd show these people what a real hot combo could do! One night in Dallas they played a mixed show, where the club had strung the customary rope across the dance floor to separate the white and black dancers—and the police were in attendance to make sure everybody stayed in their proper place. The audience for the first set was rather lethargic, more intent on drinking and talking than listening to the band.

During the break, the band conferred. Walter thought he knew how to get the crowd's attention. When the second set began, the band was in place on the stand, and although the crowd could hear a blasting harp, Walter wasn't onstage. As they looked around they spotted the compact musician straddling a big man's shoulders, being carried through the crowd, a long cord connecting his mike to his amplifier, wailing as he moved towards the stand. As Walter dismounted and continued to blow chorus after chorus, the crowd jumped up and hit the dance floor, packing it. In the commotion the rope came down, and whites and blacks were all dancing together. The cops realized that the crowd had joined into a gyrating mass, but there's not much they could do about this musical integration in action.

"We was whipping it on 'em strong and sure," Louis said:

> We was killing 'em man. One time I read in the paper that Little Walter was the baddest band in the land and it wasn't but us four . . . we had something new and different . . . some of them bands didn't have a chance. They're sitting there playing horns with one or two mikes, a 10, 12, 15 piece band—but the peoples had to get up close to hear that. Do you realize how strong an amplifier is just blowing an instrument out of it? Can you imagine an upright bass gonna sound as loud as an electric bass? Here's these cats still playing in the old style, just sitting there playing drive-along-jimmy . . . and Walter could take one of them [amplifiers] he was playing out of and hang it up on the wall somewhere out there . . . We ran into quite a few bands out there with [big] names, that didn't have a chance. If they played their set before we played . . . next set them peoples just boo them off the bandstand, wouldn't let them play no more. Walter was playing like 40 horns man! His amplifier would sound like that sometimes, put his echo on and God! Music was hitting the walls and bouncing all over the place . . . they'd say, "Them cats sound like a giant band, and there ain't but four of 'em."

One night Walter and The Jukes were in a cafe having pre-show dinner when members of Roy Milton's big band came in to eat as well. Dave Myers recalled that somebody played Walter's "Mean Old World" on the jukebox, and all the horn players gathered round, debating what kind of instrument could be making that sound. They didn't figure it out until later that night at the show.

Another one of the bands they regularly overshadowed was their showmate Eddie

Boyd's ensemble—and for Walter it was sweet revenge, settling an old score. Pianist Boyd was hot then, touring with several horns, with one of Walter's mentors from West Helena, Robert "Junior" Lockwood, on guitar. Boyd's "Five Long Years" had been a hit the previous summer, and he was now a Chess artist with higher-class aspirations. "Eddie was a star, he wanted to be a more uppity kind of guy," Billy Boy Arnold later explained. "He'd started out trying to play harmonica but gave up, saying 'I quit, the harmonica is such a low grade instrument.'"

Arnold continued:

Walter was hanging around before he got famous, Boyd criticized him, "Man, you guys, playing them harmonicas"... he didn't like Muddy's guitar playing, he wanted guys like the guys that played with Charles Brown and Nat King Cole. Every night, Eddie'd get up there with the horns, Robert Junior playing them [fancy] chords—but Walter would kick Eddie's ass, he was playing with that funk! On the show it was B. B. King's big band, Little Walter and Eddie Boyd—and they say that Walter would take the show from everybody. B. B. was tops, [but] Walter was doing B. B. in. Dave and Louis told me Boyd would walk up to them and say "Hey man, tell Walter to give me a break, don't be so hard on me—." When Eddie'd go up to play, people would be hollering "We want Little Walter!"—so it served [Boyd] right, to do people like that.

While passing through Gadsen, Alabama, Walter met another local harp player who'd been inspired by his recordings, Jerry McCain. "I just went crazy over it," McCain said. "[Walter] came through here, playing right down the street, this big club, black club that burned down. I met him there, told him who I was." McCain's brother had connections with bootleggers, and used to deliver bootleg whiskey to some of the white people in the area, so Walter and McCain became quick friends:

He loved that corn [whiskey], he wanted to go find some . . . we got to riding around, and that thing Little Walter had out about "I'm Crazy About You Baby"? ("Can't Hold On Much Longer"). I changed it—I'm sitting in the back, he and my brother sitting up front. I sang "Little Walter said he was crazy about you baby, wonder did you ever think of him." I was in the back, working on the harmonica. I said, "But you know Little Walter didn't know old Jerry was the cause his light burning so dim." And boy, he just went crazy. He said, "Man you come up on stage, I'm gonna let you play tonight."

That night, the club was packed and Walter beckoned McCain onstage midset and handed him the harp "right quick." McCain continued the tune, and says the dancers didn't notice the switch till the end of the piece.

The tour continued on throughout the south, and it was obvious there was a musical and cultural upheaval afoot. More and more whites were tuning in to "Rhythm & Blues" radio shows, a term the industry coined to replace the old "race music" label. Many of the club shows were still segregated, but the airwaves weren't, and white teenagers were responding to the honking saxes and shouting vocals heard on clear-channel late night stations. White disk jockeys aiming at black audiences, such as Alan Freed in Cleveland (and later New York) and Dewey Phillips of Memphis, discovered that roughly one in five of their listeners was white, and those white listeners were buying the records and attending R&B shows as well. It wouldn't be long before Freed would take a sexual euphemism from black slang and use it as a name for this "new" music that was stirring up young blood: "Rock & Roll" had a snap to it that crossed racial boundaries. Equally important, the music was fun, and worlds better for dancing than the bland pop balladry heard on the Hit Parade.

By March, Walter and the boys had returned to Chicago for a respite from the road. That month saw the release of the biggest hit to date for fellow harpist Rice Miller, labeled as Sonny Boy Williamson, when "Mighty Long Time" was released by the Trumpet label from Jackson, Mississippi. A haunting slow blues, it featured only bass backing for Sonny Boy's plaintive vocals and warbling harp tones, and it went on to become one of his all-time classics. At the same time, a new R&B label, Herald Records, was announced from New York. They were reported to be lining up a stable of R&B stars and cutting sessions, and announced that among their first batch of releases were "some sides cut by southern blues chanter Little Walter"—but these weren't new recordings. Herald, hoping to gain a quick toehold by playing on name recognition, had made a deal to reissue the 1950 Parkway recordings Walter had cut with Muddy and Foster.

As always, Chess was anxious to get more "product" from his successful artists produced, so it was time for another Little Walter session. When they convened in the studio that month, the band, as was becoming the custom, began with an instrumental, originally given the title "You Don't Have To Hurt," but which was issued as "You Don't Have To Hunt" due to a handwriting error. It's another stab at the theme they'd repeatedly tried during the shelved January session, exploring many of the same ideas and dynamic volume variations. Some nice accents from Below's drums enliven a midtempo version that surges and eases back again as Walter swings back and forth between hard and nasty, then soft and sweet. A rather abrupt ending is the only drawback to a solid take. Some of the bugs that had caused the earlier versions of this song to be held back must have been worked out, because the tune was scheduled for release as Checker 676.

Following the pattern from the previous session, next up was a quick, clip-clop rhythm instrumental, this time modified with a vaguely Latin-esque beat (Latin-tinged numbers were then all the rage) with percussion to the fore. On the third chorus, Myers takes a chorded solo, and later in the song Walter quotes the jazzman's favored "A Tisket, A Tasket" riff. The emphasis here is more on rhythm than melody, and with the frantic pace of the tune, Walter sticks to a limited palette of notes, exploring more rhythmic variations than melodic or harmonic ones ("A Tisket, A Tasket" notwithstanding). The beat is infectious, and the Latin spice must have done the trick, because Chess eventually released the tune, aptly titled "Crazy Legs," although not until some years later, as the flip side of Checker 986.

Pianist Henry Gray, who went on to record with Howlin' Wolf and Jimmy Reed, sat in on the next number. Though he now remembers no details of the session, a few years later he did some pickup gigs with Walter. Gray recalled him as "Fast . . . played the harp fast, run fast, talked fast, act fast—I never knowed him to take his time to do nothing. If you was driving and he was [a passenger], he'd take his foot, put it on the accelerator, mash it down to the floor. He didn't care whether the police stopped him or not. He tell you 'I'm ready to go' and you stand around waiting, you look for him he's gone . . ." Gray is prominent in the mix on the recording, a slow vocal blues with the recurring chorus "I wished I had somebody to love me all the time." The cut was ironically titled "Tonight With A Fool." Like many Chess blues sessions, it was probably titled after the fact, because these words appear nowhere in the lyrics. Walter's vocals sound sincere, and as usual, he contributes a strong and original harp solo, but the final results sound rather flat, partially due to the banality of the lyrics.

At this point, the band took a break. It appears that Chess attended to a quick, two-song gospel session by Elder Beck, which shows up as the only two master numbers sandwiched in the middle of this sequence of Little Walter recordings. When Walter returned to the studio, his first order of business was yet another few tries at the new instrumental theme he'd been working on so diligently. This time he nailed it, and the result was "Off The Wall," which provided him with his second two-sided hit—and the second of three Top 10 R&B hits he'd score that year.

An alternate take of "Off The Wall" released years later shows all the elements in place: the cymbal splashes, a distinctive "head" played powerfully as the opening verse, the dynamic drops and surges in volume and intensity. Walter and the gang try a stop-time section on one verse, but instead of building intensity, it only slows the surging momentum. A verse or two later, Below solos for a couple of bars with a drum roll. Unfortunately, there seems to be a moment's hesitation as everyone wonders exactly where to come back in. Walter misjudges, and comes back in a beat behind the rest of the band. This was the most powerful version of this now-familiar theme yet attempted, but Chess wisely called for another take. As Louis Myers put it, "Chess would call you down if things ain't right out there . . . Chess was a very funny kind of cat man, but I tell you when it gets down to that music and that ear, ain't no way you could fool him. And his brother Phil was the same, they had that ear on them. He knew what the people wanted and he wanted to sell what the people buying." The next take provided the master Chess had been looking for, and all the polishing was worth the effort. Everybody is finally on the same page, and clicking together like a well-oiled machine, as Below's drum accents propel the band throughout. Walter jumps in right on time following the drum fill this time, and his tone is fat, lively, and very horn-like. The number is now a fully realized creation.

For his last recording that day, Walter yet again follows up his new instrumental "theme song" by pulling out a fast-paced, driving number utilizing a modified "clip clop" beat. This time he puts some lyrics to it, though; it's a remake of a novelty tune first recorded in 1937 by Washboard Sam as "Back Door" for the Bluebird label. Below imitates the washboard rhythm using his woodblock with a rickey-tick beat. Walter sticks closely to Sam's lyrics, though slightly sanitizing some of bawdier aspects of this song sung by a cuckolded man. Walter's harp has a power and lilt that was lacking in the original's piano/clarinet backing. This version is a good example of how the hard-driving new Chicago style was successfully applied to traditional, older material. Now titled "Tell Me Mama," it was paired with "Off The Wall" on Checker 770, and issued as Little Walter's next single. "Tell Me Mama" peaked at #10 on the R&B charts in April, but by then DJs had begun flipping it over and featuring the rollicking instrumental "Off The Wall," and in May the instrumental surpassed the vocal side, peaking at #8.

But they weren't yet done in the studio that day; the entire band was also pressed into service to back guitarist and singer John Brim, a regular on the Chicago scene who was friendly with Walter. Kentucky-born Brim had moved to Chicago from Indianapolis in 1945, and began playing at the Purple Cat and on Sunday sessions at The Du Drop Inn. Brim's wife Grace was a vocalist, harp player, and drummer. Chess wanted to record the Brims, but he was more interested in Grace, hoping to pair her with another band, maybe the tried-and-true Muddy conglomeration, and only promising vaguely that *maybe* he'd record John on the next day. According to Brim, it was Walter who insisted that Chess record him: "[Chess] told Little Walter 'Well, I'll call John sometime . . . .' Walter said, 'Hell no, you gonna call him tonight, 'cause I already told him to be in the studio!' Little Walter was in command then."

Two numbers were cut: Brim's "Rattlesnake," a thinly disguised remake of Big Mama Thornton's "Hound Dog"; and "It Was A Dream," a gently loping shuffle with evocative original lyrics. Walter plays amplified harp on the first, and acoustic, old-style blues on the second; both cuts are enlivened by his energetic playing. (Scheduled for release as Checker 769, Brim's tracks were quickly withdrawn when Chess learned that Peacock Records was suing any label that released anything similar to their issue of Thornton's "Hound Dog.")

Soon the boys were off on the road again. Among other stops, they were scheduled into The Royal Peacock, an upstairs ballroom in Atlanta, Georgia, for a long weekend gig in late March, stretching over into a "Blue Monday" show. That spring they also were part of a southern package tour that included Ray Charles, lasting well into May. Ray wasn't yet the big R&B star he would later become; in fact, he was one of the opening acts, appearing on solo piano before Walter took the stage. Charles had only done one session for Atlantic Records, and the results were some Nat King Cole and Charles Brown sound-alike ballads that didn't do much on the charts, as Ray was still searching for his own voice. One night during Walter's set, in the midst of a swinging instrumental, Charles grabbed his saxophone (his second instrument after piano) and came back out on stage, unannounced, and joined in. It sounded good, and the crowd responded, so for the duration of the tour, Charles played sax with Walter almost every night. Although Dave Myers enjoyed the musical results, he wasn't too happy about having to guide the blind musician around for the rest of the night. At any rate, everyone agreed that the addition of the saxophone augmented the sound of the swinging, up-tempo numbers the band was doing. This wouldn't be the last time Walter worked with a sax man on the road.

Walter must have had mixed feelings about package tours. On one hand, he didn't have to work so hard; with several other featured artists on the revue, he only had to put together a short set comprised of his latest hits. Even on the weekends when there were matinees or multiple shows scheduled, a day's onstage work might only add up to an hour or two, tops. That left plenty of time to check out the local action—particularly the ladies who were impressed by the flashy visitors. Or maybe get a little crap game or some cards going in a back room somewhere. Still, he had to work just as hard to prep for these shows as he did for a solo gig: shine the shoes, get his processed hair right, try to find someplace to get a decent meal, and get his stage clothes cleaned and pressed. Then they all had to haul the gear, carry in the amps, instruments, and drum set: Why were so many of the union halls or ballrooms up two or three flights? Then plug in, make sure the amps were working, tune up—by the time they finished all that, they might just as well play a full night's gig. It seemed that just about the time the band was warmed up and the crowd was up and dancing, it was time to make way for the next act on the bill. The next night, another town, another hall, more opportunities for adventure, but after a while, inevitably, all the faces began to look the same.

On the other hand, the clubs back home took their own toll. Some of them were open till 3:00 or 4:00 AM, and a lot of owners ran by the union clock: 45 minutes off, 15 minutes off, and no fooling around. If the band started at 8:00 PM, that meant they might have to put in the same eight hours that a guy with a regular factory job did. Pacing themselves was important; if the band was grooving, people would be buying them drinks, and as nice as it was to keep a nice mellow buzz going to gain a little extra cushion, if a musician wasn't careful, soon his fingers might get too thick or his lips too loose. Still, they really had a chance to work the crowd on a club gig—get them riled up and then cool 'em down, take them on a ride; and maybe most important of all, try out new material, maybe see how that new lick they thought up that afternoon worked on the crowd. By the end of the night they'd be drained, sweaty, and drooping—and tomorrow night they'd do it all over again.

Not everybody had Eddie Boyd's high opinion of Texas; some musicians found that, like everywhere else, the cops there knew they were easy targets. They couldn't help but draw attention; a car full of black men, packed with gear, with the drums lashed on top, driving off from a gig late at night, heading for the next town as fast as they could get there. It was possible that some "illegal activity" was occurring in the car; maybe somebody had an open bottle or was carrying a little weed, and unlicensed pistols stashed under the driver's seat weren't exactly uncommon. All in all, a touring band was a choice target for bored, small-town law officers, if for no other reason than idle curiosity. Dave Myers recalled that after one gig:

> Ray Charles had left before us, that morning, going to the next gig [in] Beaumont, Texas. Walter and us, we drove so fast man so that we could catch up with him. We got on that highway, drove up on Ray Charles, and there's seven policemen, they got him out there, pulling off his socks, looking in his socks and shit. They started looking at us hard, we drove on, we said, "Don't stop, don't stop."

Walter's personality could get a group in trouble, too; he didn't take any shit, from anyone, without a confrontation or at least a threat of one. "When we were down there in Texas, Walter was driving," Dave said:

> Every time Walter [was] driving and they stop us, we had to go to jail. This guy told Walter . . . he called him nigger, he was saying all those things. Walter was kind of sensitive, Walter would respond. He turn around and say, "Man, you got my license, my name is Marion Walter Jacobs." Man said, "You getting smart with me boy?" He come and hit Walter across the head—"Get that goddam car and get in it!" Had to drive us into the middle of town, he want everybody to see "I got this bunch of whatever—." It got really terrible, but we had to learn to live with this.

They eventually did come up with a solution. "We couldn't let Walter drive no more," Dave said. Not long after returning to Chicago, they hired a "chauffeur," a local truck driver named Bennie Rooks, to make sure they got safely from one gig to the next while on the road.

Chess wasn't quite sure what to do with the results of the March session. A couple of the tunes were originally scheduled as the next single, "Don't Have To Hunt [sic] No More"/"Tonight With A Fool," but it seems that Chess had second thoughts. After mastering it and listing it as Checker #767 in catalogues that went out to dealers, apparently it was never actually pressed up and released. No ads or chart entries have been found in any of the trade magazines, and no copies of '50s pressings have surfaced. However, it was mistakenly included in a series of Chess "reissue" singles in the '60s, and a small number of bootlegged "collector's pressings" circulated in the 1970s.

By mid-April, Walter's "Tell Me Mama"/"Off The Wall" on Checker #770 had appeared on the trade charts as a "territorial tip" for New Orleans, and it got a four-star (excellent) rating in the New R&B Releases. Meanwhile, Walter was up to his usual antics. The *Cashbox* "Rhythm N' Blues Ramblings" column had an item mentioning that "Checker Records harmonica ace Little Walter has been bedded for the past couple weeks due to head injuries suffered in an auto mishap." It's possible that this may have been the result of an accident Walter laughingly recounted, along with guitarist Louis Myers, in an interview years later. Walter recalled that, in the pre-air conditioning days, one way he would cool off in the summer was to:

> ... drive cars with no doors on 'em. You remember when I had that Lincoln [Zephyr]? ... took all the doors off of that, police stopped me at 27th and Canal, said "Be careful, don't let me see you back in the street in this thing no more, long as it ain't got doors on it!" It was hot in the summer, too ... I turned that thing over when me and Big Walter [Horton] was together, I thought I'd killed him [laughter]. You know them old safety zones they used to have here, the big, high ones? "Island" they call it—we were running down 22nd Street running our mouths, landed on the thing, I'm up on top of the thing, and the car turned over. Walter out on the ground, and I'm trying to get out. We got out and turned that thing back over, got started man and *flew* away from there. It happened right there in Chinatown, by that fire station.

Or maybe he was simply recovering from the results of another fight—Walter's bantam rooster attitude, coupled with the seeming immortality of youth, sometimes resulted in occurrences of physical combat with those who got in his way.

On Monday, May 4th, Walter was back in the studio, rejoining Muddy as a sideman on a session for the first time since "Juke" had been released. Whether or not Chess could accurately distinguish between the sounds of Little Walter, Big Walter, and Junior Wells backing Muddy, the fact was that Muddy hadn't recorded anything that had made the charts since Walter left the band, and Chess clearly wanted to reunite the winning team. Muddy led off with "Baby Please Don't Go," a traditional delta number first made famous by Big Joe Williams on the Bluebird label in 1935. Walter and Muddy immediately meshed like they'd never separated; the call-and-response between guitar and harp running through the piece shows that the old musical telepathy is still there, as Edmonds lays down a steady shuffling, almost march-like drum pattern. On an early run-through, Walter takes three separate solo choruses, each time turning the heat up a notch. The later, released take was retitled "Turn The Lamp Down Low," and Walter's solos cook even more than on the earlier take, and this time Rogers also takes a guitar solo chorus. The flip side "Loving Man" is a mid-tempo number, with nice slide guitar-harp interplay on the break chorus. Walter's musical conception was evolving, and here he manages the neat trick of playing simultaneously with down-home funk and contemporary swing.

As was frequently the case with Muddy's sessions at the time, it was then Jimmy Rogers's turn to step up to the vocal mike. His "Left Me With A Broken Heart" is a great example of what is so seldom accomplished: a slow blues that doesn't sound slow, thanks to perfect ensemble work by the band. It has an easy rocking groove, with the intermeshing guitars of Muddy and Rogers laying down a mellow lope. Walter fills in with fat chords, and powerful solo hits. "Act Like You Love Me" followed, an uptempo, jazzy romp, which suited to a tee Rogers's mellow, articulate vocals. On an early version, Rogers takes a guitar lead on one break, while Walter takes a superb two-chorus solo with some dazzling single-note chops, zig-zagging and toying with the beat as if defying any harp player to try to copy him. The issued take (number 3) was in the key of G, up one step from the previous take in F, and the resulting sound is brighter and a bit more sprightly. Walter is just as adventurous here: new ideas and phrases burst forth as if he's overflowing with them. He takes three solo choruses over the course of the song, and sounds like he could have continued pouring out new ideas all night.

That same day, John Brim was back again to cut another couple of titles, backed by Muddy's band (possibly with Eddie Taylor taking over the guitar duties from Muddy and Jimmy, as listed in some discographies). "Lifetime Baby" is a prisoner's song, a slow mournful lament about being deserted while doing time. When Brim takes a guitar break, Walter plays sparsely in the background. Brim's other number "Ice Cream Man," with its catalogue of summer-time flavors, would became a staple of bar bands, but not until it was finally released on a compilation LP years later. Again, Brim's sides were held back at the time. Leonard said he'd never heard of "pineapple ice cream," but Brim knew that wasn't the reason his cuts went unissued. "He was still angry, he kept it against me a long time. It's a funny thing, he recorded a session, paid me session money and he put them records on the shelf . . . stayed on the shelf over 20 some years. [When it was finally released] he was dead, he never knew that 'Ice Cream Man' with Van Halen sold over 8 million copies."

Later that month, Walter was on the road again, according to the trade magazines, who reported "Little Walter touring California through the end of May, then into Texas." Following the death of their mother, his half-sister Marguerite had moved from Louisiana to California and was sharing a house there with Walter's older sister, Lillian, who'd moved to Oakland and remarried after divorcing Floyd. The first time Marguerite saw Walter play professionally was on a big "Battle Of The Blues" show at Richmond Auditorium in Oakland, sharing the bill with blues balladeer Charles Brown. "It blew me away," Marguerite recalled, "The place was jam packed, my brother jumped off the stage and they was gonna tear his clothes off, they almost went crazy . . . [he played] 'Sad Hours,' I literally cried."

Both sides of Walter's latest single were doing well on the charts. In fact, "Off The Wall" had attracted the attention of white, big-band bandleader Buddy Morrow, a trombonist and former member of Artie Shaw's and Tommy Dorsey's bands who'd started his own successful outfit, playing instrumental covers of contemporary R&B hits; his biggest hits were "Night Train" and "One Mint Julep." Morrow recorded a big-band version of "Off The Wall" that followed Walter's arrangement and dynamics closely, right down to the mistakes. At one point in Walter's original, he and guitarist Louis fall slightly out of sync for a few bars before gracefully finding each other again, and Morrow's arrangement reproduces this section faithfully. But Morrow's release lacked the subtlety and nuances of Walter's, and it failed to find an audience. Later, Morrow also covered Walter's mood piece, "Quarter To Twelve." It must have been both a vindication and vexation for Walter; on one hand he was being noticed by the jazz community and "serious" (i.e., non-blues) musicians whose company he aspired to join, on the other, a successful cover version might siphon off sales and cut into his royalties.

On June 8th, Walter's friend and competitor Junior Wells was back in Chicago. Wells lined up his first recording session as a solo artist for the new black-owned States label, and cut some of his finest recordings ever. Backing him on the six-song session was the group Walter had commandeered from Junior the previous year, The Aces (aka the Jukes). Slide guitarist Elmore James was in town at the time, and ended up in the studio that day, guesting on "Hoodoo Man," a remake of a Sonny Boy Williamson I number. Wells had by then developed an appealing style of his own that included roughly equal elements from Rice Miller (whom he'd first encountered down south as a kid), John Lee "Sonny Boy" Williamson I, and Little Walter. After Walter, Wells was probably the best of the local harp players then working regularly in Chicago, and on this ses-sion all of his talent is in evidence. Picking up on Walter's recent successes, Junior's harp is heavily amplified and is the loudest element in the mix. Also inspired by Walter, two instrumental titles were recorded that day. Neither of the Sonny Boys, nor few other blues harp players in recent years, had regularly recorded instrumental harmonica pieces, mainly because so few were able to create anything that sustained the listener's interest for very long. But on the strength of Walter's two Top-10 hits in the last year with harmonica instrumentals, that trend was changing. Wells was one of the few who possessed the talent and youthful drive to go head-to-head with Walter, and he acquitted himself admirably in the studio, playing with fiery energy.

Walter's activities were being reported regularly in the music trade journals, as they noted in July that "Little Walter plays the Royal Peacock [in Atlanta, GA] from July 21 to August 3, then goes on a one-nighter binge through Florida and along the east coast." That month, Chess released new singles by Muddy and Jimmy Rogers from the May session, and once again Walter's harp was all over the radio and juke boxes. But it looks like the Royal Peacock dates must have been postponed so that Chess could stock the shelves before Walter hit the road for his lengthy "one nighter binge," because on Thursday, July 23rd, Walter was back at Universal for one of his most pro-ductive sessions yet.

The date begins with Walter introducing the title of the number by gently cajoling, "Baby, don't go yet, it's only a quarter to twelve—," then the band falls in with a heavily echoed, slow and easy beat. Walter sets aside the amplified harp sound that was by then his trademark, and instead plays acoustic style into the vocal mike, alternating long, swelling phrases, subtle warbles, and vocalized tones utilizing hand techniques, to paint an effective, late-night mood piece.

"That's It," a walking-boogie instrumental, was recorded next. It is noteworthy for two reasons: it's the first recording to show Walter playing "3rd position" harp; and the first to feature, on its fourth verse, a new instrument in his arsenal, the Hohner "64 Chromonica," a 16-hole chromatic harmonica. In "3rd position" harp, Walter plays a harp tuned one full step below ("B♭") the key that the rest of the band is playing ("C"). This technique allows him to play some licks in a relative minor scale. The standard blues harp techniques until then had been to play a harmonica either in the same key as the band ("C" harp played in "C") for a standard chromatic scale, or a harmonica tuned five half steps up from the band (second position: "F" harp played in "C") for a bluesier, pentatonic scale. The Hohner "64 Chromonica" sold for $17, big money compared to the standard 10-hole Marine Bands, which sold for around $2 at the time. Besides offering the full chromatic scale (the white and black keys on a piano) at the push of a button, it also had a first octave that was a full octave lower than the Marine Band, providing a new range of possibilities and tonal effects. Although he was almost certainly using it on stage for a while before trying it in the studio, Walter sounds a little out of his depth on this first recorded attempt at using his new musical tool. He apparently forgets which key the band is in, and hits a few sour notes on the chromatic harp, before wisely switching back to the B♭ Marine Band harp he'd started the song with. The number bounces along nicely and features some new and interesting ideas from Walter, but the slip-up midsong caused this track to be held back until it was finally issued on a 1995 compilation of his music.

The next tune became one of Walter's standards: "Blues With A Feeling," with most of the lyrics and general arrangement coming from a 1947 Jack McVea release (written and sung by McVea drummer Rabon Tarrant). Again, Walter puts his own contemporary spin on it. The first take has an urgent vocal from Walter and nice interplay between the guitar and harp, but the harp crackles in and out during Walter's solo, due to a faulty mike cord. The later, issued take is a perfect slow blues, with Below providing momentum with his shuffling brush work, and an effective stop-time vocal verse from Walter near the end. Walter's vocal is right on the money, as is his harp playing.

Following "Blues With A Feeling," the generically titled "Last Boogie" is a fast-rocking swing piece featuring Walter's usual cavalcade of original phrases and ideas. The band is locked together and Louis adds tasty filigrees to Walter's rhythmic and lyrical excursions. By any other standard, it would have been worthy of release, but judged against Walter's other instrumental releases, this one may have lacked a strong or distinguishable hook, and consequently was held back at the time. "Too Late" was written by bassist and producer Willie Dixon, who'd recently become a regular at Chess; although he's listed in discographies as playing on a number of earlier Little Walter sessions, this is the first one on which you can actually hear him on several numbers. Unlike the previous number, "Too Late" is based on a strong and memorable instrumental hook, and includes some catchy lyrics like "I can't stand your cooking, and you ain't good looking—I'm gone." The wry lyrics are suited to Walter's jaunty delivery, and it's another little gem.

Another untitled instrumental was up next. Assigned the designation "Fast Boogie" (and titled that way when it was finally released years later), it again shows off the tight ensemble working together as one on a jumping instrumental. This time there's a more memorable opening hook, and Walter's playing sounds well-composed and completely focused throughout. Why it wasn't issued at the time is a mystery. It's possible that it was held back because there were more instrumentals than vocals recorded at this session, so there was nothing to pair it up with on a single, following the by-then standard practice of issuing Walter's records with a vocal number on one side and a showcase instrumental on the other.

By now the band was on a roll in the studio, and the songs just kept on coming. "Lights Out" features a relaxed guitar lead-in, then develops into another "late night" mood piece, with Walter ably redeeming his earlier gaff with the chromatic harp; he uses the instrument with unfaltering skill and power, creating an eerie feel. When the record was released a few months later it started a run in music stores, with blues-harp men all scrambling to add the chromatic harp to their tool kits.

Walter then kicked the band up into high gear, once again using the chromatic, to show another side of the sound palette available with the instrument. "Fast Large One" is Walter's take on the riff from a Gene Krupa cut from 1941 (featuring vocals by Anita O'Day) on the Okeh label, "Let Me Off Uptown." Below's bebop jazz background comes to the fore here as he liberally "drops bombs" and accents in what becomes almost a drum/harp duet, kicking a song that was probably just a starting point for a jam session on stage into another level altogether. Next up was a number that became another of Walter's signature pieces, the swinging shuffle "You're So Fine." With the chorus "You're a fine healthy thing, I wanna love you all the time," it's a direct but eloquent statement of lust.

The marathon session wound down that day with one final vocal piece, "My Kind Of Baby," which took a slightly different approach to the previous number, using a similar structure with stop-time vocal verses. The lyrics sound rather throwaway—it may well have been a quick attempt to come up with something—anything—to pair one of the instrumentals with—but as usual there were plenty of new and unique ideas flowing from Walter's harp. Altogether it was one hell of a good day at Universal; five of the tracks eventually were released on singles, and most of the rest could well have. It was an embarrassment of riches that Chess was faced with: there was more good stuff here than he could handle.

Walter went on to play his southern dates, with the band augmented by a couple of young hornmen Walter had encountered while out on road. He recruited sax player Albert Ayler to accompany him on tour while Ayler was on summer vacation from a Cleveland high school. Ayler, who went on to notoriety as a proponent of "free jazz" playing in New York City in the 1960s, said that he met Walter when he and his pal Lloyd Pearson were sitting in at a jam session at Gleason's Musical Bar. Walter liked what he heard, took the pair on to some gigs at local clubs, and Ayler said he ended up spending two summers on the road with Walter. Ayler's father remember how excited he was when he got the job: "He came running home, shouting about 'They're gonna take me with 'em, they're gonna take me!'" But it was a tough gig for a young man from a middle-class home, his father said: "The rest of the musicians were hard-drinking, barely literate country bluesmen from the deep south. He carried his food with him because the pay was poor." Ayler recalled, "The manner of living was quite different for me—drinking real heavy and playing real hard. We'd travel all day, finally arrive, take out our horns and play." At first Walter criticized him for his inability to sustain a chorus-long held note, a standard crowd-pleasing trick, but in time Ayler had mastered it and was fitting in, and in later years he reminisced fondly about his early education on the road.

In mid-September, "Blues With A Feeling"/"Quarter To Twelve" was released and spotlighted in the *Cashbox* magazine "Award Of The Week" section, complete with a Chess publicity photo showing a handsome and dapper young Walter grinning, holding harps in both hands. The blurb reads:

> Little Walter still makes with mighty intriguing sounds on his mighty mouth organ, and the result is a pair of interesting decks. Walter sings on one side, "Blues With A Feeling," and his portrayal of a lonesome man is excellent. Teaming his pipes with the harmonica playing that has lifted him high in the ranks of R&B entertainers, Walter chants a slow blues emotionally and blows a wild and weird harmonica support. The under deck, "Blues With A Feeling" has all the vocal effort condensed in the first line when Walter sings "Baby don't go yet," and it's instrumental from there on in. A penetrating and stirring side. Like 'em both with perhaps a light nod in the direction of "Blues."

On Thursday, September 24th, Walter was back in the studio with Muddy's band, which now included Otis Spann on piano. (This was Spann's first recording session with Muddy, although he'd been gigging with the group for a while.) With his addition, the classic Chicago blues combo was in place; two guitars, harmonica, piano, and drums. (Walter Horton later claimed in an interview that it was him on this session, but Muddy confirmed that Horton did only one session with him for Chess, in January of 1953. It's clearly Little Walter's distinctive "off the beat" swinging phrasing on the harp on this session.) Spann gets a solo on "Blow Wind Blow"; to make room for the piano, the harp is a bit laid back in the mix, and used more as a rhythm instrument than Little Walter had done previously. (Although Spann later expressed his admiration for Walter and stated that "The harmonica is the mother of the band," Walter's feelings weren't mutual; on his own sessions, pianists were featured on a scant handful of tracks. "They try to do too much," Walter said, feeling that they interfered with his own efforts.) The other track, "Mad Love (I Want You To Love Me)," is the first of several times that Muddy used his stop-time da-Dah-da-da rhythm. Walter's solo begins with him bubbling under, then surging out with some powerful phrases. Muddy's vocal is pure sex, and the number is an insistent and unambiguous come-on from beginning to end.

That October, Walter sent a train ticket to his older sister Lillian in Oakland, and she came to Chicago for a visit and stayed with him about a month and a half, at an apartment Walter shared with Ella Mae. Despite the fact that Walter had several long-term relationships—some women were even referred to as wives by those around him—he was never interested in getting married. "I asked him, 'Why don't you get married?'" Lillian said. "He said, 'What's the use in buying a cow when you get your milk for free? What I'm gonna get married for? All this milk out here, all I got to do is churn it. Ain't no reason for me to go buy nothin', I don't stay long enough. I'm over here tonight, and that's all.'"

Lillian was unaccustomed to the winter weather she found in the city:

THE CASH BOX
★ AWARD O' THE WEEK ★

"BLUES WITH A FEELING" (2:41)   [Arc-BMI]

"QUARTER TO TWELVE" (2:39)   [Arc-BMI]

LITTLE WALTER

(Checker 780)

LITTLE WALTER

● Little Walter still makes with mighty intriguing sounds on his mighty mouth organ and the result is a pair of interesting decks. Walter sings on one side, "Blues With A Feeling"; and his portrayal of the lonesome man is excellent. Teaming his pipes with the harmonica playing that has lifted him high in the ranks of r & b entertainers, Walter chants a slow blues emotionally and blows a wild and weird harmonica support. The under deck, "Blues With A Feeling", has all the vocal effort condensed into the first line, when Walter sings "Baby don't go yet", and its instrumental from thereon in. A penetrating and stirring side. Like 'em both with perhaps a light nod in the direction of "Blues".

Figure 7.2 Cashbox Award O' The Week: "Blues with a Feeling," September 12, 1953.

It had started to snow, [and] Ella Mae called down to ask the man to turn the steam heat down, it got so high. He said it was broke, he didn't fix it. I got hot, [so] I pulled my bed up to the window. Next morning I woke up, I was covered up with snow. I said, "Oooh!" I couldn't talk. So brother Walter had come in, from New York or someplace, he said, "What's wrong with you? What'd you—?" I said, "Oooh, I can't talk." [Walter went downstairs to the landlord and yelled], "What did you do to my sister?" And boy, he took me to the hospital, it looked like he was on two wheels! You know he could drive!

Walter went on the road for a couple of weeks after Lillian arrived. One night after he returned, he took her out club-hopping with him:

Everywhere he went, I went with him. [There was] a bar and a nightclub, in the back they played pool. Walter took me over there with him, said "Don't be looking at my sister, 'cause that's it! This is it, you know, you gonna have to play the game with me, 'cause if you talk to my sister, you know what's gonna happen!" So nobody would never say nothing to me, they was scared of Brother Walter. I was married then, I hadn't went down there for nothing like that anyway.

While visiting the clubs, they ran into former heavyweight boxing champ Ezzard Charles, who'd won 59 of his 96 bouts by KO's. Walter, nattily attired in white from his wide-brimmed hat to his toes, posed with him for a club photographer, the pair shaking hands. Another night, they went to an after-hours joint. "Muddy and all them would come, after they got through with their gigs at night. All-night place," Lillian said. "I went down there with him, and boy I was so sleepy, I said, 'Brother Walter, when you gonna go home?' He said, 'I'm gonna send you home in a cab baby.'" But Lillian didn't want to go alone; "Oh no, they find people in garbage cans and stuff over here." So, fighting back yawns, she stayed on, and witnessed an outburst of Walter's temper: "That's the night he broke Below's jaw. Below hit him first. [Walter] hit him, but he didn't intend to break his jaw, he was defending himself. He said it looked like Below was gonna hit him again, so he broke Below's jaw. Then he took him down to the hospital to get it set. Had it all wired up, still was [wired] even when I left weeks later." It didn't seem to cause any lasting acrimony between the men, and Below was still a band member on gigs. "Below knew that he had did wrong," Lillian explained. "So they stayed friends, until the band broke up . . ." Lillian recalled Walter sleeping a lot during the day, and in the evening either Ella Mae would cook or he'd take them out for dinner. "She cooked greens, beans, stuff like that, he didn't like no pork." After about six weeks, the noise and hustle of the city finally got to Lillian: "I was gonna stay longer, but it was too fast for me! I left."

Walter's new single was on the charts for several weeks that fall, ". . . showing strength in Cleveland, Dallas, St. Louis, Detroit, New Orleans and Atlanta, good reports from Chicago," according to the trades. They also announced the lineup for "5th Annual Goodwill Revue for Handicapped Negro Children" to take place on December 4th at Ellis Auditorium in Memphis, sponsored by that city's WDIA, the first all-black formatted radio station. Walter was originally scheduled to appear among a stellar cast, featuring groups like the Spirit Of Memphis Quartet, The Caravans, and Soul Stirrers, as well as bluesmen like B.B. King, Lloyd Price, Eddie Boyd, and Muddy Waters. It was noted that all artists were donating their time, and that their respective "diskeries" were defraying travel expenses to and from Memphis. Then the following month's R&B column in *Cashbox* reported:

> Len Chess reports a mishap in the lives of two of Chess's biggest artists this week. Seems that Willie Mabon and Little Walter were on their way by car to the Goodwill Revue . . . just about 20 miles outside Cairo, Illinois, they were involved in an accident which left them unable to continue the trip to Memphis. They returned to Chicago the following Monday with Willie's "I Gotta Go" and Walter's "You're So Fine" both wearing out jukebox needles in this town.

Whether there was really an accident, or if Chess was just trying to cover for his two stars who'd found better things to do than play a free gig 800 miles from home, it was obvious that Walter's activities were considered newsworthy in the trade press.

In any event, *Cashbox* also reported "Checker Records with a brand new release by Little Walter, 'You're So Fine/Lights Out.' Walter heading for Atlanta, GA and the Peacock Inn for a three day stint beginning December 11." Walter and guitarist Louis Myers later reminisced about one of their numerous trips down to Walter's southern stronghold in Atlanta around this time. "Remember that amplifier I throwed in the river down in Georgia?" Walter began:

> We started playing, around nine o'clock—amplifier played just as good as a P.A. system, brand new! Played that good till about 12:30, 1:00, then the volume would drop down to where you couldn't hear ... Louis said "Get your amp [fixed]," I said "Naw, naw, ain't but one thing to do with this one." When we crossed that river I stopped the car. Threw it in the river. You *know* I had to go get me another one then, bought one in Atlanta.

That reminded Myers of when he was coerced into buying a guitar. "We was down there in Atlanta, 1952" Louis recalled. "And I was just looking for a guitar, 'cause Walter had broken my guitar the night before ..."

"Yeah, I done busted it," Walter said. "I fell on it, didn't I?"

"Yeah," Myers agreed, "B.B. King and Walter out there clowning in Macon, so I had to get me a guitar. Went in this place, mean people down there boy, was so *mean*. I was just looking, [the salesman] says, 'Don't put your black hands on all the guitars up and down this line—we got white people coming in here to buy guitars.' I said, 'I'm just trying to pick one.' He says, 'That's your guitar.' I said, 'I don't want this guitar,' he said, 'Yes, you gonna take that guitar.'"

An argument developed, and Myers was surrounded by salesmen who were shouting obscenities. The manager overheard the shouting, and called Walter and Louis into the office. Louis recalled, "I wanted to get my guitar repaired, but we didn't have time. Walter was gonna buy me a guitar so I could have something to work on that night ... I was using Gibson, man, best I could get, cost me $400 ...." The upshot was that the manager, who recognized that Louis was from up north and told him that he was a Yankee too, sold him the guitar (including a DeArmand pickup) for $57, $40 off the listed price. Business concluded, he walked with them to the door, escorting them past the angry salesmen. "Them other guys gonna get us boy ... all them white cats walking around in there, spreading their chests—[saying] 'I'll break that nigger's back,' you know." As he told the tale, Myers managed a wry laugh.

Myers also spoke of the time in Dallas when booking agent Howard Lewis bet the club owner $600 that their group couldn't beat out Ivory Joe Hunter's 12-piece band in front of an audience. Lewis saw The Jukes loading in, Below carrying drums, Louis with an amp, Walter with an amp. "He said, 'Where is the horns at, the bass? Where is the band?' [The owner] says 'That's the band, right there.' Lewis says, 'Oh man, that ain't no band, I don't see nothing but drums and a guitar.' I said, 'Well that's all, drums, guitar, and harp.'" The bet was placed and Below held the money. "We *stole* that show,"

Walter said quietly. "When we played they didn't want to hear that 12-piece band no more," Myers confirmed. "Those cats gave Below $40, and you know what that cat did? Bought about twenty quarts of champagne. I drunk so much I got sick, I wasn't nothing but a kid . . ."

Walter continued burning up the roads, and found himself in Ohio on Christmas night, where Cleveland R&B DJ Alan Freed threw his annual Holiday Ball at the Armory in Akron. On the bill were Billy Ward and The Dominoes, Little Walter, and the Ralph Williams Orchestra, and tickets sold fast at $2 apiece. The show drew almost 3,200 fans, with the building so packed they had to turn away another 2,500 according to reports.

A couple of other blues musicians told of noteworthy encounters with Walter around this time. Willie Foster from Mississippi, who claimed to have done road trips with Muddy's band in the '50s, said he was the beneficiary of some harmonica pointers from Walter. He said that when he met him, Walter told him, "Do your best. All you got to learn is timing. Make that harp say what you want it to say. Anything you think you can say, make it say it. If you miss a word, make that harmonica say it for you." Foster noted, "Every time he said four or five words, he take that harmonica and do it." Foster says Walter also showed him a trick that became Foster's musical signature, an extended single-note solo Foster says he sometimes holds for minutes. "He said he had one thing he would give me, and that was make the harmonica go Innnh, Innh, Innnh, like that, that's a chorus." (Alternating between drawing on the 2nd hole and blowing on the 3rd hole, which produce the same note, can simulate the effect of a long, continuously held single note.) "He said, 'I brought that here and I want you to keep it, 'cause if I die before you—although I'm younger than you—if I die before you, then it keeps going with you. Put that in every song—' Sometimes I holds it a minute and a half," Foster said.

Out on the road, the band began encountering a new phenomenon: local blues harp "gunslingers" were starting to show up at the gigs, looking for a chance to show the brash young star what they could do. With the help of his multitalented guitarist Louis Myers, Walter developed a method for dealing with these challenges without wasting his breath. Louis had been playing harp almost as long as Walter, and although he was concentrating primarily on his guitar skills, Louis still kept up with his harmonica playing. "See, the one thing, he taught me a whole lot about a harp, when we was travelin' together on the road," Louis said, and from time to time, he and Walter would trade off instruments. Walter thought enough of Louis's harp playing that when a local harp hotshot challenged Walter, he'd choose that time to trade places with Louis; "I'm out there, steal the guitar, he get the harp," Walter said.

Louis continues:

And he used to shove me out there, knowin' that them cats be laying out there . . . and he stay here [on guitar], so I just go on out there and play harp . . . It's a competition. You know, Walter had so many cats that was on his tail . . . naturally cats want to go after cats . . . They used to come up all the time and tell him, "Man, I can, I can blow you down."

If the challenger was worthy, Walter might take the harp back from Louis and put him in his place. But, with amateur harp players who may have had a few drinks and just wanted to show off in front of their home town crowd, Walter trusted Louis to do the dirty work; he'd ". . . let [Louis] go on out there and KILL 'em. I didn't want to be bothered with 'em, 'cause it wasn't helpin' none for me," Walter explained.

Louis recalled a tour that took them to Saginaw, Michigan. "We used to go up there *all* the time, I *hated* to go up there because every time I go . . . Walter wanted me to play the harp, 'cause there was a cat up there named, I'll never forget this cat's name, named James . . . Well this cat, man, every time we go to Saginaw, he come up . . . this is his hometown." The band played there for several nights, and each night James and his friends insisted that the band let him sit in.

Louis continues:

> Finally, one night Walter made up his mind, said, "I'm tired of this boy, I'm tired of this boy," said, he told me, said, "You gonna play the harp this time." I said, "Naw, Lord have mercy," I didn't want to play no harp . . . Naaww, I didn't wanna . . . this cat looked tough, man, you know . . . everybody around him, he had everybody on his side, and the people knows that he was deadly. So I said, "Well, I don't know." And Walter said, "Go on out there and play." And I went on up there, and [Walter] took the guitar, and we played.

As Walter described it, they "Warmed 'em up, too . . . sure enough," to which Louis laughingly added, "Warmed 'em up . . . before we got through, he was *gone!*"

Both Muddy and Walter had singles in the Top 10 in January of 1954. While the winter winds of Chicago howled, Chess scheduled another Muddy session, with Walter on board as sideman, that would produce one of Muddy's signature numbers. On a lucky Thursday the 7th, Muddy began by working on a Willie Dixon number, "I'm Your Hoochie Coochie Man."

Legend has it that Dixon first pitched the number to Leonard, who liked it, and said if Muddy okayed it, they'd cut it. Dixon hustled over to Muddy's gig at the Zanzibar, and on a break taught Muddy the tune in the washroom, ". . . just get a little rhythm pattern, do the same thing over and over," Dixon advised. The tune proved to be so popular that for a years afterwards, the group was frequently billed as Muddy Waters and his Hoochie-Coochie Boys. The signature riff consisted of the same sort of stop-time chord hits utilized in "Mad Love," then the band kicks into a swaggering slow blues on the chord change as Muddy shouts, "You know I'm here, everybody knows I'm here!" It's a declaration of manhood that mixes hoodoo and sexual prowess, a no-fooling boast tune. The band has a raw edge that conveys the macho feel, and you can almost hear Muddy strutting. It took sixteen takes to get everybody stopping in the same places at the same times, but the hard work paid off.

The flip side, "She's So Pretty," is an uptempo boogie number; Walter's harp is hot throughout, as he switches effortlessly between a dazzling flutter-tongue technique and accented riffs, and he and the pianist (credited in discographies as either Otis Spann or Henry Gray) trade off on the solo chorus. The number ends on two pounding instrumental choruses with the whole band bouncing in unison, then an abrupt and surprising cold ending going into the turnaround chord rather than coming out of it as was the tradition. It makes for a unique effect that leaves the listener hanging, and must have gone down like gangbusters in the clubs.

Immediately following this number, Rogers stepped up, and switched around some of the back-up players, but kept Walter on harp and probably Muddy on second guitar. It took thirteen takes to get a master on "Blues All Day Long." Walter plays wonderful support harp warbling behind the vocal lines, then deftly coming in with some swooping single notes between the vocal lines; it's Chicago blues ensemble playing of the highest order. "Chicago Bound," based on Memphis Slim's 1947 release, "Harlem Bound," is a walking-boogie traveling number, with the singer gradually working his way north, name-checking the towns he's left along the way. Walter's solo is a bubbling cascade of notes and rhythmic twists and turns; this is the type of up-tempo number that he really was able sink his teeth into. His solo sets the pace for later instrumental breaks by Rogers and a pianist (later credited as either Gray or Johnny Jones), and then he solos out at the end of the tune, with the end result another top-of-the-line, good-time blues.

If Walter was riding the crest of the wave, it was inevitable that the hidden rocky shores would cause some froth sooner or later. Guitarist Louis Myers was still unhappy with the way things were being run in the group; the billing still bothered him, and there were grumblings that the money wasn't right either. "I was what you call 'one foot in the door and one foot out,'" Louis explained. "Walter was a greedy man, he want it all for himself . . . I got on to him time after time . . . said, 'I'm not trying to get into your business out here, but one cat ain't nothing without the other one.' [He said] 'Yeah, but I got the name, I'm Little Walter.'" One night in California, things came to a head when Louis and Below overheard the promoters talking about cheating Walter out of his percentage money. (Contracts often guaranteed a flat amount, with the artist then getting an additional percentage based on the "the door," the number of admissions above an agreed-upon minimum number.) "We went and hipped Walter, he came, we saved him $900," Louis said. "And his salary was only something like $300 that night; Walter gave me [only] $10!"

Myers had had it:

> I said, "Man you don't like me. Not only don't you like me, you don't like nobody in the band, you don't need me." "What you mean?" he said. I told him, "Look, I saved you $900 that you wasn't about to get and you give me a measly $10. You take your ten dollars back, you need it more than I do. When you get back to Chicago get yourself a guitar player, I'm giving you my notice out here. I don't like to play with nobody that thinks so little of me, I don't want to be around you."

Soon, Louis was gone.

Walter sought out the best-available sidemen; often this meant people who had led their own bands, and this caused problems when a sideman still thought of himself in bandleader terms. Guitarist Floyd Jones turned down an opportunity to go on the road with Walter, echoing Louis's complaints about money:

> Me and Snooky and Moody, whatever we made we broke it in half, if it was four of us we broke it down to the same thing. With the average guy, he want to take all the money and

give you a little something: "I'm paying you scale." That's what Muddy Waters and them was doing, that was Little Walter's pitch, $12.50 and $18, that was scale. I know at the time Little Walter was making $375 a night and he gave the fellas $25. He was paying their transportation and room and board, but they wasn't getting but $25 a night. And he was getting $375. He might not be going but ten miles; he got his $375. Plus, we got to take care of his car and whatnot. I told him, I said, "Man, what am I on the road for, making $25 a night? Sometimes you don't work but two-three nights a week. I can do better than that here [Chicago]. And I got two expenses, I'm out on the road, and I got my light, gas, rent and phone bill and everything here." He say, "Yeah but I'm gonna take care of you, I'm gonna take care of your food money." I said, "What about my clothes, haircuts and all that?" [He said] "Well yeah, that's right . . . I'll get somebody else then, 'cause you're leading too."

There were also stirrings of discontent on the home front. Ella Mae Taylor, who'd been Walter's one more-or-less constant companion from the early, lean days onward, finally moved out. While all the attention and acclaim might have been good for Walter's ego, it didn't salve the feelings of his lonesome lover. "When he got really popular after 'Juke,' he was gone all the time," Marguerite said. "Women was calling the house bugging her, she couldn't handle all those groupies calling all the time. My brother truly loved her—but she just left, couldn't handle it." Things were moving fast for Walter and he was racing full speed ahead to keep the momentum going. He was now living the kind of life he'd mock in the lyrics of one of his later songs; "You had diamonds and Cadillac cars, touring the world and setting up bars. . . ." But it looked like he was losing things that mattered, things that might have kept him grounded, along the way.

8 *you gonna miss me when i'm gone*

Chicago/The South and East:
February–Fall 1954

When Walter next entered the recording studio, he had a new guitar player on hand. "Louis, he stayed with Walter a little over a year and a half, something like that," Dave Myers said. "Louis got kind of fed up and he just quit. I stayed on a little longer. One time we had to go [on tour] by ourselves, just Walter, Fred, and me. When we came back we rehearsed Robert [Lockwood, Jr.], that's the first time I met him, we tried to make a way for him to fit into the combo. We give him a chance and it worked out."

In a 1995 interview, the ever-acerbic Lockwood said:

> I was like a father to Little Walter ... the Myers brothers stayed with him for a while, they were gigging all the time. Finally Louis quit. Walter come to me on his knees, "Please come help me!" Well, really, I don't especially care about a harp, I don't really like a harp that much. Walter's the first harmonica player I ever had—the very first. I told Walter, "Okay man," I said. "I'm gonna help you 'til you find somebody. That cost me two or three years."

Lockwood took over the lead guitar role on the session, with Dave as usual playing bass lines on his guitar.

On Monday February 22nd, Walter was back at Universal, and recorded three new songs. "Come Back Baby" is an urgent plea, with Walter driving hard with his third-position harp playing, although there are no full-chorus instrumental breaks. "My baby left me, and I don't know where to turn/Last thing she told me was that was a lesson I had to learn" were lines that sounded awfully close to home; he could easily have been referring to the recent departure of Ella Mae. The song uses an unusual, modified rhumba beat, with several stops and rolling drum fills from Fred Below. "Rocker" is an uptempo instrumental, an angrier sounding cousin to the earlier "Fast Boogie." Walter's harp has a harsh, nasty edged tone to it, soaring above the chopping guitars with a bite, spitting out his phrases with a vengeance. The distorted tone comes from the overdriven amplifier, but the angry attack comes from the player, who sounds like he's got some fires raging within.

The next tune continued the overall aggressive tone of the session, with

Walter's machismo on full display. Walter takes the melody and a verse from Tampa Red's 1942 Bluebird recording, "You're Gonna Miss Me When I'm Gone," but adds his own tough edge. The first run through was later released as an alternate take, given the title "I Love You So," with the refrain "Oh baby, you gonna miss me when I'm gone/I thought that you loved me but you always treat me wrong" putting the blame on her while he swaggers away unconcerned. But a couple of verses later—"You was my first love, I thought you would be my friend /You gone and left me baby, I know this is the end"—shows that the boastful chorus was mostly wishful thinking.

The master take was titled "Oh Baby," after the words that begin each verse, and the track solidifies all the elements of the previous warm-up, with the emotion intact. The harp chorus is close to a scream in intensity; for the first and only time on record, Walter pulls out another new toy, a Hohner "Koch" harmonica. This instrument is a cross between the big chromatic harp and the standard Marine Band, and it allowed Walter to further confound his harp-playing competition (along with later generations of players) by playing in the rather unusual blues harp key of A-flat.

In the winter of 1954, Phil Chess told the trade papers that the newly released "Hoochie Coochie Man" by Muddy Waters was "... taking off, selling 4,000 copies a day," while Walter's "You're So Fine" was top-ten in most of the major markets. Once again, Walter's harmonica was being heard on jukeboxes, radios, and record players across the country. Walter headed out on tour, hitting spots in Battle Creek, Pontiac, and Grand Rapids, Michigan before pointing his Cadillac southward. While on the southern swing, Walter picked up his baby stepsister, eleven-year-old Sylvia, in "...a spanking new kitty-cat" (a two-toned Cadillac), and brought her up north to stay with him. Sylvia's older sister Lula had earlier moved to Chicago after marrying a serviceman out West, and stayed with Walter until her husband's tour of duty was up. Sylvia recalled that her move took place early in the year: "It was winter, I went to a full semester of school, I think it was maybe February."

After their mother Beatrice's death in 1950, Sylvia had gone to live with her paternal grandmother. When her grandmother too died, Sylvia's father, Roosevelt Glascock, thought she ought to move to a bigger city with more opportunities. Also, his life as a gambler probably wasn't too conducive to raising a young girl. Roosevelt spoke to Walter about the situation. "My brother had a decent lady living with him," Sylvia explained. "That was my daddy's first concern, by me being a girl. [Walter] had a lady that was a nurse at Cook County [Hospital], she was a church-going woman, Madeline Walls." They all shared a flat at 1101 South Albany on Chicago's West Side. "Maddie was like a mother to him," Sylvia said. "She was an older woman, at least twenty-five years older [than Walter]. She had her own room, I had mine, he had his." But apparently it wasn't strictly platonic; Sylvia chuckled as she recalled, "I guess they went to bed sometimes, 'cause there were times he would come out of there."

The picture Sylvia paints of life during the five years she spent living with Walter is at odds with the image of the marauding bluesman driving a reckless Cadillac cross country and roaring around the South Side bars. "He was on the road some, I'd say 50/50," she said. Sylvia remembered his time on the road as mostly short tours: "He'd be gone, but he'd come back home. If he was booked three or four days, he'd come home, then go back out again. When I was there, he'd never been away even a whole week. Sometimes he drove, sometimes he flew. When he'd go on the road, Muddy Waters would stop by to check on us. When Walter worked in town at clubs, he'd leave the number on the refrigerator magnet, in case of an emergency." One night she got a quick glimpse of her brother onstage at a local club (probably the nearby Zanzibar): "Miss Maddie had taken me, I could see from the dressing room—they had a little window. But Walter didn't like that either, he didn't want me to be in the atmosphere of night club life at a young age."

Sylvia continues, "[Walter] was a person, when he was home, he'd like for us to sit down at dinner, and Maddie would bless the table. Walter loved Creole foods, like gumbo, and Gar fish, smothered in gravy. He didn't like pork ribs; liked to broil a steak, he loved beef, veal. But none of that other stuff, no ham, no bacon, not for brother Walter!" In the morning, when Walter slept in after late-night gigs, Maddie would take Sylvia to school, and later on, Walter would pick her up. "I was going to private school, St. Agatha's Catholic School, I wasn't allowed to walk," Sylvia said, recalling a strictly-run household. "He picked the company, I wasn't allowed to be around anybody that had any [police] record, or was in any kind of gangs." There were no late-night parties or carousing going on around the house, because Madeline worked nine and ten hour days. When musician friends dropped by to visit, they'd often play cards, ". . . but not for money, just for fun. See, he didn't have no gambling for money at the house." Sylvia recalled that Muddy came by quite a bit; "They was like two brothers." She also remembered Jimmy Reed, James Cotton, and Bo Diddley dropping in, and occasionally Walter's own band members like Fred Below. "They'd be coming there, always bringing me popcorn, Walter didn't allow candy, right?" Walter's former lover, Ella Mae, would sometimes stop over to visit as well. "She'd come by to check on me too, she was very nice to Maddie, she respected her, would call her Miss Walls. My brother [and her], I guess they had an understanding, she'd say 'Hi Walter, how's your little sister?'—during Christmas she always brought something for me."

Walter always had a reputation as being a sharp dresser, which Sylvia verified: "He had his clothes tailor made, he'd carry like a suit—the lining of his coat would be the same color as his underpants, he was an excellent dresser. He loved alligator shoes, Oh Lord, had all different colors. He was very sharp, took two showers a day. When he left out, he was smelling like he was coming from Neiman-Marcus—he loved colognes. And jewelry—rings, bracelets, nice watches with diamonds, everything." While staying with Walter, Sylvia met Leonard Chess, who she thought was:

> . . . a respectable person, I liked him a lot. During the years I was there—this is what I found out later to be true—most of the musicians, during the time they were with Leonard Chess, they didn't handle any of their business. All these new cars and stuff they was purchasing, Chess would pay the bills. In my brother's case, I think he'd taken it out of the royalties. When I became an adult, after Leonard died, we found out that my brother was getting all his clothes out of Hong Kong, so was all the other musicians—probably [Chess] was buying in bulk. Now, I know my brother had to pay his own rent and union dues, but I can vouch that our Blue Shield [health insurance] at the time was paid by Leonard.

Sylvia also confirmed that Walter had an occupational problem: he was subject to severe nosebleeds. "He'd come home, have to lay his head down with big bad nosebleeds.

The doctor told him he'd blown it out, blowing that horn." As for his drinking, she didn't see much around home: "He'd have a beer, every now and then a little Hennesy cognac. The rest of that stuff, uhh-uhh." Walter didn't rehearse around the house; mostly they'd go over to Muddy's place. But Sylvia remembers Walter's fondness for jazz: "People thought he liked that down-home Mississippi blues ... he liked Miles Davis, he loved Billie Holiday's music, Dakota Staton, yes indeed. And another person he loved was Lawrence Welk." Sylvia also said he was a chess player, another image that doesn't quite fit the usual picture of Walter. Somehow, it's hard to imagine Walter sitting down to enjoy the popular Midwestern accordion-playing bandleader and his All-American crew on their weekly television broadcast, and then enjoying a thoughtful game of chess!

One of Walter's regular stops on southern tours was Atlanta, Georgia, where he played clubs like The Royal Peacock (on Auburn Avenue, in the heart of downtown) and the Magnolia Ballroom (at Sunset and Vine, in the northwest part of the city). A poster from the Royal Peacock advertised his appearance with a photo of Walter, the "Creator of 'Juke' and his orchestra," appearing on Wednesday, March 10, with a $1.25 admission. The club was on the second floor, entered via a stairway paneled with alternating mirrors and red vinyl upholstery; over the years acts like Count Basie, Aretha Franklin, and Sam Cooke all played there, as well as a young Little Richard. A couple of weeks later, on Tuesday, March 23rd, Walter was headlining a bill with The Five Keys at the Magnolia, with the same reasonable cover charge. The newspaper ad for the latter also brought to light that the political consciousness of Black America was growing; emblazoned across the top was an early civil-rights movement slogan, "Fight For Freedom."

Years later, Walter was asked if there was a special time that stood out in his memory as an especially good sounding gig. "We had a good sound in Atlanta, Georgia, at the Peacock," Walter responded. "The ceiling was low, you didn't have to play as loud." Louis Myers chimed in, "I remember one time them chicks fainted—boy, I ain't never seen peoples faint. I ain't never seen people that the music gets to 'em so they faint. Them women just stood up and hollered 'Woooo,' and then *boom!* At the Royal Peacock ... they enjoyed the music, had what you call a fit—to hear that show ... boy!" Possibly referring to the same gig, Walter added, "Remember that time that broad pulled that pistol on me? I went off the bandstand, they brought me back, and I started off [playing] again. I looked in the corner, 'Yeaaaah, lookee there, something, look—pistol!'" Then one broad throwed her drawers up on Below's [drums], told him (imitating woman's voice) 'If I kept 'em, you all hadda missed the thing.' Said, 'What are you doing?' 'Drawers, drawers, Up on top of his cymbal!'"

A fifteen-year-old white Atlanta boy, Joe Lee Bush, made every one of those gigs he could get to. Bush was a fledgling harp player, and hearing Walter on the radio had inspired him. In fact, Bush entered a Saturday afternoon contest held during an old-time burlesque stage show that played between features at the Eighty-One Theater on Decatur Street. Besides an emcee "Jonin'" (aka "doing the dozens," stringing together rhymes insulting the listener's mother), and blackout skits with comedy routines, girls, and firecrackers, there were also musical acts, including a contest with a $10 prize for the best amateur musician. Bush got up, played one of Walter's instrumental numbers, and won the prize.

'Fight For Freedom'

LITTLE WALTER   FIVE KEYS

Little WALTER

Creator of the "JUKE"

Five KEYS

TUESDAY MARCH 23, 8:30

THE MAGNOLIA

Admission $1.25

B.B.BEAMON, promoter

Figure 8.1 Magnolia Ballroom poster, 1954.

Bush recalled the south in the '50s as being socially integrated, if not legally. "A lot of people think they discovered racial justice or equality in the '60s—it was happening in the '40s and '50s . . . there was a close knit tightness between blacks and whites that's been lost," he said. "We all grew up in the same slums—me and my black friends would go downtown. 'Course, they had their section of the bus, we had our section—so we'd find out where the two sections met and we'd just sit there, them on the seat behind us." The odds were tipped in a white's favor as far as going to clubs however, as Bush explained:

> Black cats couldn't come into white clubs, but white people could get into black clubs . . . if you went in there and acted like a gentleman. The problem was that because it was seg-regated, they'd put a sign out on special nights, like when The Midnighters or Five Royals came to town: "Reserved section for white patrons—twenty-five white patrons only tonight." And you better get there first—once they hit twenty-five, that was it! See, the club was primarily for black people, hell, they couldn't go nowhere else! If you didn't seg-regate it, the white people would come in and take it over.
>
> When there were big R&B shows at the city Auditorium with 15 or 20 acts on the bill, people like the Clovers, Jimmy Reed, Tiny Bradshaw, they'd run a portable chain link fence down the center of the dance floor. The crowd would be maybe 25 percent white, . . . but you'd be talking back and forth, 'cause you knew a lot of the guys, worked with 'em, been hunting and fishing with 'em, so everything was pretty cool.

Bush wasn't yet old enough to drive when he heard on Daddy Sears's popular after-noon radio show that Walter would be playing at the Magnolia. But he did have a learner's permit which allowed him to ride a motorcycle, so he hopped on his BSA and headed on over. While black music was growing rapidly in popularity with the white audiences on radio, the clubs were a bit of a different matter, and often Bush found himself the lone white teenager in the midst of the black crowd:

> When you came to the door, the man would say, "Now, what do *you* want?" I'd say, "Well, I want to come in here and hear Little Walter, I play harmonica, too." He'd say, "Let me see"—so I'd pull out my harmonica and do my little lame old shit . . . I'd have to memo-rize passages and struggle with it . . . He'd say, "Yeah, all right, you get over in that corner there and don't start nothin'." Of course they'd always emphasize to you, "Don't you do no dancin'! Don't you go out here dancin' with one of these colored girls—get your ass shot!" So I'd say, "Hey, listen, I ain't looking for no trouble."

Bush points out that he heard no such warning when he was learning to dance at the all-black Miss Carrie's Cafe a year or two earlier. He remembers the club as holding about 150, ". . . people dancing, drinking, arguing, having a good time." Over the years, a number of harp players seeking information about Walter have queried Bush about every detail he can recall of the number of times he saw him: what Walter wore, what kind of amp he played, how he acted, what he said, who was in his band. "For God's sake, I was only fifteen!," Bush chuckles. "He could've had three people up there or six and I'd probably never knowed. All I was interested in was the harmonica player." Nonetheless some details imprinted strongly on his young memory:

I remember Walter wore a blue suit . . . he looked like a serpent, a snake up there on that stage. He was just weaving, his body language was synonymous with the passages that was being played. Sometimes he'd be like in almost a cat stance, like he was ready to do a side-kick in karate. He'd come back on his right leg, you know? Like that left leg was gonna come up for a side-kick.

Bush paid special attention to Walter's gear: ". . . a National amplifier . . . it had a two-speaker set-up, one speaker went way on one side of the stage, and the one on the right side of the stage had the control knobs on it. He had two microphones [wand mikes] that were taped together with adhesive tape. He put one plug in one side of that amplifier, and one plug in the other side, and he'd mess with his tones—it got quite a sound."

While on breaks between sets, the band stepped out to the sidewalk for some cool air, and Bush summoned up the nerve to approach Walter, and show him what he could do on harp:

He was very nice, very courteous, extremely interested in my playing. I probably hung out around that Magnolia Ballroom three or four nights a week for three months. You see, bands would come to town, stay maybe 60 to 90 days working all the clubs around. I heard stories that in the '60s he turned into a real son of a bitch, but [to me] he was very polite. His English was not infected with a lot of foul language, and he was very happy to talk harmonica with me. Stood out on the sidewalk, he showed me third-position stuff.

Bush also explained how Walter tongue-blocked (covering several holes on the harmonica with his tongue while playing out of the sides of his mouth) to get octaves, and curled his tongue into a "U" shape to get heavy single tones. Bush was also adamant that Walter didn't achieve his two-note warble effect by shaking his head, as many subsequent amplified players would do, but instead did it by moving his hands: "He said that waving your head from side to side made you look like an idiot, and it gave him a headache. He moved his wrists from side to side."

Walter revealed his breath-control secret that he had previously shared with Willie Foster, which allowed him to create a sustained-tone effect: he'd alternate between drawing on the #2 hole, and blowing on the #3 hole, which each produce the same note, giving the impression that he was actually playing with one long, sustained breath. "He'd jump from one to the other, like on 'Flying Saucer,' and that's why he looked like he's never out of breath," Bush said. Walter also gave him a tip on bending notes on the big chromatic harp, a relatively difficult thing to do: "He had a piece of paper, he wrote it down for me, where you could take a 64 Chromonica apart and take the wind valve loose off of certain notes—it would enable you to really bend those notes well. He did pull about four or five off. Of course, I promptly misplaced the piece of paper . . ." Years later Bush decided to try taking all the plastic wind valves off, figuring "I'll be the greatest harmonica player in the world—[but] all I did was ruin a harmonica!"

Back in Chicago, on Tuesday, April 13, 1954, Muddy Waters was in the studio to cut another Willie Dixon number, "Just Make Love To Me," as his new single, with Walter

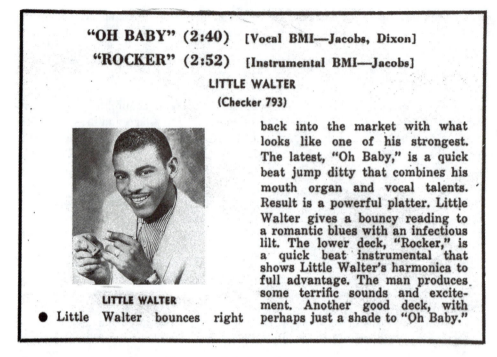

"OH BABY" (2:40)   [Vocal BMI—Jacobs, Dixon]

"ROCKER" (2:52)   [Instrumental BMI—Jacobs]

LITTLE WALTER

(Checker 793)

LITTLE WALTER

● Little Walter bounces right back into the market with what looks like one of his strongest. The latest, "Oh Baby," is a quick beat jump ditty that combines his mouth organ and vocal talents. Result is a powerful platter. Little Walter gives a bouncy reading to a romantic blues with an infectious lilt. The lower deck, "Rocker," is a quick beat instrumental that shows Little Walter's harmonica to full advantage. The man produces some terrific sounds and excitement. Another good deck, with perhaps just a shade to "Oh Baby."

Figure 8.2 Cashbox Award O' Week: "Oh Baby," April 24, 1954.

again on board as a hired gun. It was another Muddy classic in the making, with its slinky, insidious stop-and-start rhythm, Spann's piano, and Walter's darting harp. It was the first time Walter used his big, 16-hole Chromatic harp on a Muddy session, and its distinctive, somewhat ominous sound was a perfect match for the material and the mood, enhanced in the studio by some deep echo effects. When Muddy first heard Walter fooling with the new harp, he told him, "Don't rehearse on my session, motherfucker!" But when he heard the playback, he changed his mind, and really liked the new sound. The flip side, "Oh Yeh," was a swaggering, in-your-face reprimand to a faithless lover: "Oh yeah, some day I'm gonna catch you soon/gonna whup you in the morning, pet you in the afternoon." Walter's harp underscores and enhances the power of Muddy's full-bore vocals, and it's another little three-minute gem.

At the end of the session, Walter backed Jimmy Rogers on a track, a remake of Sonny Boy Williamson's 1941 "Sloppy Drunk." Seizing the opportunity to pay tribute to his early hero, Walter recreates Sonny Boy's original melody line, but uses it as a jumping-off point for various improvisations that become wilder and more original as the song progresses, eventually cranking what was originally a country shuffle into urban overdrive, while anchoring the proceedings with solid chord backup throughout. The tune was a moderate hit for Rogers.

However, bad luck continued to dog Walter. The Rhythm N'Blues Ramblings column in *Cashbox* on April 17th reported that:

More tough luck has befallen Little Walter. He and his Jukes were playing the Club Hollywood when fire struck. Walter and the boys barely escaped with their lives. And all their instruments, which happened to be brand new, were completely demolished. Just to make things worse, when leaving the scene of the fire, Walter, in his nervousness, was involved in a car accident. On the brighter side however his "You're So Fine": continues to sell and he is set to leave for a second tour of Texas very shortly.

It's possible that this accident may have resulted in one of the rather prominent scars on his face visible in later photos; his youngest sister Sylvia said that some of these scars were caused by an auto accident. There have been other explanations for the scars, stories implicating Chicago plain-clothes detectives in some vicious police misconduct, aggravating a previous wound. Other accounts mention that Walter was hit with a bottle in a dance hall brawl. In later years, Walter gave an alternate explanation for these scars when he told an inquiring aspiring guitarist, perhaps in jest, "My old lady hit me with a wine bottle."

Nonetheless, by Tuesday, April 20th, Walter and His Jukes had replaced their equipment and were on the bill at the 708 Club on 47th Street, with the Monday, Wednesday, and Thursday slots filled by Muddy Waters & His Hoochie Coochie Boys. Sax player Ernest Cotton & Trio were holding down weekends at the club, which advertised its late night hours "Open late 4 & 5 AM"—good news for partiers, but notoriously long nights for the band. The following week's ad listed Eddie Boyd taking over Walter's regular Tuesday nights.

While he was playing at The 708 Club, Walter's new release "Oh Baby"/"Rocker" was highlighted by *Cashbox* magazine with their Award Of The Week, again with a photo of Walter. The blurb made it obvious the reviewer hadn't paid much attention to the lyrics:

> Little Walter bounces right back into the market with what looks like one of his strongest. The latest "Oh Baby" is a quick beat jump ditty that combines his mouth organ and vocal talents. Result is a powerful platter. Walter gives a bouncy reading to a romantic blues with an infectious lilt. The lower deck, "Rocker," is a quick beat instrumental that shows Little Walter's harmonica to full advantage. The man produces some terrific sounds and excitement. Another good deck, with perhaps just a shade to "Oh Baby."

It was also listed as a "Buy O' The Week" in the trades, with mention that "Reports from Atlanta, Nashville, and St. Louis were strong. Buffalo, Cincinnati, Cleveland, Chicago, Detroit, Durham and Los Angeles also reported good action." Both it and Muddy's "Hoochie Coochie Man" were settled in nicely in the Top Ten charts across the country.

The May 1st "Rhythm N'Blues Ramblings" column in *Cashbox* reported that "Len Chess was off for the south again, which will keep him busy for the next three or four weeks. While traveling, Len and leading Memphis DJ Dewey Phillips of station WHBQ are running a dance at the Hippodrome Ballroom, Memphis, where Little Walter, Muddy Waters and Howlin' Wolf, three of Len's hottest properties will appear." Chess knew the value of having powerful and influential DJs on his side. He also allied himself with Alan Freed in Cleveland, and back home in Chicago with black DJs Al

Benson and McKie Fitzhugh. The label was now starting to expand its horizons, buying masters of New Orleans musicians, as well as cutting smooth-sounding doo-wop groups like The Flamingos. That same month the Chess/Checker operation moved a block or so north to larger headquarters at 4750 South Cottage Grove, in a one story red-brick building. Leonard said the idea was to have their own recording facilities there, and eventually they did set up a small studio in the back room behind the storefront offices.

According to Willie Dixon, Chess bought a used two-track, reel-to-reel recorder from Reverend C. L. Franklin, the preacher from Detroit (and father of Aretha), whose recorded sermons were big sellers in the gospel market. The machine was set up on a table by the window that led to the back room, where the mikes were. Although the studio was primitive compared to Universal, over the next few years several sessions took place there. Chess also experimented with microphone placements in an effort to get the best drum sounds, because the beat was considered to be of prime importance.

Early in May, the Supreme Court handed down its long-awaited *Brown v. Bd. of Ed.* decision that declared school segregation unconstitutional. Though the changes it mandated would be sweeping, and would alter the face of racial politics across the country, it wouldn't be without strife. But for Walter & The Jukes that May, it was business as usual: they were back at The 708 Club on Tuesdays, with Muddy again doing a three-day-a-week stint.

Although Chess rarely scheduled sessions on Saturdays, on May 22nd, another Walter session took place. But before he and the Jukes got their turn, Chess used them in an attempt to punch up some sides he was cutting on a doo-wop vocal group, The Coronets, by adding Walter's distinctive harp and the band's swinging backing to the tracks. "Cobella" was a pretty standard up-tempo number with a high falsetto lead up until the break where Walter, pianist Otis Spann, and Below's drums kick the number in the ass. Walter wades right in with a fat-toned solo, honking with his best saxman chops; then, after his break, he drops out of the mix altogether. The other track, "Begging And Pleading," is a slow number, with Walter adding little fills throughout, but he doesn't take a harp break this time. The sides were rather raw compared to the slick vocal group sound that would be featured on Chess's later recordings of The Moonglows, and these cuts went unreleased at the time.

Walter started his own two-song session with a remake of a Dr. Clayton 1941 Bluebird release, "I Got To Find My Baby." Spann's keyboards open the tune, with punctuation by Below on the stop-time chords that open each verse. Walter is in fine voice, and everybody's playing at the top of their form. A slower warm-up version lacks the focus of the issued take, where Walter takes some nice, rippling high-end riffs. Lockwood adds bubbling guitar lines, and Spann's syncopation is right on the money; it's a fine team effort. The other track, "Big Leg Mama," is another remake; this time Walter takes the distinctive "head" from Sonny Boy Williamson's "Apple Tree Swing," a 1947 Victor recording, and turns it into a swinging shuffle instrumental, complete with a jazzy, descending-chord bridge for variety. Walter starts easy and loping, then gradually builds the intensity with warbles, dropping back down before reprising the head theme for a solid finish. Although strong efforts, both tunes were held back at the time.

A couple of weeks later, another harp player and friend of Walter's met a violent end:

Figure 8.3 708 Club advertisement, *Chicago Defender*, May 8, 1954.

Henry "Pot" Strong, who'd been playing with Muddy since Walter Horton had gone off one night without warning to play another gig, and sent Strong to Muddy as a replacement. Strong and guitarist Otis "Big Smokey" Smothers had started out working on the street around 35th and State Streets, ". . . going door to door" working as a duo for tips. Strong's earliest band in Chicago had been with guitarist Jody Williams and pianist Otis Spann, in 1953. Williams had then been recruited into Howlin' Wolf's band, and would later record backing Bo Diddley and Billy Boy Arnold. Williams recalled, ". . . We all used to play together—me on the guitar, Otis Spann on the piano, Pot on the harp, and another harmonica player we had occasionally who was Little Walter's uncle [Carlton]. All four of us had a little flat together at 38th and Wabash, and in those days we played at the Tick Tock Lounge . . . and little by little the band started to scatter . . ." Muddy thought Strong was a good replacement. "I'd been knowing him, 'cause Walter was teaching him how to play harp," Muddy said.

"He was the best harp player in Chicago next to me," Walter said:

Because I taught him all I knew. He was only in his teens—very small, we used to call him Pot. He got messed up with a woman. She got angry with him, and just meaning to cut him she went and killed him. He died in the back seat of Muddy's car, on the way to the hospital.

Strong, 25 years old, died of a punctured lung.

Williams was a witness to the incident. He said that Pot's jealous girlfriend Juanita turned up ranting and raving in the middle of the night at the South Greenwood Ave. building where he and Strong shared an apartment, in the same building where Muddy lived. When Strong tried to calm things down, she grabbed a knife and stabbed him in the chest. As Strong ran through the apartment trying to escape, Muddy attempted to intervene, and was attacked as well and almost stabbed for his efforts. Williams locked himself into a bedroom, but Strong decided to try an escape through the back door; when he turned and ran back through the apartment, he once again encountered Juanita and was stabbed yet again. He and Muddy eventually made it outside to Muddy's car, and raced for the hospital. Strong lost consciousness in the car, and was pronounced dead on arrival at the hospital. "There was blood from one end of the apartment to the other . . . ," according to Williams. Juanita was later arrested and charged with Strong's murder, but pleaded self-defense and was acquitted.

Walter was navigating other troubled waters as well. Jody Williams remembers seeing Walter onstage, bearing visible effects of the aftermath of a fight:

> . . . The guys had the street all blocked up, over on the west side somewhere. [Walter] took out his tire iron, because they wouldn't move the car and let him through. They took his tire iron, almost beat him to death out there with it. His head was all bandaged up—matter of fact, the doctor told him not to play, 'cause he blows pretty hard. You know, you blow hard, things [veins] pop all out on your head . . . but he was playing out there . . .

Myers said Walter was out for two or three days:

> He couldn't come to work. We talked over the telephone, I asked him when you coming to work? He said, "I don't feel so good, I'm hurting." I asked him what happened, but he would just tell me so much, I doubt if he'd tell me the whole truth, it just went that way. . . .

While Walter was recovering from the beating, he began performing again at the Hollywood Rendezvous, and was interrupted mid-set one night by a "family" emergency. Walter was onstage—with his head still bandaged up—when someone ran into the club and got his attention. As Dave Myers tells it:

> He had his black fish-tail Cadillac parked right across the street in the vacant lot there, by Brown's Funeral Parlor. Billie, one of his girlfriends, was throwing a brick at it, trying to break the window. I don't know what he did to her, he pissed her off about something. Somebody went in and told him, "Billie's out here, trying to tear up your Cadillac." He dropped the harmonica and everything, ran out. She pulled her dress up round her waist and tore off down the alley. He didn't catch her, she's too fast for him!

Myers followed Walter out of the club in time to see that Billie had succeeded in putting a brick through the window of Walter's car. As she ran off down the alley,

Walter retrieved his gun from the glove compartment and fired off a few shots, although Myers thought he just meant to scare her, since ". . . he wasn't aiming at her." Myers also recalls another incident from around this time that took place in the alley behind The Zanzibar, where Walter was attacked and beaten by a group of men who accused him of fooling around with the wife of one.

The months of June and July found Walter and crew continuing their regular Tuesdays at The 708 Club, while the trade papers announced an upcoming Alan Freed extravaganza. Called "The Moondog Jubilee of Stars Under The Stars," it was scheduled to be held in August at Ebbets field, the 30,000 seat home of the Brooklyn Dodgers. The budget for the show was put at $25,000, with $15,000 of that going for talent which included The Clovers, The Dominoes, The Orioles, and the Count Basie and Buddy Johnson bands, along with six combos including Muddy Waters, Fats Domino, and Little Walter. There were no followup reports on this event, but it certainly would have been one of the biggest shows of Walter's career to that point.

On Thursday, July 1st, Walter was in the studio for what amounted to a demo session, because nothing from that day was issued. It's of interest mainly for the first run at "My Babe," a Willie Dixon tune that was tried out rather awkwardly here, but which would later become one of Walter's biggest hits (and the first Dixon composition to top the R&B charts) after going through a drastic rearrangement. The version here has a droning, one-chord, Howlin' Wolf "Smokestack Lightning"-like arrangement, and is slower, more ominous, and less lilting than the later, hit version, although many of the lyrics are already set. Walter plays minimal harp, as he tentatively tries out the lyrics, and sounds rather uncomfortable with the fit.

The other tune attempted that day, "Last Night," is a somewhat plodding early version of what would become one of Walter's best-loved slow-blues numbers. With this version it seems likely Walter still was thinking of Ella Mae; a line used here but dropped from the released version goes: "You was my first love, you should had been my wife." The fact that this is the only Little Walter vocal recorded for Chess that doesn't also feature his harp has given rise to speculation that it's Walter playing the basic, chopping guitar chords heard throughout; the guitar work does have more of Walter's down-home rawness than Lockwood's finesse. But that raw sound may actually have been simply the result of the band being called into the studio unprepared for this session, as Dave Myers relates:

> Chess was a funny guy. He did things when it popped up, on the spur of the moment. If he got something set up to cut you, when the day comes you're supposed to record, you don't see or hear from him. After that he would call you right in and say "We're gonna cut it," and it throws everybody off. On "My Babe," I was in pool hall that day shooting pool, so how the hell is [he] gonna find me [in time to be prepared]?

Only a few days later in Memphis, at the same Sun studios where Howlin' Wolf and Walter Horton had recorded, a white youth from Tupelo, Mississippi would take his first steps towards changing the face of American popular music—including the blues, even if indirectly. Sam Phillips was cutting a tryout session with a 19-year-old named Elvis Presley, who was enamored of Dean Martin and the Ink Spots, and so far had produced only average ballad numbers. On a break he picked up his guitar and began belting out a Big Boy Crudup blues number, "That's All Right Mama"—and everybody knew that *now* they had something. The record was released within a few weeks and the rest is history.

On Wednesday, July 14, Walter was back in the studio, and although only two tracks were recorded, they were both gold. The first cut was a hard-hitting vocal with stop-time verses and a rocking chorus. "You Better Watch Yourself" is a cautionary tale; "I've got my eyes on you," the singer growls. Walter plays with a drive that belies his ironic vocal delivery. The distorted amp and vocal sounds hint that possibly this may have been cut at the primitive Chess studios rather than at Universal—or maybe it was just overdriven when it was mastered. The flip side was a masterful mood piece, the reverb-drenched instrumental "Blue Light." Walter later bragged that he used four different harps while recording it: at least two are aurally obvious, a 10-hole diatonic and his big, 16-hole chromatic, used on the last couple of choruses. Lockwood plays some lacy arpeggio fills that perfectly underscore Walter's moves. Walter is playing full out, just on the edge of getting a squeal of feedback from his amp during his first chorus. As he paints his finely detailed aural picture, he holds a long, slow, bent tone, slowly raising the pitch with a spot-on control that would have harp players shaking their heads as they struggled for years to duplicate it. He plays sparsely, making every note count as he alternates between low organ-like tones and high, screeching sounds that climax in a dizzying reverb overload at one point. The engineer at the controls plays a large role in the final sound, as he boosts and cuts back the reverb effects. The result is a true masterpiece, an instrumental that raised the bar for every harp player since.

"YOU BETTER WATCH YOURSELF" (2:40)
[ARC BMI—Jacobs]
"BLUE LIGHT" (2:45)
[ARC BMI—Jacobs]

LITTLE WALKER
(Checker 799)

● Little Walter's latest release pairs a rhythmic blues vocal, "You Better Watch Yourself," with a mood instrumental, "Blue Light," the later featuring the harmonica work of Little Walter. On the top deck, Walter warns his gal she had better watch herself 'cause he has his eye on her. Deck has a strong beat and could prove to be the side. However, the flip "Blue Light," is a moving instrumental waxing that could catch fire. Both sides are strong material.

LITTLE WALTER

Figure 8.4 Cashbox Award O'Week: "You Better Watch Yourself," August 21 (?), 1954.

In August, there were more package shows, but now they were close to home. Deejay Sam Evans hosted occasional weekend "Jam With Sam" shows at the Madison Rink, a rollerskating rink on the West Side of Chicago. Announced for Saturday the 7th were Little Walter, along with The Clovers, Sunnyland Slim, and Big John Greer. A show publicized in *The Defender* for the following Friday was noted as the first rock and roll package concert in Chicago. Headliners "Direct from New York," shown in a photo montage, included Roy Hamilton, Lavern Baker, Big Maybelle, The Spaniels, The Drifters, Faye Adams, Rusty Bryant, and the Erskine Hawkins Orchestra. Added on to the bill were the local draws Memphis Slim, Muddy Waters, and Little Walter. According to later accounts, 7,000 fans jammed the 4,500-person-capacity space.

Both Muddy and Walter continued their respective nights at The 708 Club. The club also announced a "Meet your favorite star" Sunday matinee show, featuring Muddy, Sunnyland Slim, Willie Mabon, and Elmore James. Late in the month, Walter's hot new single "You Better Watch Yourself"/ "Blue Light" was out, and drew another *Cashbox* "Award O' The Week" featured spot. In their typical lingo they gave the nod to the vocal "deck," although "the flip, Blue Light, is a moving instrumental waxing that could catch fire. Both sides are strong material," they concluded.

Popular deejay Sam Evans would soon begin using "Blue Light" as the theme for the 11:00 PM deep blues portion of his nightly radio broadcast. Sam would tell the audience how he was going down to the basement, sitting on a beat up old orange crate in the soft glow of blue light. He'd say he hadn't had much to eat, just some greasy greens with side meat, or grits and black-eyed peas. Then he played an hour of down-home sides by Sonny Boy, Hooker, Wolf, et al.

On August 22nd, Walter and the gang were back on the road down south, playing Atlanta's Magnolia Ballroom. A newspaper advertisement for the gigs pictured pianist Amos Milburn, and announced a big jam session with him, Little Walter, Austell Allen and Band, and many other acts. Admission was $1, and the show ran from "5 PM until . . ." Dave Myers recalled the continuing touring hassles:

> We was playing in St. Martinville, Louisiana, right out of Alexandria. The white ladies, some of them got the nerve they come over and try and talk to you, try to find out about your playing. It's exciting to them. We got to fooling around there, this policeman came over. He hit Walter across the shoulder with that stick, said, "Stay in your goddam place!" Walter said, "I ain't never been outta my place, Mister. That lady came over and talked to me!"
>
> I know what they wanted, [but] I don't let them smoke me out. I don't say nothing . . . I don't want to do nothing to make them think I'm smart. They want to get me, and they don't need but a little bit to get you.

This kind of pressure, combined with Walter's miserly ways, contributed to Dave's decision to follow his brother Louis, and he quit the band. "I left because I had to stick with my brother," he said later. "I put a lot of my life into it, and I just got shit out of it . . ." Looking back on it now, he adds, "But I was glad to do it." First, Myers made an attempt to talk to Walter about the situation:

> . . . man-to-man. I dealt with the contracts a lot, saw some things—they was taking advantage of him. I got him in a hotel room, said, "You're losing a lot of money." I said, "I believe

if you was making more money you'd pay the band more money . . . there's a lot that can be done, you'd have to get yourself together and try, it don't seem like you care about any-thing—you just have to care." He took it as an insult, says, "You don't feel I'm doing my business right?" He says, "You talk to me like Leonard Chess or somebody"—like I'm trying to make a child outta him. I knew then; time for me to go now . . .

Walter was out "cabareting, drinking" and sometimes missing gigs, which meant the band didn't get paid either. The final straw had come earlier that spring, when Walter blew off two weeks of work in Texas to play instead with Wolf and Muddy at the one-night gig that Leonard had set up at the Memphis Hippodrome. Myers continues:

> It woulda done the band real good to work fourteen more days, it would hurt us to miss a night, we wasn't getting very much, we just couldn't afford it. Lewis [the Texas promoter] was gonna cancel us out if we didn't stay and work. Walter told him he was gonna run to Memphis, play this thing with Wolf and come back, but he wasn't gonna go for it, he told him no. "I got you down here to work for me—you leave, we gonna cancel you out." Sure enough Walter left, packed us up, we left, went to Memphis and played, lost fourteen days and after that had to come home. He didn't even bother to think about our benefit.

When Myers returned to Chicago, he found Louis working a regular gig with Otis Rush, and he told them that he would soon be leaving Walter as well. He stayed on just long enough to get funds to buy a new PA system for The Aces to use.

Walter's hard-nosed attitude was evident when his uncle Sam Leviege came to Chicago for a visit while on a trip to Louisiana from his home in Alaska, where he'd become the ". . . biggest black painting contractor in the state" after leaving the armed services. Sam and his wife stayed at Walter's apartment, although they didn't see much of his famous nephew; Walter was out on the road until just before Sam planned to leave town. Sam didn't witness much evidence of Walter's wild side; in fact, he said that he'd "Never known Walter to drink," but "I know he was a stubborn young man." One night, the two were returning home from a gig Walter had played in nearby Gary, Indiana. "The police stopped us. [Walter] had a sack of money in the trunk of his car, I guess that was his take from where he played," Sam said. "The police wanted Walter to give him some money so he could let us go. Walter refused. He kept us there about an hour. Walter still didn't give up none of his money . . . You know Chicago, got some dirty cops in Chicago . . ."

Eddie "Jewtown" Burks also encountered Walter's rolling bank vault. Burks was another Mississippi transplant, a mill worker and erstwhile harp blower who frequented the Chicago clubs, and played regularly on Maxwell Street. He hung out in Douglas Park near Walter's West Side apartment as well, where he says he played checkers with Walter, and claimed to have beat him all the time, going home with Walter's money. Burks remembered Walter showing up at his house with a new Cadillac. "That was when he recorded 'Juke,'" Burks said:

> He showed up that Saturday morning and I was on my way to work at the steel mill. He flagged me down and told me to come on over and get some money. I went over there and looked in that car and saw all them tens and twenties stacked up in there. I said to myself, "This cat done robbed a bank." So I went to work and didn't take any money. That Monday he was broke. I had to give him wine money.

On Wednesday, September 1st, Muddy Waters had another recording session, and once more Walter got the call, taking the place of Muddy's then-regular harp man George Smith. This time, Muddy also tapped Below to fill in on drums; it was said Muddy had wanted to replace his regular drummer Edmonds, but out of loyalty Below wouldn't take his friend's chair. Sessions however were another matter, and at the behest of Chess, sidemen were frequently replaced in the studio without any real effect on the gigging band. Another big change was that, for the first time, Muddy didn't play guitar on his session. He felt it wasn't needed any longer, and for the next few years he fronted the band as a singer, leaving his guitar at home. If Jimmy Rogers was to be believed, this came as some relief to Walter: "Muddy couldn't play with a slide in natural tuning, he'd have to tune his guitar in Spanish [to an open chord]. So he'd have two guitars he'd take with him all the time," Rogers explained. "When he'd grab that guitar with that doggone piece of slide—Oh Lord man—that's when Walter would have a fit, Walter hated that. He'd say, 'He's just scratching on that guitar!' I wouldn't tell Muddy." Perhaps Walter was put off by the "in-between" notes sounded by the slide; according to Rogers, he had a sensitive ear. "He'd hear something, its just like a tape, once he hear it, he was taping it in his mind," Rogers said. "He'd go off by himself, get in a room and close up, and when he come out he'd know it. He might not be playing it exactly like it's s'posed to go, but he played close enough."

Willie Foster, a Mississippi harp player who said he did tour dates off and on with Muddy, claimed he helped inspire the first of three tunes cut that day, Willie Dixon's macho strut, "I'm Ready." Foster says he arrived from St. Louis to join Muddy for a short Canadian tour leaving the following day (although later Muddy would refute Foster's contention that he'd actually toured with the band). He went to Muddy's place, and Dixon answered the door, as Muddy was shaving. Muddy stuck his head out to ask, "Are you ready?" and Foster replied, "I'm ready as anybody can be." Dixon and Muddy looked at each other, said "That's a song," and they all sat down and wrote the tune with lyrics like "I'm drinking TNT, smoking dynamite / I hope some screwball start a fight—'cause I'm ready . . ." In the studio, Spann's piano opens the cut and sets the pace, then the band kicks in with a solid back-beat, power-driving Muddy's macho boasting. Walter is on his chromatic harp here, with fat chords filling in behind the vocals. On the harmonica break, he hits a hard sustained tone, lays back, then hits hard again; his use of space is as effective as the notes he plays. The tune is pitched rather oddly for Muddy in the key of $D_\sharp$. This meant that Walter was using his chromatic with the slide held in all through the number. Whether it was done to accommodate Muddy's vocal range or because Walter liked to confuse the competition is hard to say. But it was a trick he used again a couple of years later on another Muddy session.

The next tune cut that day, "Smokestack Lightning," is credited to Chester Burnett, A/K/A Howlin' Wolf. The Wolf had come to Chicago from the Memphis area the preceding fall, stayed with Muddy for a couple of months, and Muddy had helped him get his first Chicago gigs. The band uses a modified version of the musical phrase that would later become known as Wolf's trademark when he finally cut his own version of the tune a year-and-a-half later. Despite some powerful singing, the track seems rather tentative and never really catches fire, and Muddy's version went unreleased at the time.

Father, Adam (Bruce) Jacobs.
(Courtesy Lillian Jacobs Marshall)

Mother, Beatrice Leviege.
(Courtesy Lillian Jacobs Marshall)

Riding on Maxwell Street,
c. 1948 ??
(Courtesy Jim O'Neal/Lamarr
Chapman, BluEsoteria Archives)

The gang in Marksville, Louisiana (l to r):
stepsister Marguerite Glascock, Walter (with
gun), uncle Louis "Carlton" Leviege, Junior
McGhee, Louis McGhee, unknown toddler,
c. 1942 ?? (Courtesy Lillian Jacobs Marshall)

Back down south, in Marksville. On porch,
grandparents Canelia and Louis Leviege,
Walter's aunt Rita Leviege, Walter, c. 1950 ??
(Courtesy Lillian Jacobs Marshall)

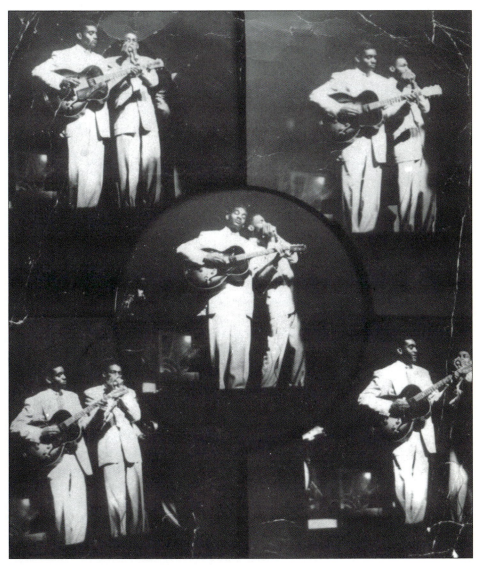

Walter and Louis Myers, Apollo Theater, October 1952. (Courtesy Bill Greensmith collection/*Blues Unlimited*)

With daughter Marion, 4 months old, February 1958.
(© Marion Jacobs-Diaz Reacco, 2002)

California beaming (l to r): unknown (Walter's uncle?), Walter (behind), Aunt Celine (Jacobs), unknown cousin, chauffeur Bennie Rooks, c. late '50s.
(Courtesy Lillian Jacobs Marshall)

Boxer Ezzard Charles won the heavyweight title in 1949. Walter looks impressed. Fall 1953.
(Courtesy Lillian Jacobs Marshall)

Chess photo sessions, mid-'50s.
(Don Bronstein/MCA/Chess
Archives)

**Gigging at Rickey's Show
Lounge, December 1957
(l to r): George Hunter,
Luther Tucker, Walter.**
(Yannick Bruynoghe, courtesy
Margo Bruynoghe)

Sitting in on guitar at the Zanzibar, spring 1958 (l to r): Walter, Earring George, unknown fan, Luther Tucker. (Billy Boy Arnold, courtesy Bill Greensmith Collection/*Blues Unlimited*)

Sitting in with Muddy, Chicago, September 1959 (l to r): Otis Spann, Francis Clay, Andrew Stephens, Walter, Pat Hare. Note amp and speaker on ledge behind Walter. (© Jacques Demetre/Soul Bag Archives)

Clubbing in Washington, DC (l to r): James Cotton, Matty Rollins, Walter, unknown, Muddy Waters, c. 1959. (Courtesy Matty Rollins)

The lord and lady.
Matty Rollins and Walter,
Chicago, mid-'50s.
(Courtesy Matty Rollins)

Checking out
in Chicago,
c. 1963.
(© Marion Jacobs-Diaz
Reacco, 2002)

Arriving
UK, Sussex
Gardens, London,
September 15, 1964.
(© Val Wilmer, 2002)

Opening night, September 17, 1964, Marquee Club, London. (Sylvia Pitcher, London)

Good times in the UK, fall 1964. (Courtesy Mike Rowe)

At the Black Prince, Bexley, UK, September 20, 1964. (Courtesy Mike Rowe)

GQ dapper in the UK, 1964. (Courtesy Mike Rowe)

With the Sheffields, a rare signed shot for *Blues Unlimited* magazine, 1964.
(Courtesy Mike Rowe)

Boston, March 1966. (Mark Power)

Mandell Hall, University of Chicago, May 20, 1966, flying high, with Sammy Lawhorn, guitar. (Ray Flerlage)

Ready to tour, American Folk Blues Festival, fall 1967. (Horst Lippman, courtesy Sylvia Lippman)

"Uncle" Walter,
AFBF tour, 1967.
(Courtesy Jim O'Neal/Koko
Taylor, BluEsoteria Archives)

Hanging at the hotel, AFBF tour (l to r): Skip James, Walter, Son House, Hound Dog Taylor,
Koko Taylor. (Christer Landergren)

1967 AFBF tour.
(Christer
Landergren)

1967 AFBF tour.
(Christer
Landergren)

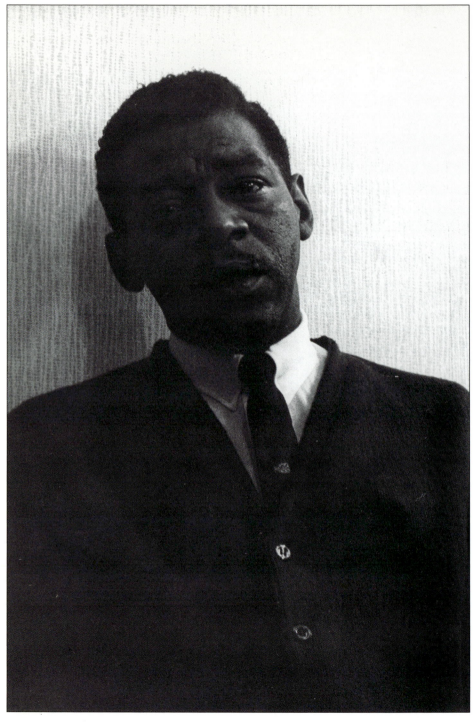

Worn and weary—AFBF tour 1967. (Sylvia Pitcher, London)

9 *roller coaster*

Chicago/Alexandria, Louisiana/Boston/Chicago: Fall 1954–Fall 1955

As the summer of 1954 began to cool down, Walter and company continued with their residency gig on Tuesdays at The 708 Club, with Muddy Waters again filling out the other weeknights and weekends. Walter was also regularly featured in major events and benefit concerts, a recognition of his importance in the community.

Sometime in October, Muddy was called to the studios for another two-song session, with Walter once again on board. The rather muffled recording quality suggests that this was another session cut at the primitive Chess backroom studio rather than downtown at Universal. "I'm A Natural Born Lover" is yet another macho-strut boasting piece. Walter uses his chromatic harp for his two solo choruses, soaring over the rather lost-in-the-mix band sound. "Ooh Wee" is a slow cooker, another Willie Dixon man-in-lust piece that Muddy performs with conviction.

With Dave Myers gone from The Jukes, Robert Lockwood brought in his protégé, 18-year-old Luther Tucker, to fill the musical void. Tucker was born in Memphis, moved to Chicago with his family when he was nine, and, when barely into his teens, was sent to jail for theft of a police car. One visiting day, his blues-pianist mother brought along a guitar-playing friend, Lee Jackson. His sound inspired Tucker, and when he was released he sought out Jackson to learn guitar. Soon he met Lockwood, who took him under his wing, showing him more chords and patterns. Lockwood had been playing with Sunnyland Slim; when he quit and went to work with Walter, Tucker joined up with Slim. "He's just like a dad, too," Tucker said of Slim. "He used to come pick me up, take me to work, bring me back. I practically used to live with him ... We'd be playing out in Elgin, Illinois, the ladies would say, 'Who's that fellow?' Slim would say 'Don't bother him, that's my son, he's too young.' He'd take all my girlfriends! [laughs]." Tucker definitely looked underage: "I used to sit in a chair, my feet would barely touch the floor. I had a hollow box guitar, I could just barely reach around to where the strings were to play it—it was a trip watching me play."

Lockwood recommended Tucker to Walter for the spot Dave Myers had vacated; Walter agreed, and the two of them went to Tucker's mother to get her blessing. "They say, 'We'd like to have Junebug in the band with us,'" Tucker said:

> My ma said, "Yeah, it'd be a good idea, just don't let him get in with no people that drinks or smokes—he can't do that." They said okay—little that they knew! [laughs] . . . I had to join the union to play, they say you have to have somebody co-sign for you . . . Robert Junior said okay. We were going to play this 708 Club, I take my amplifier and guitar in there—this security guard at the door, he say "Hey, you ain't s'posed to be in here, you get outta here!" Robert Jr. told him that I was gonna be playing with them—that really surprised him, I could see the look on his face, he wanted to put me out.

When he first met Walter, Tucker found him reserved, maybe even:

> . . . snobbish a little bit. He never did talk to people he'd just met—he wouldn't just walk up and have a conversation, most of the time they had to come to him. But if you knew him, you couldn't find a better friend. He didn't talk too much, but he sure could play the harmonica, guess that did his talking for him. He liked to drink, he liked to smoke and he just loved the womens. He'd have about five or six ladies in the nightclub at the same time. It'd be a fight every time he played, so many womens he didn't know what to do with them . . . He'd try and divide them, say "Robert Jr. you take that one, Below you take that one, Tucker you take that one—and maybe I can get away with one." All of them be looking at Walter, they all knew each other, [saying] "What you gonna do this time? We know you got four women here . . ." When it's time to go home, Walter'd say, "Yeah, I'm going home." One of them would say, "Nah, you going with me!" Walter say, "Okay, meet me outside, over there." The others say, "You gonna meet her?" and Walter say, "Nah, I ain't gonna . . . ," then all four of 'em would get to fighting, just tear up the club! Throwing bottles, a couple times pistol plays . . . Yeah, he was a playboy.

Tucker took over the bass guitar role, playing bass licks on a low-tuned guitar. "You try to wind it down to the bottom without making that scrunchy sound, when you hit a string and hear it rattle," Tucker explained. "Robert Jr. have really been a help to me in playing music. He give me some bass lines to try to learn, just go home and practice all night 'til I get 'em. I was still trying to play lead some. By Robert Jr. being something like a dad, he'd say 'Okay, you take the lead on this, I'll play background,' but he had most of the leads." Tucker honed his craft on the Sunday jam sessions at The 708 Club. He recalled sit-in guests like Muddy, as well as Ike Turner's Kings of Rhythm. Tucker also remembered how ". . . people would come up and open up [Walter's] hand to see what he had in there to make that beautiful sound."

Even at this early stage, other harmonica players wanted to know how Walter achieved his distinctive sound. Many blues harp players have attempted to imitate his sound by trying to obtain the same types of microphones and amplifiers he used. For some, the quest to recreate Walter's exact equipment setup has taken on aspects of the hunt for the holy grail.

Unfortunately, there are no known photos of Walter in the recording studio that show what kind of amp he used on any given session, nor are there any known photos of him playing live using his own amp. The only time he mentioned gear was in a 1968 interview, "I had an amplifier built . . . and it had four speakers on each side . . . little bitty speakers too. Amplifier up and one down. If I blew a fuse out of one, I just . . . plug my line in this. And I got a terrific sound out of it. I still got that amplifier." However, the musicians who played with Walter over the years almost universally agree that he used many, many different amps, and seldom kept any one model for very long.

Marshall Chess remembers:

> Walter had these little shitty little fucking amps ... it was small, I don't think it was any major big amp he brought in [to the studio]. I think he went through diverse equipment. He said that he pawned shit, he got rid of it, it got stolen, he got drunk, he got another one—he had all different ones. He might've had some favorites—but I don't think he always had them with him, he lost track of 'em.

Listening to his recordings from over the years shows that there were many dramatically different versions of "the Little Walter sound," which changed noticeably on almost every recording session, due at least in part to the use of different amplifiers. It seems that he used whatever the best thing was available to him at any given time. Dave Myers reported that, early on, Walter used portable P.A. systems rather than guitar amplifiers, because he was both singing and playing through his harp setup. Portable P.A. set ups were specifically designed to accept microphone inputs, whereas most guitar amps were not. Jimmie Lee Robinson confirms this by recalling that, on local club gigs in Chicago, Walter usually would not bring an amp at all, and would sing and play through the house P.A. system. (It should be noted that a standard club P.A. system of the day usually included a "bullet"-type crystal microphone and tube amplifier, both of which would have been well-suited to Little Walter's harp sound.)

By all accounts, Walter was relatively unconcerned with his equipment; his main criteria seemed to be whether an amplifier was reliable and loud enough to fill the room, and if it fit that bill, it was good enough for him. In the final analysis, it's clear that Little Walter's sound was not the product of a "magical amp," or any other special equipment. As Billy Boy Arnold has said, "He had that Little Walter sound no matter *what* he was blowing through."

On Tuesday, October 5th, Walter was recording again. At this date, he cut the tunes for a single that would be one of his longest-lasting favorites. First off, he took another shot at the slow blues number he'd tentatively run down in July, "Last Night" The band had probably spent some time working it out in the clubs in the interim, because this time the arrangement works perfectly: It is sparse, but heavy and full of meaning. The tune opens with a gentle bass riff by Tucker, then the band and Walter come in hard. Walter's heartfelt vocal is strong and moving. Walter's lyrics now are more evocative, too; "It's early in the morning, and my love is coming down for you" conjures up an intimate, personal emotional picture that hits home. For the harp solo, he makes effective use of warbles and slow phrases, and the effect is at once laid back and intense. Ten years later, Walter told an English journalist, "I made 'Last Night' after my best friend Henry Strong got killed ... he was my best friend, so I made 'Last Night' as a tribute to him." Although the chronology was right, with the earlier version cut barely a month after Strong's death, the lyrics (other than the opening line "Last night, I lost the best friend I ever had") seem to be more about a lost lover than a lost friend. Otis Hunt, the bartender/harpist who had lost his wife to Howlin' Wolf, recalled encountering Walter in The Stadium Sports Club on the West Side one afternoon, where Hunt was working, cleaning up and waiting for the evening trade to come in. Hunt said, "He was on the bandstand, hittin' on the piano . . . he's going on 'Last night' . . . ' I said 'What is that you're doing now?' He said, 'I'm gonna make that motherfucker! . . . I'm gonna sing a couple verses for you; 'Last night I lost the best thing I ever had/now she's gone and left me / that makes me feel so sad.'" There's not much evidence of Strong in these lyrics.

Next up was "Mellow Down Easy," a Willie Dixon number, sort of a rhumba/shuffle, with prominent tom-toms by Below (reminiscent of Louis Prima's 1938 big-band tribute to "jungle rhythms," "Sing, Sing, Sing"). Lockwood tosses off some nice, subtle rising fills, and a repeating phrase that sounds like it ends with a question mark, behind Walter's vocal lines. On the harp choruses, the rhythm shifts to a fast walk as Walter takes off on a wild ride. Somebody (possibly Dixon) urges him to take another chorus: "Blow!" and he does, with a fierce tone. Then it's back to the verse and syncopated rhythms again. With its lyric "Jump jump here, jump jump there" and its infectious tempo, this was a bouncing dance number. Paired together, the lonesome blues lament of "Last Night" and the uptempo, rocking dance number "Mellow Down Easy" made for an ideal single, and they were issued on Checker #805 in a rare example of a Little Walter record with a vocal on *both* sides.

Tucker recalled that his first meeting with Leonard was at this session:

> I'd been recording with Walter for a couple of songs, then Leonard Chess walks in. He's telling Little Walter, "Yeah, do this, do that . . ." I said, "Robert Junior, who is this cat, who does he think he is?" I didn't know he was the main man. I said it pretty loud, Leonard heard me. He said, "Yeah, keep that little punk down, tell him to turn down the volume." We had a feud going . . . before he passed away we had a chance to make it up with each other . . . but when we first met it was war.

One more tune was cut that day, an untitled instrumental. Walter uses his chromatic harp on this mid-tempo number. However, although Walter does some nice jazzy blowing, once more showing his mastery of the big harp and utilizing its low octaves to nice effect, the type of strong and distinctive melody or "hook" that Chess liked was missing. Consequently, this track went unreleased until many years later, when it was issued with the catchy title "Instrumental" on a bootleg LP.

Walter's gigs at The 708 Club continued through October. *The Chicago Defender* advertised slide guitar master Elmore James ("For a limited engagement . . .") also at The 708. Texas guitarist Little Son Jackson was over at Fat Man's Corner, (provocatively advertised as featuring "Original Walter on harp, and Horse Collar on drums"). In one of the jazz clubs, the Pershing Lounge, you could catch "The exciting professional and his trio—Ahmad Jamal." Just up the street at the "Spectacularly ornate" Trianon Ballroom, ". . . with vast reaches extending into high balconies and multiple stage settings," teenage parties were advertised for Saturday nights, with 50 cent admission; adults were admitted only if accompanying kids. The ballroom had reopened in May 1954 with a new policy welcoming the black community, and the first shows were geared toward an adult R&B audience, but within a few months "Rock & Roll" artists were performing there for teen crowds.

During the fall, Chess released Muddy's "I'm Ready"; it soon entered the R&B

charts. At one point, Chess and Checker releases held down five of the top ten slots on the important *Cashbox* charts. By November 1954, Walter was off on another southern tour; the trades announced that he and Muddy Waters were touring Texas separately but would "... join forces Nov 29th for a joint tour of 16 one-nighters, ending in Dallas on Dec 14th, both then return to Chicago, their home base."

Tucker remembered good times on the road:

> The whole band, we just lived like a family. Someone didn't have some money, need some money? There'd always be some money to help go along ... Everybody look at Robert Junior like he's their dad ... he taught me how to play, how to drink, quite a few things ....Walter and I, we used to talk. I'd say "Walter, how you get all these solos?" He'd say "I just listen to the saxophone players, different pieces of the band, and just pick out parts of what they're doing—mix it with [my own] and it's a whole different style ..."

Keeping expenses down was important, and Tucker helped to fulfill a role that Walter had filled with Honeyboy Edwards and Sunnyland Slim down south ten years earlier. "We'd go get us a kitchenette, got all the pots and pans. Little Walter and Sunnyland Slim was excellent cooks—I learnt how to cook a little behind all that too. Cook us up just about anything, black-eyed peas, cornbread. I learned that, ham hocks, sweet potatoes, greens, chitlings. I didn't know how to cook nothing [when I started], it was very educational." But food wasn't the main item on Tucker's appetite list; "All I knew how to do was to try to find out from Little Walter ... what was his conversation with the women? It was very exciting ..."

Also exciting was the competition that developed to see which could "... have the most girlfriends." In Lakeview, California, at the end of a tour, it looked like Tucker was ahead:

> ... I think I had topped him. He said, "This car gotta go back to Chicago, and you gotta drive it." I said, "Oh man, I wanna party here tonight, I got me a girlfriend." He say, "Nah ... you might have a girlfriend but you ain't gonna see her tonight. You gonna drive this car back to Chicago." And he taken *my* girlfriend ... I get a girlfriend before he did, so then he make me do the detail work, like "you gotta go set up the amplifiers, you gotta drive the car someplace ..." I'd go take the car, come back, look around, it's too late. Little Walter talked me out of it.

Tucker laughed about it. "We never did have any hard feelings towards one another though, we knew exactly what was going on with each other ..."

One of the swings took the band out to the West Coast, where Walter kept up his family connections. Whenever possible, it seemed Walter would find friends to stay with rather than get a hotel room. In California, he found his first cousin Rosa Brown living in the projects. He arrived there, she fixed him dinner, and he happily stayed a couple of nights. He located his sister Lillian sharing a house in Oakland with his half-sister Marguerite, who was causing Lillian some concern. "I had smoked some herbs with some Mexican kids," Marguerite said:

> My sister told Brother Walter I was gonna rob a bank or something. He came upstairs, I thought, "Oh God, he's gonna kill me." He came in the bedroom, said he'd square it. We borrowed her husband's car—they had a Lincoln—we were going to San Francisco.

We was heading towards the bridge, the damn thing was smoking, hot as hell— finally the highway patrol is following us. My brother hand me, said "Baby, take this s—." I said, "Walter, turn your head, so I can put it in my panties." I was so messed up it wasn't funny! When he pulled us over, my brother said, "Man, I'm Little Walter, I'm going in about a gig and I'm late, blah-blah-blah . . . ." They said, "But your car is on fire!" We took the guts out of the car, the radio . . . I know they could smell the stuff in the car, because we had been smoking all the way from Oakland, the windows was up because we wanted to feel good. We went to the city, I forgot the name of the club he was gonna play in San Francisco, 'cause I was so messed up it wasn't funny—him too. When we came back . . . Lillian said to him "Did you talk to that girl?" He said, "Yes, I spoke to her." "What did she say?" "Oh," he said, "She told me the truth, she never gonna do that no more—and get caught." [Laughs] Lillian said, "I'm not gonna put up with that stuff, me and my husband gonna move." My brother was my friend.

"My brother's whole life was harmonica," she continued, "He really wanted to play tenor sax but he had the next best thing, harmonica. He could play guitar too, better than Muddy; he was gifted." Marguerite said Walter didn't do much for recreation, but she described an outing with him and the band to an amusement park:

He liked to go to amusement parks, in spite of being a grown man—he'd never had a childhood. I must've been out of my mind to get on the rollercoaster with my brother and them, we all got on the rollercoaster. I'm sitting with my brother, and I'm going out of my mind, 'cause I am so messed up. I never was a drinker, we were drinking some kind of wine, sherry? San Francisco, right on the Pacific Ocean. They had all these dummies, mannequins that was going round and round—we were just cracking up. At that particular time, my brother dressed like an artist, he had sorta like ballet shoes, slip-on, Bermuda shorts . . . very preppie. Very preppie, very *GQ*, yes. Until in the '60s when he was shot two times in his leg—and he had a hell of a complex. Guys wear these long overcoats with the swingback and the belt on it? He might wear sandals, Bermuda shorts, and one of those coats if he felt like it. He was an artist, he was weird.

While on tour in the southern states, Walter connected again with Waver Glascock, the daughter his stepfather Roosevelt had fathered by another woman before meeting Walter's mother Beatrice. She became another sometime girlfriend/road companion for Walter. Waver was ten years older than Walter and they had met when Walter passed through New Orleans when he first left home a decade earlier. Walter got her number from her daddy and called her in Marksville, where she was then living. She remembered that the band played an open-air gig in the Marksville town square one afternoon where his music had the locals, both black and white, dancing in the streets. Walter's young cousin Latelle Barton (the son of Beatrice's sister Mildred) was born after Walter left Louisiana, so this street dance was the first time Latelle met his now-famous relative. "Everybody was jumping up hollering and screaming . . . overwhelmed to see this character perform." Latelle was so impressed with the music and the reaction it got that he "swiped a harp at the back of his amp," and began a lifelong quest to recreate Walter's sound, getting some lessons from Uncle Carlton before Latelle's family moved away.

Waver says that she then joined Walter on tour and helped drive the station wagon with Walter's name emblazoned on the side for:

One-night stands all over the US. Alabama, Arizona, in Atlanta, Georgia—the motel dining area was at the entrance. Some local paper came to take pictures, Little Walter asked me to join [him] . . . the sign stated "Colored, not white"—we were told a lot thought it was for whites. I was very proud to walk onstage in Texas and hand him a hanky . . . Fort Lauderdale, Florida, was great, they had a beautiful motel. The club was just across from the "Africa In America" park, with real animals. I took a photo while straddling a cheetah, held by a couple of chains, Walter didn't like the idea, he watched.

On the package concerts, Waver recalled cheering crowds, and by the end of the show: "Black/white security lines were down—they were trying to get on stage but the front was too high."

While he was on the road, Walter's new single was again given the *Cashbox* "Award O' The Week" slot. The blurb noted that Walter was still strong with "You Better Watch Yourself," but extolled the "Slow tempo dirge-like blues 'Last Night' . . . and 'Mellow Down Easy,' a change of pace. A rhythmic jump that comes out an infectious piece of wax." One of the teenage buzz phrases of the day, heard on WGES DJ Al Benson's afternoon show in Chicago, echoed the lyric of Walter's "Mellow Down Easy": "You jump here, you jump there, you jump *everywhere!*" By early December, both sides were appearing on the regional charts; "Mellow" was hot in Atlanta and Detroit, while "Last Night" was showing action in St. Louis and New Orleans. The disk was also selling well in Buffalo, Cincinnati, Cleveland, Nashville, and Durham. Chess wasn't the only local blues label seeing chart action; Vee-Jay was hitting with Jimmy Reed, while Parrot had a hot title with J. B. Lenore (a/k/a "Lenoir").

With two weeks left to go in the 1954 *Cashbox* Magazine Reader's Poll to choose the year's favorite musicians, the editors published the vote tally so far. In the Best R&B Record category, Muddy had two titles, followed by Walter's "You're So Fine"; in the best R&B Male Artist listing, Muddy was leading by a couple thousand votes over Walter—but both were ahead of Ray Charles, Louis Jordan, and Memphis Slim. When *Cashbox* announced their final poll results, Walter came in sixth out of the 20 listed in Best Male R&B Artist 1954, garnering 39,767 votes over Muddy's 38,206; Joe Turner topped the list with 54,016. The nation's Best Record for 1954 (a category dominated by white pop music stars) was headed by Kitty Kallen's "Little Things Mean A Lot"; the only black artist mentioned there was Nat King Cole.

Besides the usual road work, the fall also featured special appearances at benefits and larger concerts. In Memphis, the first radio station to feature an all-black staff of broadcasters, WDIA, known as The Goodwill Station, announced their 6th annual Good Will Revue to be held December 3rd at the Ellis Auditorium. The previous year's show, a 1953 benefit for crippled Negro children, drew 6,000 attendees and raised nearly $7,000. Besides gospel groups The Spirits Of Memphis and The Southern Wonders, others billed included Big John Greer, Little Walter, and Muddy Waters. While on the road in Florida, Junior Wells again left Muddy's band; in Memphis, Muddy picked up his replacement, James Cotton, who'd spent time as a lad following Rice Miller (a/k/a Sonny Boy Williamson II) around.

1955 started off with an item in the trades noting that "Checker artist Little Walter reportedly has just been released from Mt. Sinai Hospital, where he has been since Xmas morning. Seems he was rushed into the hospital a very sick man. Walter is now at home recuperating . . ." Over the years, various explanations of this incident have cropped up. Drummer Sam Lay, who a few years later would room and play with Walter, heard a story about Walter taking a vicious beating at the hands of the Chicago police, and attributes some of Walter's prominent facial scars to the incident. "I didn't witness that, but I knowed about it," Lay says. "Plain clothes detectives, the way they did him, the top of a fire hydrant, where you put a wrench to turn it on? That's where he hit [him,] right on top of a fire hydrant." Another version of this "police beating" story that made the rounds had Walter being discovered unconscious in a vacant lot, and being transported to the hospital by the one person who seems to have been a constant source of stability in his life, Muddy Waters.

Dave Myers has firsthand knowledge of an incident which, if not the same event, tells of a disturbing pattern beginning to emerge in Walter's life. Myers was driving home one night when he saw what looked like Walter's car, parked on Indiana Avenue near the Hollywood Rendezvous Club on the south side. "The damn car was just sitting right in the damn street, in my path. I had to go over and see if I could find anything going on wrong with the car." A lady who lived in the building in front of which the car was parked was standing on the sidewalk. She told Dave, "I tried to stop them . . . they left just before you pulled up," and told Myers that the cops had beaten Walter. Dave saw the passenger side door hanging open, and looked in and saw Walter laid out on the seat, ". . . just covered with blood, oh man, they beat him badly, something like terrible. They beat him with those billy clubs across the head, back, everywhere—that cut him up like that." Dave thought that this is how Walter got the prominent scar on his forehead. "They was hitting against that hard-rock bone on his head, they hit him with so much pressure it just splits it wide open . . . I had to move as fast as I could to get him to the hospital. I went and got another fella to call [Walter's] old lady for me while I stayed by him. I already called the fire department, they came right away." He was taken to nearby Michael Reese Hospital, where Armilee Thompson, Walter's girlfriend at the time, met Dave while Walter was treated in the emergency room.

Later, Armilee told Dave that the doctor had told Walter he had to be very careful; he'd been permanently damaged, and wouldn't survive another blow to the head. (Dave later felt that this beating, coming soon on the heels of the one Walter had taken outside the Zanzibar, was a contributing cause to Walter's demise—after yet another beating.) Walter was conspicuously absent for several weeks from the weekly ads in the *Defender* for the 708 Club, where Muddy was now alternating with The Four Aces Combo (which Louis and Dave Myers had reformed after leaving Walter). Muddy was also playing weekend gigs at Silvio's with his "Hoochie Koochie Boys."

On Tuesday, January 25th, Walter was back in the recording studio. Great things were to come of this session, by way of a hit record. Robert Lockwood says he did double duty, overdubbing Tucker's bass guitar parts as well as playing lead on the two-song session. "We couldn't find Tucker that day," Lockwood said. "I don't know where the hell Tucker was. I played the session by myself . . . me, Willie Dixon, and Below. Dixon was playing bass, but you couldn't hardly hear what he was doing—that happened all the time." (Because the "lead" guitar drops out completely and only the drums and bass guitar can he heard at one point during the session, it seems likely that Lockwood actually played the bass guitar line live along with the band first, then came back and over overdubbed the "lead" later.) An instrumental was the first number completed; titled "ThunderBird" (after either the cheap wine, the sporty new Ford model that had just debuted, or maybe both), it's a jaunty number with an easy swinging drive to it, with a nice if not a particularly memorable melody hook. Walter takes three choruses on diatonic harp, then switches to his big chromatic to finish out the piece with a steady rock.

Following was another stab at the Dixon gospel takeoff, "My Babe," which Walter had tried six months previously without much enthusiasm. Dixon later said:

> I had been trying to give Little Walter "My Babe" because of his style of doing things but it took him damn near two years to record it. I felt [he] had the feeling for this song. He was the type of fellow that wanted to brag about some chick, somebody he loved, something he was doing or getting away with. He fought it for two long years and I wasn't going to give the song to nobody but him. He said many times he just didn't like it, but by 1955, the Chess people had gained enough confidence in me that they felt if I wanted him to do it, it must be his type of thing. The minute he did it, *boom*! it went right to the top of the charts.

The session files tell an interesting story. If the master numbers are to be believed, Dixon took part in a gospel session with pianist Reverend Ballinger immediately preceding Walter's recordings that day. One of the two tracks cut was "This Train," the gospel standard that is the direct source for Dixon's chorus, rhythm, and melody for "My Babe." When Walter's crew took over the studio, the files list four unissued titles attempted before "ThunderBird" was cut and deemed acceptable. Chess needed a vocal number for the flip side, so Dixon again pressed his tune, this time suggesting a bouncier arrangement, closer to the spiritual in feel than the one-chord version that they'd previously attempted. (Below later told a British journalist it was he who arranged it, and after his version was played for Leonard over the phone, Chess decided to record it the next day.) This new arrangement was the charm, although according to Waver Glascock, it was a bit arduous task to complete it. "I was at the studio all night when Walter decided he wasn't leaving until he recorded "My Babe" right for the hit, and he made it." From the opening drum hit and walking bass guitar line, the tune has "hit" written all over it. Walter sings with energy and conviction, and his lively, swinging two-chorus harp solo is a nice controlled power surge. The riff seems to get catchier as it rolls on, and it's another built-for-dancing number that would be heard on radio and jukeboxes for some time to come.

A week later, Walter was back in the studios, for a Muddy Waters session. Three tunes by Dixon were recorded. "This Pain" came first, a melodramatic and rather ponderous slow blues, featuring plonking bass, plodding drums, and sparse band backup. Walter's harp shadows Muddy's vocals closely but nonetheless the number drags, and never develops much excitement. "Young Fashioned Ways" fares better. Played at a sprightly tempo, it has nice piano-harp interplay. Finally, "I Want To Be Loved," after a plodding early take on which Walter tries out some third position harp licks, eventually came together as a swinger with stop-start rhythm. He offers a simple but effective solo, then afterwards drops back into the mix. The last of Muddy's cuts, "My

Eyes (Keep Me In Trouble)" was credited to Herbert Walker again. Walter starts out playing 1st position harp in the key of "C" up to his break, where he switches to the chromatic to take a truncated, somewhat awkward ride, dropping out completely for the last four bars of the solo section.

After Muddy's songs were recorded, Jimmy Rogers again stepped to the mike, to take his first stab at the number that would ultimately be his next hit, "You're The One." The piano is prominent throughout, and Walter solos with long swooping notes for the first chorus, and chopping chords and bursts of short phrases on the second. Although it is a seemingly solid performance from Jimmy and, as usual, an entirely unique and original offering from Walter, it went unissued at the time.

Meanwhile, Walter continued to take a devil-may-care approach to his life and career. Bobby Rush, today a successful soul-blues singer with several bawdy classics to his credit, took up the harp in the '50s, inspired by Walter. Rush recalled an adventure they shared, similar to a tale told by Eddie Burks. "I lived on Troy, and he lived on Albany, which was right behind me," Rush said:

> Walter said, "I got a gig in Waukegan, come go with me." He had a Cadillac, Chess I guess bought him a Cadillac. Old car, but it was a Cadillac. We goes out to Waukegan. He got a little amplifier, took an amplifier himself . . . I think Tucker was playing on guitar, Below I think was on drums, three pieces . . . So there's about eight or ten ladies in the bar. Walter's setting the bar up, he just bought 'em all . . . if I had $5, I had a lot of money, Walter must have spent $25. At the time beer cost 25 cents, it wasn't much. Walter told me, "Hey blood, come with me, I got to go get some more money." I said, "Get you some more money? How you gonna get some more money?" He went to the trunk, he raised the trunk—this is God's truth—the trunk was full of money! But in nothing, just [loose] in the trunk . . . every time he go to close the trunk, it go whoosh! dollars flying, he had to pack it down. Believe me, I thought he was a millionaire! Looking back now, it was five dollars [bills], one dollar bills, maybe a few tens—it couldn't have been more than a thousand dollars but it looked like a million to me, all up in the trunk.
>
> Apparently Walter couldn't count well, because he'd grab his money. He'd never count it, just get it and stuff it in his pocket. He probably had $30, $40, just in ones. He said, "Get you some . . . blood, get you a handful." I didn't want to be greedy, I must have got $18, $20 in ones. We goes back in, now I got money to spend! What impressed me, I said whatever I do as a young man, I'm gonna play harp . . . I never saw this kind of money before in my life! Walter was rich to me. Trunk full of money? He was rich. So I've been trying to get a trunk full of money ever since with the harp . . .

During February and March, Walter played at the popular blues hot spot, The Zanzibar, advertised as "The best in blues five nights a week at the West Side's most beautiful Zanzibar." Beginning in March, radio disk jockey Big Bill Hill hosted regular Tuesday night live broadcasts from the club on WOPA from 10:30 to 11:00 PM. Wednesdays featured "The Howlin' Wolf and his 'Evil Going On' combo," while Walter and his Jukes held down the Thursday through Sunday slot. It was another long-hours gig, running from 9:00 PM to 4:00 AM. Willie Foster, who'd gone to school with Jimmy Reed in Mississippi, wound up at The Zanzibar after migrating to Chicago to work the railroad. "I went in and listened to him," Foster said. "Me and him got to be friends. Nobody ever taught me [harp], Little Walter told me, 'You do

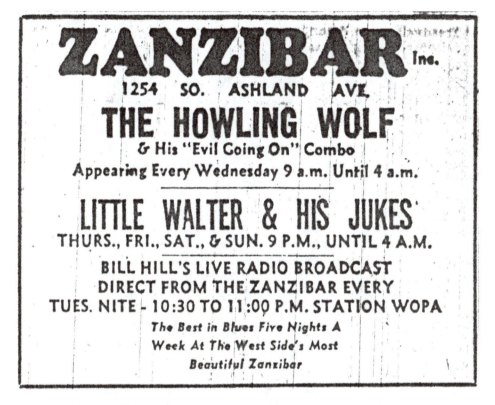

Figure 9.1 Zanzibar Club advertisement, *Chicago Defender*, February 26, 1955.

good, but you got to learn timing.'" Eventually Foster was skilled enough to feel he was ready to sit in with the band:

> Walter told me, "I don't need you on my show unless I go and get me a woman." I said, okay. He'd say, "I'm gonna turn it over to Mr. Foster," then I'd play with Robert Lockwood Jr. That weekend I quit [the railroad], I was supposed to go back up there and play with Little Walter. But I knew he got it sewed up there with harp. So I said all right, I'm going back to Detroit and get me a band.

Although up-and-coming harp player Billy Boy Arnold also recognized Little Walter's supremacy among harp players, he decided he'd take his chances at a career playing blues locally. The 19-year-old had earlier auditioned for Phil Chess. Chess had wanted to hear a few songs, so Billy pulled out his harp right there in the stockroom and sang and played a couple of solo numbers. Phil told him, "Well, I can't use you right now, but if you get anything else come in and see me." A few months later Arnold, who'd been working some small gigs with Bo Diddley (then still known as Ellas McDaniel), got Bo to cut a few tracks of their group on his home disk recorder. They used the disk as a demo for United Records, and rehearsed there for a week. They were finally told they were welcome to record for the label, but that they wouldn't be paid.

So, they left and went over to Vee-Jay Records, where a secretary on her way to lunch listened to their record ". . . for about a second." She said she didn't like that kind of music, and walked out of the office. Undaunted, Arnold headed across the street to Chess Records, where he came across Walter at the counter, packing some mail-order boxes for Leonard, who'd run up to the bank. Walter recognized Bo and Arnold from the clubs, and perhaps saw them as potential rivals; he told Arnold, "Well, we don't need nothing right now." At that moment Phil came out from the back, and recognized Arnold from the audition. They talked, Phil put their demo dub of "I'm A Man" on the turntable, and was impressed by the compelling beat and the strong, macho lyrics—a hallmark of some of the label's most successful recordings by Muddy Waters. He asked the guys to come back at 2:00 the next day with their equipment, saying, "I want Leonard to hear this."

The group came in the next day, set up in the back-room studio, and ran down their repertoire for Leonard, who listened, nodding his head. He liked the sound of their ribald novelty song "Dirty Mother For Ya," a/k/a "Hey Noxema." Arnold recalls, "Leonard kept telling Bo to give him more tremolo, he had an acoustic guitar with a pickup on it, Leonard say, 'Turn it up, give me more of that.'" But the risque lyrics were a problem; Arnold says he suggested using the phrase "Bo Diddley" instead, and they came up with a couple of new, less racy verses as they jammed on the number in the studio. Chess liked it so well he wound up christening Ellas with the name "Bo Diddley" on the record's release.

As the group rehearsed in the back-room studio for a couple of days in preparation for their official recording session, visitors and other Chess artists dropped by from time to time. "Muddy Waters came by and heard 'I'm A Man'; he wanted that," Arnold said. "[Muddy said,] 'Man I like that, I want that—man that's great!' [Muddy recorded his own version as "Mannish Boy" a couple of months later.] And Little Walter liked 'You Don't Love Me,' and we had another called 'Little Grenadier' [eventually issued as 'Little Girl'], Bo wrote it after a waitress at the club [The Sawdust Trail], that's where [Walter's] 'Roller Coaster' came from." A few days later, on May 2nd, the group cut four titles downtown at Universal Studios, augmented by pianist Otis Spann, who was pulled off a Muddy Waters gig at The 708 Club. Chess may have noticed the difference in sound quality between the studios, or maybe the Cottage Grove site was already booked for another session; at any rate, he decided to pay the hourly rate downtown. After Bo cut four titles, Arnold pushed to do his own vocal numbers. Leonard okayed it, and a few tracks were cut, but were shelved at the time.

By mid-March, Walter's "My Babe" arrived on the market, and it soon began a steady climb into the charts where it would hold sway for some time, eventually becoming his second #1 single. A trade column item noted that "Little Walter, whose 'My Babe' is heading for the top, leaves April 1 for a southern junket, to be gone it is said indefinitely."

While Waver Glascock was still visiting in Chicago that March, Walter showed her his old haunts, introduced her to his ex, Ella Mae, and took her to dinner with Leonard. "Walter took me around Chicago like a child," Waver related. "He showed me how he had to make a living to survive, before he got to playing with Muddy Waters. He had a room which faced the streets in Jewtown, he connected his amp inside the room and dropped the cord out the window, to play for hours on the street." Waver thought that "Many disliked Walter because he did try to be a gentleman, he dressed well for stage, tried to look good . . . Walter was kindhearted, he once said, 'I believe in God, although I don't sit in church.'" Waver said she fed him well. "Walter didn't drink hard the first year I was there, because I cooked and he ate more than drank, [though] we drank Coffee Royale together," a drink made by soaking a sugar cube in brandy, lighting it on fire, and then dropping it into a cup of coffee. Waver also said she influenced Walter's appearance: "We had a gold star cap put on the very same front tooth, I had mine first, his after." Waver also recalled, without apparent rancor, another of Walter's women, Armilee, spending ". . . days with Walter, in my home."

Early in April, Bo Diddley's first single was released on Checker, and the new sound caught the ear of DJs and kids across the country, selling in both black and white markets. Walter was due to hit the road soon, so Chess called another session for Thursday, April 28th, to get some more material in the can. The three-song session began with a roaring instrumental, "Roller Coaster," one of two tunes Arnold recalled as being inspired by one that he and Bo had been playing, this one eventually called "Little Girl." There is some melodic resemblance at the outset, but "Roller Coaster" surges with a fiery intensity absent from the Diddley tune. Bo was deputized to play guitar on the session. Arnold says:

> They went round to Bo's house, right around the corner at 48th and Langley, in the basement—Chess was at 48th & Cottage—and got Bo to play with Tucker and Little Walter's band. Bo told me they got him to record with Little Walter, he said Walter played a thing—he didn't know the name of it, but he was really blowing on it.

That's a bit of an understatement: Walter is all over the harp, playing with an almost wild abandon, even by his standards. He seems more determined here than ever before to distance himself from the pack, to let the world know that his music was never going to stand still. Maybe he was beginning to feel the up and coming rock and rollers nipping at his heels; maybe he wanted to put all of the other blues harp players in their place; maybe he just got a good night's sleep for once. Whatever the motivation, the drive and determination that had pushed him to never retrace his musical steps, to always create something new, surprising, or outrageously different, is never more evident than here.

Walter begins by closely following Bo's opening guitar figure, and then almost immediately launches into a dizzying cavalcade of improvisations of odd and varying lengths, mixing melodies, time signatures, and accents, all reeled out one after another with scarcely a beat in between to breathe. Amazingly, he's able to knit it all into a cohesive piece—although it may have seemed more "together" to jazz than to blues fans of the day, because this type of freedom of melody, phrasing, and timing was almost without precedent in the blues world. Jazz buffs hear the influence of Illinois Jacquet's groundbreaking tenor solo in Lionel Hampton's "Flying Home" from 1947 as the source of inspiration for some of Walter's cascading riffs in "Roller Coaster." The simplicity of the backing allows Walter's tight and tasty phrases to dance and drive over the single-chord

Figure 9.2 Rock 'n' Roll Revue advertisement, *Boston Daily Globe*, May 19, 1955.

rhythm, which builds in intensity. The title is more than apt, because the piece captures the climb, rush, and breathless excitement of a rollercoaster. Fred Below urges Walter on with some fine stick work, keeping the drive solid.

Drums also are an integral part of the mix on the flip side, "I Got To Go," an uptempo rocker reminiscent of the earlier "Tell Me Mama," but given an added urgency by Walter's third-position playing. His playing of minor key scales over the major chord guitar backing adds a tension and energy to the piece. The third number from this session was "Hate To See You Go," another song that had begun life in Bo Diddley's repertoire under a different title. Walter didn't care about Bo's words, but he liked the driving groove and Bo's distinctive guitar sound, so Bo played on this one as well. The song is another insistent one-chord pressure cooker, with a guitar figure and melody lifted directly from Bo's "You Don't Love Me," which Bo had cut at his debut session in March; here he duplicates his descending guitar "hook" line. (Chess obligingly held up Bo's song until long after Walter's single was released, eventually including it as an album-only track on the second Bo Diddley album, *Go Bo Diddley*, in 1958.) In Walter's hands, the tune is a stomping rocker, with his harp just at the edge of feeding back, and the band pounding out the rhythm. Chess faded the take for maximum impact, and the result is a textbook example of just how rocking blues could be.

"I Got To Go" and "Roller Coaster" were paired up for Walter's next single release. "Hate To See You Go," as the odd-numbered cut from this session, was slated for the followup single, to be paired with "Too Late," a strong leftover from the marathon session recorded over a year earlier.

After the session, Walter probably just left his equipment in the car and hit the road immediately, headed for the East Coast. The following day, April 29th, Philadelphia radio DJ George Woods was heading a big show. The lineup included Vanetta Dillard, Gene and Eunice, Little Walter, and The Buddy Johnson Orchestra. Also announced, for late May, was an Alan Freed Rock & Roll Show, which had just completed a successful Easter-week stint at the Paramount Theater in Brooklyn. The show was scheduled first into Boston's Loews Theater, then would move on to Providence, with negotiations underway to bring the package to New York City and the downtown Paramount. It was a savvy, commercial mix of old and new acts, with Freed combining established artists who already appealed to an older crowd with doo-wop vocal groups for youngsters. As icing on the cake, he added the hip new beat of the urban blues that was capturing radio airwaves in Chicago and across the country, choosing Chess artists Bo Diddley and Little Walter, two of the label's best sellers, who would both add to the teenage appeal.

On May 10th, Bo Diddley was back in studio for a followup recording session. The group had been performing one of Arnold's tunes, "Diddley Daddy"; Leonard heard Arnold sing it on a show they did with Ruth Brown at Chicago's Trianon Ballroom, and wanted Bo to cut it for his next single. Meanwhile, Arnold had gotten the idea that Chess wasn't interested in him, so he took his tune to Vee-Jay, where it was reworked and recast with different lyrics as "I Wish You Would." In fact, he had been at Universal Studios recording it for Vee-Jay the previous day. The next day Arnold went to Bo's Chess session. "Bo started to play 'Diddley Daddy,'" Leonard said 'Hold it, hold it, let Billy sing it,'" Arnold said. "But I had a contract from Vee Jay in my pocket, a recording contract and a songwriter's contract. I said 'I can't do it . . . I just recorded it for Vee-Jay.' I showed him the contract, he said, 'Goddam! Ain't this a bitch!'"

Chess suggested they come up with some new words to it. The Moonglows were in the studio for their own Chess session, and Billy Boy remembers, "Harvey Fuqua and the other guys said 'We'll write some lyrics,' so they started writing right on the spot. I was young, I didn't realize I could've done both versions, I was under contract." Little Walter had also stopped by that day, and although he wasn't scheduled to be on the session, "He said, 'Man, lemme use your harp,' so he used my cheap little $35 amplifier and harp, The Moonglows sang the background—just one of those spur of the moment things." Walter takes a distinctive solo, holding a long, swooping note before launching into a swinging improvisation for one chorus over the single-chord backing vamp.

Later, Arnold heard Walter back in the office, talking to Bo about Billy Boy's apparent abandonment of Bo's band to go across the street to Vee-Jay: "If that was me and he did me like that I'd tell him to hit the goddam road!' He was kinda jealous . . . he didn't want a young punk coming up might give him a little competition," he laughed. Arnold did stick around to play on the second Bo Diddley tune cut that day, "She's Fine, She's Mine." As it turned out, it would be the last time he recorded with Bo for Chess, although he did another two or three live gigs before Bo replaced him.

On a southern tour, Arnold noticed how some people down South didn't care much for gut-bucket blues, preferring Fats Domino, Smiley Lewis, or Lloyd Price instead. Nonetheless, in more rural areas, Walter was still the king. "We went to a joint in Houma, Louisiana, just 50 miles out of New Orleans. Bo Diddley sung, the people just stood there and looked at us. Then Howlin' Wolf went up, pulled all his tactics, running through the crowd, crawling around—they looked at him like he was crazy," he laughs. "But Walter was it, that's why he played all over the south."

The market for R&B was growing steadily, aided by a new generation of white youths who were the original "crossover" market, as they ventured into the black areas of their towns, looking for the latest releases. It was a restless time in America, and teenagers were for the first time beginning to get a sense of themselves as individuals, rather than as just adults-in-training—and they weren't all ready to step into the gray-flannel suit routine of their parents. Besides movies starring such individualist/rebel role models as Marlon Brando and James Dean, who gave them a new image to emulate, the search for individuality spread to their music. And if that music happened to go against the grain of their parents' ideals, all the better. In the urban markets, youngsters who were sick of show tunes or novelty numbers like "How Much Is That Doggie In The Window" were turning to the new breed of DJs who played R&B vocal groups as well as jump bands and the new urban blues styles. But the majority of the country's radio markets were dominated by "Your Hit Parade"-type programming, where the top ten pop numbers rotated endlessly, or else polka or country & western records were played between farm shows with cattle prices. At night, young people looking for something else—anything else!—trolled the far reaches of the radio dial, listening through static and rising and falling signals, trying to find something they hoped was out there. Then one lucky night, bingo: They might pick up a clear channel station like WLAC at 1510 AM from Nashville Tennessee, where an R&B show started at 10:00 PM, sponsored by Stan's Record Shop, 728 Texas Street, Shreveport, Louisiana, an address burned into the memory of every early R&B fan. They sold mail-order record packages; there was the gospel package, the doo-wop package, the down-home package, each featuring five or six current titles. Living in a small nowhere town, you could order either 78s or the new 45 RPM size disks ("The big ones with the little hole, or the little ones with the big hole in the middle"), send off a money order, and wait impatiently for the mailman to deliver this "care package" from a far-away, exotic, exciting new world.

On this show on WLAC, or a similar one sponsored by Randy's Record Mart in Nashville, many future blues fans—and players—got their first taste of Muddy Waters, Howlin' Wolf, and Little Walter, mixed in with the latest from Fats Domino, Bill Dogget, and the raunch of The Midnighters. Or they may have come across the even more bizarre and exotic-sounding radio station XERF, broadcasting from Ciudad Acuna, Coahulia, Mexico, across the border from Del Rio, Texas. It had more broadcasting power than the FCC would allow U.S. radio stations to use (250,000 watts); at night their signal carried all the way into Canada! The R&B shows on XERF radio were presided over by one Dr. Jazzmo, a shouting, babbling, jive-talking, snake-oil salesman. In between playing John Lee Hooker and Bo Diddley sides, Jazzmo offered up for sale tablecloths with Last Supper paintings that glowed in the dark, or a passel of live chicks so you could start your own "profitable egg business." His finest moment may have occurred when he did a spiel for an army surplus outlet, as he ranted, "You need a jeep? We got jeeps! You need a typewriter? We got thousands of 'em! You need a battleship? Jesus Christ, we got that too!" Not long after that, he disappeared from the air, and was eventually replaced by a more manufactured character, Wolfman Jack (whose on-air shtick was based on imitating the speaking voice of blues man Howlin' Wolf).

In May, youngsters listening to Symphony Sid's WBMS broadcasts in Boston heard about a big R&B show coming to town, put together with fellow DJ Alan Freed. The bill again mixed acts that appealed to both young and older R&B fans, with the revue taking the stage at Loews State Theater between showings of the Zachary Scott western *Treasure of Ruby Hills*. Dinah Washington topped the bill, followed by "Little Walter and Quintette" [sic], vocal groups The Five Keys and The Moonglows, Bo Diddley, and songsters Al Hibbler, Dakota Staton, and Nappy Brown. The singers were accompanied by Buddy and Ella Johnson's Orchestra, who had a recent hit with a tune that probably first caught Walter's ear here, and which he'd later appropriate as his own, called "Just Your Fool." The weeklong stand opened on Friday, May 20th, with a special midnight show added. It drew a mostly black crowd, which a reporter from the *Boston Daily* figured was 90% teenagers, while noting that "It's this group that's pushing this form of entertainment high up on the pay-off ladder."

The *Daily* gave a full description of the one-hour concert. It began with Symphony Sid introducing the Buddy Johnson band, who kicked things off with their rousing "Crazy About A Saxophone." The show continued with Dinah Washington, who sang two slow blues, then rocked the house with her big number "Such A Night." Blind Al Hibbler scored with his "Hit Parade" number, "Unchained Melody," then "voluptuous" Dakota Staton sang a slow blues, following it with her hit "My Heart's Desire," dancing ". . . a provocative boogie woogie" as the crowd clapped to the beat. Alan Freed then took over as emcee and introduced the vocal groups he'd been featuring on his New

York City radio shows, The Five Keys and The Moonglows. It was a fast-paced show, each act only getting in three or four numbers, and usually closing with their current record release. Freed worked the crowd, building the momentum as the show moved along. The Buddy Johnson band finished a number with a powerful flourish of horns, then the stage went dark as the musicians took their seats. Over on the right corner of the stage, four men strode onto the stage and picked up their instruments. The shift from big band to small combo signified that something different was about to happen, and, as a spotlight picked out the group, Freed shouted out, "Lets hear it for Little Walter and His Jukes!"

The audience was on their feet clapping as the group launched into "Juke," the guitar and drum combo a vital and driving new sound behind Walter's soaring, roaring harp. Walter was sharp as usual; Waver recalled proudly how handsome he looked in the lights as the crowd cheered. He'd got a new, light-colored suit that made him stand out in the spotlight, two-toned wingtips, and his hair was newly processed and slicked into a wavy pompadour. Walter rocked slowly back and forth as he played, his shoulders slightly weaving in time to the music. A large diamond ring glittered as he cupped the harp and mike with his large hands, his eyes darting from side to side, blinking continually against the spotlight. If Walter was tempted to hide behind the harp, the enthusiastic crowd response buoyed him up. As he played, people were up and dancing in their rows of seats; Walter's harp was horn-like, its disproportionately huge sound filling the room with a cascade of ringing notes, Below's drums punctuating and driving the guitars of Tucker and Lockwood. After a couple more numbers, probably including the hopping new number "Mellow Down Easy," Walter glanced into the wings and saw Freed giving him the wrap-it-up signal, and so he closed with "My Babe," still hot on the charts and quickly becoming his signature number. The infectious, swinging riff brought the last of the seated audience members out of their seats and dancing, the more reserved ones tapping their toes or clapping along with the beat. And as Tucker and Lockwood sang the closing reply chorus "True little baby . . ." the number ended to fervent applause. Walter had captured the audience with electricity, both in the unique new sound of his combo and the sizzle and crackle of his playing. As he left the stage, the applause continued.

Next, a striking pink-suited, bespectacled figure strolled out: Ellas McDaniel, introduced to the crowd as Bo Diddley, backed on this tour by Walter's Jukes. His self-titled hit record had been getting a lot of radio airplay, and the audience responded immediately to his shimmering, pulsating guitar rhythms. Veterans like Lockwood knew it as the "hambone" beat, but played through a full-blast amplifier it had a hypnotic effect, and the whole crowd was shaking to Bo's "strange tempo and almost calypso rhythm." The write-up ends ". . . it's a new experience at the State for those who don't know what kind of music it is. With a week long engagement coming up, it appears that more devotees will be made."

Although Walter may have felt his star was still rising, it wasn't long before the trades were noting ". . . Bo Diddley reportedly stealing the show at his very successful engagement at Loews State Theater Boston, with the Moonglows and Little Walter also on the bill." Soon Freed was referring to the revue as the "Diddley Daddy" package show.

The summer of 1955 was when the teenage market made itself felt in a big way as it snapped up Bo's new release, hits like Bill Haley's "Rock Around The Clock," as well as Chuck Berry's "Maybelline," another back-room effort from the Chess brothers' Cottage Grove studio. If Elvis had caused a stir by being a white man doing black music, then Berry had now completed the circle; his number was based on an old country & western number, "Ida Red." Suddenly, the entire record industry was turning its attention towards this new market, and all their potential pocket change. Walter's "Roller Coaster" still did well, as did Muddy's "Mannish Boy," which reached #9 on the R&B charts. But it was obvious to anyone paying attention that change was in the air.

On July 14, another lucky Thursday, Walter and his band, along with Willie Dixon, were back in the studio, going for another hit. Dixon's hit-making ability had been duly noted by Leonard, and he was now on staff as a songwriter/A&R man/supervisor of blues sessions, in addition to his bass-playing duties. Leonard had a continual need for new releases from his high-profile artists, and scheduled sessions for them whether or not they had come up with new material. If they hadn't, Dixon could be counted on to step in with an original number or two—or more—which he could quickly work up with the band, and coach them through on the session. This session appears to have been one on which Walter had not brought in much in the way of tried-and-tested-on-the-bandstand material, and Dixon was ready and able to supply some new songs.

The three-song session kicked off with a filigreed guitar figure from Lockwood, which laconically opened the slow-blues ballad "Little Girl," while Tucker held down the walking bass line, doubling a barely audible Willie Dixon. Walter's singing is confident, as is his harp playing. "Crazy For My Baby," another Dixon tune, has Walter using chromatic harp on a stop-time arrangement, which stays on the "one" chord through the verses, the band playing standard blues changes only on the chorus. During the second chorus of Walter's break, somebody had a conversation, which leaked onto the track and can be heard on the released single. The third song, "Can't Stop Loving You," is an uptempo shuffle. "I can't stop worrying, 'cause you driving me insane," Walter sings before a heavily echoed harp solo. Again the band is stellar, although Walter's unfamiliarity with the lyrics is clear as he rambles his way through them with little attention paid to phrasing or timing. Things get more interesting when he puts the harp to his lips, and he tosses off a solid solo, reaching into his seemingly bottomless well of original ideas and phrases for something which, as was his trademark, he'd never played before and never would again. But a solid solo doesn't sound so impressive when compared to the dazzling work on some of his other records, and by itself it certainly doesn't make a hit record. Ultimately the only tune officially issued from the session would be "Crazy For My Baby," and that not until six years later.

Walter continued gigging in the Chicago clubs, but he was beginning to be spoiled by the easy workload of the four-song sets he was playing on the package shows. He often took the opportunity to lay back when playing on his home turf, letting other harp players sit in and fill out the sets. Tucker wasn't too happy when that happened; "Leon Brooks, he used to come around us all the time . . . great heavy harmonica blower. Little Walter would get down [from the stage], let a few harmonica blowers come up and blow with the band. I hated it, because by me just first starting with the band, I didn't know the songs, they playing some things I didn't know nothing about. Robert Junior say, 'You better learn it, 'cause it's gonna come in handy further on up the road,'" Tucker said.

But it was more fun when Walter Horton showed up. Tucker fondly recalled:

There used to be quite an argument every time [they] get together. Little Walter be blowing, Walter Horton come along, [and say] "Hey man, what you doing blowing my number?" Little Walter'd say, "Hey man, that's my number, don't nobody know that but me"... they always carried on like that. Horton get out his harmonica, say "Yeah, this is the way it goes," started blowing. Walter get out his harmonica, say "Nah, it don't go that way, it go this way" ... and they'd just start blowing with each other. It'd be a dynamite show! They was just being friendly and funny with each other—it was great, some beautiful people.

Meanwhile, Billy Boy Arnold's career was taking off with Vee-Jay Records, and the label had bankrolled him for a P.A. system and connected him with the Shaw agency. The agency booked him into a brand-new club run by an ex-prize fighter, Kid Rivera's Barrelhouse Lounge on the South Side. Walter was scheduled to open the club on Wednesday and Thursday nights, with Billy Boy and his new band coming in for the first weekend. DJ Sam Evans had been promoting the gigs on his radio program, playing Billy Boy's and Walter's records back to back; Arnold was a bit nervous, and Walter didn't see any reason to make things any easier for his young competitor. As Arnold was setting up his P.A. on his opening night, Kid Rivera came in and said, "Well, I'll tell you one thing—you look first class! But Little Walter told me your band wasn't hitting on too much." But when the band hit the stage, they were playing loud and the people liked it—and the group ended up playing the club for three months, getting union-scale wages, "Pretty good," Arnold thought, "... 'cause Muddy wasn't getting no more than scale, and he had a hit out." When that gig eventually ended, Arnold moved over to Ricky's Show Lounge, which had formerly been known as The Hollywood Rendezvous, Walter's old mainstay spot.

In August, there was another new competitor in Chicago. Rice Miller, now going full bore under the name "Sonny Boy Williamson," recorded his first session for Chess, backed up by Muddy's band. One of the numbers cut, "Good Evening Everybody," was a thinly disguised remake of his old King Biscuit radio show theme song. But the standout tune was "Don't Start Me Talking," which became an extended ribald workout on club gigs, where Sonny Boy would roam the audience, teasing women by lifting their skirts, and jiving with the men. The single was released in September and was an instant mover for the label.

Another blues veteran turned up in Chicago: John Lee Hooker came in from Detroit for an October session at Vee-Jay, his first to actually take place in the Windy City. Walter met Hooker's train decked out in camel's hair coat, snap brim hat, and gold jewelry. After a round of club hopping they wound up parked on Cottage Grove, on the trolley tracks in the middle of the intersection. Walter told Hooker not to worry about it, he could do what he wanted, because "this was Chicago."

James Cotton was feeling more than a little constrained in his role as Muddy's harpman. "He was used to hearing whatever he knowed, and if it was anything new he was scared to stretch out on it," Cotton said of Muddy. "I had to play those solos Walter made for Muddy note for note! And that kept me kinda restricted 'cause I had to play this thing night after night, every night." Muddy later told his young guitarist Bob Margolin that he was looking for harp players to "hold up" his voice, like Walter used to do, playing a warble behind Muddy's singing, then answering it with a phrase. "Muddy loved that warble, he'd say 'shake that harp' to a harp player sitting in, and the guy wouldn't know what he was talking about—so he'd just stand there, holding the harp in his hand, shaking it."

When Cotton came to Chicago for the first time to play with Muddy, he felt like a country boy, out of his element and unsure of what to do. He would go along to Muddy's sessions and watch while Walter recorded in his stead; Cotton's role was confined to bringing water and whiskey for the band, and waiting for his chance. "I played like Sonny Boy when I got in Muddy's band," Cotton explained. "Walter made the harp swing, I asked him how did he do it. I figured since I was playing in the band and he was recording with Muddy and I would have to play his parts, he would kind of help me out." As he'd proven with Billy Boy, Walter wasn't interested in helping out the competition. "He put the harp in his mouth, turned his back to me and did it. So I never did ask him anything else," Cotton relates.

Muddy was a little more encouraging; on one occasion he and Cotton heard Walter blowing some chromatic harp in a club. "He left it on the bandstand, and I picked it up and played it," Cotton said. "Muddy didn't say one word to me. The next night he walked through the door with a chromatic harp in his hand." Muddy's gift of the more expensive harmonica to Cotton showed how much he wanted to replicate Walter's sound.

In November, Muddy was back in the studios for a four-song session. Walter is listed as harpman of record, but his casual attitude may have been catching up with him. Some of the playing isn't up to his usual sharpness, and that, coupled with subsequent claims by Cotton that he played on these recordings in Walter's place, has left some questions as to the true identity of the harp player. According to Cotton, Walter never showed up at the appointed time because he was drunk: "Muddy told Chess, 'My harp player is over there. He ain't no Little Walter but I'd like to go over the songs.' Chess put us in a back room and we started playing 'Trouble No More.' They heard it and said, 'Bring that in here.' We recorded that, 'Flip Flop' and 'Sugar Sweet.' That song came out and hit, that's what got me into recording with Muddy." But the aural evidence suggests otherwise; it's likely that Muddy had performed these songs with Cotton prior to the session, and possible Chess may have recorded a demo session in the back room studio with Cotton on it, but the harmonica player on the released tracks is almost certainly Walter. The tricky and unusual "across the bar" phrasing that was Walter's trademark—which is absent from virtually all of Cotton's other recordings with Muddy—is the giveaway.

The first tune cut that day, "I Got To Find My Baby," is another Dixon lyric, with an uninspired harp solo and accompaniment throughout. But on the uptempo jump "Sugar Sweet," Walter's harp comes into its own. His phrases bounce and dance around the beat, and when someone in the studio yells out what sounds like "Play it, Walter!" after the solid first chorus of his solo, he turns up the heat a few more notches and reels out a second chorus full of tight, swinging licks and syncopated accents that leaves little doubt as to who is in the harp seat. "Trouble No More" is a reworking of Sleepy John Estes' s "Someday Baby," another blues standard. Dixon's bass and the drums are way up front in the mix driving the rhythm. The harp once again takes the lead with some inspired playing throughout, although Walter seems to lose his place a bit during his solo. The session ended with the slow blues "Clouds In My Heart," recast from Muddy's unissued 1953 recording "Flood," which had featured Walter Horton on harp. In the end, it's clear that some of the harp playing on this session fell below Walter's high-water mark, but it's also worth noting that he hadn't been playing as a member of Muddy's band for two years by this point. With little indication that he'd had any rehearsals for this or for this or any of the other sessions on which he rejoined his old boss, it's evident that most of Walter's playing was improvised on the spot while the tape was rolling.

In mid-November, R&B got a shot in the arm with the nationwide broadcast of a nine-minute segment on the Ed Sullivan show of "Dr. Jive's Rhythm Revue," an excerpt from a show running at The Apollo Theater. According to Ed's somewhat garbled introduction, the show was ". . . drawing thousands for this Rhythm and Roll . . . ahh . . . Rhythm and Color . . . ahh Rhythm and Blues show . . . ." He then turned it over to WWRL DJ Dr. Jive, who introduced Bo Diddley as a ". . . folk blues singer." Bo did a powerful if abbreviated version of his eponymous hit, and was followed by Lavern Baker ("Tweedle Dee Dee"), and The Five Keys (with their hit, "Ling Ting Tong," widely considered in white "beat" circles to be a secret paean to dope-smoking). The segment ended with Willis "Gator Tail" Jackson playing a honking and stomping sax blaster. Legend has it that Sullivan wanted Bo to perform the currently popular (and decidedly non-R&B) number "16 Tons," but Bo played his own hit instead, earning Sullivan's ongoing wrath.

The growing popularity of the new Rock & Roll performers must have annoyed Walter. He was the first star Checker Records ever had, he'd helped make the label a success, and now he was being eclipsed by these other men with more teen appeal, performing what he must have thought of as novelty music. Why was it that Bo was on national TV, and not him? Walter had been on the road and gigging steadily around Chicago with his own band for three years now, and it was beginning to get a bit old; the thrill and sense of adventure wasn't what it used to be. Whether or not Cotton's story of Walter being too drunk to record with Muddy was true, it was a fact that Walter was beginning to have some problems that were affecting his career. On the road he'd been exposed to jazz players who had needle habits—some even say he dabbled with smack himself, but almost everyone who knew him in his later years refutes this allegation. Sure, he drank hard now and then, and he'd begun to smoke a little pot (he pronounced it to rhyme with "boat"), but didn't everybody in his business? Wasn't that just an expected part of everyday life when you were a bluesman? And didn't things seem better when you were mellowed out enough not to notice how sharp the corners of reality could get?

10   *i've had my fun*

Chicago/The South/Chicago:
December 1955–December 1957

In December 1955, Walter stepped back into the studio again, and made a noticeable attempt to appeal to a younger market with more pop-oriented material. He led off the four-song session with one of his own numbers, "One More Chance With You." The title was taken from the hook line in the chorus of this bouncy number with stop-time hits on the verses. Jazzy guitar chords from Lockwood, and Below's smooth brushwork lay a back-drop for Walter's three-chorus solo of mostly chorded phrases; the third, and most interesting, sounds like it was improvised after Walter forgot the lyrics and failed to come back on time with his vocal. "Who," a slow shuffle with an easy swing and a steady rock, was cut next. Walter delivers the Dixon-esque lyrics convincingly, but for a change plays a laid-back harp solo that doesn't add much excitement.

Walter followed "Who" with a tune guaranteed to raise hackles today, "Boom Boom Out Go the Lights." The singer is looking for his baby, with evil intent in mind: "If I get her in my sights—Boom! Boom!—Out go the lights." Lyrics aside, the number carries on with the musical theme of the session, with jazzy guitar-chord backing, swing-style brushwork from Below providing an insistent drive, and again, a three-chorus solo break from Walter.

Finally, Walter cut another tune credited as an original, "It Ain't Right," a fast shuffling guitar-boogie in the same musical mold as his "I Got To Go" from earlier in the year, given a decidedly jazzier spin by Below's use of brushes on the drums. The cymbal splashes on the harp break perfectly accent Walter's improvisations, and propel the tune onward adeptly. This infectious number closes one of Walter's more productive sessions from the company standpoint; all four titles were deemed usable, and were eventually issued as singles. Following Walter's session, Jimmy Rogers came in to recut "You're The One," backed by Walter and his band. The ten-month ripening process seems to have helped convince Leonard Chess to release the cut. Other than a harp break that is slightly more dynamic, the new recording is fairly similar to the abandoned version.

Figure 10.1 St. Louis North Side Social Club advertisement, *St. Louis Argus*, December 16, 1955.

Walter was heading south and working over the holidays. An ad in the *St. Louis Argus,* placed by the North Side Social Club, billed him as the "Vice President of the Blues" for a Friday, December 23rd dance at the Masonic Auditorium. Down in Georgia, the lineup for a Christmas weekend gig at Atlanta's Magnolia Ballroom provided ready fodder for DJs plugging the event. It must have been easy to come up with lines about the "big 'Little'" show, because it was headlined by Little Walter, and, pictured on the poster alongside him, Little Richard, "The Tootie Fruitie [sic] man." The bill was filled out by the established New Orleans vocal group The Spiders, whose fifth Top-Ten R&B hit in the last two years, "Witchcraft," was high on the charts. The "Xmas Show" played at 5:00 and 9:00 PM on the 25th, and on Monday the 26th it was billed as a "dancing" event, from 8:30–12:30. Both The Spiders and Little Richard had records currently in the R&B Top 10; Walter was coheadliner by virtue of his #1 hit "My Babe" from earlier in the year. "Roller Coaster" had charted briefly in July, but Richard was the new sensation, with a hot hit on the charts in the form of his tidied-up version of a raucous, bawdy, juke-joint number ("Tutti Frutti"), and a wildly exhibitionist, flamboyant stage show. The crowd's response must have given Walter a hint at the direction that the audience's tastes were heading.

Walter returned to the studio with Muddy within the month, in January 1956, cut-

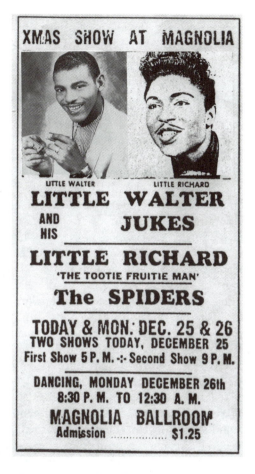

Figure 10.2 Magnolia Christmas show: Little Walter and Little Richard, December 25, 1955.

ting two tunes for Waters's next single. Muddy's fierce vocals on the first, "40 Days & 40 Nights," made for one of his most intense numbers in some time. The burning guitar work is credited to Pat Hare and Hubert Sumlin, the latter lured away from his mentor Howlin' Wolf by Muddy's offer of triple the salary. It was Muddy's first recording without Jimmy Rogers since 1951. Both Sumlin and Hare played with their guitars turned up to the edge of distortion, each took a modern, oblique approach to both melody and rhythm, and both played with passion. The number begins with the title shouted out by Muddy, then the band falls in, guitars twined together, Walter blowing high warbling chords to provide an intense cushion for Muddy's lyrics. The harp break is white hot, with a searing tone, and overall the number is a killer track.

The flip side features the debut of James Cotton on harp on a Muddy recording, although he's relegated to a background position. He plays the train-whistle sound effects on a small Marine Band harp behind Walter's driving lead work on the chromatic harp. Walter plays mainly in the lower registers until he bursts forth for a dynamic solo. "All Aboard" was a remake of Big Boy Crudup's "Mean Old Frisco," although Cotton claimed it resulted from Muddy hearing him do a version of Junior Parker's "Mystery Train" on the bandstand. Below's propulsive brushwork on the drums results in an effective train rhythm number.

1956 was a good year for Chicago bluesmen. The local scene was jumping, with many opportunities to play. Luther Tucker was still a regular member of Walter's touring band, but he also took some side jobs, recording and occasionally gigging with Rice Miller. Robert Lockwood Jr. introduced Tucker to Miller; when Miller next recorded for Chess he'd requested Lockwood to accompany him, and Robert Jr. brought Tucker along. This January 24th session produced Miller's next single. Things clicked musically, and Tucker ended up on all of Miller's sessions for the next couple of years.

On January 29th, the entertainment page of *The Chicago Defender* featured a one-column photo of Walter, captioned "Famed blues chirper and his combo are featured at the Rocket Show Lounge at 5114 Prairie, Tuesdays through Thursdays." Muddy Waters was "rocking the audience with his blues and ballads" at a huge gala event celebrating the 25th anniversary of a chain of South Side dry cleaners. Another item in the trades mentioned the various acts the Shaw Agency was booking into "Gleason's Bar Of Music" in Cleveland for February, including Walter, Joe Turner, Lowell Fulson, and The Moonglows. Walter & His Jukes began a steady engagement in February at the New Rickey's Show Lounge where they'd work off and on during the fall. Muddy moved back into The 708 Club for regular four-day stints working week nights, as well as midnight shows at The Indiana Theater.

At the same time, The Chess Brothers debuted yet another label, this one aiming to "insure pop coverage." Marterry Records (named after a combination of the names of Leonard's son Marshall and Phil's son Terry) signed Savannah Churchill and Bull-moose Jackson, as well as purchasing masters from other labels, including ballad singer Kay Starr tracks. The Marterry name didn't last for long however, with only two releases before bandleader Ralph Marterie voiced objections over the similarity to his name, and the label's name was changed to Argo.

On Friday, March 9th, another Walter session was held, resulting in only one title, yet another jumping instrumental. This one seems to have been titled with an eye to the teen market and a current craze. "Flying Saucer" begins with Walter on chromatic playing soft single notes, before adding some fat, ominous sounding chords. After a couple of choruses he switches harps, picking up his Marine Band to quote the jazzman's standard, "Salt Peanuts." Walter once again dips into his bottomless well of improvisational tricks to pull out another minute and a half of licks that were all his own, all new—and all left behind after this session. The number has a lot of the same kinetic energy of "Roller Coaster," building steam as it goes along, and is heavily drenched with studio reverb.

March was a bonanza for blues fans in Chicago, with The 708 Club featuring Howlin' Wolf on Monday, Elmore James on Thursday, and The Four Aces with Otis Rush on weekends. Over at Silvio's on the West Side, Elmore and "Sonny Boy Williams" [sic] were advertised in the weekend slot. The Crown Propeller featured a full-blown revue with dancers and guest vocalists, headlined by T-Bone Walker, and

Big Maybelle was at The Stage Lounge. At the same time, Walter's "It Ain't Right" / "Who" was released. The combination of the peppy, driving blues and the more pop-oriented flip side clicked with the record buying public, propelling the record to #7 on the *Cashbox* charts—although it would be the last one of Walter's singles to make those listings for a couple of years.

Recording sessions frequently took place on Thursdays; Chess may have scheduled them to catch his artists before they headed out of town for weekend gigs. At one such session, on Thursday, April 5th, John Brim was back in the studio, backed up by Walter's regular crew. After Chess had left Brim's previous recordings on the shelf, Brim went over to DJ Al Benson's Parrot label and scored there with his signature number "Tough Times." Brim's first cut back in the Chess studio three years later, "Be Careful," had stop-time verses, a rocking chorus, and a tough, two-chorus solo by Walter. With Brim singing lines like "Come here baby, look me dead in the eye/You know if you 'tempt to quit me, that's when you're gonna die," and the repeated chorus (with Walter joining in on harmony vocals) "Be careful, baby what you say and do/You know I'd hate mighty bad to have to do away with you," the violent imagery of the lyrics reflects the less enlightened times. The flip side is led off by Willie Dixon's thumping bass intro, then rolls into a steady jump. "You Got Me Where You Want Me" is a tough, rocking Chicago remake of Buddy and Ella Johnson's 1953 Mercury release "Ain't Cha Got Me." Again Walter improvises a powerful two-chorus solo, and perfectly complements Brim's vocals during the verses. The cuts were released promptly this time, in May, as was Walter's "One More Chance," splitting a Checker label ad in *Cashbox* with the Flamingo's new one, "A Kiss From Your Lips."

Through the spring, Walter continued to play at Rickey's Show Lounge whenever he was in town. He also made several higher-profile appearances, including a show at the Milwaukee Theater on May 11th. The following weekend, Walter was listed as splitting a bill with Muddy in South Bend, Indiana. Walter and The Moonglows headlined a sock hop at the Trianon Ballroom on June 21st for the teen crowd. By the end of June, Muddy was playing Tuesday and Wednesday nights at Rickey's, while Walter covered the other nights.

In July, Muddy was called back into the studio, with Walter on board, for a three-song session that would feature one of Walter's highwater marks as a sideman. It started with another of Muddy's powerhouse numbers, "Just To Be With You." After a shouted out catalogue of the hardships the singer will endure "... just to kiss your sweet lips, honey," he steps back for an instrumental break from Walter. Walter, who'd been playing short, fiery, but barely restrained answering phrases to Muddy's vocals up to that point, pauses for a cymbal splash from Below, then comes roaring in with a short but blistering solo, stopping to exclaim "*woah!*" a few beats in, then unleashing enough intensity to blow the listener's hair back. Muddy responds by returning with an even more impassioned vocal for the last verse. This is one of those rare and lucky times when a song at its absolute peak of performance was somehow captured on record.

Next up, "Don't Go No Farther" opens with prominent guitar from Hubert Sumlin, soon joined by Walter's burbling low-register work on his chromatic. Again, on the solo Walter burns in with white-hot tonality that is virtually screaming by his strutting second chorus. The last tune cut that day, " Diamonds At Your Feet," was a remake of

Figure 10.3 Rickey's Show Lounge/Silvio's advertisements, *Chicago Defender*, June 23, 1956.

one of the tunes Muddy had cut for Alan Lomax's 1942 Library of Congress field trip to Mississippi, the gospel-based "You Got to Take Sick and Die." The tune shows Chess's fine hand in arranging; Walter sneaks in quietly under the last few words of Muddy's second vocal verse, then plays a two chorus mid-tune solo, again using his chromatic, and lays out for the rest of the song. It sounds like he's having mike cord trouble, because the sound cuts out in a couple of spots, although Walter is still playing with surging energy.

Walter played weekends at Rickey's in July, while Muddy held down Tuesdays and Wednesdays as before. Elsewhere, both Dinah Washington and Billie Holiday were working in the local jazz clubs. Walter also played in Rockford, Illinois for a couple of weeks before moving on to Cleveland, then returning to Chicago for another studio session on Friday, July 27th. By now, drummer Freddie Below had quit the touring band, but after a vacation in Florida, he returned to Chicago and continued to play on some sessions with Walter, including this one. "It's Too Late Brother," a number written on the spot by Chess session drummer Al Duncan, was first up. Duncan had been at the studio recording with The Flamingos and The Moonglows earlier that day, and stayed afterwards to hang out with the guys in Walter's band. He later said that Leonard Chess didn't like one of the songs Walter had brought in, and asked if anyone had any other material. Duncan volunteered that he didn't have a song, but could get one, and went into "the shitter," sat down, and wrote the song in the time it took to answer nature's call, basing it on the musical arrangement of Walter's big hit "My Babe." The band starts out with a swinging, jazzy groove, and after an instrumental lead-in, Walter jauntily sings the fatalistic lyric, "Ain't no need of going no further, brother," which leads to the lines about having diamonds and Cadillac cars and touring the world, setting up bars, etc., but eventually losing it all. The last verse includes an ominous "Your money's gone and your health is bad/All you can tell is the fun you had." Duncan may well have had Walter in mind when he wrote it, but Walter sings it as if he doesn't have a care in the world, and plays a casually swinging but effective solo. The band fades out at the conclusion, a rare occurrence on Walter's sides, which more often ended with a flourish.

An instrumental with the same jazzy groove followed. Walter uses his chromatic harmonica without an amp for the first time, and Tucker contributes a funky and tasty guitar solo. The band plays a repeating one-chord figure throughout, allowing Walter to really cut loose with some inventive, swinging phrasing and melodies without having to concern himself with following chord changes. Hearing Walter without amplification shows just how much of his sound came from him and not his equipment. The number sounds like a spur-of-the-moment jam, with the band improvising on the appealing pulse set by the opening number. This one also ends with a fadeout, suggesting that the band may have continued playing for some time longer than the usual three or so minutes allotted for a single. It was titled "Teenage Beat," obviously with the emerging youth market in mind.

A second guitar player—probably Lockwood—joined the trio for the next couple of numbers. "Take Me Back" is another Walter composition with impassioned singing on a medium tempo shuffle; the solos feature tasty guitar/harp call-and-response phrases.

The last number that day, "Just A Feeling," was based on a Big Bill Broonzy record from 1939, "Just A Dream." This version has the same easy loping tempo as Broonzy's, but as usual, Walter raises the intensity level when he plays his solo, and when he plaintively sings the verse "Black night is falling, my pains is coming down again/I feel so sorry, people I ain't got no friend." During the take, everything came to a halt when Leonard cut the band off mid-tune and burst out into the studio after Walter sang this verse. "You can't say that Walter, you can't say 'My pants are coming down!'" "No, no," Walter replied, "It's 'My *pains* is coming down.'" According to singer Bobby Charles, a recent addition to the Chess roster who was present that day, the entire cast and crew burst out laughing—including Leonard. The released version leaves the line intact.

Walter may have been inspired to record the song as a result of recent encounters with his old friend and mentor, Big Bill. Walter had known Broonzy since his early Maxwell Street days almost a decade earlier, and he'd been running into him again when visiting a South Side girlfriend, Armilee Thompson, who happened to be Broonzy's cousin. Thompson lived across the hall from Broonzy in an apartment building at 47th and Parkway, on the third floor of a six-flight building directly across the street from The Regal Theater. Armilee later smiled, "Bill would always tell Walter, 'Come on man, when you gonna get married?' Walter would say 'Oh, cuz'—by Bill being my cousin—'I'm gonna get 'round to it.' But I just wasn't in no hurry, you know?"

Alex "Easy Baby" Randle was another southern musical expatriate, who'd moved to Chicago in 1956. He'd played around West Memphis with Willie Johnson, Joe Willie Wilkins, and James Cotton before moving north. When he checked out the club scene in Chicago, "First place I went was Rickey's Show Lounge . . . Little Walter and them were playing down there," Randle recalled:

> I always wanted to meet that guy to try and find out what he was doing with that harmonica, I could never pinpoint it. I went there, sat down and looked at him and listened. Finally I made myself known—"Yeah, I'm from Memphis, West Memphis." I was a little bitty fella, weighed about 135 then. He let me get out there on stage and I forgot half the song. Little Walter, he told the people, "He did good, let's hear it for him." But let me tell you something, it was two or three weeks before I got enough nerve to try it again. Then I went back to Rickey's and blowed them a-loose.

Randle said he and Walter got to be good friends, that they understood each other:

> Walter used to smoke a lot of pot. I tried it but discovered I couldn't inhale it, which was good . . . his ways and my ways was two different things, but we still got along good . . . [On breaks] he'd leave his stuff there and I'd use it, he'd yell "Go on, blow blow blow! Blow your ass off!" And that silly son of a bitch would steal your stuff too, boy, shit! He'd come around where you play at, if you had a new "D" harp, Little Walter would steal the hell out of it. . . .

Honeyboy Edwards and his wife had settled in Chicago in 1956, and he reconnected with old pals like Walter Horton and Little Walter, working the clubs with Horton, paying off the musicians union steward to let him work without a card. Edwards frequently hung out at Sunnyland Slim's gambling joint over on South Prairie, where Slim had a piano in the basement and two crap tables; he sold whiskey and sandwiches as well. Slim had it all worked out with the beat cop, who sometimes came in, got drunk, and nodded out for a while before resuming his patrol. There, Edwards ran into people like Muddy, Floyd Jones, and Little Walter drinking and gambling. Sometimes the music would start up with everybody jumping in, for a good old southern time. Sunnyland would get a game running when the people were drawn in off the street.

Blues club activity continued through the summer and early fall. Muddy and Jimmy Rogers held down different nights at The 708 Club in August, while Silvio's featured weekend shows with Muddy, Wolf, and Billy Boy. The September 8th *Defender* had an ad for an all-time dream slate scheduled at Rickey's, featuring Howlin' Wolf alternating with Muddy during the week, while Little Walter covered the weekends, providing "A full week of the top in blues bands," a column item noted. In the trades, Chess/Checker ran a large display ad with photos featuring new releases by Chuck Berry ("Brown Eyed Handsome Man"), The Moonglows, Bobby Charles, J. B. Lenoir, Muddy ("Dont Go No Further," which would hit #12 on the *Billboard* charts), Wolf ("She Gave Me Water" [sic]), and Walter ("Just The Feeling").

The trades also had this rather mysterious item: "Little Walter reported recovering from a very serious recent illness and now discussing series of one-niters around the country." There's no indication of the nature of the "illness," but Walter's old Maxwell Street buddy Jimmie Lee Robinson provides a possible clue. He stated that "Walter

Figure 10.4 Rickey's Show Lounge advertisement, *Chicago Defender*, September 8, 1956.

was always getting into some sort of trouble, was in and out of the hospital a lot after getting cut, stuck, shot, beat up by the police, whatever. . . ." One of the announced dates had Walter at Ernie Busker's Palms Club in Hallendale, Florida, "The great southern oasis for tour weary R&B performers . . . just about the only spot in the southeast where an act can play for a full week." The Shaw Agency had a number of stars booked into that club; Walter followed Bo Diddley, Joe Turner, The Cadillacs, and Ruth Brown. On the heels of Walter's September 10th date were Ray Charles, followed by Guitar Slim.

Figure 10.5 Club Riviera advertisement, *St. Louis Argus*, September 21, 1956.

As he worked his way back towards Chicago that month, Walter spent some time in St. Louis, working at the Club Riviera on September 14th and 15th, splitting a bill with Eddie Johnson's Orchestra, doing "Two floor shows—11:15 and 1:15." The same ad in the *St. Louis Argus* announced the two would be sharing a Sunday night gig the following weekend at The Blue Flame, a jazz spot where Miles Davis would play when he came through town.

A couple of years earlier, Walter had befriended radio disk jockey Bernie Hayes. Hayes had his first on-air experience in the Air Force, and by the early '50s was working in Chicago on WGES, a station that featured a variety of ethnic block programming, with Polish, Italian, and African-American programs on at various times during the broadcast day. Hayes played the doo-wop and R&B hits of the day, and had met Little Walter in ". . . the juke joints on the West Side . . . you couldn't go three or four blocks without having a name, Muddy, Little Walter, or Wolf. Understand me, Little Walter was a King then." In 1956 Hayes took a position at WDBS (the Dixie Broadcasting System) in Alexandria, Louisiana, Walter's early boyhood hometown. As the only black disk jockey on the station, he did two daily segments, from 10:00 AM until 2:00 PM, and then again from 6:00 to 9:00 PM. He described Alexandria as ". . . a typical southern town. Lee was the main street, there was a two-story black hotel, The Hollins House, several small businesses on both sides of the street, storefronts, two or three small clubs, a cab company, funeral home. You had two prominent black doctors, it was a wonderful small community." The population of 30,000 or so would swell when servicemen from nearby Air Force and Army bases came to town on leave, looking for some action. There was a black section called Samtown, ". . . where they did a lot of partying, naturally attracting a lot of prostitutes, too."

In the summer of '56, Walter was finishing the tail-end of a southern tour and wound up spending several weeks in the Alexandria area, where he and Hayes reconnected and hung out; Walter even took him out to the family farm. Across a bridge over a small creek from Alexandria was the adjacent community of Pineville, ". . . where Little Walter hung out mostly, his family was over in Pineville. He'd get homesick sometimes, he loved his family on both sides of the river, that's primarily why he came," according to Hayes. Walter worked clubs and taverns in Alexandria ("That was a big event, like a homecoming"), Monroe, Shreveport, and east-central Louisiana. Hayes said Walter worked every weekend, maybe some weeknights as well, and the places were always packed: "They'd flock out to see him, loved every minute of it, he always left them wanting more. Play maybe an hour set sometimes, mostly with a smile. If he'd been drinking a lot, he'd get right into it, other times he was more introverted." Walter drank ". . . before, during, and after a show—but it never affected his talent, in fact it may have increased it." Hayes commented that Walter usually kept a half-pint bottle; "They wouldn't buy pints, figured half pints taste better." There was a large Creole population, and Walter was comfortable there; he knew many of them, although he only spoke Creole ". . . every now and then, especially when he got angry or hot, he would go into it, geechee-type speaking, sometimes when he wasn't feeling good . . . ." He also liked the women there. Hayes recalled that he kept up his womanizing ways, and ". . . had two different ladies in different spots, I wouldn't call them girlfriends, acquaintances, they would party and have sex sometimes."

Around the time Walter was due to return to Chicago to fulfill some dates there, Hayes had vacation time scheduled, so he caught a ride with Walter and the troupe back up north to see his family. It was the usual two-car caravan, with Walter, his driver Bennie Rooks, maybe one other band member, and Hayes riding in the Cadillac, while the rest of the band drove the wagon with the gear packed in. According to Hayes, they did the 900-and-some mile stretch to Chicago in one long haul, only stopping every couple hours for something to eat, drink, or hoping to find restroom facilities they'd be allowed to use. As the trip progressed, the car radio was kept tuned to R&B stations in the various big cities they passed, and sometimes one of Walter's records would be heard. "Turn it up, turn it up!" he'd say. Hayes recalled a fair amount of joking, and talk about gigs past and upcoming. At times during the long drive, Walter would open up a little. "He talked about what it was like growing up in that area, how he hated to work, how he hated to go out in the fields ... that's why he tried to get out of Louisiana, he said. He was very bitter about the way they treated black people, the prejudices, the second class citizenship. He knew he should've been a superstar, he felt bad." Now and then things got musical. "He'd be writing new tunes in the car sometimes, experiments with different things ... he'd occasionally write something down on the back of an envelope, ask the musicians what they thought about it ... He told a story about how a sheriff didn't believe it was musical instruments in the car. He made then unpack 'em and play him a tune—then he let them go." Hayes recalled that Walter "... kept three harps in a little case, a leather bound case, like a little satchel, a briefcase."

Hayes made several such trips with Walter over the next year or so. One time, on the way through Memphis, they took a detour down Beale Street and spotted singer Little Willie John sitting on the curb, taking in the air between sets at a club there. "Looka that, looka that," Walter said, and got out of the car, then Willie saw him. "They were real happy to see each other. We stayed about an hour, they had a good time talking music, talking records," Hayes recalled. Then it was back in the car and onward into the night. Forty-five years later, Hayes still recalls the pre-interstate route: "... come up through Memphis to St. Louis, pick up Route 3 coming through, 61 was mostly the route, cross the old McArthur Bridge over the Mississippi, up Route 3 to 66, 66 was flourishing then, 66 into the South Side of Chicago."

Back in Chicago, the blues scene continued to grow, with Memphis Slim, Howlin' Wolf, Big Walter Horton, Sunnyland Slim, John Brim, Lee Jackson, and Otis Rush all actively playing the clubs. However, *The Defender* already noted a change in the air; rock and roll was overshadowing the blues, and many artists were having problems getting recognition. Nonetheless, the paper assured its readers that "Elvis Presley won't be around in a year ... rock and roll in a year or so won't appeal to the wide audience it has today." The article's writer also commented that "Chicago had been the starting point for many personalities down through the years, from King Oliver and Louis Armstrong to Joe Williams and Little Walter," placing Walter in some pretty heady company. But Rock & Roll seemed to be the phrase of the day: Memphis Slim & His House Rockers were at the House Of Rock And Roll, while, at the Grand Terrace, Elmore James was billed as "King Of The Rock & Roll." Everywhere you looked, someone was appending variations of the words "Rock & Roll" onto an event, a club, or a musical act in an attempt to cash in on the new "craze"—whether or not the words accurately reflected the content.

On Saturday, December 1st, Muddy was in the studios for a four-song session, one that has caused a degree of controversy among discographers; some credit James Cotton on harp, others split the date between Cotton and Little Walter. The first two tunes used acoustic harp, which some sources list as Cotton, then there was a break in the master number sequence, and finally two more tunes were cut with amplified harp, which most sources credit to Walter. To further add to the confusion, immediately afterwards was a Jimmy Rogers session, during which he cut the followup to his hit "Walking By Myself," using yet a third harp player, Walter Horton. Regardless of who's credited, most likely it's Little Walter on all the Muddy tracks; Cotton himself has stated it was Walter on the version of "Got My Mojo Working" recorded this day, while he played on a later, live version. Walter's unique stylistic idiosyncrasies are evident in the harp playing throughout the entire Muddy session, marked by subtlety and control that Cotton hadn't quite mastered yet, judging from his later, known recordings.

Even though Willie Dixon had gone over to the Cobra label for a time following a salary dispute with Chess, he was still feeding him material, and the first tune recorded that day was one of his better efforts, the philosophical "Live the Life I Love." The harp leads in with a phrase that's repeated between verses throughout the number, with a tricky switch of harps on the solo. The difference achieved by this switch was so subtle as to be almost musically invisible, even to most fellow harp players. The only conclusion that can be reached is that Walter switched not for any special musical reason, but did it simply because he knew he *could*. Walter would later say that on occasion he used as many as four different harmonicas while playing a single number, at least in part with the aim of confounding other harmonica players. He said he'd "Pick one up, put it [down], pick one up, while I'm playin' another one . . . They didn't know what you doin', then."

Up next was "Rock Me," an updated version of Muddy's 1951 cut, "All Night Long," using a couple of verses from that track, as well as mixing in a few lines from Lil' Son Jackson's influential 1951 hit "Rockin' And Rollin'." (B. B. King's later hit version was based on Jackson's recording as well.) There's an almost sweet feel to the tune; Walter plays a delicate, lacy harp that floats in and out of the vocals, tightly meshing with Muddy's mood of laid back lust. "Look What You've Done" comes after the session break. Muddy sings somewhat tentatively, as if he's not completely at ease with the rather busy lyrics. Although credited to Muddy, the lyrics sounds more like Dixon's poeticizing. But the harmonica solo is pure Little Walter, playing forcefully and inventively, utilizing bent notes to create some unique melodic phrases of a sort seldom heard from the small Marine Band harp.

The final track cut that day, "Got My Mojo Working," became a signature tune for Muddy. He'd picked up the song while touring the south the previous month; singer Ann Cole was part of the package and Waters' band backed up her set, which included this number. Once home in Chicago, Muddy changed the lyrics a bit and added a new verse, making it more down-home. Although Muddy gets label credit, the tune was actually written by Preston Foster. However, it's easy to see why many thought it was a Muddy original, with all of his trademark hoodoo references, including "Going down to Louisiana to get me a mojo hand." Spann kicks it off with the now-familiar piano chords, then the band kicks in with a beat that won't quit, the cyclical rhythm pushing the beat, building the kinetic energy. Walter's harp break is quietly dazzling, with more intricacy bubbling under the surface than meets the casual ear.

In January 1957, Checker released Walter's "Too Late Brother"; it had some chart action, although Walter seemed to be keeping a low profile, not turning up in ads or trade columns much at that point. However, a significant event occurred early in 1957. One of Walter's girlfriends, Armilee Thompson, became pregnant with the child that would later be deemed in court to be Walter's only living descendant. Nonetheless, there is much controversy over the child's paternity, with Walter's sisters insisting that he did not have a child.

Like most of Walter's road companions, Armilee served as Walter's sometime manager, sometime bookkeeper, and sometime lover. When she traveled with Walter, Armilee was "Keeping his books, collecting the money, pay the boys, making sure the boys paid their taxes to Uncle Sam." She also said she helped deal with the door counts:

> Most of the time I'd be working with the guy booking the gig, to make sure he was saying the right amount of people being there, you understand? Some, you'd have to check behind them. You'd have one of those little clocks you would carry and every person come in, you would press this little clock, to make sure the right amount of people he said was in there ... Some of the guys would say, "Oh, there wasn't that many in the house." Most of the time I would stand at the door, to make sure he was clocking it exactly like I was clocking it, to make sure the money would be right.

Armilee also noted that Walter was picky about the gigs that the Shaw Agency offered, taking only the ones he felt like doing, and turning down some of the work that was offered. One of the tours was a several-week long southern swing, and Walter took her along to his home town. Armilee says she met several of his aunts and uncles, and that Walter took her to the cemetery to show her where his mother was buried.

On Tuesday, March 5th, Walter was in studio for his first session in seven months, the longest gap between sessions yet since his first hit, "Juke." "Nobody But You" takes the same swinging tack as the numbers from Walter's previous session, with drummer Below once again providing the jazzy beat with his brushes. Walter sings confidently, but his voice has a slightly ragged quality; his harp dances delicately around the changes on the first chorus of his solo, but on the second chorus he emphatically stabs out his musical phrases, pushing the energy level up a notch. Second was an attempt at "Temperature," a Dixonesque novelty number with stop-time verses, and some tricky vocal phrasing that Walter didn't quite have a handle on yet. It would be put on hold, and tried again at a later session. The instrumental "Shake Dancer" has some nice guitar-harp interplay with chords answering and supporting Walter's lead melody lines. Last was "Everybody Needs Somebody," a slow blues with an almost martial beat, and a strong vocal by Walter. He's playing through his amplifier's tremolo channel, using its pulsation to good effect during his solo. Walter was obviously on the lookout for any distinctive effect he could adapt and use in his arsenal. This tune along with the first one cut that day would become the next single.

Later that month, Walter did some moonlighting, recording over at Cobra Records where Willie Dixon was producing. It was an Otis Rush session with pianist Lafayette Leake, tenor sax man Harold Ashby, guitarist Jody Williams, drummer Odie Payne, and Dixon on bass, cutting tracks for Rush's third single. Walter is mostly buried in the mix on the two numbers cut that day; if you didn't know it was him there you probably wouldn't pick him out.

Muddy's "Got My Mojo Working" was released in March, and a month later Walter's "Everybody Needs Somebody" hit the streets; once again Walter was omnipresent in jukeboxes and on the airwaves. On March 18th, Walter stopped by the AFM union office, and changed the beneficiary on his union death benefit from his mother's name to his youngest half-sister and ward, giving her name as Sylvia Blair Scott. Meanwhile, a column in the trade press raved about the new facilities that Chess was building on Michigan Avenue ". . . with redwood trim for the executive offices," and added this intriguing tidbit: ". . . no, don't rub your eyes, that was Little Walter bicycling down the street. Seems he lost his drivers license and has taken up the bicycle."

In May 1957, Chess opened up their newly remodeled building at what became one of the most famed addresses in blues history, 2120 South Michigan. The two-story storefront building is only 25 feet wide but runs 125 feet deep back to the alley. The offices were on the first floor, with the street door opening onto a small lobby area. Through the lobby and a few steps down the hallway on the left were the offices of Phil and Leonard, the latter now, according to the trades, "back in harness and looking great following a rough illness" (Leonard suffered a heart attack in late January, an ominous sign for the future). Across from the offices was a stairway to the second-floor studio area; straight back down the hallway past the offices was a large shipping and packaging room. At the rear, next to the back door, was another stairway, which gave easy access for the artists to unload their gear. At the top of the stairs was a small back room used as a tape-storage vault; to the left was a tiny rehearsal studio, which opened to the recording studio proper, which measures about 20 by 37 feet. Beyond that, closer to the street, was the elevated control room with a 12-channel mixing board (photographs show a simple radio-station type console with large rotary volume controls). In a room behind the back wall of the studio control room, overlooking Michigan Avenue, was an area for the disk mastering equipment.

The facilities were known as Sheldon Studios, and were built and operated by a 22-year-old former employee of Universal Studios named Jack Weiner. Chess had worked out an agreement whereby Weiner would do the recording for their labels, but could also take on outside accounts on his own. Expenses were split three ways between Weiner and the two Chess brothers. In order to make the space suitable for recording, Weiner totally overhauled it, putting in new cork and concrete layered floors and spring-mounted walls, to isolate them from adjoining rooms, and to cut out traffic rumble leaking in from the busy street outside. He also installed nine adjustable panels to control the acoustic dampening of the high-ceilinged room. An echo chamber was built in a tiled room in the basement; the signal from the studio was fed into speakers there, and that sound was then picked up by microphones at the other end of the basement and sent back to the studio to be remixed into the original signal. Now Chess had state of the art gear allowing them to record freely at all hours as their whims and the performer's schedules suited them.

Walter had been looking around for another guitar player. Lockwood had given his notice, because, he explained, Walter refused to hire a bass player—but money may have been just as big a factor as well. Otis Rush recalled Walter approaching him sometime earlier. "Oh, he was bullshitting, I guess. He'd try to bullshit me, said he wanted me to play lead guitar for him. When he first heard me play, 'I like you man, I want your phone number' you know, shit." But Rush demurred, partly because he had heard rumors about Walter's temper. "He didn't pull a gun on me, [but he] pulled it on Fred Below, Louis Myers, and Dave Myers . . . I don't know, just musicians arguing. That was at a place on Indiana, Hollywood Rendezvous. I never saw the gun myself, I wasn't there. I just heard about it," Rush said. Instead, Walter once again hooked up with his Maxwell Street running pal from his early Chicago days, Jimmie Lee Robinson. Robinson had been working in a trio known as The Every Hour Blues Boys with Freddie King and drummer/guitarist Frank "Sonny" Scott, appearing on the West Side at the Stadium Sports Club and occasionally on bills with B.B. King and Little Walter. When that group broke up, Robinson went with Elmore James, who was putting together a group to go on the road with him to Atlanta. "Walter lived around the corner from me," Robinson explained. "I lived on Roosevelt, he lived on Roosevelt and Albany. He came to my house and asked me would I go on the road with him. Elmore came at the same time, he really loved me, we'd be together every day, so I didn't give Walter no answer." Robinson sought advice from another former Maxwell Street musical partner; "I asked Eddie Taylor, what should I do?" Taylor's advice was to go with Walter since he was hot and had more jobs lined up, so Robinson did, and spent the next few years in Walter's band. He already knew Tucker, and commented on how Lockwood looked after him: "He tried to take care of him, he was his godfather, his mother had let him be responsible for him. Walter was on drugs, marijuana, whatever else he was on, Robert tried to keep [Tucker] from getting on anything with Walter . . ."

As Robinson recalled it, Walter had Otis "Big Smokey" Smothers working with him at the time he joined the band. "Robert Junior wasn't with him, neither was Tucker," Jimmie Lee said. "We went out and played St. Louis, but the people didn't like his attitude. They told me to tell Walter if he didn't change his attitude, go around and give himself to the people, that they was not gonna have him back no more. He didn't like to go out and be with the people." Walter controlled the money and, like many bandleaders, sometimes got a little funny with it, according to Robinson. "He's selfish, you know. We went over to a gig in Evanston one night, got through and Walter said, 'Who want their money tonight? Whoever want their money tonight is fired.' I said 'Okay then, pay me my money, I'm fired.' He paid me, I guess Smokey let him keep his money, I dunno. Next morning I had a phone call, Walter told me to come over to the house. We sat around and listened to some jazz records . . ." Simple as that, Robinson was back in the band. The money was in the neighborhood of $20 or $25 per man, actually above the union scale. Band members were paid in cash each night after the gig while on the road; the union didn't have as much control over band business away from home. As for hotel and travel expenses, "The booking agency set all that up in advance," according to Robinson.

Luther Tucker didn't remember Walter working with Smothers, suggesting that Smothers may have just done a few fill-ins during this period when Tucker wasn't available for one reason or another. He said that after Lockwood left, Robinson immediately replaced him: "He was the next person to come into the band. He knew a little about playing background. Little Walter say 'I wanna hire this cat. He may not know the material right now, you show him what to do. Although we don't have Robert Junior, you take Robert Junior's place and he'll take yours.' We just got together and started practicing." Tucker thought that Robinson had a good ear. "He could hear what we were doing, 'cause none of the music was wrote down, none of it. We all just played by ear. It turned out okay, coulda been better, but at the time it was a rush thing. We had to find someone to take Robert Junior's place, to take my place [when Tucker moved to the lead guitar spot], all this was sort of nerve wracking."

In May, the trade papers reported that "Little Walter [is] enjoying a short rest and vacation in Alexandria LA, in preparation for big things up and coming." According to Robinson, it was a working vacation: "We played all over the country, all through Florida, a week at the Palms in Hallendale, Pensacola too, Texas, Nebraska, Kentucky, down in Louisiana. We gave 'em hell, took the show from the big bands—Joe Tex, Little Richard, Chuck Berry, all of us be on the same shows together. They'd be leaving out, we'd be coming in, criss-crossing." He remembered that the band dressed onstage in matching blue tuxedo jackets, while Walter would wear something contrasting to stand out, like a yellow jacket. Robinson recalled Leonard Chess coming to Atlanta to take care of some business and staying at the same hotel, The Majestic, as Walter and the boys. The hotel was just across the street and down the block from the Royal Peacock, where they were performing. Robinson didn't like hanging out around the club; "The police down there tried to mess with me and Tucker a few times, so we didn't really care too much about hanging out there in the street [on breaks]. I might go to the movie down the block . . ." Walter's prowess as a lover was made audibly obvious to Robinson at the hotel, and he became both envious and curious: "He'd have women moaning in there, you could hear it out in the hallway. I wanted to know, what the heck is he doing? I wanted to learn how to do that myself! So I told Tucker, 'I'm gonna peep through the keyhole tonight and see.' He went and told Walter, and Walter covered the keyhole up!" Robinson concluded it was probably Walter performing oral sex on his female guests, although he also mentioned his impressive physical endowment: "Walter had a thing on him so big it was pitiful."

One of the shows took place at the Atlanta Prison: "It was Little Walter, me, Luther Tucker, and Odie Payne. Also Piano Red, the real one, and Jump Jackson. They gave us a big dinner there, big table and everything, a big auditorium full of prisoners. Playing the blues, we had a nice time, they gave us a party." It was on this trip that the group stopped off in Marksville to visit Walter's grandparents, and where Robinson says that "Papou" Louis showed him Walter's birthplace, pointing out a place under a tree outside one of the family's two houses. The band stayed there a while, working the area. Walter's first cousin Rosa Brown remembers him returning to Holy Ghost, the

Catholic school he'd attended, to play a "big gig." She remembered, "It was 50 cents in those days. He was a good performer, he did talk to the audience in Marksville, everybody there was his folks, real friendly. The whole family is there, he played the whole night." Walter also played in Alexandria, but was upset when a parade was thrown together to celebrate B.B. King's appearance in town; Walter, as a native son, felt he was deserving of the same type of honor. One night while out driving drunk by himself, Walter flipped the band's station wagon over in a ditch. He wasn't seriously injured, and the battered wagon lasted for the rest of the tour.

Down in Baton Rouge, guitarist Phil Guy, Buddy's younger brother, caught Walter at the Purple Circle Club. "Me and [harp player] Raful Neal got to play with him that night," Guy said. "Raful still talks about that. He had that drummer, a very quiet man, Odie Payne, and Louis [Myers] was playing the guitar. I'll tell you how long it's been, 'Honky Tonk' was new then and he played it on the harp, just like a sax. I didn't really know him well, I only saw him one time. By the time I got to Chicago, he was gone further up the road."

It might have been at the end of this same tour when Walter found himself strapped for cash down in Meridan, Mississippi, and had an encounter there with pianist Lovie Lee. When Walter came through town, he found Lee (who years later would join Muddy's band) working a local club with a small combo that included a young harmonica player, Carey Bell. When Walter let it be known that he was in need of financial help, Lovie volunteered some. He told Walter:

> "I got some gigs here I could give you, but I know I couldn't pay you over $30. You folks, you been making big money." The boys and me wasn't making but about $25 then. He say, "Where you get that?" I say, "Two blocks down, but c'mon, you probably got that much money in your pocket now." He say "I'm broke as hell right now—you really gonna take me there?" I say, "Yeah," he say, "Well then, I'll have some gas fare home!" So I let him play with me. The gig at the Al-Miss Club, right near the Alabama-Mississippi line, lasted five nights. He go down home with me, ate everything. I told him he could stay with me, he didn't have to get a hotel. Oh, he thanked me. 'Cause whatever money he made before, he'd done drank it up, messed it up. I was giving Little Walter $30 and it look like he was glad to get it.

While in town Lovie says he overheard Walter complimenting Bell's harp playing to his bandmates, "Said, 'That black motherfucker can play!'"

If Walter occasionally took advantage of his band members, he sometimes watched out for them as well. Following the final gig of one road trip, Robinson and the others were gambling, and Robinson says he "... beat them out of their money." While on the road driving back to Chicago, Walter told him to give Tucker his money back, and when Robinson refused, Walter stopped the car and put him out at gun-point. "Took my clothes, guitar, I got out, black dark. Out in the wilderness, wasn't a house ... I don't know where it was, we were on our way back to Chicago." As soon as he walked across a bridge up ahead, a car with a "white brother" driving pulled over and offered him a ride. He got in the car, and as they drove off towards Chicago, they passed Walter, who'd turned around and was coming back to look for him. Understandably upset, the next morning back in Chicago, Robinson went to the union hall and lodged a complaint. There was a formal hearing before the union officials, and for his actions, Walter was ordered to pay a fine, some of which went to Robinson. "After he paid me, I got ready to walk out the door. He come running up behind me, 'You coming to work tonight?' [Laughs] I said, 'Yeah, I'll be there.'"

In June, the trade paper reports had "Little Walter headed east from Atlanta to meet up with Muddy Waters where they plan to combine for a southern tour." Another item mentioned that "Cream City swung to Little Walter's big band, then verra [sic] busy fella headed to Chi for a Chess recording session." Around this time Walter also was contributing his talents to another Otis Rush session at Cobra. This time his harp is more prominent, particularly on "Jump Sister Bessie," another Dixon novelty number, with somewhat trite lyrics. It's distinguished mainly by a strong and distinctive opening chorus with Walter's harp taking the lead. Walter plays nice answering phrases to Rush's vocals, although he doesn't play a solo; the guitar takes the middle break.

On Thursday, June 20th, Walter was back at Chess, for his first session in the new studio, which would ultimately result in three completed masters. The session started at 3:00 PM, and the engineer dutifully wrote down on the tape box the instrumental lineup for the session: "2 guitar, 1 bass, 1 drum, 1 harmonica." First up was a number that had been tried with unsatisfactory results at Walter's last session three months earlier, the somewhat lyrically complicated "Temperature." Dixon was the "ringmaster," supervising the activity out on the studio floor, relaying directions from the booth, and counting off the takes from behind his bass.

Even under the best of circumstances, recording sessions can put everyone involved on edge. Not only is there a man in the booth making sure that everybody in the studio knows that the time is *his* money, pushing to get takes completed as fast as possible, there's also the knowledge that any little mistake might be released on a record to haunt the artist forever. There's also the pressure to create the same level of excitement that a band generates in a club, not an easy task in the sterile confines of a brightly lit, large, otherwise empty room. At the end of a tune, instead of appreciative applause and adulation, a player gets only silence back, or maybe a terse, "Lets do it again" from the booth. There's also the pressure to be creative, to come up with something new, to top the last effort. Under the best of circumstances, it's a less-than-relaxing situation. And if one of the characters involved has a hangover, is having a disagreement with a woman or another band member, or is just plain ornery, look out.

"Temperature" took 38 takes to record, with the tempers and nerves of all involved severely frayed by the time they were done. During the first take, Walter appears to have made the painful mistake of getting too close to the vocal mike while holding his harmonica microphone, which was plugged into his ungrounded amp, resulting in a nasty electrical shock. Midway through the first verse Walter suddenly goes off mike, and the band stops. Sounding surprised but amused, Walter says "Shit! This motherfucker's *hot* Jim! Blue! Blaze! Me no like! [Laughing] No shit!" he jokes. The band finally manages a complete run-through on Take 6; by this time, Walter has the arrangement and lyrics pretty well under control. It's a good warm-up version with a casually tossed-off solo that, like most of his improvisations, reveals more complexity when studied. But, while technically acceptable, the track is missing the excitement deemed necessary for release.

Dixon immediately urged another run at it; "One more while we're in the groove! Hold it right there. . . ." Walter obviously thought they had just completed a satisfactory version of the tune, and clearly frustrated, he mutters "Oh, your dick! Shit!" Dixon counts it off and they go into another attempt, this one with Walter singing much more softly, and apparently liking what he hears the band doing this time; he suddenly shouts out "Yeah!" as he launches into his harp break. Walter plays a wild solo, alternating longer phrases with a rapid-fire, single-note attack as he works his way up and down the instrument, and then coming back to sing the final verse much more forcefully. Still, another take is attempted, with somewhat different arrangement, the guitars laying out completely when Walter sings the verses. Walter cuts it off quickly, complaining that he can't keep up with all the rearranging. Nevertheless they make a couple more attempts with the new arrangement, with Walter starting half-heartedly and then conveniently forgetting the lyrics before either take builds any steam. In the booth, Leonard is convinced; "Back to the old riff," he calls.

When the tape rolls again, Walter seems to have warmed up to the tune. Take II is a complete take, played in the key of "A," with two strong solo choruses from Walter's harp, the first played on the high end of an "A" harmonica, and the second on the low end of a "D" harp. It's a beautiful performance, but as it ends, Dixon breaks in with a critique of Walter's solo on the high end of the "A" harp; "It's too high," he says. As one of the other band members counters with, "Well, that's Walter's sound . . . ," the tape is stopped.

Apparently at this point it was decided to let the tune rest a while and move on to something else. Next up on the session reel is "Ah'w Baby," a tune with a distinctive descending guitar hook line, and rapidly picked guitar fills. According to Jimmie Lee, it was a tune he'd been working on, and "Walter just took it." Robinson continued, "I went by Chess one day, and they was recording up in the studio. Robert Junior and all of us was up there. Walter wanted to do that tune and Robert Junior couldn't do it [right], so he gave me his guitar and I did it. But I didn't know they was recording it." He said it wasn't until he later heard it on the radio that he realized it had been released on a record. "Thugs and thieves, that's all they was," he opined. However, with at least a couple of complete takes of it surviving from this session, it seems unlikely that he could have been completely unaware that a recording was being done.

On the first take, Walter's casual approach to the lyrics gives the impression that he's improvising them on the spot, and his harp mike is too low as he starts his solo. A between-vocal lines nostril-clearing snort marked this take as a reject. After clearing his sinuses, Walter is heard commenting to a female companion who had apparently joined him in the studio, "You're looking good. . . ." Obviously the inspiration helped, and the take that follows is better focused with smoother lyrics and playing, with a nice slow bubbling simmer to it; it became the master take.

For the final tune, somebody suggested the St. Louis Jimmy (Oden) classic blues "Going Down Slow," recorded in 1941 for Bluebird. In comparison to the original, Walter's rendition, renamed "I've Had My Fun," is a sprightly romp. He sticks to Oden's lyrics, but his version rocks compared to the slow bass and piano (played by Roosevelt Sykes) original version. The first attempt was rejected due to a rather abrupt stop in the last verse. Walter's woman friend encourages him, "Please make one more, the next one—." The problem is ironed out, and the next attempt is the keeper, after which Dixon comments, "That was good and fast."

Then, they went back to work again on "Temperature." Apparently they kept rewinding and reusing tape as usual, the takes piling up to no avail. This reel opens with Take 25. A couple of takes break down immediately, then a slow, rather plodding take is completed. Walter is clearly getting frustrated, angry, and tired of this song. "God damn! They can't . . ." Leonard interrupts calmly, "You got forty more [takes] to go, you'll break the record" for the most attempts at a single song. Walter, clearly caught off-guard by Leonard's joke, laughs heartily, "No shit?" breaking the tension. More takes follow, as Walter and Dixon argue over the tune's tempo, with Walter wanting to take the tune slower. But when Dixon counts it off at a snail's pace, it's clear that the band can't stay together at the plodding tempo.

By Take 30, it's obvious that things were deteriorating, getting worse rather than better with all of the repeated takes. "Lets make *another* record, maybe get together," Walter is heard muttering. Now taking Leonard's "Break the record for the most takes attempted" comment seriously, he complains, "Ahh, you motherfuckers! Gawwwwwd damn, you motherfuckers break the record and it's all my fault? Anything you do, it's always my fault!" Trying to get things back on track, Chess calls out "Take 30!"; "I don't want to take no thirty . . ." Walter begins to protest, but the band starts another take anyway. As the band kicks in, Walter's tirade continues: "God damn, motherfuckers! It ain't right!" The band stops mid-beat as Walter continues, "Fuck that shit! You got the thing so confused, I don't know, nobody know . . ." Pointing out that the tape is still rolling, somebody reminds Walter, "It's a take man." "Aww right, but let me know when I sing," Walter says petulantly, "Go!" The balance of the session included more fragments and a couple of complete takes. After almost 40 excruciating attempts, according to a note on the tape log, it was an earlier take, Take 24, that wound up being used as the master.

In August, Walter's hard-won new single, "Temperature," was released. It did okay, but didn't exactly burn up the charts, and must have been a disappointment after all the effort put into it. However, this was balanced by an item in the trades noting that "Jim Fleming called with news that Shaw [Agency] had pacted Little Walter for another five years. [Headman] Milt Shaw planed in for the occasion," encouraging news for Walter. Shaw could continue to book him into the larger venues and on the package tours that Walter liked. Playing the Chicago clubs was okay as a fallback, but Walter liked those high-profile jobs better. The hours were shorter and the bread bigger. And unless he did something to screw it up, a five-year contract seemed like a guarantee of a profitable future.

On September 18, 1957, Jimmy Rogers cut a session at the new Chess studios, backed by Walter, Otis Spann on piano, possibly Luther Tucker on second guitar, Dixon on bass, and Muddy's drummer Francis Clay. All three tunes cut that day have a prototype Dixon cast to them. "What Have I Done" has a slinky, minimalist arrangement, with Walter playing restrained harp throughout, providing counterpoint to Rogers's vocals. After a laconic run through, on the issued version Walter takes a hard-edged, two-chorus solo, and adds twenty-plus seconds worth of much-needed meat to the tune. "My Baby Don't Love Me" is a fairly lightweight pop number that taps into the then-current Latin-beat craze; Walter echoes the vocal lines in a deliberately sparse call-and-response pattern. The arrangement is structured, alternating between the Latin beat and a shuffling backbeat rhythm on the chorus. Despite a very pop, eye-to-the-market arrangement, the track wasn't released at the time. "Trace of You" puts Walter in the rare position of back-up singer; he duets with an otherwise unknown singer named Margaret Whitfield (who also happened to be the proprietor of the Hollywood Rendevouz and the tiny local El Bee Records label), singing answering phrases like "Not a trace of you" to Rogers's lyrics. On the first take, Walter's vocal is prominent, but on the issued version his singing is mixed down. His harp work is limited simply to backup behind the vocal chorus, and a short solo marked by some high-end riffing in the style of Jimmy Reed.

A couple of weeks later, on Tuesday, October 1st, 1957, Walter's sometime girlfriend and occasional road companion, Armilee Thompson, was taken to Cook County hospital in Chicago by her friend and roommate Lolita Scott, for the birth of her baby. Scott says Walter met them at the hospital and waited for the birth to take place, while she returned to the apartment. Afterwards, Walter told Lolita that the child born to Armilee was a girl and said, "I've got a daughter." (Armilee has more recently said that Walter was on the road at the time, and not present for the birth.) When the hospital official came to collect data for the birth certificate, Armilee gave her daughter's name as Marion Blair Jacobs, even though the couple had never married. Armilee listed her birthplace as Pine Bluff, Arkansas, her address as 4716 South Parkway, and said she was 28 years old. Under "Father's information" she listed Walter Jacobs, age 31 (which indicates a birth year of 1926, close to the 1925 date he gave the draft board). Curiously, she gave his occupation as delivery man for a record company. When Armilee brought Marion home she didn't yet have a bed for her. Walter came by to visit and found the baby sleeping in a dresser drawer, wrapped in a blanket. He pulled out a wad of cash and sent the roommate across the street to a furniture store to buy a regular crib.

One night at Rickey's, Big Bill Broonzy came in to catch Walter's show, bringing with him a white Belgian couple, the Bruynoghes. There was a small but devoted cult audience for blues developing in Europe, and Yannick Bruynoghe was one of the first to make a pilgrimage to the U.S. to catch his heroes in action on their home ground; he was in Chicago helping Broonzy put together his autobiography. If there was any animosity towards the white visitors in a black club, it was soon dispelled when it was learned that the foreigners had crossed an ocean just to come to these clubs. That night the band was seated behind a railing, all wearing suits and ties. Yannick saw a youthful and earnest Luther Tucker, picking a hollow-body electric guitar, while next to him Walter was playing on his big 64 Chromatic, eyes slitted as he concentrated on blowing. Off to the side was drummer George Hunter. An onstage photo from around this time caught Walter sitting in on guitar with a group that included Luther Tucker and harpist Earring George—Walter casually dressed in a shirt and slacks as he picks a hollow-body model. Big Bill had also given Bruynoghe a photo that caught an impressive street group; Elmore James, Rice Miller, Tommy McClennan, and Little Walter striding down an urban sidewalk. Walter looks dapper in a slim tie and two-toned shoes, grinning widely. He's strutting, a real cock of the walk.

11 *crazy mixed up world*

Chicago and On the Road:
January 1958–Autumn 1959

In January 1958 Walter returned to the studio for a two-song session. With him were guitarists Luther Tucker and Jimmie Lee Robinson, Lafayette Leake on keyboards, and Willie Dixon on bass; Odie Payne replaced Fred Below on drums in the studio for the first time, although he'd been playing with the band since Below quit touring with them. Jimmie Lee noted that Payne, who'd spent time playing and recording with Elmore James, Tampa Red, and others, was one of the best drummers in blues, "Young and fast, faster than Below."

Robinson felt that a good drummer could really drive a band. "You don't hardly need a bass when you got a drummer that know how to use his foot, know how to make his drops in the right place and time, with the feeling, with the turnaround," he opined. "A lot of times [when] you hear the bass real strong, you think it's the bass, but it'd be the drummer's foot, pushing. The bass [guitar] and the drum got to work together or else it's no good." Robinson remembered that at their record sessions, they'd usually do tunes they'd already worked out on gigs; the stage was their rehearsal hall and testing ground, because there were never any formal rehearsals during the time he was with the band. Walter knew that they understood his music—what he wanted to do and how they would support him—so he'd just start playing and they'd fall in behind him. However there was a logistical screwup at this session, as neither Tucker nor Robinson brought his own guitar amp; both ended up having to plug into the single beat-up studio unit, resulting in some rather funky, distorted guitar sounds.

A slinky, minor-key instrumental, "The Toddle," came first. Tucker claimed it was his arrangement, saying that he'd suggested a few things for Walter to play. The guitar is twangy a la Duane Eddy, with a tight guitar/ harp call-and-response arrangement running throughout the tune. Walter gives a short break to Tucker and Leake, who briefly trade off guitar and piano licks, before returning to step out himself. He tosses off some nice phrases and the tune has a catchy sound to it, but it lacks some of the visceral excitement most of his early instrumentals had displayed;

he sounds as if he's taking a more studied, jazzy approach, instead of from-the-gut blues wailing.

For a vocal side, Walter reached back to 1941 for a number done by both Jay McShann and Dr. Clayton, the now-standard "Confessing the Blues." Walter gives a very literal reading of McShann's recording vocally, with some nice B. B. King-influenced guitar backing from Tucker, and Leake on droning organ. Walter's fine, forceful vocal is abetted by solid if relatively unspectacular harp work. The sides were released as Walter's next single in March; it failed to chart nationally.

Although accounts vary widely, it was most likely during this winter that an incident took place that deeply affected Little Walter's future: He was shot in the left leg during some sort of altercation. The few details that are known of this incident have been told and retold so many times by so many people in the Chicago blues community that the story has passed into legend, becoming something of a touchstone for those discussing Walter and his career. Consciously or unconsciously, most people who were around Walter at the time seem to divide his career into "pre-shooting" and "post-shooting" eras, and it seems as if there are as many versions of the circumstances as there are narrators.

Luther Tucker says:

> We was working on the West side of Chicago, and Little Walter had a girlfriend, which he didn't trust her too much. That night about twelve o'clock we was playing, Walter said "I'm gonna take a break, Robert Jr., you take over the band"—since Robert was like a dad to us all. [Walter] said, "You play this set, by the time you get through with this set, I'll be right back." He taken off and went over to his girlfriend's house, she live about three miles away. And he caught her with her boyfriend. They got to arguing, got to fighting, got to wrassling over a gun—and it went off, hit Little Walter in the leg. That night we was looking, where is Little Walter? And we found out he was in the hospital.

Walter's half-sister Marguerite tells a somewhat different story, which she heard later on:

> He was tussling in the projects, down on State Street, he had a .32, slipped in the snow, it went off and hit him in the leg. Of course the police was called and the ambulance . . . they took him, not to Cabrini [Hospital] but to Cook County . . . the cops and the doctors cut the cuff of his pants, he was saying "Please don't cut my pants"—he had a lid of weed. They busted him right there, Leonard had to pay to get him out of that trouble.

In Robert Lockwood's version: "Him and his woman supposed to have some kind of little problem, and they was scuffling over a gun. Gun went off and shot him in the leg. When the police came to the scene he had his hand closed up, they pried his hand open. He had three sticks of marijuana in his hand . . . so when they got him to the hospital they chained him to the bed." Lockwood said he asked Muddy to talk to Leonard about the situation, but:

> . . . [Muddy] grumbled. Leonard say he don't want nothing to do with him . . . I went on down there and got on Leonard's ass. Leonard called over there and told them to take the chains off him, that's all, he had a lot of power. I got over there and Walter said, "My

white father got them chains off me." I said, "You're goddamn lying, your black father got them chains off you." He laid up there and looked up at me just as funny. I said, "Leonard and Muddy was going to let your goddamn ass rot right here."

Walter was released from the hospital, and got around on crutches while his leg healed. His sister Lillian noted this was the beginning of a major change in Walter's personality, "After he got shot in the leg, that's when he *really* started getting depressed." Billy Boy Arnold also commented on the effect that the shooting had on Walter:

> Before he got crippled, Walter had a real cocky walk, real self-assured. I saw Junior [Wells] try and imitate that walk . . . see Willie Anderson was so caught up in Walter's spell that he'd go up on stage and blow, and come off limping just like Walter. Everybody was cracking up—he wasn't even crippled. But when Walter got crippled he still had a unique way of moving, he'd grab his nose, like you squeeze the tip of your nose and close his eyes and shake his head? Willie Anderson did all those gestures when he'd be blowing, he wore the same type of hats Little Walter wore, he did everything.

Willie Anderson was born in West Memphis in 1920, making him ten years Walter's senior. He came to Chicago in 1939 and first played with mandolin player and guitarist Johnny Young (as Walter himself had done shortly after his own arrival in Chicago). Once Anderson heard Walter, he became totally captivated by his style and followed him religiously, eventually becoming a drinking crony, and Walter's occasional driver. He was so immersed in Walter's music that it was said that he sometimes substituted for Walter onstage and got away with it, because he both looked and sounded like him. It was a complex relationship; Walter must have been flattered that the older man looked up to him, yet by most accounts he never acknowledged Anderson's talent or publicly gave him any signs of respect. According to Billy Boy Arnold, Anderson ". . . followed Walter around like a puppy dog," but this devotion was rarely rewarded. According to some, Anderson was his valet. But Tucker took him seriously: "He's truly a musician. He had a day job, a good day job, he's got some knowledge behind him—but he would be at the club *every* night that we play. He'd bring Walter a pint of whiskey, ask how do you do this, how you do that?" Billy Boy Arnold added, "When he got off work, he drove Walter's brand new, midnight blue four-door '57 Cadillac all around, carrying Walter, be four or five guys in the car. Willie was hanging around, trying to learn licks and get in his corner—he would've died for Walter at the time."

Muddy had been holding down a regular gig at Smitty's Corner, where ". . . everybody came in," according to his drummer Francis Clay. "People from the blues world, also modern jazz too, like Cannonball [Adderley], and Roy Eldridge. Sonny Boy, he'd come in, Big Bill Broonzy before he died, after he came back from Europe. And everybody . . . B.B. and Bobby Blue Bland." It was there that Walter sustained yet another injury:

> See, he'd been shot by a woman, he wasn't quite well, he shouldn't have been out yet. One winter night there was ice out and everything—he said he just had to come out and jam with us, so he came to Smitty's Corner. Played a hell of a show like he always did—or

most of the time. Sometimes he couldn't get it together, but when he did—I'm sorry! Anyway, he slipped and fell on the ice and broke his leg, I don't know how many places. But he was crippled up ever since then. Ever since, harmonica players have been limping on one foot as though they were crippled, a whole lot of them!

Waver Glascock, Walter's sometime traveling companion, said, "He slipped and broke his leg on the ice, coming home where I lived on Douglas Boulevard off Kedzie. It had snowed and melted inside the entrance. He could have sued the man but he didn't. He didn't want to go to the hospital, Maddie and I put him in his Cad and I drove, his leg was swollen and in pain, he decided to go." While Walter was still laid up, Waver decided to leave Chicago and return to California. She visited him in the hospital, kissed him goodbye, and left the next day.

Guitarist Jimmie Lee Robinson hadn't been too happy with the way things were working out. He remarked in later years that the band he'd first joined was a hot unit, and probably would've gone on to record some of the jazz-based numbers they were doing on stage, such as the instrumental standard "Canadian Sunset." However, he was dismayed by the changes in the drummer's seat; after having worked with the jazzy stylings of Odie Payne, he was disappointed by the replacements:

> Billy Stepney was the first drummer after Payne. He played another kind of drum, a free drum—he might've had some soul with his hands but not his feet. [After Stepney left], that left George Hunter, old straight-ahead George. We could play the same songs with him but it wasn't the same—he didn't have the speed in his foot and hands—the feeling was gone. I know Tucker liked him, they smoked joints together. But it was just killing me, my bass never sounded right with him.

According to Jimmie Lee, things came to a head during a regular gig the band held down at The Zanzibar, where they'd moved following a long run at Ricky's Show Lounge. They were scheduled to play there the same night Jimmie heard that Walter had been shot, so he, Luther Tucker, and George Hunter showed up anyway and did the gig as a trio, with Robinson taking the vocals. The trio continued the regular gigs they'd been scheduled to play with Walter (sometimes aided by sit-in harpist George Maywether) while Walter was in the hospital, but Hunter's rather plodding rhythm got to Robinson. By mid-summer of 1958, he'd left the group and hooked up with Magic Sam, replacing Sam's army-bound bass player. Jimmie Lee confirms that after the shooting, Walter always walked with a noticeable limp. Although no longer a regular band member, Jimmie Lee still did occasional fill-in gigs with Walter over the next few years.

If Walter was fading in record-sales popularity, he nevertheless remained a big attraction in the clubs, especially with the women who still found him boyishly handsome, despite the scars that were beginning to mark his countenance. Some of Walter's scars came from run-ins with the law, Jimmie Lee said: "Ignorant cops found Walter an easy target, they'd call him over, get him to stick his head through the cop car window, then roll it up on his neck." Other scars came from fights that Walter either instigated, or refused to turn away from. Tucker remembered one that occurred when they were playing at The Barrelhouse:

This chick, she worked down at the union hall. I didn't know she was going with Walter at the time. She came to the club, said, "Walter, I'm gonna tell you something." Walter say, "Okay baby, you tell me [later] . . . I gotta go up there and play right now." What she wanted to tell him was that her husband was coming down later, and he knew that both of them was going together. Little Walter didn't know that, so he's up there playing. When he come down, her husband had walked in the door. She's on the other side of the club, she seen her husband but Little Walter didn't see him. So Little Walter get down and go over there, give her a little kiss. She said, "Don't do that, my husband!" He said, "Well why didn't you tell me?" He looks around—big fella too, six feet six, built like superman. Oh Walter, how you gonna get out of this one? This cat was mad, he go over to his wife, says "You go over there and tell him I wanna see him outside!" She come tell Walter, he say "That's okay—come on, Tucker." I say, "Oh boy, you got me into this, now both of us gonna get beat up!" So Little Walter walks out the door, this cat says "Yeah, I wanna tell you about my wife. . . ." Just when he said "wife," Little Walter slapped him upside down, he slapped him so hard his heels went up in the air and his head hit the ground. He's a little fellow, but big hands. He said "Come on Tucker, let's get him!" I say, "You just about killed the man already; you want me to help you?" The man got up and start running to his car. We had an equipment man, [he] outrun him to his car—he realized he couldn't get to his car so he kept running down the street. He ran down the alley, that's where Little Walter caught him again. Little Walter had whipped the fellow so bad his shirt was hanging off him, his pants was hanging off him, his nose was bleeding. Then the police come: "All right, you going to jail, both of you for fighting!" Walter said, "We ain't fighting, we just wrassling"—the fellow says "Yeah, we were just wrassling." And that saved us from going to jail that night. We had so many nights like that you wouldn't believe it. [Laughs]

It wasn't uncommon for Walter's troubles to have roots in his insatiable appetite for collecting girlfriends. Jimmie Lee recalled a beautiful young girl Walter brought back to Chicago; Walter met her while the band was out on the road, stole her away from her man, and brought her to Chicago, where she stayed for a while. Walter eventually tired of her, and she went back home, but not all such relationships ended so cleanly. Robinson thought that the woman who was involved with Walter's shooting might have been one he'd brought back after a road trip as well.

Another night, another gig; this time Walter found himself in the middle of some trouble caused by a frustrated fan with a gun. "It was a club over on the West Side by the stadium," Tucker recounted:

We had a tremendous house, it was packed, any place you could stand people was standing. This fellow, he's got one hour before he's gotta go to work. He say, "I wanna see Little Walter, we gonna dance tonight." The cat tell him, "I'm sorry sir, the place is so packed there's not even standing room." The fellow say, "I gotta get in there, I wanna see Little Walter, I wanna hear him blow—there's gotta be one place on the side!" They say, "No, there's not." So the bouncer closes the screen door and just as he's walking back to the bar, this fellow taken out a .38 and he shot. First shot hit the bouncer in the back of the neck. Didn't kill him. Second shot went up against the wall someplace. Third shot—I'm over here playing—third shot hit this guy right near me in the eye. I jumped behind the bar with my guitar, I just dived—I didn't know whether this cat was gonna shoot again. Shot this fellow in the eye, it was terrible. Then when the police come they arrested Little

Walter and the fellow who got shot in the eye. The guy who did the shooting, they caught him about four hours later. He got outta jail but Little Walter had to pay his way out, the other fella, too. I'm sure glad the fellow didn't die, it was terrible. Just 'cause he couldn't hear Little Walter blow, ain't nobody else gonna enjoy it either!

At Chess Records, the wind was definitely shifting. Sales figures and chart trends made it obvious to the brothers that there was a larger market for the Rock & Roll records by Chuck Berry and Bo Diddley, and vocal groups like The Moonglows, than for the straight blues acts on the label's roster. Blues, while not being completely ignored, was being moved to a back burner, and newer, younger artists were getting more attention. Also changing were the recording techniques used, thanks to new advances in the type of equipment available. Where in the past everything had been done "live" in the studio with singer and band all recorded at the same time, Chess was now starting to occasionally cut band backing tracks without the vocals. This had a twofold benefit: not only did the band not have to keep repeating their part while a vocalist struggled with lyrics or phrasing, it also meant that now the vocalist was on an isolated track and could be mixed down into the final track later, and with more accuracy.

Chess was also taking big steps in the marketplace by compiling some of their successful singles onto long-playing albums for the first time. Their initial LP offerings a year earlier had concentrated on jazz artists like Ahmad Jamal. When it looked like the twelve-inch disks were here to stay, they turned to Chuck Berry and doo-wop groups for material. A mid-April 1958 release was the real break-through for blues fans; *The Best of Muddy Waters* was the first collection of straight-ahead urban blues ever available on LP. There had been some previous folk-blues collections on the market, by Big Bill Broonzy, Lead Belly, and Sonny Terry and Brownie McGhee. Sonny and Brownie were playing to rapt "folk" audiences in April of that year, but Muddy's album was the first to feature modern, relatively contemporary urban blues styles, ranging from his solo "Rolling Stone," to full-out band tracks like "I'm Ready," in all their funky glory. Walter was well represented on the disk, with his harp playing heard on six of the twelve tracks, and his guitar on two more.

Not long after came *The Best of Little Walter*, twelve tracks compiled from his hit singles to date, including of course "Juke" and "My Babe." The cover photo was a striking black-and-white studio shot by Don Bronstein: a close up of Walter's face and hands as he plays his big chromatic harmonica. A younger generation of harp players studied Bronstein's cover photo, eventually figuring out that he was holding a Hohner 64 Chromatic, then ran out to buy one and tried to mimic his records. Some very basic biographical information was found in the liner notes, by writer Studs Terkel; Terkel had probably only had a brief conversation with Walter. The liner notes stated that Walter started to play at age six, and moved to Chicago with his family at age eight. In response to a question about his choice of such a "humble instrument," Walter is quoted as saying, "If a guy could pick up a peanut and make something out of it [an oblique reference to the agricultural achievements of George Washington Carver], I figure I could take the harp and make something out of it." Asked about his singing, Walter responded, "I needed breathing time. If I blowed that harp without any rest, I'd never make it. Not the way I blow. So I began to sing in between my blowing, just to rest my lips and harp." Walter also bragged a little about his popularizing the instrument; "Not so long ago, a harp sold for a quarter. Now it cost two dollars. It'd be nice if the company remember who helped raise that price." Walter also told Terkel that he wasn't familiar with the gospel number "This Train," on which Dixon had based "My Babe": "I didn't know when it was given to me. I never heard that spiritual. You see, I'm not a regular church-going Christian, though I'm a good believer. Maybe I should go more often, then I'd've known where it came from." The overall impact of the album was stunning; the four instrumentals set the standard for harp technique and tonal qualities, and the vocal tracks had a fresh updated feel. Although it wasn't necessarily a "hit" at the time, this LP went a long way towards establishing Walter as a true master of his art to the world at large, and ultimately found its way into the collections of a large number of important and influential musicians in the years to come.

On August 14, 1958, Big Bill Broonzy died of throat cancer. He'd last sung in 1957, before an operation had accidentally damaged his vocal cords. There was a large funeral with the musical elite turning out, and a photo of the crowd at the service shows a serious Little Walter in attendance. The pallbearers included Muddy Waters, Tampa Red, Brother John Sellars, Otis Spann, Sunnyland Slim, Francis Clay, and others. In many ways, Broonzy's death marked the end of an era, coming at a time when the market for deep blues among its original audience was fading.

At the same time, Walter's drinking and careless attitudes were escalating to the point where they were starting to affect his gigs. Jimmy Rogers recalled that Walter would let just about anybody up on the bandstand if it would allow him an opportunity to take it easy: "A harmonica player'd come in, if he could play pretty good, that's right up Walter's alley. Little Walter would come down, get in his car and go drive and get some whiskey or something. When he come back it's closing time and he's drunk. The [owner] man is mad, people done walked out. And then Walter starts cussing, wanting his money, you know. There's a lot of tricks about this stuff."

Billy Boy Arnold remembered a problem at The Barrelhouse. His and Walter's bands split an opening week there. "When Walter was in town, a couple times they had him on weekends," Arnold recalled. "I went over one weekend, the guy says 'Man, that goddamn Little Walter passed out in here the other night!' They had to carry him out hand and foot, put him in the back seat of his Cadillac." Some club owners were bothered by Walter's tendency to spend his break times keeping to himself, isolated with a woman, or away from the club altogether. They were more used to gregarious bluesmen who'd work the crowd between sets, making an effort to curry favor with the audience by mixing with the customers.

Even before Jimmie Lee Robinson's departure, Walter was looking to make a change in the group. He'd approached a 19-year-old guitarist—coincidentally also named Robinson—who'd played some gigs with his shadow, Willie Anderson. Freddie Robinson (later known as Abu Talib) had come up from Arkansas, moving to Chicago in 1956. He played with Birmingham Junior and His Lover Boys, who cut one record on the Ebony label, and was hanging out on the South and West Side scenes when he met Walter. "He told me he was gonna hire me in Jimmie Lee Robinson's place," Freddie said, "and he hadn't even heard me play. I guess Willie Anderson had brainwashed him. [Walter] told me he wanted me to come around and listen to him, become familiar with the situation." Freddie was a bit leery, since he'd heard about Walter's notorious reputation for the way he treated his musicians, but in his case the fears were unfounded. "He liked me for some reason, I don't know to this day why," he said. "I really wasn't up to par as far as my professionalism was concerned. He gave me on-the-job training, he let me hang out with him."

Robinson later recalled:

We used to go by Muddy's gig all the time, because he was the only person I know Walter had any respect for. Everybody else, he considered them less than an artist . . . Tucker and Hunter, they used to give me a hard time, but Walter told them to just leave me alone and let me develop. Tucker really did help me a whole lot . . . in terms of showing me the ropes both musically and otherwise. . . . We did some stuff that was just unbelievable. We'd get high and go in there and just blow the roof off the place. That's why it was so difficult for me when I first started, I couldn't keep up with those guys. They were doing "Lester Leaps In" and a whole bunch of other stuff that required some skills. But I was able to stick with it.

Robinson recalled that Walter was on crutches when he initially began working with him. He knew the stories of Walter's shooting; he too had heard the version about Walter being busted at the time for having some pot stashed in his pants cuff. Robinson said he wasn't on crutches long:

. . . not nearly as long as he should have been, that's why he wound up limping. He was determined he wasn't gonna be on crutches, so he didn't let himself heal the way he should have. He started walking without crutches, putting weight on his foot way too soon . . . I lived a few blocks from him, I was at his house every day. We would go down to Jewtown, he'd show me the ropes down there. He had a bunch of ladies working the streets, he was pimping. He showed me how he collected his money and kept everybody in line, how he handled his business . . .

Speaking of Walter's women on the street, he added, "That was one of your requisitions for being a rough hombre back in those days. Everybody tried to do that, to be that, so yeah, he had a lot of women."

Billy Boy Arnold also knew that Walter had ". . . several whores out on Maxwell Street," but he didn't think it was any kind of serious business proposition. "It was more like they was women he could screw anytime he wanted, and tell them to go get him some money," Arnold said. "He'd act rough with women, he always had that rough, whoopin' ass tactic type of thing . . . You know, he was a big time celebrity, so they wanted to be with him anyway, they come and give him money just to be in his company."

In August of 1958 Chess called a session which found both Muddy and Walter's bands in the studio, an event which has caused considerable confusion among discographers. Muddy laid down three new titles that day, while Walter completed two, but the sequence of events and personnel have been a matter of some dispute. If the chronology of the master numbers is to be believed, the session began with Muddy cutting two numbers, then Walter doing a couple. The numerical sequence then takes a giant leap ahead some 150 numbers, and shows Muddy returning for one more tune, followed again by Walter, for another take at a number attempted earlier that day. Adding to the confusion, there was some personnel trading going on as well, with drummers being swapped from one band to the other.

Muddy led off the session with a slower tune of his, "19 Years Old," which may have been inspired by his latest young girlfriend. Like all three of Muddy's tunes that day, this one is in the key of "B," with Walter accompanying here on an "A" harp played in third position. For once Dixon's bass is prominent in the mix, as is Spann's piano. Walter weaves his accompaniment tightly into Muddy's vocals during the verses, then on the break he works his way up the harp, fashioning an interesting solo, although he seems to be fighting for space with Pat Hare's rapidfire guitar picking. "Close to You" is another Dixon novelty lyric: "I want to get close to you as the white on rice." After a run-through take, Walter seems concerned about being drowned out by the band, and says to the drummer, "Hey man, dig it, why don't you play with your brushes, get a better sound?" "Why don't you let him drive it?" someone says, and Muddy concurs, "Let him drive it." Walter begins to protest, "I want 'em to hear me . . . ," but Muddy interjects, "Let's make it," and they do, with the drummer using sticks, not brushes. The mid-song solo goes to Pat Hare's guitar, while Walter just accompanies in the background.

Muddy's third tune, "Walking Through the Park," was another mid-tempo number. After a first run-through as a straight shuffle, Walter came up with a syncopated Latin-tinged intro, demonstrating it to the band on his harp while snapping his fingers, and then vocalizing the riff: "Bamp, Bam de Bamp!" The drummer murmurs, "That's a Latin American intro, I don't know . . . ," then counts it in. Walter takes his harp intro lead-in and the first verse on an "E" harp in second position, then switches harps and plays the rest of the song on an "A" harp played in third position. He plays a simple but effective solo, breaking through with some dynamic rhythm stabs, making sure that he's heard this time. A second solo chorus later on is taken by guitarist Hare; it's clear that although the harmonica was still pivotal to Muddy's sound, current trends dictated that it was now going to be sharing the solo spotlight with a flashy young guitarist.

Walter then stepped up with *his* band, and his new guitarist Freddie Robinson ran into a problem. "My main humiliation came when we were doing 'Key To The Highway,'" he said. "And I had never done any eight-bar blues, so I wasn't able to get that on the first go-round. Of course it didn't take me but a few minutes to get it. But they wouldn't accept that, because they were riding me anyway. That's how Muddy Waters wound up playing on that . . . they would not let me recover that day." There may have been other motives beyond Chess's impatience at work; it had been a couple years since Walter had a chart hit, and perhaps Leonard wanted to reunite the winning combination of Muddy and Walter for the single. So Muddy, who had put away his guitar and was performing exclusively as a singer at that point in his career, picked up his instrument once again, and they worked out an old standard, "Key To The Highway," putting it in the can on the second take. The tune had been cut by two artists within a few months of each other in 1940, first by its composer Charles Segar on Vocalion, then by Jazz Gillum on Bluebird. A year later Big Bill Broonzy recorded a third version, with Gillum playing harp; Broonzy's version was the hit, and the song would be associated with him from then on. With this session taking place right around the time of Broonzy's death on August 14th, it's possible that the song was chosen as a kind of informal tribute to one of the best-known and well-liked elder statesmen on the Chicago blues scene. Walter and crew do a fairly straightforward cover of Gillum's version of the song, and Walter tosses in one of Bill's original verses. Overall, it's a very subdued recording; whether overcome by emotion, or by something else, Walter delivers a heartfelt but low-key vocal, and his harp playing is—for him—pretty rudimentary. Nonetheless, Chess may have had thoughts of a tribute stirring some sales interest, because the number was chosen as the "A" side of Walter's next single.

Next was a heavily-reverbed instrumental jam. Muddy tuned his guitar down to an open "G" chord, recapturing the sound of some of their earlier days together. The first take was listed as "Walking On" when it was finally issued on a compilation in the 1990s. It's arranged in a call-and-response pattern; Walter leads off with short riff that Muddy answers in kind, then Walter gradually ascends the scale over the course of the first verse, reversing the process on the following one. Muddy's guitar gets two solo verses, then Walter and Muddy trade back and forth one chorus apiece, before a final duet verse that fades out mid-chorus. In many ways, this one is the most interesting of the three existing takes of the number, but apparently somebody didn't like it, because they went on to take several more shots. By Take 9, Walter suggested Muddy tune down to an open "D" chord, which would suit the tuning of Walter's big chromatic harp. Walter opens up playing his small diatonic harp for a couple of verses, using some of the ideas developed on the earlier takes, then the guitar takes a couple of choruses. Walter then comes in blowing the chromatic, giving the number a decidedly different feel, but also muddying up the easy-rocking bounce of the tune. (This take was finally issued in the '90s with the title "Rock Bottom—Alternate.") Muddy then tuned back to "G," and after an admonishment from Leonard, "Don't fuck with the mike, man, let's go!" Walter did something totally out of character: he opened the tune with an intro borrowed right out of one of his earlier recordings, "Juke," a fact noted on the session log attached to the tape reel. This take, number 10, was the keeper. Guitar and harp trade a couple of verses, and Walter creates a bouncing solo that zigs and zags unexpectedly before reprising the opening figure, after which the number fades abruptly. This one was released as the "B" side of the single as "Rock Bottom."

According to Francis Clay, the session was intended to record a full album worth of material from Walter, but was cut short. "There would have been the album, but Walter was too out of it—he drank too much. So we couldn't add any more songs to complete the album," Clay said. He remarked that the attempts to cut "Rock Bottom" deteriorated to the point that it turned into a "jam," with plenty of leftover "footage" that wasn't usable. Clay also recalled Walter's pied-piper way with women; "I met Tina Turner through him, she must've been about 15 or 16 I guess . . . I think he met her in St. Louis, brought her to Chicago. I don't know if she stayed any length of time, but she was something; there's some beautiful women down in St. Louis!" Clay said he can still picture young Anna Mae Bullock, before she became known as Tina, turning and laughing as she walked out of Smitty's with Walter.

The August 1958 trade papers had an item regarding a possible Atlantic/Chess Records exchange deal. "As we overheard it, Chess would lend Muddy Waters to

Atlantic who would wax twenty-four sides with Waters and [jazz pianist] John Lewis. Then Atlantic would release one of the sets and Chess the other, or both labels would issue both sets together. There was also a chance that Little Walter would appear on some of the tracks. Nothing was concluded, but don't be surprised if something on this order eventually happens between the diskeries. And it isn't such a bad idea anyway." Apparently the "execs" had thought better of this overheard conversation, and nothing ever came of it, although if Clay's account is true, the album he referred to may have been intended for this project. In October, Chess released Muddy's "19 Years Old"; it reached #9 on the *Billboard* charts. A couple of weeks later, Walter's "Key To The Highway" was issued, climbing to #6 on the charts. It was to be Walter's last Top-Ten hit.

Walter's band was making regular short road trips, mostly in the south, within a day's drive from Chicago: Memphis, spots in Ohio, Indiana, Missouri, and Kentucky. "We weren't on the road for months at a time," Freddie Robinson said. "Some times less than a week, but we did it frequently." They played venues ranging from taverns to arenas, sharing the bill on the larger shows with artists like Ruth Brown, James Moody, and The Paul Williams Orchestra.

Robinson felt that Walter never reproduced in the studio what he could achieve— on a good night—in the clubs:

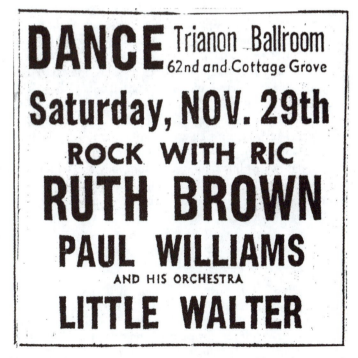

Figure 11.1 Trianon Ballroom advertisement, *Chicago Defender*, November 29, 1958.

His best work, that I've been privileged to hear him perform, on the bandstand with him—none of the recordings even measure up to that at all. You had time to do what you wanted to do on the bandstand. Back in those days recordings were kept under three minutes. A lot of stuff we played on gigs we wouldn't record: Lester Young, some jazz things. If we heard something on the jukebox, Lou Donaldson, Horace Silver—that wasn't the kind of stuff we were gonna record for Chess. Even on the blues stuff, you had more room to experiment and create [on gigs]. Once you go outside and get high and come back— even if you had played a song, it wouldn't be like that the next time. We would decide that we were going to go in there and burn the roof—that's what the objective was.

Near the end of October, Muddy Waters and his pianist Otis Spann left for their first tour of England, playing mainly as a duo (although joined by Chris Barber's "Trad" Dixieland-style jazz band on their encores) for the growing contingent of white jazz and blues enthusiasts there. Although it was a dramatically toned-down version of what Muddy's band was capable of, the electric slide-guitar and rocking piano were too much for people accustomed to—and expecting—solo/acoustic folk-blues concerts like those by Broonzy and Sonny and Brownie, who'd played in England earlier. The local press complained about "Screaming guitars and howling pianos," although judging from the enthusiastic crowd response heard on a recording of one of the shows, at least some of those in attendance appreciated the "screaming" and "howling."

Back in Chicago, full-blown urban blues and R&B was still a big live draw; *Defender* ads ran for a November 29th "Rock With Ric" dance, hosted by popular R&B radio DJ "Ric" Ricardo at the Trianon, headlining Ruth Brown, featuring the Paul Williams Orchestra and Little Walter. Ric was back with a Christmas Night dance at the Pershing Ballroom featuring "Muddy Waters, Wade Flemmons ('Here I Stand'), Chicago's own L.C. Cook and J. B. Lanore" [sic].

Mississippi harpist Carey Bell and pianist Lovie Lee had moved to Chicago, trying to make it there with their five-piece group. They started out at Rickey's Show Lounge doing a fill-in gig for Jimmy Rogers, then scuffled for other jobs. But the band was mostly underage and had trouble getting into clubs. Bell and his pregnant wife wound up staying with relatives of hers, but Bell was soon tossed out, and he hooked up with Honeyboy Edwards. "Honeyboy took me in," Bell said. "Kitchenette, one room with a kitchen and a bath, rent wasn't but $14 a week. Honeyboy was on relief, we would go to Jewtown and play, pool the money." One night during the last part of '58, with nothing else to do, he and Honeyboy headed over to the Zanzibar at 13th and Ashland, where Little Walter was playing. Bell wasn't allowed in because he was underage, so he sat out in the car.

When the band took a break, Honeyboy brought Walter out. "He told Walter I was playing, that I was a good harp player," Bell says:

He told more lie than truth. Walter says, "Let me hear you hit a tune for me." I'm bashful, ashamed, whatever, goddamn, I don't wanna do this. . . . He said "Come on son, you can do it, lemme hear you, Junior." I played a little bit, "Juke," I said "That's the only thing I know Mr. Walter, I heard a little bit of what you do on the radio." I know how to start it off, I was doing pretty good . . . [but] there's a break in "Juke," that's what I couldn't get. Walter says "What happened to the break?" I says, "I ain't learned it yet." He says "Let me see that harp, I'm gonna show it to you." He showed it to me—I still couldn't get it. He said, "Junior, you can get that, if you don't get it man, I'm gonna whip your ass!" Just like that, scared the fuck outta me. He showed me a couple more times, I kinda half-way got it. He said, "Now you getting it—next time I see you, you gonna have it." Anyway, we got to be friends.

Walter encouraged Bell musically, teaching by example. "He'd take the harp and do something, then he'd give it back to me and say, 'See can you do what I just did?' Sometimes I'd get it right off, sometimes I'd have to take it along. That's how I really got to [know] Walter's stuff. He'd be on his gigs, I'd just be around, sitting in . . . he'd say, 'Everything I do, Junior, answer me back with the harp.' He'd hit a note, sometimes I'd get it real good . . ."

Walter also gave Bell a hand with his love life. "My kids' mother, when I started going with her, she didn't know I was a musician," Bell said:

She wanted to see Little Walter, I took her. We got there, I know he was gonna call me up. I went and told Walter, "Don't call me up—this girl I got, she don't wanna go with musicians." He says, "Okay Junior, come on in." We goes in, Walter gets up on the bandstand, plays two numbers. Goes, "Ladies and gentlemen, we got a young man, I call him Junior—give him a nice round of applause to come to the bandstand." Goddamn, I could've shit right there! I went up and played, turned around and played a little bass, and I come down. She said, "You lied to me!" I said, "Awww, I used to do this, I don't do this no more . . ." Walter come down and encouraged her to let me play—and she went for it.

Besides music, Walter and Carey shared a taste for drinking:

At first he wouldn't even have a drink. Third or fourth time together, he asked me did I drink? I drank white port wine at the time, I think he was drinking scotch. He said, "Well, I'm not gonna give you none of my scotch, what else do you drink?" I said "I drink a little wine." He went and got a whole pint of white port. Put some Kool Aid in it, that's what they call Shake and Bake. I drink that wine and got to feeling good, kinda got used to him, the way he talk. I thought he was gonna bother me, but he didn't, he was trying to make me learn. After that we hung out quite a bit, Walter got so he'd come by the house kinda often, we'd hang out all night long . . . wake up in the car lotsa times, he's in the front seat, I'm in the back seat, police picking on the damn window [laughs] . . .

Bell had heard of bad Walter's reputation: "A lotta people told me, you don't know what you're doing hanging out with that guy. He'll get drunk, do this, do that. Tell you the truth, I ain't never knowed Walter to get in no fights that I saw . . . I never saw Walter do nothing, no more than to hisself. Like driving them cars, tear up a Cadillac every six months . . . Chess was putting up them cars for him, he'd tear 'em up."

Muddy's harpman James Cotton seconds this last statement; he later told a story about Walter collecting his royalties in the form of new Cadillacs. ". . . he wrecked the car, so he called Chess said 'I want another car.' The man said 'I just bought you a Cadillac.' Walter said 'I can't help that, I need some other car.' He called Chess four, five times, Chess kept turning him down. So he was traveling up the street [Michigan Avenue], studio right there—he drove right into the office. Him and his secretary just sitting there. Walter got out and left it, said, 'Tell Chess I need a new car.'" Marshall

Chess, however, discounts Cotton's story: "No, I'm not sure that's true—again, I wasn't always there . . . I can't believe I wouldn't have heard about that one. Unless it [just] went up on the curb, if it was really a major smash-through I would've known about it . . ."

Like many other label owners of the time, Chess would "reward" artists with new cars and other gifts, often in lieu of paying royalties. Marshall Chess recalls:

> We had different deals with different artists, I can't remember the details. Sometimes they wanted the company to buy the car and deduct it from their royalties, sometimes we advanced them the money, they bought the car. [But] there wasn't any perk Cadillac plan. It was what the guy wanted, how he wanted to do it, and how it could work out best for all of us. Might even have gotten 'em hooked up with a finance company, had payments . . . [Leonard] knew a Cadillac dealer, my dad loved Cadillacs, he got one every year. We would help them get the best deal. How it was paid for, there was no plan, every artist wanted a Cadillac . . . [My dad could] make it work for everyone. He took care of artists— it wasn't that easy then for a black guy then to walk into a car dealer and buy a Cadillac. Maybe cosign for it and stuff, I don't know, there wasn't any formula.

Muddy was back in the studio in January with Walter on board for a recording date that was spent almost entirely working on songs based on the same slow groove. The session is notable for a couple of other reasons: for the first time, Muddy was recording with a Fender electric bass player (Andrew Stephenson); and for the first studio date in years, Walter was playing acoustic harp exclusively. It's a safe bet it wasn't his idea; Chess continued to insist that Walter record without his harp amp. The studio outtakes show Walter taking an active role in the direction on the music. He admonishes the band (which included his guitarist Tucker) to "Cool it down now," as he starts a countoff for the first take of "Blues Before Sunrise." Muddy gets one line out before Chess interrupts the take: "Hold it Muddy. Say, ah, guitar, ah . . . Tucker, where he says 'Blues before sunrise,' you oughta come in with a figure in there, right after that. 'Blues before sunrise'—dom-do-do-dom, play those fill-ins. All right, let's take it again, that was a good start too. Aww right, take two, Walter . . ." Again Walter, sounding slightly loaded, says, "Go on, count it off then," then counts it in himself, but the take again breaks down on the intro. The third try is the charm. Muddy sings the old Leroy Carr standard from 1934, as Walter interjects harp replies to the vocal lines, at one point shouting out encouragement to Muddy—"I hear ya, man!"—and squeezing the most out of his un-amplified harp through the generous use of hand "wah wah" effects.

The second tune, "Mean Mistreater," differs only in lyrics; it's in the same key, and the melody and backing are virtually identical, save for a stop-time bridge. Muddy's vocal is stronger than on the first number, and this was the song that was picked for his next single. Again, Walter does call-and-response harp fills, and switches harps a few times over the course of the tune.

The third number also uses the identical melody. "Crawling Kingsnake" is a delta standard that had recently hit for John Lee Hooker. On one early take, Walter plays most of his solo chorus on a different type of harmonica than he'd used briefly on the previous number: probably a Hohner Echo Harp. This type of instrument is almost never heard in a blues context, but was popular with polka and old-timey harmonica players; it consists of what amounts to two sets of reeds sandwiched together, one atop the other, tuned an octave apart. When the player blows one hole, he produces two separate tones, which gives a wheezing, almost accordion-like sound to the instrument, although with less volume; moving twice as many reeds requires double the wind power. These harmonicas also have the notes laid out in a slightly different pattern than the instruments more commonly used in blues, which means different tonal and chord combinations are possible. The last take finds Walter using this harp all the way through the tune, and although it's a bit limited melodically, it adds an interesting and unique ambiance. On the very last notes of the song, Walter picks up his usual Marine Band harp to blow a high-end tag line. This version has a good harp break in it, but it wasn't released until 1970 on an LP collection. After experimenting on these songs with a new instrument and creating some interesting new sounds, Walter left the Echo Harp behind and never recorded with it again.

Backed by almost the same group (minus Pat Hare on guitar and with George Hunter subbing on drums), Walter took a stab at a new single that carries on the slow-groove theme established on Muddy's numbers: Once again, it's virtually the same melody and backing. Walter's tune, "You're Gonna Be Sorry," is loosely related to the standard "Someday Baby," first done by Sleepy John Estes in the 1930s. The band is very laid-back in the mix, and Walter crowds the vocal mike, almost crooning. After a rather desultory harp break, Walter forgets the lyrics, and calls out "Hold it!" But the band continues, and as Walter again shouts "Hey!" they keep right on playing, finishing up the verse. Walter complains to the control booth, "They can't hear me!" Another attempt starts with Chess demanding, "Put some feeling into it, will ya? Take six!" Walter responds, "Okay Phil, just a minute . . ." He moves the key up a step to "B," and plays an "A" harp in third position, and this time manages to create some energy both in his vocal and playing. But all in all, it was not one of Walter's best days in the studio, and the track was shelved for the next four decades.

On Wednesday, February 25th, Walter returned to Chess studios to take another shot at a new single. Dixon was again added to the recording ensemble; he'd brought along a couple of his numbers to cut, and was acting as an arranger. "Dixon was the floor general, so to speak, 'cause most of the time we'd be dealing with his material," Freddie Robinson said. "When Dixon gave us the lyrics in advance, we'd go rehearse and arrange this stuff the way we wanted it to go, then we'd get to the session and Dixon would change it."

The first tune off the blocks, "Baby," was a bouncing mid-tempo shuffle with solid guitar by Tucker throughout, and an arrangement that called for a full stop by the band and singer at the end of each verse. Like all of the numbers from the session, Walter was playing acoustic harp, and, at times, he was a bit lost in the mix. Before the band starts, Walter can be heard trying to work out the vocals, learning the lyrics, and trying to find the right pitch. On the first take, Walter comes in singing off-key. Leonard immediately calls a halt and says, "Lighten up on the drums, lighten up." Walter, still getting his bearings, takes the opportunity to go over the song's arrangement with the band: "I'm gonna take the two [verses], then a solo, take one [more vocal verse], then I'm going out." Dixon counts it off, but Walter is now out of sync with his vocal timing. They continue working on it, and by Take 10, Walter's singing is now impassioned and his harp has some nice, subtle, rhythmic and melodic touches on a very nice mid-song solo, although that's the only place his harp is now actually heard. Walter's vocal phrasing is still a bit off, and his voice is starting to sound a bit strained as he bears down and sings emphatically.

They try another take, but Leonard isn't satisfied, and decides to try another tactic. By this time, Leonard was doing rudimentary overdubbing in the studio, recording the band track first, then having the vocalist come back later and spend the necessary time perfecting and overdubbing vocals when the entire band wasn't on the timeclock. Leonard says, "Okay, we'll take it straight, all you have to do is blow the solo when you're supposed to, Walter." Walter groans, "Awwww," obviously not happy with the idea; "Wha . . . I ain't gonna sing?" Leonard reiterates, "No singing" The band then lays down a solid instrumental track with Walter heard only on the midsong harmonica solo; they never got around to overdubbing the vocal; the previous take, #11, complete with live vocals, was chosen as Walter's next single.

"Baby" was followed by a tune with a similar title. Freddie Robinson said: "I'll never forget this one song we did, 'My Baby Is Sweeter.'"

> Walter had a thing going on that, we had patterned it off of Little Willie John's "Country Girl." As soon as Willie Dixon heard it, he was, "Oh, no, no, no!" That was the end of that . . . Dixon would change everything and just throw the whole thing into another dimension. He made it real bad for us, because we had what we thought was hip and up to date. He changed it into something else.

"Crazy Mixed Up World" was a Dixon-composed song aimed at the feet of the teenage market. It's a little odd to hear the hard-living, 28-year-old bluesman Walter singing lines like, "I'm a crazy mixed up kid, I love to dance like this." The other lines may have had a deeper ironic meaning for the situation Walter found himself in; "Well, I'm crazy ain't you heard?/I'm in a crazy mixed up world." There's a touch of bitterness in his voice. The first take is a bit slow but solid, with the band vamping as the song fades at the end. Walter had been playing his Marine Band harp in second position, but decided to have the band switch keys to "D" so he could use his chromatic harp for the takes that followed. It took several more tries before Walter got his vocal timing down and the band really started to swing. Walter's playing on the chromatic on this tune has been a required course for those studying Walter's style; his hard-swinging solo can be clearly heard here naked, sans electronics. "Crazy Mixed Up World" wound up as the top side of the next single with "Baby" on the flip.

The final tune recorded that day was a cover of pianist Big Maceo's 1941 Bluebird release "Worried Life." It was probably an attempt by Chess to capitalize on the strong sales of Walter's last cover of an older blues standard, "Key To The Highway." Tucker closely follows Tampa Red's guitar lines from the original version. Two takes of the number were completed, but both ended up on the shelf until many years later.

According to Freddie Robinson, it was at the Chess brothers' insistence that Walter record his harmonica acoustically, without an amplifier. "That killed his spirit," Robinson said. "Things were never the same. It was their idea, it wasn't Walter's idea." It also made things more difficult in the recording studio; without the benefit of an amplifier, the other musicians had a hard time hearing him and following Walter's lead. Robinson would set up close to where Walter was sitting in the studio in order to hear what he was playing, but with every instrument in the studio louder than the unamplified harmonica, it was rough going. Headphones had not come into regular use in recording studios, so Walter had to hope the other band members were watching him for their cues. In a bit of between-songs rap, Walter makes it clear that he was not at all happy about having to play his harp into the studio vocal mike. "This mike is a bitch, Leonard!" Walter can be heard complaining. "Damn, Walter, what do you know?" snarls Leonard. "Why doncha try something?" Walter responds plaintively, "They can't hear me though." Leonard snaps, "Don't . . . Will you try it?" "Yeah, yeah, I'll try it," Walter mutters dejectedly. Leonard rants, "You're condemning something before it happens! Kill a person, *then* say you killed him!" Apparently genuinely amused at how flustered Leonard has become, Walter shifts gears and diffuses the tension, chuckling good-naturedly, "I don't mean to kill nobody, sheeeit . . . Okay, ready when you be ready . . . "

In an interview done several years later, Walter reiterated his feelings about the way he should be recorded. "All my best records, I made 'em with amplifiers. They started putting me on the [acoustic recording] mike, that just took my drive, take my drive from me when they take my mike." Louis Myers added, ". . . he don't know what's going on, young engineers don't know what's going on." Walter continued, "Don't know where your *sound* is coming from. You getting your sound from here [your amp] . . ." Myers said, ". . . he just take an ordinary mike . . . and just play out in the open, nobody could hear . . ." Walter interjected, "The band can't hear you . . . they got to miss you 'cause they can't hear you! They feel for you, but that's no good." Walter felt that this was a large part of the reason for his declining record sales. "That's a *big* mistake they're making, they start doing it with me. That's the reason I ain't had nothing out on the street worth nothing [since then]."

But it wasn't just Walter who was beginning to fall on harder times. All of the big-name Chess blues acts were having a more difficult time on the charts and on the road; the hits, and the big national tours, weren't coming as frequently anymore. Nonetheless, Walter continued to work the clubs, even getting some upscale dates at fancier venues like McKie's Lounge. *The Defender* announced the booking:

> Little Walter, and his great combo take over the musical chores at McKie's Disc Jockey Lounge tonight for weekend of swinging for star-studded program. Little Walter, a huge favorite has arranged some special music and cuttings-up for the five nights. In addition to Walter there will be several guest stars on the program night after night. This plus the fun, and gayety [sic] in the adjoining Jockey Room means gayety on solid side. McKie also rates with radio listeners. His midnight program over WOPA features request calls from phone in patrons, as well as the spotlighting of on the scene patrons.

Perhaps the "cutting-ups" referred to the food service: "The usual deliveries of chicken as result of orders being called in will prevail tonight." A later display ad featured a glamour portrait of Walter under the heading " 'Crazy Mixed Up World Nite'—tonite, 9:30 'til 4AM. Rock'n good time with the blues. In person Little Walter and his Juke Men." The gig at McKie's would be a steady one throughout the summer.

Billy Boy Arnold described McKie's as a nice, upscale place:

Figure 11.2 McKie's advertisement, *Chicago Defender*, c. 1959.

It wasn't no jive joint, they had steaks, chops, frog legs, all that. It was a jazz club, didn't feature blues regularly. They'd have people like Horace Silver, Jack McDuff, Gene Ammons. Like I said, all the harp players would come to see Walter. One night I came in, and Junior Wells came in. McKie said, 'Hey, I got an idea—tell the photographer to come here, all you guys come on, take your picture. [Many nightclubs had regular staff photographers who would shoot pictures of the patrons at their tables, develop, print, and sell them complete with a custom cardboard commemorative frame to celebrate their night out on the town.] So we went out in front of the club. He say, "I got an idea—Blue-sarama." So he hired me, Junior Wells, and Little Walter together with Walter's band. They wound up calling it "Landlady's Night"—we were there every Wednesday. First the band would come up and play, I'd go up and do three or four numbers, then Junior'd come up and do three or four—then Walter would come up and play the rest of the set out with the band. We'd start at ten, it went on 'til 4:00 AM, so about five sets, forty minutes on, twenty off."

Walter had also acquired a new Cadillac, as Billy Boy noted: "He got a '59—he mighta had one or two in between, I don't remember all of 'em. But I knew he got that blue '59, fishtail, real pretty one—we was playing at McKie's when he had that."

Arnold wasn't too impressed by Walter's current band: ". . . Luther Tucker and Fred Robinson, George Hunter on drums. Walter was really losing ground, George wasn't the type of drummer who could do anything good really, Tucker would stand us up sometimes, [we'd] have to get Lacey Gibson or somebody" to fill in. One night, Walter's band hadn't arrived yet by starting time:

Me and Junior Wells was sitting there waiting, the show started at 10:00, it was 10:30, they was just coming in from St. Louis. Tucker walked in, said "Billy Boy, Walter wanna see you." I walked outside, there was a liquor store next door, he said, "Go in there and get me a couple half-pints of gin." So I went in, got two half-pints. While the band was setting up, everybody was out there hitting on the bottle.

After a few passes of the bottle, Walter got around to the real reason that he'd called for him:

He asked me, "You wanna go on the road with me?" I said no, I had my own little band, working weekends at a club on 63rd called The Rock 'N Roll. He said, "Well if you want, I'll take you on the road with me." Now, how would he use me on the road? I'll tell you what he needed . . . on the road, a lotta times he'd be too drunk to make the show. He can't remember none of his lyrics, he was a spontaneous guy. I knew "Juke" note-for-note, he didn't. I learned it note-for-note 'cause that's the only way I could play it. He didn't have to learn his songs, when he got out on the road, he couldn't sing a lot of the songs, he'd forgot the lyrics or be too drunk. He needed somebody to carry the show. When he got blasted, he couldn't sing, Luther couldn't sing, Fred couldn't sing, drummer couldn't sing—everybody would be mad.

Billy Boy pointed out that, by contrast, Junior Wells was the opposite of Walter at that time: "He'd frown on us drinking, he'd criticize that—then Junior turned out to be the biggest damn drinker of all!"

Walter's youngest half-sister Sylvia was growing into a young lady and was getting to be more of a handful than Walter could deal with. So she left Walter's place, returning to Louisiana and staying with her Uncle Sam briefly before finally joining her sisters out in California. With Walter absolved of his direct responsibility for Sylvia, on June 1st, 1959, he made what amounts to a semi-official acknowledgment of the daughter Armilee had given birth to: He went to the American Federation of Musicians union office and changed the beneficiary of his death benefit from Sylvia to Armilee's daughter Marion.

It was around this time that Walter met the woman many thought was the true love of his life, a stunning woman with exotic, almost oriental, features named Matty Rollins. Given Walter's sometimes brutish behavior and his tendency to associate with both men and women who operated at the outer edges of polite society, Rollins's soft-spoken, cultured demeanor seems ill-matched to Walter's. But he'd had more than enough experience with women to learn how to charm, and probably just as importantly, he *was* still a famous entertainer. In him she probably saw someone worldly in a way that seemed exotic, and he must have been attracted to her as a member of the stable, respectable, sophisticated world that had seemed to be out of his reach.

Matty was born and raised in Memphis, and moved to Chicago around 1952 after a divorce. She was at The Zanzibar with friends one night when Walter approached. "Walter just come up to the table and said, 'Is this your boyfriend?' I said, 'No, this is a friend of mine.' He said, 'Well, I'm gonna go over to [another club], why don't you come and go with me?' I said 'I just can't go with you.' Walter had the wrong conception of a lot of things, he felt, 'If I see a lady tonight, and she goes with me where I'm

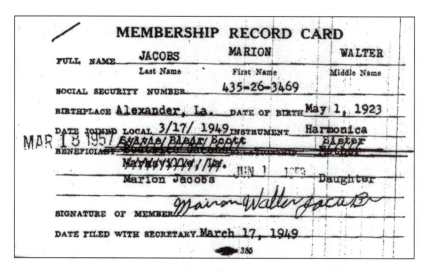

Figure 11.3 Little Walter's 1949 AF of M Local #208 union card.

supposed to play, then she's *my* lady.' The girl I was with—this went on for days—she asked, 'Did you ever call Walter? Why didn't you?'"

After more urgings, Matty finally did call, and arranged to meet Walter the next day at a restaurant on 39th Street. But he again embarrassed her: "He asked me some questions that I didn't like so I got up and left, he was being kind of forward. Then he was almost feeling guilty . . . he called somebody and asked if they would call me. He was playing at McKie's, I went down that night, a girlfriend was here from Memphis, she went down with me. This fellow came in we knew from Memphis and we started talking to him. Walter got so mad he tore my dress, I had a pretty dress." Matty sighs. When she left in her car, Walter followed: "He passed us, pushed me over to the side of the street, got out, took my car keys and threw 'em over in Washington Park. I had to get a cab and go home and tell a lie, say I lost the keys at a party. . . ."

For all the turmoil, Matty doesn't hesitate to add, "I loved him dearly, I loved the ground he walked on. Then he was good, he was kind, but I don't know, I just don't know . . . People wondered why I didn't marry Walter? Those are some of the things . . ." Matty saw continued signs of his possessiveness and jealousy when she went along on gigs, traveling out of town with him. "He had a station wagon," she explained:

He would always ride in the Cadillac with me and the chauffeur, just the three of us, the other boys would ride in the station wagon. I hadn't been with Walter too long, I was going to a cocktail party, I said, "Walter, let me have the car to go out to 95th Street." Walter let me have the car but this chauffeur, he says, "Why you gonna let her have the car?" Walter says, "Well, she's used to things like that." I think I'm the first woman ever drove a Cadillac of his . . . but he was jealous. All of his gigs was big dances, places were full wherever he played. We went out of town, I couldn't dance one time with one man. He would say over the mike, "It's time for you to sit down now." He wouldn't call no names, but I knew who he meant, that's right. And I would sit down.

Apparently that situation was a one-way street: "He carried me all over the world, we went to Mound Bayou, down south somewhere. We got out of the car and a lady there said, '*This* is beautiful—can I kiss him?' I said, 'Yeah, go on and kiss him.' He was a cute boy, he was beautiful. I couldn't tell you today why I didn't make a [scene], I wished I had ..." Walter apparently had no problems holding himself to a different standard, and he continued to see Matty regularly while still sharing his apartment with Madeline Walls, who provided stability, if not excitement.

Pianist J. D. Nicholson had met Walter in Cleveland while touring with Jimmy Reed, and after leaving Reed's band he and his wife Leona traveled to Chicago. Nicholson was another Louisiana native musician from an older generation, born in Monroe in 1917. He grew up in Los Angeles, and gigged with Lowell Fulson and Ray Agee before hooking up with Jimmy Reed. Leona was a cousin of Little Walter's. Once Walter found out that J. D.'s wife Leona was his cousin, he brought the couple to his place, where they stayed for three months. "When Little Walter wasn't playing he would just stay at home, he was kinda crippled, he couldn't walk too good," Leona said. "I think somebody shot him in the leg. When he would go out to play, J. D. didn't always go with him and when Walter came home some nights he would holler for J. D. to take him upstairs because he couldn't walk too good. J.D. would carry him to his room. He was high, stayed high. Just drinking whiskey, beer, whatever, and he would speak French! He'd get pretty high sometimes, but he was a good guy."

A mid-June ad in the *Defender* announced a weekend "Dine & Dance Concert" at The Coliseum in Joliet (some 40 miles out of Chicago). Fifty cents admission got you in to see Little Walter and The Jukes. Apparently the gig was a success, because they were back for another weekend in mid-July.

The Chicago blues scene was very competitive, with musicians enjoying challenging each other to "musical duels," particularly in the informal jam sessions that often took place on Sunday afternoons. Guitarist Fred Robinson remembered the competition on the scene:

At the time the term was "headcutting" ... Walter didn't have any competition on harp, but all of us did ... two people that all the guitar players would cringe and try to sneak to the corner when they'd walk in was M. T. Murphy and Earl Hooker—those were the men. Freddie King was bad for everybody too, including Walter, because of his showmanship and his ability to vocalize a set. When Walter would look up and see Freddie King coming in he'd say, "Hey Tucker, here comes Fat Daddy. Fat Daddy gonna wipe your ass!"

Carey Bell told of another kind of friendly competition:

Every time me and Walter and Honeyboy and Big Walter got together it'd be great, hanging out, we'd be in the alley drinking, they'd be on the back porch, shooting craps, playing poker. See I don't gamble, Big Walter didn't gamble neither. [We'd have] jam sessions. What would happen, I was on the deep end, I would play the chromatic, Big Walter would play the "G," and Little Walter playing the "C" in third position—that was an odd sound. I was doing the bass line with the chromatic ... that was cool.

On a Tuesday, July 21st, Walter returned to the studio, with Otis Spann joining in on piano. Although the Chess personnel listings for the session include Robert Jr. Lockwood on guitar, for what would have been his first time in the studio with Walter in two years, it is more than likely that the strings were being picked by Luther Tucker and Freddie Robinson. On hand in the booth were both Leonard and Phil; Phil's producing style was a politer, more diplomatic version of Leonard's.

"Everything Gonna Be Alright" was a reworking of Walter's 1957 recording "Ah'w Baby." This one again features staccato, rapidfire picking on the descending guitar line, with Spann adding some rich chordal fills on piano. It took five difficult takes to capture. On the first take, Walter is playing with drive and fire, but he was interrupted from the control room after one verse, due to problems with the miking. The next take has more piano in the mix, and the lyrics are tighter. Walter's harp is more complex too, using more chords and octaves, and he plays a wild, intense solo, punctuated by his shout, "Yeah, yeah!" But the vocals are a bit distorted, and Chess may have felt the song was going on too long, because he breaks in as Walter sings, saying, "All right, all right, all right . . . ," stopping the band.

The next take comes together well, with the band settling into an easy groove, and Walter playing a slightly different "head" on the intro, and a completely different and unique solo. But when he tries a stop-time finish, repeating, "We can make, we can make, we can make . . . ," the band stumbles, trying to find a resolution. Things finally grind to a dead halt, and Walter chastises the band: "What the . . . what the hell is wrong with y'all?," annoyed at the screwup. Before the next take begins, he demands, ". . . Listen, hold it. Don't break that goddamn drive. When you start to driving, stay on that drive, don't slow down for shit! Ya'll gotta knack for slowing that sonofabitch down, make me say 'Yaaah, yaaah.'" To his new drummer Billy Stepney, he says, "Same beat! Keep that same drive Billy." The next take is played solidly through to the end, and Walter tries a simpler ending that will be easier for the band to follow, but it still doesn't quite work. On the fifth and final take, the arrangement jells, with the band finally coming together on Walter's stop-time ending, although Walter's voice was getting noticeably more ragged, particularly at the end.

After going through the trials and tribulations of working out a new number on-the-fly while the tape was rolling, the band then tackled a blues standard, although it would go through a number of changes before they achieved a satisfactory take. "Mean Old Frisco" was written and recorded by Big Boy Crudup on Bluebird in 1942, and a number of variations on the theme had been recorded by other artists over the years. Robinson's primary role in the band was to play the bass lines on his tuned-down guitar strings, but on this number he took the lead part. "Some things I knew Tucker didn't know. I'd been listening to that on the plantation, so I knew the style, trying to imitate Big Boy Crudup."

Chess again insisted that Walter play acoustically through the vocal mike, even though he had his amp set up. Frustrated with the band's inability to hear his harp, and his inability to get "his" sound, Walter shouts loudly through his harp amp, "Can you hear me real good? Now wait a minute—couldn't you hear me if I was singing through this here?" Persuaded to return to the vocal mike, they try a run through, but the vocals are heavily distorted. Walter is practically touching the mike with his lips as he shouts the lyrics, ruining the take in frustration. Afterwards he mutters, "You wrecked the sound," then, with rising irritation, "I wanna know one thing man. Why did you all used to let me record with my mike, now you done CHANGED this shit?" The brothers attempt to explain, but Walter is yelling, "This is such a nauseating situation ... ," as the tape is stopped.

When the tape starts again, Freddie Robinson is working out a bass line, and Walter is still annoyed, both by the recording conditions and now by the plodding bass line. "Fucker may come in here and get one, he's a lucky motherfucker. Ahmad Jamal, see he ain't got a damn thing to do but hit the mike over his piano and wail!" he complains. (Jamal was a popular jazz pianist who had recorded several one-shot live club recordings for the Chess subsidiary Argo.)

"I'm blowing to who?" Walter asks. "I gotta feel it, [otherwise] I'm blowing to myself. Them motherfuckers can't hear me over there. I want them motherfuckers to know which way I'm going! Sheeeit, they don't know which way I'm going! I'm going by my goddamn self ... I make a turn, they just keep 'doot—doot—doot—doot!' Fuck that motherfucker up, do something else with it! I'm getting tired of all this ..." he complains, clearly annoyed at Robinson's monotonous bass line. Trying to calm things down, Len mildly interjects, "Come on baby, let's try one more, please...." Walter is right on mike as he mutters, "God damn! Shit! Going the same fucking way ... twist the motherfucker, put something else in! Put some sugar in the motherfucker!" Chess tries again, "Let's try one more?" Walter snaps back, "Shit, goddamn!"

Two abortive takes follow. As they prepare to start one, the engineer calls out, "Hey, Len, I think he wants a little taste," apparently referring to one of the musicians who's fidgeting between takes. "No tastes," Walter mumbles. "He wants a taste, but it's not whiskey; go!" Leonard jokes as he tries to get them rolling on another take. He's apparently referring to some of the musicians' preference for stepping out into the alley and smoking their refreshments on band breaks. Leonard's levity seems to relieve some of the tension, and Walter responds, "He's a gobala goola, don't get nothing," suggesting that the taste the musician wants—but won't get—is neither whiskey nor pot, but the taste of oral sex (Dave Myers's translation of Walter's "gobola goola"). Walter giggles like a kid at his joke.

Next, Walter switches keys up to "B," puts down the chromatic and picks up his Marine Band again. Though this take doesn't quite work, the tune is obviously on the right track. The take is at a slower tempo and now the band has a more interesting pattern going. One more try, at a slightly quicker pace, and they finally nail it. The track would eventually be issued, but not before six years elapsed.

The session ended with an instrumental with Walter at last able to use the mike and amp he'd brought along, and perhaps in an attempt to prove himself, he really makes the most of it. The rocking shuffle is fittingly titled "Back Track," and is a throwback to Walter's powerful amplified instrumentals of yore. His warbles have a nasty edge to them, and he works the dynamics of his instrument for all they're worth. It sounds as if he's releasing all the pent-up energy and frustration of the day, finally doing things the way he wants to. This number must have vindicated his feelings, as it was chosen as the "B" side of his next single, issued two months later.

Walter continued to make short road trips, sometimes with pieced-together backup bands. One tour included Frank Thomas, Jr., on guitar, who Walter called "Wooden Finger" because he always had a pencil in his hand for sketching. Thomas gigged frequently with his band, The Illinois Flames. For Walter, he was a handy fill-in player, because he lived just across the hall in Walter's building on Albany and Rooselvelt.

Walter continued to impress younger harp players in his road performances. Louis McTizic grew up near Memphis, hearing Walter on the radio and trying to blow harp like him. He wound up living in the town of Waterloo in northeastern Iowa, where guitarist Earl Hooker held sway in the 1960s. One night Walter came to town. "Shit, you know I wouldn't miss that!" McTizic said. "I was damn near right up on the stage with him. He played at the Masonic, that used to be the place where all the black people went in '58, '59. In fact, that [was] the onliest place black people had then, that and the Elks . . . [Walter] was evil, man! I tell you that shit now. He was so damn evil, people ask him to play something, he wouldn't play it. He wasn't like Howling Wolf and some of them guys, come laughing around your table. Little Walter, when he wasn't playing, he just kind of stayed away from you."

Little Cooper was another harpist, who'd played some with Walter's old buddy James DeShay in St. Louis and cut a few tracks for a small label. On August 2nd, 1959, he got a chance to meet Little Walter: "There was a place out in Bolton's Oak Grove and they had a big picnic out there, he came out to do a show for them . . . he had a good band. One thing about him, somebody had caught him and beat him up that night, he had a big knot in his head, a whale of a knot right up there. I asked him what happened and he said somebody had beat the hell out of him."

Matty Rollins remembered nights on the road when Walter beat the hell out of himself: "We'd go to a place and he would be so drunk he couldn't get on the bandstand. The place would be just packed with people, and the lady sometime have to give the people their money back." But there were good nights as well: "He played in Iowa, I never will forget that. It was on the water, some kind of resort, I think they were having a banquet there that night. He knew these people, we talked and laughed, had a good time. He would send me to get his money, I would just put it in my bag." You never knew what might turn up on a gig, Matty recalled: "This was in St. Louis. We were dressed fine, he had on a seersucker suit, I had on a suit. I didn't feel good that day, I was sitting off by myself. This girl was out there and she had two babies. I never did ask who the babies was or nothing, but somebody came to me and told me they was Walter's babies. [Walter's] got a friend in St. Louis, James DeShay. I talked to him later, he said Walter didn't have no child."

Barely a month after the previous session, on Wednesday, August 12th, 1959, Walter was back in the studio again. He's once more on acoustic harp, and his rather ravaged voice fits the "You got my face all wrinkled and my hair is turning gray" lyric of the first number, "One Of These Mornings." The lyric has Walter swirling out some rather vengeful warnings to a bad-acting woman while the drummer pounds out a driving backbeat. Tucker provides fleet-fingered guitar fills, set off by Walter's deft third-position improvisations. This track went unissued for years, possibly due to the violent imagery of the lyrics: "One of these mornings, about nine o'clock/You're gonna come in drunk, girl, and we are gonna rock!" Walter shouts threateningly—and convincingly—in one verse.

The other tune of the day was "Blue and Lonesome," a slow blues that verges on harrowing, done in a doomy-sounding minor key. Tucker leads off with his trademark staccato picking over a bed of pulsating tremolo rhythm-guitar chords. Walter sings several tortured verses before coming in with eerie-sounding chords on his chromatic harp, on the long first take. This one seems to come from the same emotional territory as Robert Johnson's "Hellhound On My Trail"—only Walter's demon here is definitely a woman. If the harp break on the first take was eerie, on the final take it was fiery—but Walter jumps a chord change and comes back early with his vocal. No problem, the band follows him, and the piece resolves just fine. This take was paired with "Mean Old Frisco" from the previous session, but they weren't issued as a single until 1965. The intensity of this track seems to act as a marker of what Walter was going through. The last lines paint a vivid picture of how dark his moods could get as he rasps:

> I'm gonna cast my troubles in the deep blue sea,
> let the waves and the fishes have a fuss over me.

12 *i ain't broke, i'm badly bent*

Chicago: Fall 1959–February 1963

In September 1959, Checker released "Everything Gonna Be Alright," which ironically marked the beginning of an era where almost nothing was going to be all right for Walter; as it turned out, although "Everything Gonna Be Alright" reached #25 on the charts, it would be his last hit single. However, the mediocre chart showing didn't dampen the enthusiasm of two French chroniclers of American jazz and blues who were making a pilgrimage to the "Land of the Blues"; Walter was one of the musicians they specifically sought out.

In the fall of 1959, Jacques Demetre and Marcel Chauvard, writers for the French magazine *Le Jazz Hot*, traveled to New York, Detroit, and Chicago looking for musicians who were previously little more than names on records to them. Demetre began writing articles on blues for *Le Jazz Hot* in 1955, noting with apparent disdain that previous reviewers for the magazine had commented on early Muddy Waters releases that "Little Walter's harmonica sounded like a mewing cat."

During their trip, the pair met pianists "Champion" Jack Dupree and Memphis Slim, and boogie-meister John Lee Hooker. But one of their prize finds was hearing the Muddy Waters Band at Smitty's Corner in Chicago. However, they were disappointed to discover that Muddy no longer played guitar, and now had James Cotton on harp in place of Little Walter. "We all the more so had the desire to make Little Walter's acquaintance, which several days previously at the time of our sojourn in Detroit, John Lee Hooker had declared to us this was his singer of preference," Demetre wrote. Before leaving the club, they asked Muddy where they could find his old friend; Muddy answered that he would go to hear him now and then, and that with luck they might catch him at Smitty's on another night.

Three or four days later they got their wish:

> As the band took a break, Muddy came out to greet us. [He] introduced us
> to a small man sitting quietly at a table, "This is Little Walter, my former

harmonica player. He left me to start his own group." We had a very interesting conversation . . . he told us how much he admired the late Sonny Boy Williamson I. "I'm from Alexandria, Louisiana," he told us, ". . . and I can speak Creole." Muddy interrupted, "Come on Walter, come sit in with us." Walter needed no encouragement and replaced James Cotton for the rest of the evening. Gradually the tension grew and the band played like never before. Each of the musicians crafted the most beautiful blues phrases, underscoring perfectly Muddy's voice.

Muddy's guitarist that night was the talented Pat Hare (who would die in a Minnesota prison after carrying out the promise of his recording "I'm Gonna Murder My Baby"); while Eddie Boyd and Hare did a duet set, Walter returned to the visitor's table, where he was interviewed. Demetre noted that:

> . . . Contrary to his reputation, he showed himself to be very cooperative and amicable about our endeavors . . . if his preferred singers were Sonny Boy Williamson #1, Big Bill Broonzy, Leroy Carr, Walter Davis, and Big Maceo, he cited other artists such as Roy Hamilton, Dakota Staton, Red Prysock, Ahmad Jamal, and the English pianist George Shearing. At the mention of the name of Sonny Terry, he made an expression of profound distaste. It is evident on reflection that the styles of the two harmonicists are too difficult to be compatible between each other.

Demetre commented that, although the jazz artists Walter mentioned seemed odd influences at first, that "Walter was equally an innovator in his genre . . . the method he had of playing his instrument and of cutting out his musical phrases called back enormously the punch of a tenor sax." The irony of it all couldn't have escaped Walter: while he was so highly regarded by foreign journalists, at home he was having to scuffle harder for gigs, and more of them were now in neighborhood clubs rather than at the lucrative concert venues.

In November, Jimmy Rogers was back at the Chess studio, recording with Walter and his band—augmented by Otis Spann on piano—working towards a new single. Two songs were recorded—"You Don't Know" and "Can't Keep From Worrying"—both in 2 similar takes. Walter's playing is strong on both tracks, but, ultimately, neither was issued. After Rogers finished, it was Walter's turn. Walter must have convinced Chess to let him record his harp with his amplifier once again, because he contributes some searing amplified tones to both tracks he laid down that day. He began, again probably at Chess's urgings, with another blues standard, "Me and Piney Brown." The Kansas City favorite had been popularized by blues shouter Big Joe Turner on a 1940 recording. Walter's version features Spann on piano and is taken at about twice the tempo of the original. While Turner's version is a clarinet-and-piano based slow blues, Walter's is a rocking juke-joint number. It sounds like Walter spent some time with Turner's record, because the lyrics and arrangement are a virtual duplicate. Walter's harp is only heard on the middle solo, but he plays a fiery and highly original twelve bars.

"Break It Up," another woman-threatening number, is an odd one. The reissued CD version is in stereo, with Walter's vocal isolated on the right channel, and with the band at full strength on the left; it's possible that it was recorded this way with the idea of going back and re-recording the vocals at some later date, although apparently this never happened. Walter gets composer credit on the label, but close listening clearly shows that Walter was unfamiliar with the lyrics. As he sings, another voice can be heard speaking faintly in the background, feeding him each line just before he sings it. At the beginning and end of the tune, Walter blows his harmonica acoustically into his vocal mike, but the middle harp break is played through his amp, which is on the left channel with the rest of the band. These two cuts were paired for his next single, released soon after the recording date.

Barely a month later, Walter was back in the studio; once more the session began with a blues standard, this time a remake of St. Louis Jimmy's 1941 Bluebird recording "Going Down Slow." Originally a slow, mournful blues, Walter's version is a bouncing shuffle, with the guitar chopping out staccato chords through the verses. Walter plays a nice two-chorus amplified solo, putting the tremolo effect on his amp to good use. Listening to Walter's vocal, with its whiskey rasp, makes the tune especially poignant. As upbeat as the delivery may be, the true meaning in the lyrics of the singer's failing health and fortunes isn't far from the surface. "You're Sweet" finds Walter experimenting with some interesting licks in third position. Although Walter fluffs a lyric in the first verse, the tune is solid and sounds comparable to the previous month's efforts. Apparently Chess didn't see it that way—possibly due to the harsh, poorly recorded sound of the vocal—and both of these recordings went into Walter's growing stockpile of tunes that were left on the shelf.

John "Pops" McFarlane is now a forty-odd year veteran bass player, whose resume includes a stint in Luther Allison's band. Back in the winter of 1959–60, he was working in Peoria, Illinois with Wild Child Gibson and the Violators, playing R&B cover songs. Sometimes after his gigs he'd head downtown to a "4:00 AM" club, a would-be swanky (with a canopy) Black-and-Tan spot called Harold's Club, run by an ex-boxer who hung larger-than-life paintings of himself behind the bar. The club brought in acts from Chicago for six-week engagements, among them Little Walter and his band. One night while his own group was on a break, McFarlane went into Harold's club still dressed in his band uniform, and it was there that he first met Walter. Pops was playing the jukebox while waiting for Walter's band to resume, when Walter came over and asked what tune was playing. "I told him it was 'Big Boy' by Bill Doggett," McFarlane remarked:

> He says, "That's a cool tune—you're a musician?" and all of that. We shook hands, he bummed a dime off me, wanted to play it again. He played it again, maybe twice, standing there listening to it. I didn't see him pull out a harmonica and mess with it, he just listened to it a couple times, real attentive. Then he went on stage, looked over at me and called off the tune, named a key and off he went. They played the tune, which has a pretty simple head two times through, then he played the sax solo just like the record, just about note-for-note ... I thought, Wow man! He really impressed me, I thought, my God, I never heard anybody play harp like that ... he sounded like a damn saxophone. And I played with horn players all the time, in fact they would go down there with me, they thought he was great. It was late on a weeknight, not that many people in there.

Walter returned to the club two or three times over the next year with backup groups that included guitar players Robert Lockwood, possibly Hubert Sumlin, and probably George Hunter on drums. The gigs were long ones, running from 10:00 PM until nearly

4:00 AM, with only Sunday nights off—however the job did include room and board. McFarlane recalled Walter's band wearing "... cheap Towncraft coats you used to buy through union magazines, a pair of tux pants, probably a continental tie. Another time it was blue suits, Walter had a yellow jacket." McFarlane thought Walter was a:

> ... scary looking guy. Did he have scars? He had this big one that went down through his nose and over across his chin, another couple on his cheeks. You knew they were razor scars, kinda raised up off the skin, like they hadn't been stitched ... The guy was big boned, had big cheeks, big facial features and all these scars ... seemed to me to be a powerful man, but broken down, didn't seem to me to be all there, kinda scrambled, cut up as much as anybody I'd ever seen. Even me, I was kinda shocked when I looked at his face ...

The band's sets were aimed at dancers, with more up-tempo than slow numbers, each player sometimes going on and on for extended choruses, the guitars weaving intricately behind Walter's harp. McFarlane remembered Walter not talking to the men there much, but regularly pursuing the women:

> He was quite a ladies man, he used to walk up to the women and wanna dance with them or talk, kinda made a nuisance of himself ... black women, white women, any woman that looked good. Seems to me he liked 'em pretty hefty. The guy that ran the club, he kept tabs on these guys pretty good, he ran a tight ship. If Walter was over there bothering somebody too much, he would send his bouncer over and drag him off. I remember him telling [Walter] to get away from people a few times.

When Walter returned home in February 1960, he took in some more boarders: drummer Sam Lay and his pregnant wife. Lay had first moved from his home state of Alabama to Cleveland, Ohio, and was working the second shift at Riser Steel, which left him an hour after work to catch the music at Gleason's, a favorite Cleveland nightclub. The first band he had ever heard live—Guitar Slim's—was there; the second was Little Walter's. In time, Lay joined a band, Tommy O'Neil and The Thunderbirds. O'Neil was a harp player, so they played Jimmy Reed numbers and most of Walter's tunes, learning the records as soon as they came out. Lay next encountered Walter after riding the Greyhound bus to Chicago; he soon found out that Walter had a regular gig on the West Side, at a club called The Playboy, just down the block from Walter's apartment. Lay had done a few gigs with Hound Dog Taylor by then, and had gotten Walter's phone number from him. When he called, Madeline answered, and Lay asked her if Walter knew a band he could play with? She told him to go where Walter was playing, because he was looking for a drummer.

Lay went over one Tuesday night and sat in. He remembered the band (which he thought was a pickup group) had Jimmy Rogers and Poor Bob Woodfork on guitars, and "... some old fella" on drums. When Walter asked if Lay would play some gigs with him, he was so tickled, "I didn't even want to get paid." In point of fact he barely did—sideman pay was then about $12–$15 a man per night. Soon after, Lay and his wife moved into Walter's flat. "I wasn't in the way, 'cause he was hardly ever home," Lay recalls. "He give up his bedroom to me and my wife. It was a three-floor apartment building, he had two bedrooms. He gave up his 'cause he was never home, come in for a little while, get sharp again and he was gone again."

Walter had family down the block; his half-sister Lula and his uncle Carlton were both in the area then, but Lay didn't get the impression that Walter spent much time with them. Lay recalled that Walter knew a lot of women whom he'd visit: "He loved for 'em to cook and stuff—I can't say he was actually going with 'em, but I knowed him to go to different women's houses and eat . . . When he cooked for us at home one day he cooked a big old pot of pinto beans and ham hocks. They had so much black pepper in 'em that my wife and me was sitting there eating and crying. He was from Louisiana, so that spicy stuff didn't hurt him—we wasn't used to that! [Laughs]"

Walter soon was keeping Lay busy, although not always musically. "He depended on me to run things for him—not the band, but to get musicians and whatever was to be done at his household, I had to be responsible for everything like that." Walter was working only sporadically then, not even every weekend, and when gigs came up, he asked Lay to scout up a band. Lay noted, "I didn't have a car, I used to have to do that on feet. He kept a regular band as much as he could, but they didn't stay a hell of a lot . . . There were times I went to Tucker's house, he would say he'd play, but he'd hocked his guitar. I'd go around to Big Moose Walker's house, occasionally when he would use a piano I'd go get Roosevelt Sykes to play with us. I remember I got Lee Jackson a couple times, Robert Junior traveled with us, so did Matty, she was always with us. She was clean as a whistle man, about the sharpest woman you ever saw in your life." Although they mostly did gigs around the city, when they occasionally did go out on the road, sometimes it was in a two-car caravan with Walter's Cadillac and the band's Chevy station wagon, like in the earlier days, but at other times five people and a drum set crowded into one car.

Lay remembered gigs in New York, New Jersey, Detroit, Moline, Iowa, and parts of Missouri. Although a few of the jobs were high profile—they split the bill with Louis Jordan and The Tympani Five at McKie's—more often they were farther down the scale, ". . . different little hole in the walls, little juke joints." A typical night ran from 9:00 PM to 2:00 AM, playing 40 minute sets with 20 minute breaks. Walter wasn't tight on the sets, ". . . we was kinda free to do whatever we wanted to, relax and play like we wanted," Lay recalled. Walter had a little rap he'd do at the end of a set, telling people to "Stick around—and if you wanna take us to the bar, here we are." There were never any rehearsals. Although Walter was the leader, he sometimes let players like Jimmy Rogers or Poor Bob sing a few. Walter did mostly his own material, but would some-time ignore shouted out requests, ". . . mixing it around. He'd play something else, and finally he'd play something they'd asked for." Things had changed, and Walter wasn't getting the respect that he was used to. "People where we played at, most of the time acted like they didn't care if he was there or not. He had kinda wore hisself out with people for some reason," Lay said.

With opportunities for big concert shows getting rarer, Walter worked local clubs more often. Thanks to this reversal in Walter's fortunes, local players like harpist Carey Bell were able to hear him more regularly. Bell thought that Walter could clear as much as $3000 after paying off the band when he eventually got a few high-end college jobs. But in the clubs, "He wasn't making that much, maybe $400, $500 a night," Bell recalled. "One particular time I went to see Walter on Madison Street at The Happy Home Club. He wouldn't let me sit in on account of the drummer, Sam Lay. He told Little

Walter not to let me sit in and they had a big argument. Walter knew me, but Lay didn't. At the last song Lay let me come up, then we got to be friends."

Bell recounted Walter's spontaneous generosity:

I still ain't got no day job, had a little jacket on, cold, man! Walter said, "Ain't you got no other coat than that?" I said, "No Walter," this was on a Sunday night. He said, "Look, I'm gonna come by your house, we gonna go to a Monday jam"—they used to have jam sessions at Theresa's Lounge, in the basement. He come by about two or three in the afternoon, and we got to riding. He was drinking, I was drinking Shake and Bake. He said "Man, I don't see how you stand it here, ain't got no coat." So we went to Jewtown, stopped by a thrift store. He goes in, I wonder, why in hell he going in there—he's sharped out, tie, suit, all that stuff on. He said, "Come on"—he went and bought me a topcoat, first overcoat I ever had. I think he only paid about $10, $15 for it, but it was a good one. He said, "Put this on, it's too cold for you out there with that little old jacket you got on." I put it on, it fitted me okay. And he bought me some shirts, some pants—I guess he spent about $35, $40. You could get a whole lotta stuff at cheap then. I had a whole bag full of stuff to take home.

Bell also recalled some wild nights on the highway:

I used to race with [Walter]—he had a '61 Cadillac, white, I had a '59 Catalina Pontiac convertible. We'd get out on the Dan Ryan [Expressway through the south side of the city] about two o'clock in the morning—it said 120 on the dashboard, that's what we did. Sometimes he'd be ahead, I'd get up alongside and wave. We passed everything like flying colors. Out run the police too, if they didn't watch it. We used to do that quite often—I was in jail every weekend just about. Walter would get away, I couldn't get away for shit! Walter'd go one way, I'd go another. Looks like all them motherfuckers forget about Walter, come up on my ass, damn! [laughs] I remember one time they took his driver's license. He had tore the car up, didn't have no car. I used to have to drive him around in that convertible. The top was kinda ragged but we didn't care ... that was some great times.

On April 23, 1960, Walter made his first trip into the studio in the new decade, for a four-song Muddy Waters date for Chess, with Spann and Jimmy Rogers also on hand. Leonard Chess, working the booth, halts the first take of "Woman Wanted," telling Muddy, "Give me a good strong intro." The group would go through seven more attempts before nailing the track, mostly due to Muddy forgetting lyrics or fumbling with his guitar.

The second tune taken up that day, "Read Way Back" is credited as a collaboration between Morganfield and James Oden; however, it has a Dixon/novelty feel with its biblical references to Adam and Eve, and "Daniel in the lion's den." The raw session tape shows the trust Leonard had in Muddy where the choice of material was concerned. Chess asks, "What's the name of this?" Muddy tells him, and Leonard misunderstands the title and slates it: "We're rolling on take one, 'Rip Way Back'—who got the intro on this? Piano? And Walter takes the solo?" "Right," Muddy says, adding "... and everybody's singing." Chess says, "When you're ready to blow, stand up Walter, so I'll know, stand up just before you're ready to blow, so I know when to bring you up." "Awright, boss," Walter says agreeably, rising to his feet. "No," Chess says, "... sit now, but stand up when you're ready to blow . . . take one." Again, the band falters through several attempts at recording the tune, although Walter's breaks, on his chromatic harmonica, are fiery and exciting. Eventually, Leonard decided to try for just a band track with no vocals. The resulting instrumental track is strong from beginning to end, and meets Leonard's approval; the finally issued version, with Muddy overdubbing his vocal, also includes an unidentified basso voice singing an answering vocal to Muddy's lead, interjecting "Oh baby," "My darling," etc., which is mixed louder than Muddy's vocal throughout. It was a gimmick that doesn't quite work out, and detracts from the strength of the track.

"I'm Your Doctor," the third tune covered that day, finds Walter on acoustic harp again, accompanying Muddy on one of his standard mid-tempo pieces. The last tune to be recorded, "Deep Down In My Heart," has Muddy back on slide and Walter using his amp again. The whole band has a distant reverbed sound to it, and the mix is rather odd. This cut was the only one from the session not issued at the time.

St. Louis was still the home of Walter's lifelong friend, James DeShay, whom he usually visited when in town. The city seemed to have a special attraction for Walter, which more than one person would later observe. More than likely, Walter had a lady friend in the city with whom he spent extended periods of time. In the late '50s, when Walter was gigging around the St. Louis area, there were two Moonlight clubs: one in St. Louis called the Moonlight Lounge; the other, across the river in Illinois in an area now called Centerville, was Ned Love's Moonlight Inn. Both were among the few spots that still booked blues acts regularly, featuring people like Jimmy Reed and Elmore James. After arriving in the neighborhood to play the higher-paying weekend slots, Walter would pick up other fill-in gigs, playing Tuesday and Wednesday off-nights at smaller taverns for less money, sometimes $100 for two sets.

Radio DJ Gabriel Hearns, an acquaintance of Walter's then living in St. Louis, describes how Walter operated:

> He used to take his band with him at first, but in the later days he did like Chuck Berry, just go by hisself and have a rehearsal with the band for an hour. That cut expenses, he didn't even have to bring his amplifier, he could plug in to somebody else's. We booked Walter, must've been about '59 or '60, me and some buddies got together and booked him for a dance, in a place in Alton called the Ex-GI, give him $500. He didn't draw much of a crowd, but it wasn't his fault—people were going for Chubby Checker, blues was taking third place to Rock and Roll . . . he wasn't as precise in his later years as he was before. I don't think it was because of age or nothing, he was just sort of despondent . . . blues was going down the drain. There wasn't that many people there. I figure he saw the handwriting on the wall . . . his gigs were few and far between, his records wasn't selling . . . It's bad for a guy to have been on top: when he'd walk in, you'd think Michael Jackson was there, people, women crowding all around him. Two years later you walk in, nobody knows you.

Hearns had previously met Walter at Chess Records around 1958 or '59, when he'd gone to Chicago with a tape of his band, hoping for a record deal. "Chess would buy Walter a new Cadillac a year, every year a brand new Fleetwood, and he would drive to St. Louis," Hearns recalled. The two met again, by accident, in St. Louis at a "process parlor" where Walter would get his hair straightened. "It was at Leffingwell and Cole—

it seemed out of all the process shops in Chicago, he liked this one better, in St. Louis. He'd come in the morning, get his hair straightened, then disappear until tomorrow. I figured he must've had a woman here, though I never saw him with her. He never talked any of his personal business."

It looked like not only was Walter beginning to wear out his welcome with audiences, but that his luck away from music was turning as well. While still in Cleveland, Sam Lay had heard about the first time Walter got shot; now he was staying with Walter when yet another shooting occurred:

> One night somebody came down [to Walter's gig], telling Walter that Buddy and his half-sister Lulu was into it—down the street, where she lived. Buddy was his sister's old man. So he goes down there. Everybody knew Walter's reputation for carrying a pistol, and he did—had a snub-nosed .38 Colt in his pocket. He goes into the house to ask what's the problem there. Buddy was, "I know you got your piece on you . . ." Walter had his hand in his pocket, and the guy thought he was gonna pull it out, so he grabbed at Walter's hand, and the gun discharged while it was in his pocket. It popped him right in the kneecap . . . I didn't see it, but Walter told me. When I heard he got shot I run out of the house and he was coming up the sidewalk. Couldn't get him to go to the hospital. He went on up in the house and I gauzed him down. A day or two later it was swelling up, had something like green pus running out of it—and he still didn't go to the doctor with it!

Lay thought that the bullet might have stayed in him, and said the leg never really healed completely: "It made him limp even worse than he was from the last gunshot. When we traveled, Walter would sit in the car where he could extend that left leg, he hardly ever would bend it. Sometimes he would sit in the back seat where he could put his legs across the seat."

Frank "Little Sonny" Scott, a drummer/guitarist who'd worked in bands with Freddy King and Walter's friend Jimmie Lee Robinson, told of helping Walter after the injury: "I was a pretty strong guy. I used to carry Little Walter upstairs on my back after he got shot in the leg. He had a cast put on it, I carried him up to the second or third floor there on the corner [of] Fillmore and Albany. He'd get drunk and couldn't go upstairs. He was real heavy for a little guy—especially with that cast on his leg—and I used to carry him up on my shoulders."

By this time, Walter had a long history of trouble dealing with police officers going all the way back to his teenage days in New Orleans, and the outcomes were seldom in his favor. Marguerite told of another such incident that had now-predictable results. This one took place in Kansas City ". . . on Juneteenth. He was playing music and there was a fight. The police was sorta like involved, shoving a woman too much. My brother jumped in and they beat him in the head." Yet another unfortunate incident she recalled was literally highway robbery. "He was playing in St. Louis somewhere, and he was driving hisself back to Chicago. Somebody flashed a bright light in the car and pulled him over—he thought it was a policeman. They hit him in the head and robbed him. They aggravated an old injury, he didn't even go to the hospital that time." The cumulative effects of these repeated head injuries were piling up; eventually the consequences would prove dire.

The summer of 1960 was a busy one for Muddy. June saw release of one of the first blues "concept albums," *Muddy Waters Sings Big Bill*. The Chess marketing department was obviously aiming for the folk-music fans, and the growing opportunities for blues performers to play for white audiences. In July, Muddy's band, along with John Lee Hooker, made an appearance at the Newport Jazz Festival. His show was filmed by the U.S. Information Service as part of a series of jazz films and at the same time recorded by Chess, a rare live-concert recording for a blues act. The energetic version of "Got My Mojo Working" (featuring Cotton on harp) cut that day was released as a single and became a minor hit, becoming Muddy's signature song and show closer for the next 20-plus years.

The marketing department wasn't altogether ignoring Walter either. The label had recently had some success with a Dale Hawkins rockabilly cover of "My Babe," and apparently felt they could get even more mileage out of the song by re-releasing Walter's five year old number one hit. In order to "update" Walter's original recording, a female chorus chanting "My babe, ooh, aah!" was grafted onto it, and it was released as Checker #955. While some might consider the overdubs an ill-advised and intrusive addition, the idea proved to have some merit; on June 27th it peaked at number 106 on the Billboard Pop Music charts. Not exactly a smash hit, but it turned out to be the only time Walter's music crossed over onto the pop charts.

Around the time Muddy was playing Newport, Walter was working as well, but in a more down-home fashion. An ad in the *St. Louis Argus* announced that the Highlanders and Minnie's Lunchroom were presenting a "picnic-outing-dance" (the illustration showed a clean cut, All-American family camping and fishing!) at Bolton's Grove in Maryland Heights, Missouri, on Monday, July 4th. Little Walter of "My Baby" Fame [sic] and his orchestra were featured as part of "12 continuous hours of entertainment." This event was not as prestigious or well-attended as the Newport Festival, but undoubtedly funkier.

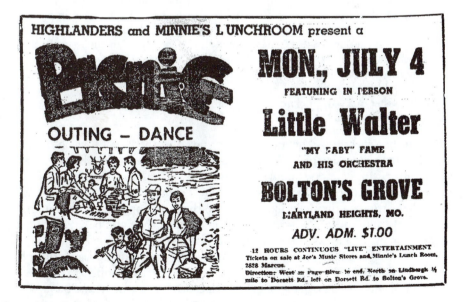

Figure 12.1 Bolton's Grove advertisement, *St. Louis Argus*, July 1, 1960.

In July 1960, yet another overseas blues fanatic made a pilgrimage to the blues mecca of Chicago; this time it was researcher and author Paul Oliver from Britain, who was traveling with his wife Valerie in the U.S. on a State Department research grant. Oliver and Valerie drove through the United States from June through September, interviewing ". . . over sixty-five blues singers and their associates" with a field tape recorder. The interviews were used as a basis for a series of lectures Oliver gave on American blues music at the U.S. Embassy, London. They were also incorporated by Oliver into a BBC radio series, "Conversation with the Blues," and ultimately into his book of the same name, first published in 1965.

On his first visit to Smitty's Corner, Oliver found Walter and Cotton onstage, trading choruses; then Walter held sway until Muddy took the stage. When Oliver interviewed Muddy he was told, "I had Little Walter on harp—I picked him up in Chicago 'cause he was playing on the streets then. He's real tough, Little Walter, and he's had it hard, got a slug in his leg right now! But he's the best damn harp player there is." Oliver saw Walter in a club where Muddy was playing and he joined the party and they talked a bit, Walter telling Oliver that he was flying around, doing one-nighters in New Orleans and Cincinnati.

Oliver appreciated Walter, but had some trouble relating to him, perhaps due to his British sense of manners. While finding him annoying as a person, he still admired his music. "Walter came alive through his harp," Oliver said:

> He was just difficult the rest of the time, and could be a damn nuisance; he was a bit of a barfly. Also he had a certain amount of jealousy which was not very overt, but if I talked to Muddy too long he would always find an excuse to interrupt. He was a very odd person. Very unreliable and quite . . . he could be very friendly and you'd get on fine, then he'd be kind of bare-faced in a lie a moment later. I mean, call for another round of drinks, then the guy would come, [Walter would] say, "I didn't ask for it," looking at me with his eyebrows raised, "Did you see me ask for that?" [It's possible that Walter may simply have been expecting his unsuspecting interrogator to be buying him drinks.] He had this curious, almost clowning way—but he meant it, and he got away with it most of the time. He'd been shot in the ankle . . . somebody had shot him with a shotgun. He was heavily bandaged and finding it difficult to walk. When I expressed some concern he ripped open his shirt and he was just covered in scars, he was actually quite proud of it . . . He just courted disaster in a way, you know? I thought he had been shot at but I think he probably almost called it on himself.

During the several days he and his wife stayed in the city, Oliver hung out at Muddy's house, witnessing days-on-end jam sessions with people like Roosevelt Sykes, Little Brother Montgomery, Sunnyland Slim, Otis Spann, Robert Lockwood, Jump Jackson, James Cotton—and Little Walter. Oliver shot several photos, including one with Walter sitting on the sidewalk, with Little Brother Montgomery and Sunnyland Slim standing above him. Walter is dapper in a striped shirt and beret, but the dour expression on his face looks more suited for a mug shot.

Walter's living situation was about to change again. According to Lay, although the apartment was in Walter's name, Madeline had gone down to the office to pay the rent: "I went down with her. The man there, Mr. Lane, had made some remark to upset her. We got back, she said 'I'm gonna call Mr. Lane and tell him I don't appreciate the way he talk to me, I been with him a long time.'" Lay and his wife were sitting in the next room when she made the call. "I heard her say 'Oh Lordy, oh Lordy' and—Bam!—we jumped up, ran in there and Madeline was lying on the floor. We picked her up, got her downstairs and into Walter's station wagon in the back, laid her on a mattress and rush her to the hospital. They say she had a stroke."

Lay and his wife wound up taking care of Madeline once she returned home. "I had to carry her back and forth to the bathroom. We wasn't paying no rent to stay there, so that's the least I felt we could do." Madeline stayed on a while at the apartment, but soon went back to her native Cleveland, where she later died. Walter must have missed not only her steadying influence, but her steady income as well. Matty Rollins, who Walter had been seeing for some time, moved in shortly after that.

That fall, Lay was in need of cash, with his wife about to deliver their first child. "Walter didn't work regular enough, we wasn't making much. The money used to be $12 a night sometimes . . . Somebody called me and told me that Wolf's drummer had hurt his foot, could I play with him that Wednesday at the Playhouse on 43rd and Lake Park? I went and played that first night, he wanted me to keep playing with him—and I did. Walter was okay, he didn't know I was playing with Wolf." That changed when Lay hired Frank Thomas, Jr., the musician/artist living across the hall, to decorate his bass drum head. When Walter came in, smelled paint and saw the drum with the Wolf's head and song title "Spoonful" on it, he got angry. Lay recalled, "He said 'What's with Spoonful and Wolf? Looks like you been trying to do something real franticky here—.' That's when we got on bad terms, got rocks in our jaws at each other. I started playing with Wolf in November, he was working four nights a week. I needed to work, it was that simple. [Walter] pretty well told me to get out, and I did." At first Lay and his wife stayed with friends across the hall, then they moved out to the South Side, to the home of one of Walter's girl friends. "He told us we better not to go out there, and that's where we went," Lay said.

The breakup would be a blow to Walter; Lay had been a good musical influence on him, helping him work out more jazz-influenced pieces: "He loved Cannonball and Nat Adderly. There was a tune, "This Here," he went all around looking for that, trying to find a 45 so he could play it in his car. You could buy them things that would play 45s like a portable radio; he had one he got at a pawnshop." Lay also says he helped Walter prepare material to record. He was working on a couple of songs that autumn, "I Don't Play" and "As Long As I Have You." "Every time I saw him rehearse he had a guitar in his hand," Lay said. "I never saw him pick up a harmonica other than onstage. He didn't have nothing wrote down, he was just singing it, wasn't like he was reading it. He worked it out on guitar, he knew how he wanted the guitar to go when he got ready to record . . ."

In December 1960, Walter was in the Chess studio for his first session as a leader in over a year. In honor of the occasion, he decided to hold some rehearsals, which had been unnecessary when he was working steadily with a regular band. Freddie Robinson said that the only time the band rehearsed was for recording sessions. "We'd go over to Walter's house, get high, rehearse for whatever length of time, once we found out when the session was gonna be . . . the whole band, the drums wasn't set up, we didn't use any amplifiers, just be acoustic. The drummer would be beating on whatever was available

. . . just all acoustic 'til we got to the studio." Robinson didn't remember much drinking going on during sessions. "We would usually get high before we went up there, we were basically getting high off marijuana at the time. Even though Walter was drinking, when it came to taking care of business it was marijuana . . . that's what we wanted to be into when we got into the studio."

Marshall Chess later commented on his father's attitude about musicians getting high in the studio: "Yes, there'd be a bottle maybe, and sipping. Was there getting drunk? No way! Getting mellow to play, yeah, definitely. I knew [pot] was smoked at Chess, but never done in front of my father or uncle—they would not stand for that. It was done in the bathroom, or the alley. They probably knew it, but it was never done in front of them."

On hand for this session were Tucker and Freddie Robinson on guitar, with Spann barely audible on piano and Dixon lost in the mix altogether. "I Don't Play" is an odd musical mix of rhumba and shuffle. Much of the musical arrangement is lifted from Roscoe Gordon's hit "Just A Little Bit," which had reached #2 on the R&B charts earlier that year; Walter even borrows part of his solo from the sax player on Gordon's record. Walter is again on "enforced" acoustic harp, and plays with a nice solid attack, making the most of his solo despite the sonic handicap. "As Long As I Have You" is a mid-tempo number featuring some nice guitar work, with Walter reaching not entirely successfully into a falsetto vocal-range for the first time on record. It was paired with "Play" for the single despite Walter's little goof: going into the harp solo he picks up his Marine Band upside down and blows a squeaky high note, but quickly rights it and redeems his mistake with a solid solo. On the session tapes, a snatch of studio talk is heard before the next tune. Walter is grousing again about the acoustic set-up, and the difficulty of interaction with the band: "This is just a nauseating situation. A fella don't know which-a-way you going!" The track "You Don't Know" was based on a 1936 Tampa Red release on Bluebird. Jimmy Rogers had previously tried a different version on a session with Walter in November 1959.

For the final tune of the day, Walter pulled out one he'd heard while playing in the package shows. "I'm Just Your Fool" had been a Top 10 hit for Buddy and Ella Johnson on Mercury in 1954. Their version is a slow blues ballad; Walter's is a pounding rocker with an exploding intro, the harp and piano coming on strong. Walter's vocal is expressive, and his harp is right on the money.

In January 1961, Walter was back in Peoria, doing another six-week stint at Harold's Club. Pops McFarlane explained:

> Peoria had Caterpillar, Hiram-Walker, all these three-shift plants, Keystone Steel & Wire, that's why they had those 4 o'clock places. Harold's was about the only place you could go to hear live R&B, all the clubs had just switched over from jazz, had all these little bebop combos. On weekends the joint would be packed. During the week there wasn't much of a crowd, the band looked like they were tired, half-asleep sometimes. Even then those guys looked old.

When James Cotton left Muddy's band in 1961, Muddy hired Mojo Buford. George "Mojo" Buford had come up from Mississippi to Chicago, and was playing harp with a group called the Savage Boys (after their drummer Sam Burton's nickname). Muddy

Waters heard them, and liked them enough so that when his group left on tour he'd have the Savage Boys hold down his gig as the Muddy Waters Junior Band.

"My first trip on the road with Muddy's band was to Washington, DC," Buford said:

> Him and Little Walter were on the same show and I didn't have to do nothing! But I got paid, I just sat and listened to Muddy and Walter. They were booked on the same bill and Walter knowed more about Muddy's stuff than I did. That was the first night, but when we go to St. Louis, Walter told me "You're on your own 'cause I ain't going to St. Louis!" Though me and Walter ran together he wouldn't show me nothing, he told me to pick it up from looking and watching him.

The place on Albany that Walter had called home for years and now shared with Matty was about to be torn down, and the two moved apart for a while, although they continued to see each other. In 1962, Walter's half-sister Marguerite moved to Chicago, and they roomed together. "He had moved from Albany, and we lived in a hotel where it wasn't nothing but gay dudes," Marguerite said. "4140 Drexel, right on the corner, a restaurant downstairs, which wasn't far from where Muddy lived. James Cotton used to come by, drink white port and lemon juice with my brother, have battle of the harps . . . My brother thought he was a pool whiz, he used to go to Turner's Pool Hall on 40th and Indiana, hang out there all day, he thought he was a pro at it."

But if times were getting lean professionally, Walter was still doing all right with the women. Marguerite recalls that he attracted the attention of a young Tina Turner and confirmed that ". . . yes, they had a fling." She continued:

> She had eyes for my brother. She called the hotel, "Is Little Walter there?" I met her in '62, and she wasn't all that. It was Albert, Freddy King, and Ike and Tina. Ike had those platform high-heel shoes, a bandana on his head, a vest and a shirt. He tried to get a cousin of ours to book him. He looked ridiculous, they had a cardboard suitcase . . . I wasn't used to countrified people like that, they were really " 'bama." She had a Hong Kong knit suit on. You know Roy Rogers horse, Trigger? Brother Walter called her hair "Trigger"—she had a wig on with hair long as Roy Rogers horse's tail, with bangs. Money makes you change, she wasn't as light as she is now . . . but she had eyes for my brother . . .

Eventually Walter and Matty found another place on 8125 Vernon, renting in a building owned by singer Dinah Washington's father. Marguerite moved in for a spell there as well, until she and her husband Ernest found their own place together. Walter traveled to St. Louis for occasional gigs, and Marguerite met him down there once, when he had a gig at DeShay's nightclub. "Then we went on to Memphis, to meet Matty's mom and them," she said. On one of the forays, Walter took Ernest along as a doorcounter at the gig. Marguerite recalled, "He told Walter, 'Man, I'm sick of counting, it's a lot of people!' Walter said, 'Keep on counting un-till you get tie-yered!,' he spoke with a more southern, Creole accent than I had. Even the cats and dogs didn't understand English when I was little. My first language was Creole . . ." Marguerite used to cook for Walter, ". . . soup, Creole dishes, I'm a pretty good cook. Red beans and rice, 'cause my beans have gravy to them, they're thick. Those groupies used to call me up and say, 'He never eats my beans', [he] says 'You not my sister.'"

Walter made it clear that he didn't much appreciate the way Ernest sometimes mistreated his sister. "One time he was babysitting my baby. My husband had beat me unmercifully while my brother was out of town. We came back, [Walter] was standing up there on the balcony. He said to Ernest, 'I want you to come up here—did you bite my sister's lip?' And Ernest didn't answer him. I said 'Please God . . . ', my brother was getting ready to kill him. Ernest ran and Walter cut him across his neck, with a kitchen knife." The wound wasn't serious, and Walter himself stopped the bleeding with one of the baby diapers. But the point had been sufficiently made: Don't mess with Walter's family!

Walter took Marguerite out night-clubbing now and then. Elmore James was a favorite, as was Big Maybelle. "One night he said, 'We gonna see Wolf tonight,' and Matty was with me and Walter. Brother said hi to Mrs. Wolf, told her she was fine." Walter's party spent the night in the club, ". . . but Wolf never even said that my brother was in the audience. I could see the hurt in his face." Another time, "He took me to Robert's Motel Lounge to see Gene Ammons. Ammons was playing 'Satin Doll' and I went crazy. Walter said, 'You never holler like that for me!'" But Ammons had heard of Walter and knew his work. On a break ". . . Gene Ammons told him, 'You the man.' I don't know of any musicians who didn't like my brother . . . but there was a lot of jealousy there."

August 1962 brought the first of what would be an ongoing series of blues revue tours through Europe called the American Folk Blues Festivals. Blues musicians had long been more popular in Europe than at home; beginning with Lead Belly's European tour in 1949, promoters discovered that traditional blues musicians could draw good crowds. Subsequently, Big Bill Broonzy and Muddy Waters, among others, had successfully played Europe. It was natural to assemble a group of blues performers for European tours. Willie Dixon hooked up with German entrepreneur Horst Lippman and contracted talent in Chicago, who then went to Europe for several weeks of gigs, playing to jazz, folk, and the growing blues audiences there. On the inaugural program were John Lee Hooker, Memphis Slim, Sonny Terry and Brownie McGee, Shakey Jake, T-Bone Walker, Helen Humes, and the rhythm section of Dixon and Jump Jackson. Muddy flew over later and joined on some dates as well. These shows proved quite popular and developed into annual events, becoming a seminal force of inspiration for the British blues boom and such groups as the Rolling Stones and Animals. The annual tours would continue on well into the '80s; Walter would have to wait until the fifth year to be included.

At home in Chicago there was a growing interest in blues among young white musicians as well, as they began turning up at South Side clubs to watch, listen, and eventually attempt to sit in and play with their heroes. Fred Glaser was one of a group of well-off Jewish kids who were making the rounds; he'd gone to school with Marshall Chess, and Marshall's sister Elaine was Glaser's high-school girlfriend. Fledgling guitarist Mike Bloomfield was another core member of their posse, self-described as "Weird, wild troublemakers. All of us grew up with our maids, they were nicer to us than our parents were, they became like our mothers," Glaser said. "They'd turn on WVON during the day while they were cleaning the house, you'd hear

Muddy Waters, Howlin' Wolf, Little Walter." The group used to hit the bars where they were allowed in, although only in their mid-teens, to sip Cokes and listen to the music. There was jazz at the Sutherland Lounge by Miles Davis and John Coltrane, and the blues of Muddy Waters at Theresa's and Pepper's Lounge. "Wolf was another one, Silvio's, over on the West Side. That was a rougher neighborhood there, but they just didn't bother us—we were like friends. Wolf and Muddy would call Bloomfield up on stage, say 'This is our friend Michael from Glencoe, he's a tremendous guitar player' . . . that just turned everybody around, it was amazing that these white kids from the suburbs could play." Little Walter was another bluesman they saw some-times, usually in very small, intimate clubs. "He didn't have a regular weekly gig," Glaser explained. "Wolf was there every Friday and Saturday, same with Muddy, [Walter] was a floater. These were neighborhood bars, the people all knew each other and the performers 'cause they were there every week."

Glaser was enthralled by Walter:

When [Walter] played man, he captivated the audience. He was like a mythological crea-ture when he was up onstage. He had a tremendous charisma . . . people really dug him. They'd be screaming, "Wow," "Yeah man!" "Play it!," really yelling out. And he'd go on, playing real long solos, hour-and-a-half-long sets. He'd talk, "Come on, I want you all to dance now. It's Friday night, I know you got some money in your pockets, I know you all just got paid. I know you having a good time, wanna drink some liquor. Let's get down and dance! We don't want no rough stuff here, no crazy stuff, no fights, just want everybody to have a good time!"

Walter struck Glaser as funny and quick-witted, like a black Lenny Bruce. Glaser described the club scene, "It was amazing how small the stages were, just tiny, the size of your bathroom—they wanted to get all the tables they possibly could in there. You had players holding their guitar necks vertically, sitting on each other's amplifiers, blasting their ears out. This was the early '60s, stuff would fuck up. They'd have to stop to rewire an amp, put new tubes in." Glaser, Bloomfield, and group inadvertently had a taste of heroin at a South Side diner one night after going to a Muddy Waters gig; an addicted midnight-shift manager gave it to them mixed with coffee in a cup, so they would forget about the gang of toughs waiting outside to beat them up.

Glaser said they often brought joints to share with the musicians in the dressing rooms, and Walter would usually take the joint as it was passed, but Glaser never saw them use any hard drugs:

None of those guys, they weren't junkies. That was a whole other world, they didn't hook into that at all. They drank, liked to get laid . . . but I think Walter drank more than other people did. He never looked good, coughed a lot. He was sort of a gangster kind of char-acter, he always wore a coat, halfway into summer. Hat down over his eyes, three-quarter length, black leather car coat . . . he was a shadowy figure. Cynical, chip on his shoulder sort of guy.

One night Glaser and two friends, one from England, decided to catch Walter over in the Englewood area:

... corner of 63rd and Cottage Grove, I think it was like the Three Brothers bar, something like that, not one of the better-known clubs. It was a weekend, real crowded. But they let us in, in fact we sat up right next to the bandstand. We sat down, saw Walter, one of his band members bought us a round of drinks. We're sitting there for half an hour drinking beer, listening to the music . . . these cops come in with dogs. They thought we were going in there for hookers, it was notorious for that. "All right you guys, you're under arrest, drinking underage. Let's see some drivers licenses . . ."

The cops wouldn't believe they were just there to listen to the music, thought they were looking for women or dope, and saw the beers on the table. "Walter came over, said 'They're just here for the music, they ain't drinking drinks, that's just Coke.' The cop said it looked like beer on the table, Walter said it was his, not ours. They say 'Well, we may have to take you in, too.' Walter said they could take him if they wanted, they said they might if he kept talking like that." The police hustled the three young fans out to the car, over the objections of other bar patrons, who saw that the white Irish cops were having a color problem. When Englishman Peter Brown told them he came all the way from London to see Little Walter, the cops refused to believe him. They asked Glaser what he was doing there, he told them he was a writer, and that Walter was a tremendous musician. The third fellow said he worked for a national record label, and that Walter was a huge star they were going to record and that he'd be touring colleges next year. "The cop says, 'Man, he's a fucking nigger harmonica player, don't give us that shit!,'" and threw them in a holding cell.

According to Glaser, around 3:00 AM, after Walter's gig ended, he came by to get them out. "Walter says, 'I'm the guy who was playing at the bar.' They said, 'We're not remanding them to your custody, we need somebody with a job! You're just a guy playing in the bar that was giving them underage liquor, you're the guy that got 'em busted in the first place.'" They threw Walter out. An hour later Muddy came by, also to no avail. The cops wanted a bondsman. Finally at 8:00 AM Pete Welding, then a writer for *Downbeat* magazine, put up $500 bail and got them released. The case eventually went to trial, with the bartender's license at stake, but their lawyer got it thrown out of court.

Glaser's pal Mike Bloomfield was sitting in with black bands, and the crew would go hang at Muddy's house, eat dinner, and listen to records. But they never saw Walter there; Glaser noted, "He was in like a different social set. He wasn't a real outgoing guy. Interesting, but hard to talk to . . . not unfriendly but just quiet. A great musician, a brilliant mind but less sociable, less sophisticated. He couldn't make the transition into the white people's world where others could." But Glaser thought he was a major musician. ". . . A mix between R&B and modern-jazz, like a link from Charlie Parker to Muddy Waters. He was the colossus across that chasm of urban blues and jazz, one of the first to bring blues up to a higher technical level. He played chromatic harp which gave that whole other minor key sound into blues—he put the minor key of urban life into blues."

Elvin Bishop was a scholarship engineering student from Oklahoma, who'd selected the University of Chicago when he found out that that was where all the great music he was hearing on late night radio was being made. Since 1960, he'd been haunting the clubs, watching and learning from the bluesmen whose music had drawn him there.

Before long, Bishop had let his school studies slide, and was jobbing with bluesmen like Hound Dog Taylor, Junior Wells, and sax man J. T. Brown. "There were personnel changes on every gig you were on," Bishop explained. "Like you play for $10 a night, some guys comes along and offers $11—bam! You know?" The university is located in Chicago's Hyde Park area, ". . . which was the only integrated neighborhood in Chicago at the time, right in the middle of the South Side. There was a lot of blending, where the university met the neighborhood people."

Bishop first heard Walter at a dance at the school in 1962:

> They had dances at Ida Noyes Hall, called Wednesday Night Twist Parties. Various bands would play, I gigged there myself a couple times . . . it was a lot of fun, they were pretty hip people, it wasn't just ignorant college kids. They had good jazz, good blues, and R&B. That's where I saw Walter the first time, playing with some band that wasn't so good. He seemed kind of uptight, had on a business kind of suit and tie. After a couple of numbers it was pretty obvious that nothing was gonna happen, so I just kinda drifted off, talking to some chicks or something.

But the next encounter Bishop had with Walter was a different matter altogether:

> It was at Pepper's Lounge, 43rd and Vincennes. He sat in with somebody, maybe Little Mack or Eddie King. They'd announce, "We have a special guest artist coming up now." Walter gets up in his overcoat and Stetson hat. You know how guys make a production out of taking off their coat, folding it up just so? He had on a sharp white suit, was kind of wiry looking, broad shoulders. He had a lot of scars, a lot of hard wear on his face. He played great, he was in his element there. He was hitting some licks that would've collapsed anybody else's lungs! He was sucking that harp so hard, it was real physical, really phenomenal. I heard stuff that he didn't do on his records—it was just unbelievable. When he got up there, he just took over.

Bishop would later meet another youth aspiring to play blues harp, and become the lead guitarist in his group, an early incarnation of the Paul Butterfield Blues Band.

Butterfield was the son of a lawyer, in high school and studying classical flute with a member of the symphony when he too fell under the spell of South Side sounds. He began frequenting the clubs with Bloomfield and Nick Gravenites, trying to emulate not only the music but the rough lifestyle as well. Luther Tucker recalls Butterfield coming to gigs and plying Walter with a half-pint of whiskey, trying to find out how he played certain numbers. "You think Walter was a helpful kind of guy who'd show you stuff?" Butterfield asked. "Well he wasn't, he was a nasty sonofabitch who'd tell you to get the fuck away from him." (Butterfield may be a less-than-reliable informant, however; many people found *him* difficult and arrogant.)

Charlie Musslewhite, coming to Chicago from a blue-collar background in Memphis, was closer to the bluesmen in class and style. He too began haunting the South Side clubs, sitting in when possible, always soaking up the sounds: "I had just gone up to Chicago to look for a job, I heard you could get jobs in factories real easy up there. I got this job as a driver for an exterminator, so I'd be driving all over Chicago. I'd see all these posters and flyers advertising clubs, I started writing down addresses and hanging out."

Musslewhite caught Walter at Hernando's Hideaway on Ogden Avenue on the West Side: "It was a pretty rough place, a lot of fights in there ... I've heard a lot of stories about him taking guns away from people. If somebody pulled a gun on him, he'd just walk up to him and take it." One night a familiar face caught Charlie's eye. "After a few beers I happened to say to him, 'You look just like Chuck Berry,' he said 'Yeah, I am Chuck Berry.'" Just then, Walter called Berry up to sit in, and they played a set of "... straight ahead blues." Some of the black patrons and musicians confused Musslewhite and Butterfield, confounded by the thought that there could actually be more than one white kid trying to play blues harmonica.

Norman Dayron was another young blues fan on the scene. He was active in the folklore society at the university, which sponsored what Dayron thought might have been the first folk music festival in America, beginning in 1959. The annual University Of Chicago Folk Festival brought in an eclectic mix of performers, from hardcore folk artists to bluegrass and country players like Bill Monroe and Doc Watson, to bluesmen like Mississippi John Hurt and Dr. Ross. Starting in late 1962, Dayron began recording artists for Pete Welding, the *Downbeat* magazine writer who'd founded his own Testament label. The two recorded local Chicago talent as well as embarking on field trips into tarpaper shack areas of East St. Louis, hunting down obscure bluesmen. Dayron had a half-track monaural recorder he'd found for about $15 in an Army/Navy surplus store; the modified Telefunken was a "... great bargain that weighed about 200 pounds," which he rebuilt. One of his first recordings he recalled was made on campus in Lexington Hall, with James Cotton, Elvin Bishop, Paul Butterfield, and Billy Boy Arnold doing a "Three Harp Boogie." Later he taped sessions at the Fickle Pickle coffeehouse, and concerts held at the University's Mandell Hall. He also worked with Mike Bloomfield and Howard Alk on Mike Shea's documentary film *And This Is Free*, covering the Maxwell Street Market scene from a sociological standpoint. In years to come, Dayron would produce albums for Howlin' Wolf, Muddy Waters, and James Cotton.

Dayron found part-time work as a janitor at Chess Records to supplement his scholarship:

> I was like this gofer, this assistant at recording sessions. I'd go to work at ten o'clock at night, leave at seven the next morning. What I did was clean up after sessions, clean tables ... there'd be vomit on the floor, old liquor bottles, chicken bones, crud you could not even begin to describe, beyond scientific classification. The toilet was quite interesting, a work of art, a Salvador Dali experience ...

Dayron recalled the equipment at the time including an old upright piano in the studio, and an FM circuit that engineer Ron Malo built; recording was done in mono with free microphones supplied by the Electro-Voice company. Echo effects were achieved by using two tape machines placed six feet apart, with a tape loop spanning the distance, linked electronically with the play head of one feeding a signal back into the record head of the other. By altering the length of the tape loop, they could change the rate of delay, and the echo effect.

Dayron described the Chess Brothers as "... totally out of *Guys and Dolls*, the ultimate Damon Runyan ... Phil's wearing a fedora like Sinatra would wear with a pale yellow band around the crown, tipped back on his head . . . a funky cigar, a dress shirt with a tie pulled down, open at the collar, wearing colors like yellow and purple. The guy was total gangster chic—and talked like that." A few years later, Dayron began producing sessions (starting with a November 1969 Chuck Berry session), and would bring the results for Chess to check out: "You'd do your session, cut an acetate, bring it down. Phil had this old Emerson victrola with a tone arm that weighed like a ton, he would clank this thing down on your acetate, and out would come this music. It would be 'thumbs up' or 'thumbs down,' and he was *never* wrong."

Dayron said that when he started going to clubs, he felt the live performances were kind of haphazard:

A lot of it was never up to what you'd hear on Chess records, even for somebody like Muddy. Saturday night was about dancing, entertaining people who were drunk, and the musicians were mostly drunk. There was a sloppiness, a looseness—in that sense it was good time music. You'd go into these clubs, some had dirt floors and served goat barbecue. A lot of times it seemed they didn't care which musicians showed up for gigs, they were lucky to get whoever was gonna come. A lot of the times it was very sloppy—but I also saw some very good performances.

Contrary to Butterfield's comments above, Dayron says Walter did take some time to share some pointers with Butterfield:

Walter was coaching Paul how to blow. He said "Paul, you're an all out-blower, not like me, you don't hold anything back—if you don't watch it, it's gonna kill you. . . . "He was showing him, they both pulled out their harmonicas, and Walter was saying, "Now you could play this note that way and you'll get the full edge and full tone—but you're gonna kill yourself. Now here's a way you can get exactly the same tone and it won't hurt you as much . . . ," telling him all these little things. It was really wonderful, because he just loved Butterfield, he thought he was a good player, he respected him and was trying to help him . . . Paul admired Walter but I don't think he ever went out of his way to see Walter . . . he more often would want to sit in where there was no harp player, Paul would be looking for a place where he could perform.

Walter could be just as competitive as Butterfield—if not more so. Louis Myers told about the time Walter went out gunning for Rice Miller. According to Myers, Walter would wave at Miller when he saw him, but Rice would just give him a funny look. "I used to feel sorry for Sonny Boy," Walter told an interviewer, "He blow wide open and that harp *killed* him. You know that man drank a fifth of whiskey in the morning, fifth of whiskey in the evening, go to bed with a fifth and ride that harp *all* night long . . ." Myers asked Walter, "Remember the time we jumped ol' Sonny Boy over there on 47th Street, where Miller was playing at on Monday? You said, 'Let's go up there, light him up, make this old rascal mad'? I was playing guitar when you came in, it was a little before he made 'Help Me' . . . you and me was up there, got old Sonny Boy all stirred up," he chuckled. ". . . That old coot come out with them harps, he still would blow them big old harps, he had that big sound." Walter said, "Yeah, sound like a train . . . I pulled that chromatic, laid it right on him, I knowed that would take care of him." Myers told another interviewer:

Sonny Boy, he blow Walter right on out . . . he took two or three harps, went through his bag and took the great big harp and really put on a show. Well, Walter wasn't that much of a show, but Walter could blow . . . you get on down to nitty-gritty playing you don't fool around with Walter 'cause he'd lay that tone on you. He'd lay back there, you'd see him batting those eyes, looking around at you out of the corner of his eye. You might as well turn him loose . . . he's gonna be playing tone . . . if you listen at that harp it don't even sound like a harp no more!

Myers later told Charlie Musslewhite that when "Sonny Boy saw them come in, he went straight to the bar, ordered a half a pint and knocked it right down and then just started playing his ass off. Walter was just laughing 'cause he was playing so good, Walter talking about 'Listen to that old man play!'"

Walter continued to carry an attitude on the street as well. Billy Boy Arnold recounted the time when Walter came back from out of town and he had a woman with him who was doing a lot of cursing out on the street, "Motherfuck this and that . . . ," until the police were finally called. As usual, he didn't exactly bow to the officer's authority. "A cop says, 'Stop hollering that noise!' Walter says, 'Listen mother-fucker, that's my old lady!'—and the cop hit Walter and knocked him out cold. While he was out, the conversation went—'This is Little Walter.' 'Oh, that's Little Walter? I got some of his records!' [Laughs] See Walter was at that point where if he was half drunk and somebody said something, he'd start arguing and cursing." Arnold also remembered Walter hitting up Leonard for money, ostensibly for a doctor to treat some burns he'd suffered: "He came down to Chess, had tape on his back, he had fell out of bed on a little space heater. Leonard say, 'What the fuck, you think I'm your daddy?' Walter was a guy that lived reckless."

Chuck Herron was an aspiring drummer who moved to Chicago in 1952, when "Juke" was on the charts. He began hanging out at jam sessions at Muddy's house, and when he met Walter around the Blue Flame and Walton's Corner, he began to carry himself like his idol, wearing the same kind of shades and dressing like him. Herron said that, even though his popularity was fading, Walter could still take over a gig:

He was still a star on the South Side. A band would be playing, Walter might pull out that harp and start playing at the bar. Pretty soon he'd be called up on the bandstand—and that was it for the group that was playing. That's how Walter got a band to do a little gig. He'd say, "You, you and you—meet me Monday, gig at such and such." Leave the bandleader stranded. This was just some little tavern gigs, pick up some quick bread.

Herron said Walter was a stern bandleader who'd fire band members on the spot, or turn around during a song and tell them what they were doing wrong, and expect them to fix it quick. One night Herron was door-checking at a gig for Walter, who'd told him to keep an eye out for a couple of his girlfriends. "I sneaked up and told him that two of the women were in the club, pretty soon there were more, five or more. Walter said, 'Goddamn man, all these women here and I can't fool with none of them'—Walter was worried about one finding out about another." Herron recalled that Walter was drinking Gordon's gin then, and liked to smoke pot, sending Herron out to the car to bring in joints.

Bassman Willie Kent was another jobbing sideman, up from Mississippi by way of Memphis. He told of Walter hanging out in his Cadillac outside a club called JB's Place at 21st and Pulaski: " 'Course his leg was broke at the time and he'd be sitting up in the Cadillac with his leg hanging out the window. He had Luther Tucker with him then." Kent wound up jobbing with Walter as well. "They wanted me 'cause I had good equipment," he said. "I worked some with him over on Roosevelt and Kedzie, used to be a little place there in the alley. But it scared me, 'cause I knew I wasn't good enough to work with Walter. I told him I don't know but one song, a Jimmy Reed song. He say, 'If I play it fast, you play it fast, if I play it slow, play it slow.' First night I was scared to death. By the second night I had a little more confidence. About the fourth night I thought I knew what I was doing." Kent went on to job with Wolf and Muddy as well, before forming his own band.

A young Marshall Chess was starting to hang around the studios, learning the ropes:

> I remember my father recording Walter early in the morning after a gig, before he went home. Walter was a real night person, so that was part of getting him when he was warmed up. The thing about Chess is, we would use that kind of sensibility to record each artist when we thought we could get the best performance. That's how we produced. My father and my uncle, they weren't musicians, we try to get the best performance from an artist, using any kind of psychology we can.

Marshall said that Dixon's role was more as rhythm section leader than producer for Walter. "Was Willie involved with getting more tone or echo? No, Willie was involved with the band, with the playing, getting a groove going . . . Probably Willie's main function was getting the bands together, finding the people. They didn't always go home, they didn't all have telephones in that area, they had different women . . . [Willie] knew who to call or where to go to find them." Once a young white blues harp man, who was convinced Walter's sound came from his gear, kept pestering Marshall to find out what kind of mike Walter favored. "I said 'Hey Walter, this guy is driving me crazy, he wants to know what kind of mike you use?' Walter answered, 'Whatever motherfucking mike I haven't pawned!' Meaning, *he* did it, it had nothing to do with the mike."

Marguerite said it was "tough times" in early 1963:

> When he made that record, "I ain't broke, I'm badly bent" [aka "Dead Presidents"] he had some very heavy problems . . . Oh hell, yes . . . he drank a lot, but why wouldn't you not drink a lot? You're not getting no money, you're not getting no more new Cadillacs, you can't even pay your union dues. I was at Pepper's Lounge one night, my brother couldn't even take a break, because the union man was there, and he could not pay his dues . . . We were all having a bad time. Every time my brother would leave, my husband would batter me. My husband abandoned me, I was pregnant—had I not been a Catholic I guess I would have been dead, they helped me out a lot.

Walter cut "Dead Presidents" on Tuesday, February 5th, 1963, along with three other tunes; this was Walter's first Chess session in a little over two years. He didn't have a regular working band at the time so Chess arranged for some studio musicians to back him. Buddy Guy was on guitar, Jack Meyers on bass, Al Duncan on drums, Billy "The

Kid" Emerson on keyboards, and there were a couple of saxophone players on board as well. The session started with a remake of a 1949 Regal label blues ballad cut by The Paul Gayten Band with vocalist Annie Laurie, "Cutting Out." Walter's version, retitled as "Up The Line" (and credited to Walter and Dixon), goes at about twice the tempo of the original, and opens with bass and sax riffing. His harp is only heard during the middle break and on the fade out; he's playing chromatic into the vocal mike, displaying plenty of energy and drive. The next cut, "I'm A Business Man," was coauthored by Dixon and Emerson, with some of Dixon's typical double-entendre lyrics. Walter's vocals are lackluster and the tune rather plodding, although Walter takes a nice Rice Miller-styled harp solo.

"Dead Presidents," the song Marguerite remembered, was also a Dixon number, although Walter surely agreed with its sentiments: the quest to collect dead presidents of course referring to the portraits found on various denominations of currency. Again Walter's vocals are prosaic at best and the rhythm section just doesn't swing, although not surprisingly, he still pulls a decent harp solo out of his hat. The session ended with the instrumental "Southern Feeling." Walter takes the intro, laying out a line that the horns reply to. On a second chorus, he does some tasty melodic variations. Emerson stumbles into a chorus on organ, followed by twelve bars of uncharacteristically restrained Buddy Guy guitar soloing. Emerson takes another chorus, this time on piano, before Walter takes it out reprising his opening line. Overall the tune sounds like an improvised jam—pleasant enough, but rather unfocused and not very exciting. It became the flip of "Up The Line" when the two were released as Walter's next single later that year.

It was the last Little Walter session where the Chess brothers found anything usable to release ... and the resulting single saw virtually no chart action. Walter's days as a viable singles artist with the label he'd helped to build were over. The handwriting was on the wall: it was the beginning of the end.

13 *back in the alley*

Chicago/London/San Francisco/Boston:
Winter 1963–Fall 1966

Walter's decline in health—exacerbated by his increasing alcoholism—and his lackluster attitude towards his career was growing increasingly evident in the mid-'60s. He often worked with whoever was available, and his playing was limited primarily to the Chicago area. The few concerts he played outside of Chicago for the growing blues revival audience met with only limited success.

Walter "Big Red" Smith, a/k/a "Guitar Red," began playing pickup gigs with Little Walter around this time, providing lead guitar while "Poor Bob" Woodfork covered the bass parts, and Sam Johnson or whoever else was available filled in on drums. As Red explained:

> We'd . . . get a gig over in Gary, or somewhere in Indiana, a one-night stand, Chicago Heights—play one night and get outta there. 'Cause [Walter] couldn't hold a steady gig, he'd go 'round sitting in . . . Walter couldn't do nothing for nobody, he had nothing. I could use his Cadillac any time I wanted, he couldn't drive it cause he didn't have a license . . . The gigs wasn't strong, anybody coulda had 'em. Wasn't no big house gigs, just a regular walk-in tavern, wasn't nobody paying to get in.

Big Red was born in 1925, and spent his childhood in Mississippi in the '30s. He moved to Chicago after leaving the army in 1945. His first band in Chicago featured George "Mojo" Buford on harp and vocals, in 1952. Red's partner Buford left Chicago for Minneapolis around 1962 and Red found himself working with different front-men.

Red recalled Walter's gig at Johnny Pepper's new club in south-suburban Chicago Heights. "Walter, you had to watch him," he said. "He'd start bull-shitting about the money. He was smart, he'd make 'em pay before he played." One night after the band members set up their gear and tuned up, Walter said to Red, "Lets go get high, joker," and the band went outside to smoke some reefer to get ready for the gig. When they went back in, Red demanded his money in front as well. "I wouldn't play unless he pay me—he probably wound up giving Poor Bob $25, with Walter I got $50 . . . a lot of guys thought it was a big thing to play with him, they'd do anything. Blues players was dumb-ass musicians as far as I was concerned, just to be able to say they was out there. . . ."

While Walter was only gigging sporadically in Chicago, like many American blues artists whose fortunes were sagging at home, he was beginning to draw more attention abroad. A group of enthusiasts in England led by Mike Leadbitter started a blues magazine, *Blues Unlimited*. It began as a mimeographed newsletter, eventually evolving into a slick paper monthly and becoming one of the most respected chroniclers of the blues tradition, before folding in the 1980s. One of the early issues contained a review of Little Walter's newest single, "Southern Feeling"/"Up The Line." John Broven's write-up was complimentary of Walter's playing but not so the context in which it was presented, praising ". . . a spine chilling solo but this is lost in the general mood of mediocrity." Broven liked the instrumental "Feeling" and hoped the rest was ". . . just a temporary lapse on Walter and A&R man Willie Dixon's part."

With the market growing in England for pure, electrified Chicago Blues, Chess recordings were now being successfully reissued on the British Pye label. The trendy Marquee Club in London hired a resident blues band, The All Stars, led by professed Little Walter emulator Cyril Davies on harp. Out of that scene came enthusiasts like Alexis Korner and Long John Baldry, who in turn fostered others like Mick Jagger and Keith Richards. That pair formed the core of The Rolling Stones (named after Muddy's 1950 recording), who in May 1963 cut their first sides, covering American blues and R&B numbers. The two had hooked up after Richards spotted Jagger on a railway platform with some import Chess LPs under his arm, including *The Best Of Little Walter*, and struck up a conversation about them. Marshall Chess remembers responding to mail orders for albums from British enthusiasts, and he was in turn interested in the new English groups. This initial correspondence paved the way for the Rolling Stones to record at Chess's South Michigan Avenue studio in Chicago on their first American tour in 1964. The Rolling Stones soon had competition from other English groups like the Animals and Manfred Mann, who were also attempting to recreate the Chicago sound.

In the fall of 1963, Muddy Waters and Otis Spann traveled overseas as members of the second annual American Folk Blues Festival tour. The festival line-up also included Big Joe Williams, Lonnie Johnson, Victoria Spivey, and Rice Miller. This time, Muddy was mindful of the negative headlines his amplified sound had gotten on his previous trip, so he brought along an acoustic guitar. He was surprised to find that now audiences *wanted* to hear his full-scale electric-band sound, and shook his head over white folks' confusing tastes. During the tour, Mike Leadbitter of *Blues Unlimited* interviewed Big Joe, who ". . . told us that Little Walter is not such a bad person as he is made out to be. 'A truly fine artist,' said Joe, 'although he drinks heavily. Who doesn't drink anyway?'" Joe related that he felt Walter's "mistake" was in failing to keep his fine combo together. The band members went their own ways, Joe explained, pinpointing the time when Robert Jr. Lockwood left as the most critical.

In the U.S., a growing "anti-rock-and-roll" folk movement was building on campuses across the land, with young whites discovering Lead Belly and Big Bill Broonzy as well as Appalachian ballad singers and banjo pickers. Topical singers like Bob Dylan were hitting nerves with incisive songs featuring antiwar and pro-integration themes. Folksong societies were springing up, and the coffeehouse circuit was a place where solo guitar players could "sing for their supper." In February 1964, the Beatles made their first foray to America, mentioning at a welcoming press conference that they'd come to hear bluesmen like Muddy Waters and Bo Diddley, leaving most reporters scratching their heads. "Don't you know who your own famous people are here?" McCartney quipped.

A few people did. One was *Downbeat* magazine writer Pete Welding, who was conducting interviews with bluesmen, as well as making modern-day "field recordings" of their performances. While Ed Sullivan was talking to the Beatles, Welding was talking with John Lee Hooker. "My favorite blues singer, you'll be surprised when I tell you, is Little Walter," Hooker said. "I don't know what it is about his singing, I can't say it, but there's just something about it that I like. He got a lot of soul. Songs like 'Mean Old World' and 'Sad Hours' and so forth. But now it don't seem he's as good as he used to be; it don't seem to be. But when he was doing that stuff, he was something else."

One of the primary reasons Walter had trouble maintaining a regular band was lack of steady work. Walter's final link to his successful recording days of the '50s, guitarist Freddie Robinson, didn't so much quit the band as just fade out. "Things had slowed down to the point where we weren't able to maintain ourselves without doing extra gigs. I just got to the point that whenever [Walter] got something, usually I was unavailable for it. I would have much preferred to work with him, but his situation got down to the point where he really wasn't getting enough work for me to support my family." Robinson went on to work with Junior Wells, James Cotton, Ray Charles, John Mayall, and Jerry Butler. The last time that Freddie saw Walter, Willie Anderson took him " . . . over to some little hole in the wall he was playing. It was difficult for me to see him in those circumstances, knowing his pride and personality, so I didn't remain there very long. I told Willie, 'Lets go'. . . ."

In March 1964, Walter returned from a short southern tour, and was working at a small West Side club, the Pride and Joy, on a bill with slide guitarist "Homesick" James Williamson. It was a rough place; Norman Dayron recalled a night when a jealous husband blew the joint apart with a shotgun:

> Me, Musselwhite, and Bloomfield went in there; it was rumored that people sitting in would be B. B. King, Albert King, Little Milton, maybe Chuck Berry, Bobby Bland—it turned out they didn't show up at all . . .[while] we were there, some guy came up to us at the bar, said this crazy guy was gonna come down and kill us. I said, "Why?" And he said it was because we were white, the guy thought we were fucking around with his wife. The guy says "if you want, you can go out to my car" . . . it was thirty below zero, we sat in this guy's '49 Hudson smoking reefer and listening to blues on the radio until the guy blew the place apart and we could go back in. . . .

Guitarist Bloomfield had slightly different, and grander, memories of that evening. He recalled a jam with a band made up of "Chuck Berry, me, Little Walter, Sam Lay, Sunnyland Slim on organ, and some putz on bass. I think Charlie Musselwhite played on that gig too, and our theme was 'Canadian Sunset'."

With time on his hands and the weather warming up, Walter returned to playing on Maxwell Street. He played only guitar on the street this time, picking up some spare change, but at the same time trying to maintain a degree of anonymity (and perhaps pride as well); he was still a member of the union, and if he had been playing harmonica, he probably would have drawn too much attention. One afternoon Walter stopped photographer Ray Flerlage, a white Southsider who had taken an interest in covering the local blues scene after being hired to shoot a Memphis Slim album cover in 1959. "Take my picture," Walter said, and Flerlage obliged; the resulting print shows him nattily dressed, in stark contrast with the rubble-strewn lot and tenement buildings that were his backdrop. He's holding a cheap Airline electric guitar (a brand sold through the Montgomery Wards department store) and looking quite dapper. Although he'd seen Walter in clubs, Flerlage had never photographed him before, and, because of the guitar, didn't recognize him or realize who he'd photographed until later. When he sent the print off to the fan magazine *Rhythm & Blues*, which by this time was mainly devoted to covering the soul music scene, it was published with the caption "unidentified singer."

A growing "folk-revival" scene at the University of Chicago led to several concerts being staged there featuring "rediscovered" musicians. The preference was usually for "acoustic" musicians; urban blues often was viewed as too modern and commercial to be true "folk" music. Nonetheless, these concerts helped introduce blues performers to a wider audience. On May 9, 1964, about 150 people attended a concert put on by Pete Welding and The University of Chicago Folk Society at Mandell Hall. Featured were blind street gospel singer Arvella Gray, Mississippi guitarist Avery Brady, mandolinist Johnny Young, and guitarist Robert Nighthawk, with Little Walter accompanying the latter two on their short acoustic sets. Walter had not worked regularly with these musicians, nor were they particularly sympathetic to his style of music. He had particular problems accompanying Johnny Young, a rather erratic mandolin player who had difficulty keeping his instrument in tune. Young was also accompanied by pianist Jimmy Walker. Charlie Musselwhite was there; he recalled Walker as ". . . a piano player who only played in one or two keys. I remember when they played in a key he couldn't, he'd sit there with his hands in his armpits looking real disgusted." An account of the performance at the time says ". . . despite some good tunes, the set was played with difficulties; Walker couldn't find the right key much of the time, a few times Walter was sadly out of tune, and Young broke three strings." Young also played with Walter to accompany Robert Nighthawk in the second half of the program. Walter's playing harked back to his earlier style, rich with the "wah-wah" hand effects that he had learned from Sonny Boy Williamson. Walter also played some acoustic guitar off stage, drawing praise from the concert's reviewer: ". . . [Walter's playing] reminded me of a [Peatie] Wheatstraw more practiced, and prolific . . . Someone is missing out by not recording him on acoustic guitar."

In early June 1964, the Rolling Stones made a pilgrimage to 2120 South Michigan Avenue to do some recording at the hallowed Chess studios, hoping that they could absorb some of the ambiance, that maybe the magic would rub off. Their first album, released the month before, had featured covers of tunes by Muddy Waters, Jimmy Reed, Slim Harpo, and Chuck Berry, and now they were in the very room where some of the originals had been recorded. Junior Wells later recalled that Leonard Chess called him up. "I want you to come down here," Chess told Wells. "I got these two motherfuckers sitting around here, Sonny Boy and Walter, and these motherfuckers cussing each other out, talking about cutting each other and stuff like that. And I got these Rolling Stones down there, and they're up against the wall so tight I can't convince 'em to get off and even say hello to Walter 'cause Walter and them done scared the hell outta them with knives." According to Wells, he and Buddy Guy went down, and Buddy told the Stones, ". . . don't worry about them cats man . . . people be looking at us like we crazy or something, they think we gonna kill each other and we just be playing with each other. . . ." Wells said that soon cooled out the situation.

Buddy Guy offers a different version:

> I was in the booth singing "My Time After A While" and all these guys are lined up against the wall with long hair. I'm saying "What the hell is this?" And all of a sudden, it's the Stones, which I knew a little bit about . . . the name had been getting around. Sonny Boy Williamson and Little Walter were in the studio, arguing about some young girl they had down in Kentucky. Walter told Sonny Boy that he didn't know the girl, and they got into an argument about it. Sonny Boy did know the girl! When he described her to Walter he said the first thing the girl ever had was one of his fingers. And he said the second thing was his two fingers. Then he said, "You know what the third thing was?" Walter says "No! What, motherfucker?" Sonny Boy stuck out his tongue, popped his fingers, walked off and looked around and winked at me. The Rolling Stones just fell out. They was lying on the floor laughing.

As the Rolling Stones have grown to legendary status, it appears stories of their visit Chess studios have taken on legendary proportions. Rolling Stones bassist and archivist/historian Bill Wyman recently stated he has no memory of the above incident, and remarked flatly, "it never happened."

During the course of the next year or so, Pete Welding continued his recording, dropping in several times at Johnny Young's place to tape him, often backed by Walter and pianist Jimmy Walker. Several cuts have turned up on various compilation reissues, including standards like "Crawling King Snake" and "Forty Four Blues." All have Walter playing acoustic harp much in the old style of John Lee Williamson's classic Bluebird sides, behind Young's mandolin and vocals. There's a living room feel to the music, and a mellow unhurried ease throughout. This was music being made for pleasure; Welding wasn't paying union rates, or issuing the songs on records at the time.

Meanwhile, things were percolating in England, where amateur musician Frank Weston was working for the Malcom Nixon agency, a London booking firm that handled folk, blues, and jazz artists. They sponsored concerts with American folk artists such as the Weavers, Ramblin' Jack Elliot, and Jesse Fuller, and had arranged month-long trips around the U.K. for piano men Memphis Slim and Champion Jack Dupree. Slim introduced him to Willie Dixon, who was considered "the man, the fixer," as far as lining up stateside talent. The idea of bringing Walter over was discussed. "We just thought that Walter was a name somebody'd be interested in seeing," Weston explained. "It was the beginning of the blues revival, when kids were getting into amplified blues . . . we thought we could fix up a month of dates, we had various small clubs around the country that had been taking blues musicians." Budgets were tight, and the agency could only afford to bring Walter over, so he'd be backed by whichever local groups were available at each venue. Weston set up dates, and talked Pye Records (the British licensee of Chess) into issuing a four song EP to coincide with the tour. They also arranged for several BBC television appearances.

There was only one hitch; to get a US passport, a birth certificate was needed, and Walter didn't have one. It looked like once again the circumstances of his birth were conspiring against him; he might lose an opportunity to make an overseas tour and tap into the eager English market. However Dixon and the others who were negotiating the paperwork (Dixon of course taking a fee as broker) soon discovered that the passport office would consider "secondary birth evidence" when a birth certificate was not available. This evidence could include a baptismal certificate, family bible records, or ship's logs. Also, an affidavit could be completed by an older, blood relative. It was decided that the easiest way was to produce a baptismal record; however, because that didn't exist either, one would have to be manufactured. When Lillian was wary of getting involved, Marguerite stepped forward and arranged a quick ceremony. "[The priest] baptized him, I was his 'Godmother.' I wasn't older than him, Father Prater didn't care, he said 'Marguerite, you have to learn to lie a little' . . . he got his papers to go." Although Walter wasn't fond of flying, he got ready for his first transatlantic flight.

Walter's scheduled month-long tour was well-publicized, with *Blues Unlimited* listing dates well in advance. The weekly beat-scene music paper *Melody Maker* ran a feature by critic Max Jones, quoting Paul Oliver's impressions from his American sojourn. Oliver had written, ". . . although he has featured many rock-and-roll numbers, Little Walter is a superb blues player, very exciting and exhilarating." Jones also quoted bandleader Chris Barber, who'd backed Muddy during his 1958 trip, and then seen him in Chicago two years later:

> We met him in a club in 1960 to find him holding the stage in the absence of Muddy. Walter was backed by bass and drums and playing guitar—which we hadn't expected at all. Apparently he plays guitar quite a bit because he can work with smaller groups that way. He's also an excellent singer. He asked us to join him and we became his band for the next hour and had a ball. I've never actually heard him play harmonica in person, but I have most of his records . . .

On Tuesday, September 15th, Walter was met at the airport in England by a driver for the agency and Memphis Slim, who'd just finished a Parisian tour, and who thought Walter might be more comfortable with someone from the states who also had a black face. As they headed back to the office, Walter was amazed by the un-hip shape of the London taxis. "Gee man," he joked, "those things got motherfucking square wheels!" The agency office was in Mayfair, an expensive shopping area, and the first thing Walter wanted to do was head across the street and buy some shirts. Slim warned him, "Hold on a minute Walter, you can't go throwing your money away as soon as you get here."

Slim took on the role of escort, driving Walter around in his new Mark 10 Jaguar, which no doubt gave Walter an idea of just how appreciative the foreign audiences could be. After getting Walter checked in and fed, Slim showed him the club scene, stopping at the 100 Club on Oxford street where two R&B bands, The Artwoods and Brian Knight's Blues By Six, were playing. "I was surprised, it took me by shock," Walter later told journalist Max Jones:

Memphis didn't tell me, just walked in and these youngsters were playing and I was surprised, happily surprised. I was expecting to hear the same thing as I hear from the hillbillies back home ... them young kids was really down with it, really terrific ... I thought that white boys couldn't play the blues but they were playing the hell out of the music ... them boys was as pure in the blues as many a Negro group back home. In fact there's many a player in the States couldn't keep up with them. Everything surprised me. Because I thought this boy I saw playing the piano was a girl ... I asked Memphis about her and he straightened me out. Can you explain to me why the boys want to look like that?

Walter also talked about his own playing: "I started singing to get a rest from my playing. I blow pretty hard you know—and now I do a lot of it. Singing used to stage fright me; I used to keep my hands in front of my face so the people couldn't really see me, but it's no problem now." Walter said he carried five or six Marine Band harmonicas with him, plus " ... my axe, my big chromatic harp ... I take my microphone in my hand and put the harp on top of it, then I can blow as loud or soft as I like. With the stand mike you don't get the tone from behind it. No, I don't use a stand mike. I wouldn't like to, it would take something out of me." Walter credited Big Bill Broonzy and the original Sonny Boy Williamson as his key inspirations. He ended with a diplomatic nod to the local scene: "Really, the way these boys play here, they're better than some of the so-called bands in the States."

Slim and Walter met Val Wilmer at a west London hotel. A 22-year-old music journalist and soon-to-be professional photographer, she would champion many of the younger American jazz players with her warm, open-minded friendliness. Slim had warned her, "Little Walter, he's not like Roosevelt Sykes, he's not a gentleman ..." Wilmer said, "He was a rough-house person, you could see that by looking at him. [But] he showed no violence of any kind towards me, or unpleasantness ..." Wilmer did an interview with Walter and over the course of the evening the two split a bottle of whiskey. Years later Wilmer wrote, "We got drunk together and had a little frolic ..."

Walter told Wilmer of his youthful beginnings, and opined "... music played real low is better to listen to than the loud stuff. All these young kids they blow so much 'til they forget what they should really be saying." Speaking of the American performers getting into blues, he said:

"There are some good musicians in the white race who can really play their instruments, but they don't have the feeling ... you've got to live it to know it. You can pretend but that really ain't the soul of it. All of your music has to have soul, without it it's just pluck, pluck, pluck. It's the same in what they call jazz. When Louis Jordan was making records and Nat King Cole had his trio and Erskine Hawkins and Lionel Hampton had swinging bands, there was some soul. But the bands now don't really have the feeling. Records today, only kids buy 'em. They look on the title of a record and name a dance after it!" Walter laughed wryly.

Walter's *Best Of* LP had just been released on the English Pye label, winning favorable reviews in *Melody Maker*, alongside a Chuck Berry collection, John Lee Hooker's first Vee-Jay album, and albums by jazzmen including Coleman Hawkins. Walter was getting a good amount of press attention in England, no doubt quite welcome after the low-rent gigs with little notice he'd been playing back home. The day after his arrival he was interviewed by John Broven for *Blues Unlimited*. After recapping his by-now standard biography, he ran down his band members' history, concluding that since 1959 he had had no permanent combo, although noting that recently Guitar Red, Po' Bob (bass guitar), and Scotty (drums) were playing with him.

Broven wrote: "When I met him in London I found a most charming and good-natured man ... Walter was a most willing interviewee and unlike some bluesmen has an excellent memory." Walter told Broven he rehearsed solidly for four or more days prior to recording sessions. He said that he had three contracts with Checker—possibly referring to separate deals for singles, albums, and publishing—and that they always paid his royalties promptly. He mentioned a recent session with Buddy Guy on guitar, which had actually had taken place a year and a half earlier, but was his most recent work for Checker. He also expressed his hope to record again on his return to Chicago. He said he had gigs lined up at the Pride and Joy but wasn't particularly keen on Chicago—"They don't pay enough"—and that he preferred Gary, Indiana or tours through the states. As to the upcoming U.K. tour, he said he'd be doing his own material: "I have enough of my own, why should I sing somebody else's?"

At the same time that Walter was in London, Lightning Hopkins and Rice Miller were in town as part of the 1964 American Folk Blues tour. Miller had an innate hustler's sensibility, and where Walter would sometimes come across as hard and aloof, Sonny Boy was sly and ingratiating. On his previous London gigs, he'd recorded live albums backed by both the Yardbirds and the Animals. While they were not stellar blues events (Sonny Boy was later quoted as saying, "Those English boys want to play the blues so bad—and they do play the blues SO bad"), the shows did help to further his popularity with the wider young audience of blues-rock fans. "There was a bit of tension between Walter and Sonny Boy," Oliver recalls. "Everybody was saying, 'Did you know that Walter jumped Sonny Boy?' I wasn't quite sure what jump might mean in this case, but he actually literally jumped on his back and tried to get a knife into his throat, this was in the hotel. So Walter was obviously more dangerous than I ever experienced." Walter and Sonny Boy had a friendly/adversarial relationship that went all the way back to the early days in Helena, and any real hostilities were probably little more than momentary occurrences.

That evening, September 17th, Walter played his debut London gig at the Marquee Club to a capacity audience of some 400 people. Walter was lucky; the backup band arranged for him was familiar with his material and knew something about playing it. "Long" John Baldry, a 6'7" singer, was fronting The Hoochie Coochie Men, the group that had been led by Chicago blues fan/harpist Cyril Davies until his recent death. Also on the bill were Chris Barber's band and Memphis Slim. Reviews were mixed. Jazz critic Max Jones wrote:

> ... the proceedings were informal, almost to a fault ... Little Walter making his British debut blew his harmonica with impressive drive and organ-like fullness, sounding at one minute like a miniature Jimmy Smith, at another like a soprano sax and at another like a blues whistle. His singing, rich enough and expressive so far as I heard it from the outskirts of a capacity audience brought some contrast to "Mean Old World," "You're So Fine,"

"Blues With A Feeling," "You Better Watch Yourself" and his well-known feature "My Babe." "Thunderbird" was an eloquent solo.

However another reviewer, perhaps expecting faithful recreations of the records Walter had recorded a decade earlier, found it disappointing:

The evening declined from its billed status of An Evening With The Blues to An Evening Of British Rubbish. Walter, encouraged by an avuncular Memphis Slim, blew a few fine phrases amidst the rough patches; his voice has never been his best feature and on this occasion it lost a battle with nerves and strain, cracking on some words, missing others, and failing to reach many high notes. On this showing it was justifiable to think of him as a bluesman past his peak, slumping, if not into downright mediocrity, at least into the "betwixt and between" world inhabited by many former "greats."

From this point forward, the tour lurched on, with Walter playing dates in various venues, always with different—and usually barely competent—accompanists.

To be fair, some of the blame could have been placed with Walter; he didn't bother to rehearse, according to booker Weston. "He'd say 'Oh shit man, I'll just get up and blow.' It was a bit disappointing because I knew what he was capable of doing. He just wouldn't bother to make too much effort."

On Friday the 18th, Walter played at the Chinese Jazz Club in Brighton, backed by The Soul Agents, a band that recorded a couple of singles—both featuring Willie Dixon numbers—for the Pye label that year. Journalist John Broven described them as: "... really awful, worse even than John Mayall and Company ... when I saw Walter before the show he was visibly unnerved by them; 'I'm not gonna sound like I do on my records tonight,' he said sadly." Nonetheless, Broven thought Walter's performance was "masterly," but chided promoters for using a "... group of unmusical juveniles" as backing.

Broven gave one of the few descriptions of one of Walter's British shows:

He came on and went straight into an instrumental before doing "My Babe"... here at long last was the amplified harmonica played to perfection for an English audience, and the large crowd were truly hypnotized. After "Blues With A Feeling" and "Last Night" he finished off his first set with "Southern Feeling." The second half was mainly taken up with instrumentals spotlighting his harmonica. Walter obviously realized that it was point- less trying to sing the blues to the perennial accompaniment of "Green Onions," and his only vocal was "Everything's Gonna Be Alright."

On Sunday, the twentieth, Walter was at the Black Prince in Bexley, backed by The Sheffields, a group that added organ to the standard guitar and bass setup. They cut three singles for Pye, including a cover that year of Muddy's "Got My Mojo Working," and also backed Memphis Slim on his 1964 U.K. tour. Aspiring blues journalist Dave Williams borrowed a portable tape recorder from his friend (and future Led Zeppelin guitarist) Jimmy Page, brought it along to the gig, and captured parts of three songs that evening. The home recording shows Walter struggling mightly to overcome the band's limitations. "Everything's Gonna Be Alright" was played as a straight shuffle, without the distinctive descending guitar riff heard on the record. It sounds like Walter's cupping the vocal mike to his harp and using the PA system for amplification, and despite the rather plodding backup, he manages to stir some real excitement. After singing three verses, he takes a powerful seven-chorus solo to end the song. An improvised instrumental followed, basically a repeat of the earlier song without vocals, at the same tempo, and in the same key. Walter blows with fire again, and switches harps to play in third position for a few verses, overriding the band's limitations. This is followed by "My Babe"; it sounds as though the group had actually heard the record, and they do a fair job of reproducing it. Walter's vocals are a bit ragged, but he plays his harp with inventiveness, control, and passion. Williams also recalled Walter playing a strong version of Roscoe Gordon's Vee Jay hit, "Just A Little Bit."

During the next few weeks, Walter played gigs at small clubs in Portsmouth, Bristol, and Mudeford, backed by different bands at almost every one, with sometimes sparse attendance. Walter generally did two half-hour sets at each location, and before long he was drinking heavily right out of the bottle at most of the gigs, probably as a result of becoming disillusioned by the amateurish backing and the tepid audience reception. Over the course of his tour he was backed by seemingly every local group that had even a passing connection to the blues, with varying results. Among them were The Artwoods (led by Art Wood, brother of future Rolling Stone Ron Wood), Tony Knight's Chessmen, and others now lost in time. Keyboardist Jon Lord of The Artwoods (and later of Deep Purple) saw Walter drink half a bottle of whiskey before the show, finishing it off between sets. He also noted that Walter was hard to work with, given his tendency to switch keys mid-tune, without changing harps. One night at Readings Olympia, Walter was so drunk onstage he could only remember little more than a verse or two of any song. Judging from the reviews, and depending on the night, Walter's performance could vary from mesmerizing to just passable.

On Friday the 25th, Walter appeared on British TV's popular "beat" program, "Ready, Steady, Go," in London. Also on the program were Little Eva, Gerry and the Pacemakers, Wayne Fontana and The Mindbenders, and the Band Of Angels. Walter lip-synched to his recording of "My Babe." The next day he was scheduled to record with Long John Baldry for Southern TV, and the day after that for BBC 2's "Beat Room" program, along with his Checker labelmate, R&B singer Sugar Pie DeSanto, plus the New Orleans girl group The Dixie Cups, and British pop band Peter & The Headliners.

On the weekend, Walter was booked into the Broadside Folk Club. Rather than being accompanied by one of Britain's fledgling blues-rock bands, he was partnered with folk-blues guitarists Davy Graham and Bert Jansch, along with folksinger Shirley Collins. Jansch had never heard any of Walter's music, so a friend, John Challis, loaned him Walter's *Best Of* LP, and he spent the afternoon studying it. Challis met Bert at the gig to retrieve his album. Challis recalled:

> There were only about three people in the club when we got there and one of them was Little Walter, who'd just drunk his first bottle of whiskey and was starting on the second. He was still quite compos mentis, obviously used to it, but at the same time on a slightly different wavelength. . . . I'd had several spliffs [joints] before we'd set out. So I became completely tongue-tied, thinking bloody hell, it's Little Walter! Bert and everybody else just cleared out and left me with him. . . . He's standing there going in and out of focus,

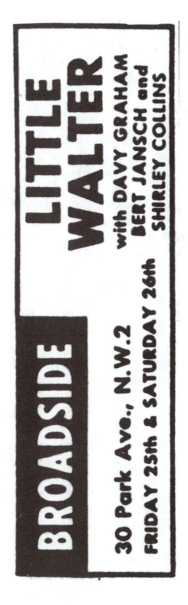

Figure 13.1 Advertisements from Walter's 1964 English tour, *Melody Maker,* September 26, 1964.

and I'm sure he was having the same problem with me, and neither of us could think of a thing to say. Suddenly I remember this record, so I took it out and said, "Would you mind autographing this for me?" He sat down, licked the end of the pen, which was a biro [a disposable ballpoint pen]—and spent about five minutes, more or less drawing his signature from memory.

The show was also awkward. One commentator wrote ". . . with unnerving instinct Jansch's gloriously slovenly playing might add or deduct a half bar from twelve-bar blues, the dictionary definition of mistake expressed as style; he took risks with all the split-second timing and casual aplomb of a high-wire act"—but Walter had no interest in the circus. He was trying to get Jansch to play as simply as possible, shouting, "Easy on the fingers baby!"

Charles Radcliffe, a writer for *Blues Unlimited*, described the next evening's gig, saying that Walter had started playing "folk," singing quietly and blowing " . . . pleasant but undistinguished harmonica, a good foot away from the microphone." During the break the writer suggested Walter use a hand mike, "but he obviously felt this wouldn't appeal to this audience," probably recalling Muddy's tales of outraged folk purists when he'd used electric guitar on his first trip. Then four or five members of the British blues fanatic contingent showed up, and Walter brightened visibly, " . . . pleased to be surrounded by people who had followed his career, knew his records and admired him . . ." On the second set he cupped the mike to his harp and took requests from his fans. "I have never before heard such beautiful or moving work on harp . . . gentle, but with real tension, echoing and continuing the vocal lines, emphasizing, underlining, extending the melody, riffing beautifully, bouncing and bubbling with vitality, energy and controlled power . . . ," Radcliffe noted. Following his set Walter returned briefly to play a number on guitar, impressing Radcliffe again with his " . . . beautiful rolling quality . . . superb down-home guitar."

Radcliffe then followed Walter to his second gig of the evening, at the Club Noreik in Tottenham, where Walter was backed by John Lee's Groundhogs, led by guitarist Tony McPhee. Although they had some actual combat experience, having backed John Lee Hooker on UK tours, they didn't please Radcliffe. They ". . . did not even begin to accompany Walter and made no apparent effort to listen to his work. Despite them he was able to play some very thrilling music, though he was visibly disappointed by the poor support . . . Here he became an R&B artist . . . Walter soared into the upper register, hitting notes with unbelievable drive and precision, holding and bending them indescribably." Radcliffe concluded his review of the evening: " . . . within six hours Walter had been a rather feeble singer, a fine bluesman and a driving and forceful R&B performer . . . a demonstration of quite exceptional quality . . . Little Walter is King."

Bob Hall, pianist with the Groundhogs that night, offers a different view of the late-night gig:

> It was a dance hall, with a standing audience. There was a good crowd, but they were underwhelmed by Little Walter. He didn't connect with them, made perfunctory sort of dispirited announcements and played a lot of instrumentals. He just didn't seem to know how to play to British audiences. He seemed in a bad mood, acted as though he had a chip on his shoulder, and blamed the reaction of the crowd on the band. They just stood around, I think the audience found it a bit dull. After the gig he complained about our

tempos . . . said he'd never played "Last Night" so slow. He told us it was customary for his backing band to buy him a bottle of whiskey before his gig but we didn't—it would have cost us more than our fee! We felt it was an honor to play with him, but I was personally brought down by the occasion. We were used to backing John Lee Hooker who had records in the Top 20 and went down a storm almost everywhere.

Keyboard player Ian McLagen, who would later join The Small Faces and The Rolling Stones, had his own Walter tale to tell. By his own admission, in 1964 his band The Muleskinners was several notches down the pecking order of bands enlisted to back visiting U.S. blues performers, chosen only when The Yardbirds and The Authentics were unavailable. They had backed Howlin' Wolf on a couple of his gigs, then were hired to support Walter for a Sunday afternoon show at the Ricky-Tick Club in Guildford. As the band waited nervously at the venue for him to arrive, they wondered whose idea an afternoon gig was, and how much chance to rehearse they were going to get. McLagen recalled:

Eventually a grey Ford Cortina with a kid who looked even younger than us at the wheel pulled up, and I saw Little Walter Jacobs in the shadows of the back seat, apparently asleep. When he stepped out into the bright sunlight of middleclass England, he was clutching a pint bottle of whiskey, his bug-eyes not yet fully open. Although he didn't look drunk, he wasn't in a great mood either, but then he had just woken up.

The kid introduced us. Walter mumbled something and walked out of the daylight into the hall and the gloom of the dressing room, where he slumped down on the sofa, evidently looking to catch up on his sleep and leaving us feeling a bit unnecessary, to say the least. We did the verbal equivalent of twiddling our thumbs, talking amongst ourselves, while we waited to see what was what. "Hey Walter, d'ya wanna rehearse with the band?" the kid asked a little too helpfully. I would've let him sleep. "Plenty of time. Let me sleep, okay?" "There isn't much time, actually. You go on in about an hour and a half. The band needs to rehearse." "Okay, then, let's get to work." He turned his attention to us. "D'you know any of my tunes?" I told him we knew "My Babe" and mentioned "Boom Boom, Out Go The Lights." "Okay, how 'bout "Juke"?" We'd heard it, but didn't know it, but said we did. Rule one: never let on you don't know the tune. He took a harp from his jacket pocket, brought it up to his mouth and started to play "Key to the Highway" right there and then. It was great. Just to hear his unmistakable sound that close was something I'll never forget. Dave, who'd brought his guitar in, picked out a rhythm part unamplified and Walter turned mere sound into beauty with his soulful wailing. The rest of us were all smiles, grinning at each other in case we were dreaming. This was as good as it got for five white boys on a Sunday afternoon in Guildford, Surrey.

But the kid was about to bring us back to earth with a bump. "Pretend you're a slave on a chain gang," he suggested. Walter stopped playing abruptly as he pulled the harp away from his mouth, glared coldly, and pointed a long-nailed finger at the kid. "Wha'd you say?" Little Walter was wide awake now. "What the fuck do these kids know, or ever have to know about a fucking chain gang, you motherfucker? They're from England, you asshole! Get the fuck outta here!" This was just the start. He tore into the kid, telling him to mind his own business, just drive the car, and leave the band and the music to him. Oh boy, we were glad to have that moment pass, but the mood passed too.

The gig was a bit of a shambles. He'd had a few and we hadn't. Maybe we should have. But it wasn't just the bad taste left from the scene in the dressing room; the lack of rehearsal, our inexperience, and the fact that Walter had changed the keys of some of the numbers guaranteed that it wouldn't have been great. Guildford was hardly the home of the blues, and even the twenty or thirty youngsters who came to this echoing hall didn't know what they were missing. The crowd, if you can call them that, didn't come down to the stage. They stood at the back and the sides of the hall as if they were hiding. It was a bloody shame that this incredibly talented bluesman had come all the way from Chicago to play to such a disinterested audience. I was and still am a big fan of Little Walter and it should have been so much better. It didn't stop him from signing a card, "To my pal from Little Walter," which I treasure to this day.

On October 1st, Walter returned to the Marquee Club in London, along with Long John Baldry and The Hoochie Coochie Men. Rod Stewart and his supporting group was also on the bill. Apparently even when Walter did rehearse with some of his bands, not that much good came of it. Geoff Bradford, guitarist with Baldry's group, reported of Walter, "He was great at rehearsal at the Marquee, but he got horribly drunk before the gig and tried to stick Rod Stewart with a knife!" The gigs continued, with Walter growing increasingly sullen as he worked the smaller clubs outside of the hip center of the swinging London scene, where audiences may not have known him and he did little to accommodate them. He played dates in Manchester, Hanley, and Sheffield, then came back to London to play the Manor House, an established blues club.

Booker Frank Weston accompanied Walter to the gig. During the interval between sets Weston asked Walter if he wanted a drink:

He said "Yeah man, get me a bottle of gin." I said, "Well hold on Walter, you've been drinking rum . . ." He said, "Not now, I want a bottle of gin!" I said, "Okay, but go on finish the gig first"; he had another set to do in the second half. He went on, did his set, he came off stage, I gave him a half bottle of gin. He just unscrewed the top and drank it straight down, without stopping for breath. I couldn't believe it! Then he picked up a bottle somebody had left, Coca Cola—he chased it with that. We went down the steps out into the corridor—and he just collapsed straight on the sidewalk. A friend of mine who had the job of driving him around on his tour took him home and put him to bed. There was a girl with Walter that night but I don't think she saw any action.

According to Weston, Walter's tour driver Mick Baker (not to be confused with the expatriate guitarist) had to sometimes threaten him with physical violence to get him out of bed in the morning. "One night they got back from a gig quite early and Walter didn't want to go to bed, so Mick thought he would take him to a black club on Carnaby Street. Called the Roaring Twenties, from midnight on they had a club aimed at the West Indian community, they played blue-beat and ska. It was almost like the South Side of Chicago, a sea of black faces, Mick thought Walter'd be more at home there. I think Walter stayed about five minutes, I think he felt even more ill at ease there, he virtually ran out," Weston chuckled.

Walter was feeling increasingly lonely and mistreated. His contract for the tour had been booked through Willie Dixon, who got a cut, as did the Variety Artists Federation (the U.K. musicians union). Weston recalled, "We used to pay Walter each week, and he immediately went down to the American Express office and wired it back to the states, back to his lady, or his wife Matty. Then he'd say 'Oh man, I need some bread.' 'Come on Walter—we just paid you yesterday!'"

The gigs ground on through mid-October, Walter competing with other concurrent club dates featuring John Lee Hooker, Jimmy Reed, and Rice Miller as well, a veritable "blues downpour" as *Melody Maker* characterized it. Mike Leadbitter would later write of the tour:

The first time I saw Little Walter was at a drab little club in North London. He looked utterly miserable and was making tinny sort of Sonny Terry sounds on his harmonica. When he saw a dozen or so drunken folk advancing on him he looked wary. But when we knew his whole name, all his records, when he was born, then he was laughing. With an unknown guitarist to provide the rhythm, Walter produced on his second set the best blues harp I've ever heard. By the time I saw him again in his dreary London room with John Lee Hooker he was again utterly fed up. Nobody seemed to know or care who he was, they were working him too hard, the only money he seemed to earn went to Willie Dixon and he hated the fucking English blues groups . . . and he wanted to stay drunk and wanted never to see England again.

While Rice Miller had returned to Chicago boasting of his overseas success, Walter was probably glad just to get back to his familiar haunts and forget all about his English sojourn, which likely left a bad aftertaste. Even though it meant Walter was returning to the same little corner taverns, gigging with pickup musicians, scuffling to make a few bucks a night, he was relieved to be on home turf once again. His sister Marguerite remembered a potential golden opportunity—not to mention a musically historical one—missed due to bad timing. Muddy had called her:

He didn't know how to find brother Walter. I knew where he was at, he was with a woman—I wouldn't give him the number. He said "Can you get in touch with Walter baby?" I said yes, he said, "Well, tell him I want him to travel with me." My brother wasn't doing so well at the particular time. I forget where he was playing, Pepper's or the Zanzibar, he had a gig on the weekend, playing as a single. My brother gave up that gig. He had hired local musicians to do these particular gigs in which he'd have more money. My brother called Muddy after doing what he did, and Muddy said, "Oh man, I've got somebody else."

Despite this seeming slight, when guitarist Mike Bloomfield and photographer Ray Flerlage went to Muddy's house to do a magazine interview, one of Walter's 8x10 publicity photos was prominently displayed in a frame on the fireplace mantle, alongside Muddy's family members. Muddy never stopped showing his concern for Walter's welfare; he had even housed Walter in his basement when he was particularly hard-pressed. Walter could generally always rely on Muddy in a crisis, as other musicians had done; the basement apartment had also sheltered "St. Louis Jimmy" Oden for a time, and Otis Spann.

Walter's pickup bands for his sporadic gigs now included Lee Jackson on guitar, Jerome Arnold (Billy Boy's brother) on bass, and Willie Williams on drums. Jackson had an easy-going point of view on letting people sit in on guitar, and once when Walter objected, Jackson told him, "Man, after all one time you couldn't even play the harmonica, you remember? You had to learn this." Walter replied, "I ain't got time to be learning nobody. I gotta have a guy that can hit." But Walter wasn't hitting all that well himself. According to his bass-player Jerome, frequently ". . . his playing was incoherent, he'd turn up with only three harps for the entire night. His downfall was his choice of friends . . . the worst riff-raff. . . . Sometimes he looked so unhappy, as if he wanted to commit suicide but couldn't do it. He was always fooling around with guns . . . he was a whole situation of self destruction."

Marguerite saw his choice of friends differently:

> My brother always gave himself to the underdog. Grassroots people that was poor, winos and bums, my brother would sit on his car and these guys would all just group up, when he was living on Albany. Brother Walter would sit down talk with these guys, or go to the pool hall with them—those were the people who made him, those were the people he never ignored, 'til the day he died.

By late 1964, Jerome Arnold had another, steadier gig, playing bass with the Butterfield Blues Band, which also included Sam Lay on drums; they would soon cut their debut album for the folk-revival record label Elektra in December, covering three of Walter's numbers. Butterfield's band—although integrated—was led by young, white musicians, and attracted a college-educated crowd. Consequently, they almost immediately were playing in better-paying and classier clubs than their black counterparts. Butterfield was working three or four nights a week at Big John's, a popular street club in the bohemian Old Town section on the near North Side, covering material by black bands that the club wasn't quite ready to hire. Fred Glaser explained:

> . . . they wouldn't book [Walter] up there, they booked white bands like Butter and Michael and Barry Goldberg, Steve Miller. I think they were afraid that black bands would get busted because everybody thought black people were doing dope, involved with hookers, just trouble . . . I think it was probably prejudice that kept him outta there.

After Butterfield's band became a success at Big John's, extra nights were added on; eventually, Butterfield was playing Thursday through Sunday. The first black stars from the South and West sides began to get booked into the weeknights, playing to a racially mixed crowd that had been attracted to the scene. Black blues bands eventually played weekend gigs at Big John's. Otis Rush was booked there, as was Muddy and band, Buddy Guy, and Little Walter at least once. Guitarist Elvin Bishop recalled Walter sitting in with the Butterfield band one night: "He was pretty good, but he wasn't loose, not communicating, he didn't look happy. You know how people get at certain stages of drinking when everything just kind of deteriorates and they start to go down fast? There was some of that . . ." The Butterfield band would become very popular in the psychedelic rock halls of San Francisco with Mike Bloomfield now a regular member on lead guitar. Their blues/raga-rock sound suited the hippie audiences at the Fillmore and Avalon shows.

During 1965, Walter was almost invisible as far as the press went, although he continued to play his neighborhood gigs and scuffle along. In October he was photographed by Ray Flerlage sitting in at Theresa's Lounge with his one-time protege Junior Wells. Louis Myers later told an interviewer, " . . . all in California, Huntington Beach, back up to Fillmore Auditorium, peoples was carried away with

Junior Wells . . . it's funny, he pretty good showmanship, put on a pretty nice *little* show . . . but he's no harp man." Walter agreed, "No, he can't operate that harp." Maybe Wells wasn't in Walter's league as an instrumentalist, but he was learning to operate in the hippie ballrooms, and he went out on frequent gigs on the white rock and folk club circuits. Rice Miller had also tapped into the white markets successfully abroad, and by spring, negotiations were underway to book him at the Newport Folk Festival, a venue that would certainly have guaranteed him a lucrative schedule on the U.S. coffeehouse and club circuit as well. Unfortunately, on May 25th Miller was found dead in his bed after failing to show up for his radio slot on the King Biscuit Hour in Helena, having returned there after his last trip to England.

Walter was playing funkier circuits. Guitar Red remembered a month-long southern tour with a lot of stops in northwestern Mississippi: "We played Greenville—that's my home town—Pace, Cleveland, Mount Baldwin—that's a black town—and Arcola. Played a couple places in the country in Tennessee. I talked Walter into going out with just three pieces and hire a drummer when you get there, and that's what we did, made about $50 a night, me and Poor Bob. Then we went to Terre Haute, Indiana, Milwaukee, Wisconsin, Waukegan, Illinois . . ." Red recalled some of the expected prejudices; there were "colored bathrooms, you had to drink 'black' water and all that," he chuckled:

> . . . outta all that you had some loving, friendly white people . . . we played for a lot of white joints, wasn't no blacks in there. We'd pull up to a service station, and the man say, "Would you like to play a party tonight?" We'd say "Yassuh" and he ask how much we charge—Walter would give 'em a price. Sometimes we'd make more money with them, they'd have us up at the farm, in the barn. They'd have a hoedown, a big dance—and give you all that country ham and bacon to take home. We stopped at several of them . . . they loved the blues.
>
> One gig we had was in South Bend, Indiana, before them highways was all through there . . . a couple of guys with us, Tucker was one, he and Walter smoking reefer, making noise in the car. Police stopped us, they was dumb about that stuff. He didn't bust em for the reefer, the man didn't know what they was smoking. He bust 'em for drinking and making noise. I was no fool, I said "Sir, I ain't making no noise, I'm from the South, I know how to act." They was lighting up in the station, rolling 'em up right in front of the man. Wasn't no big police station, little one horse town. The man refer to me as boy, he said "Boy, you the onliest one of this bunch got any sense." He didn't even lock me up, says, "I'm gonna build a cell for the rest of these niggers!" They didn't even have a jail. The man took some beaverboard, plywood, woke up some construction workers, built a big calaboose, they called 'em calaboose down south, some didn't even have no top, just a big box. The man built one, he put Walter, Tucker, the boy who drove, and another guy, I forget who. Walter says, "Call my old lady," so I called her, he had one called Dorothy I think.
>
> I talked to the man, I saw on his hand he had a Masonic ring. Well I'm a Mason and so was Walter. I said "Sir, he's a Masonic and I am too. . . ." That white guy said, "I didn't know no niggers was in the Masonics." I said "Yassuh," shake his hand and I put some signs on him. He said, "Well, maybe we can talk here—can you scrape up $50?" I says "Oh yassuh." The man didn't even search them—Walter had a gun on him. I said "Y'all gotta be glad you walking out of here," and they had me driving 'til we got back in Illinois.

Walter continued to press Chess for money and recording opportunities, and in October they threw him a bone. Shel Silverstein was a *Playboy* magazine cartoonist and raconteur, who also wrote and sang ballads with satiric-comedic, folk-styled content. Chess had recorded a live show at Mother Blues with Silverstein fronting a four-piece acoustic group. Producer Esmond Edwards decided to call Walter in to overdub harp. He appears on four of the tracks on the album, issued on the Chess's Cadet subsidiary label as *I'm So Good I Don't Have to Brag*. Walter added a nice feel to the proceedings, but the results weren't anything he was likely to be very proud of. He certainly earned his $61 sideman session fee.

With Elektra Records having successfully branched out from its folk-based catalogue to record the electric blues of Paul Butterfield, it was no surprise that their biggest competitor, Vanguard Records, would also make a foray into the growing marketplace. In December 1965, blues researcher and author Sam Charters came to Chicago to record artists for a three LP Vanguard series called *Chicago/The Blues/Today!* Junior Wells and Buddy Guy, J. B. Hutto, Otis Spann, Otis Rush, James Cotton, Homesick James, Johnny Shines, Johnny Young, and Walter Horton were all recorded, but Walter was conspicuously absent from the program. Charters later wrote that Walter ". . . was an alcoholic, and his career fell apart only a few years after he did his best recordings . . . By the mid-1960s he was working only sporadically, and it was usually when a friend like guitarist Lee Jackson came and brought him to the club. I wanted to include him in the Vanguard series, but he was too nervous to come to the studio." Charters's wife Ann did capture him on film however, photographing him in a small club while ". . . he was waiting for Lee's band to finish its warm up set, and he seemed almost apprehensive as he looked at Lee and waited for the moment when he had to stand up and take over the band." In the photo Walter eyes Jackson warily, his body leaning away, visibly tense.

On December 16, 1965, Walter took care of some business at the American Federation of Musicians union office. His membership had lapsed due to nonpayment of dues, and now he rejoined, probably in anticipation of more recording at Chess, who required union membership for their artists. For reasons known only to himself, he gave a fictitious social security number, and gave his year of birth as 1930; this was later scratched out and 1923 written in (probably to match up with the date he had given when he first joined up in 1949). At the same time, he changed the beneficiaries of his union death benefits from Armilee's daughter Marion, whom he'd added shortly after her birth, to Margaret [sic] Brother and Lula Jackson, "two sisters."

The reason for this change may have been second thoughts about his paternity. According to family members, Walter had been tested by a doctor, and was found to be sterile. What initially prompted such a test can only be conjectured. "Walter couldn't have a baby," his uncle Sam Leviege later said. ". . . he couldn't produce, if you can't, you can't impregnate a woman." Pressed as to how he knew this, Sam replied, "'Cause I took him to the doctor, that's when he was in Chicago. . . ." Marguerite said further that ". . . he used to say this all the time, 'Man, I am shooting blanks, no loaded bullets.'" She doubted that he ever had any children, and that if he did, she felt she certainly would have met them.

In January 1966, Chess released another Muddy Waters compilation LP. Titled *Real Folk Blues*, it was aimed at the folk devotee white audience; there were also albums under that heading issued by Howlin' Wolf and Sonny Boy Williamson #2 at the same time. The tracks were compiled from Muddy's singles over the course of his career, and Walter was heard on three cuts. But there was no such LP in the pipeline for Walter; according to a Chess label catalog at the time, there were no Little Walter albums currently in print.

In February, Walter was back at Chess studios for his first session as a leader in three years. Backed by guitarist Lee Jackson and tenor saxman J. T. Brown, Walter took another stab at a hit single. "Back in the Alley" is an instrumental based, directly or indirectly, on jazz guitarist Kenny Burrell's popular tune from 1963, "Chittlins Con Carne." The tune has become something of a staple, used by numerous bands as a "break song" at the end of their sets. Walter may have actually gotten the idea from Junior Wells; Wells had included it on his Delmark debut LP a couple of months earlier, and regularly performed it at his Blue Monday weekly jams, which Walter frequented. Walter's band arrangement has more in common with Junior's than with the Burrell original, although after the opening verse Walter simply improvises the rest of the song. This is one of the rare instances where Walter seems to have borrowed an idea from a "lesser" harp player, one he had thought could show him nothing new. Walter's recording features more tenor sax than harp, Brown taking five choruses to Walter's four rather uninspired ones. He plays without his usual sharp attack, and seems to run out of steam by the end.

"I Feel So Bad" was very aptly titled. The first take is somewhat reminiscent of the tune "You Don't Know" from his unissued 1960 session. The second take is a little more original, with a different chorus, and is a bit longer but not really any better than the first. On both, Walter's singing is out of time, off pitch, hoarse, and his lyrics are confused—and his harp playing is only marginally better. "Chicken Shack" was the last tune attempted, an instrumental shuffle also used by many bands as a break song, with its now-classic riff played here in unison by harp and sax. There are vestiges of Walter's old ability present, but the band is rather sloppy and the take is unfocused and repetitious. Chess wound up shelving the entire session.

Saxman Gene Barge, who worked the blues and R&B circuit as well as doing numerous Chess sessions in the '60s, had encounters with Walter around this time. "Johnny Pepper opened a place in Chicago Heights, we used to play out there with Bobby King. Every time we'd go out there, Walter would sit in with us . . . Walter used to hang out there all the time. [We] had a lot of fun with Walter." Barge was present at the "Back In The Alley" session, the last Walter would do for Chess as leader, and his recollection goes a long way towards explaining why:

They were gonna give him one shot. By this time everybody was so pissed with him anyway, because Little Walter had been screwing up so badly. [He] come in, they're telling everybody, "Absolutely no whiskey. None. He ain't allowed no whiskey. Don't let him go out, let him just do his thing." So Little Walter says, "Well, I gotta get some soda man, I gotta get some pop. Get me a 7-Up." He had this 7-Up bottle down there between his legs, straddling the chair. He had the chair turned around backwards, had his harmonicas on the floor, playing his tracks. And by the time he got to about the third tune, Little Walter was paralyzed drunk man! He had, some kind of way got some gin into the 7-Up bottle. I don't know how he got it in there man, I don't know where it came from. Man, Leonard was furious. He didn't even finish the session . . .

Walter was apparently in an advanced state of alcoholism, with very little tolerance for alcohol, and his liver could no longer absorb booze the way it used to. Billy Boy recalled Matty talking about how Walter could get drunk ". . . so damn fast. He left off, say he's going down to the corner . . . twenty minutes later, Walter couldn't walk up the steps. He'd take a bottle and turn it up . . ."

In March 1966, an East Coast promoter called Bob Koester in Chicago, who'd been involved in bringing some older blues artists out of retirement to record for his Delmark label, to ask for assistance in booking Walter into a Boston coffeehouse called the Moondial. Koester had frequently seen Walter sitting in on Monday nights at Theresa's Lounge, and thought he was always in good shape. But recently he hadn't been working much. Koester recalled, "The whites didn't know about him, he was just a name on a Paul Butterfield liner note. I guess he held himself a little high, and didn't tend to want to do local jobs. Walter's idea of working was the real theaters or those South Side clubs that almost never had blues . . . if he worked other jobs, I think it was some kind of a bring-down. . . ." But those other jobs, using pickup bands, were the only ones he was getting anymore; Koester recalls, "I never saw him work with the same musicians twice." Koester couldn't find anybody who was willing to leave town with Walter for the eastern date. Nonetheless, a fee was advanced to Walter so that he could assemble a suitable Chicago band on his own to bring with him on the trip, but he still turned up in Boston solo. As listed in the Moondial's calendar, Little Walter and His Chicago Blues Band were scheduled to play the weekend of March 25–27, then again the following week from Tuesday to Friday, with white blues singer Lisa Kindred as the opening act.

The Moondial was housed in a former synagogue, near the Boston Commons; up two flights of marble stairs, patrons found a room large enough to accommodate three or four hundred people. The place was advertised as a "concert gallery," and tables were set up around the large room. (The club would later enjoy some fame as Boston Tea Party.) The gig was eagerly anticipated by the local blues cognoscenti; among those attending were aspiring writer Peter Guralnick, future J. Geils Band vocalist Peter Wolf and guitarist Paul Shapiro (who was then a bandmate of Wolf's in a Boston group called The Hallucinations), blues fan Jim Lombardi, and photographer Mark Powers. They all stood in line for Walter's first Boston appearance for a mainly white audience.

Reactions to the shows ranged from disappointed to appalled. Shapiro, who'd seen the 1955 Alan Freed revue Walter had performed in, went with Peter Wolf on the first night, and recalled the backup band as being an out-of-town group called The New York Public Library. "They did not know the music. Little Walter was drunk out of his mind; he'd start playing and fall flat on his face. He kept falling down; he was a shadow of his former self. It was pathetic, very depressing. . . ." Lombardi, who went on a week-night, recalled that Walter was dressed very casually, just a checkered shirt and pants; ". . . he wasn't dressed like Muddy's guys at all, Muddy would never allow his guys to look like that. He didn't look well, seemed like an old bluesman. I don't remember him even completing a whole song, maybe 'Juke.' It was an extremely short set . . . I just remember him being ripped, tearing into the band all the time he played some harp. He'd get really pissed and stop—he'd grab the guitar and play awhile, then he'd stop and play drums—I remember him actually telling them [the band] how to play. . . ." Lombardi remembers a small audience of maybe fifteen people in the large room, watching with reverence; "It was so bizarre, like watching guys practicing, rather than a show."

Mark Power stood in line down on the street, ". . . hearing this harmonica come out, you could hear it a block away . . . the hairs on the back of your neck would just rise, it was an amazing sound." But, once inside the crowded hall, he too recognized that there were problems: "His pickup band was awful, he would stop in the middle and stamp his feet trying to get them back into the rhythm of it, 'Pick it up boys!' He was playing very well, the fact that the band was so bad would normally throw a musician off, but it didn't seem to bother him. I thought it was wonderful . . ."

Afterwards, Power approached and told Walter how much he'd enjoyed the show, and asked if he could photograph him. Walter asked, "Why don't you just shoot me while I'm doing the set?" When Power told him it was too dark, and that he wanted to do a portrait shot, Walter gave him the address of the room where he was staying a few blocks away from the club. The next day Power showed up at the appointed 2:00 PM, and found Walter still asleep, motionless, a sheet over his face:

> He seemed to remember saying I could come by, didn't seem too surprised to see me. He had a turban round his head; first thing he did was pour some Coke and gin into a glass and chug it down—two of those and he was ready to go. He dressed carefully in a black suit, a tie with a Mason clasp, a handkerchief minutely adjusted in the breast pocket and polished alligator shoes. In the most careful step of all he removed his hairnet and put on a black cap, just so. He said, "First we have to go down to Western Union." I drove him down to the office and helped him fill out five or six telegrams, all to different women, all with $5 enclosed—something like "Love Walter" was all it said—cost me about $30. We sent those off, then he walked into this vacant lot next to Western Union for about five minutes and I took a few head shots. He said that was it, so I drove him back to his rooms.

Power later sent a copy of one of the processed photos to Walter, in care of Chess records, as he'd promised he would. To his surprise, when the retrospective album *Hate to See You Go* was released in 1969, it was a cropped version of his photo gracing the cover, a striking closeup of Walter, with attitude and scars prominent. Powers contacted Chess, and he eventually received a lump sum payment for his work.

Mark "Kaz" Kazinoff, who would later go on to produce, and play saxophone and harmonica on countless blues and R&B recordings from the 1970s onward, was another fledgling musician who attended the Moondial shows. At the time, he was an enthusiastic 17-year-old who'd memorized every note on Walter's *Best Of* album. Kazinoff hit the club twice, and remembered a good number of people there, whooping it up. The earlier backup band had been replaced by the Blues Children, a local group:

> It's always tough for somebody to live up to their records . . . he definitely was not the player that he was earlier in his career. He was very sloppy, and just tended to be kind of unfocused in his playing. At the same time, he'd come out with something that was moving and spectacular, an incredibly phrased original-sounding lick. Unfortunately you

had to wait quite a while before something like that happened . . . I was completely cha-grined that the band didn't know his tunes . . . I wanted to pursue getting to know him, so I asked if I could take him to lunch.

So on a bright and sunny Saturday afternoon, Kazinoff met Walter at the club and took him over to Ken's, a lunch counter/diner in Copley Square, then right on the edge of the ghetto. Kaz thought him a:

> . . . very polite, actually kind of sweet guy, but very hard-bitten, hard-edged . . . my impres-sion [was] that he was living on the edge, day to day . . . felt like he was lonely and a little lost . . . it was easy to talk to him. I was just a young white guy who loved his music, I asked him about Muddy, he told me Muddy was like a father to him, said something like "Muddy has always taken care of me. . . . "We started talking about the Rolling Stones, who I loved at the time, he said "Yeah man, they're the greatest band I've ever heard . . ." He'd seen them on TV, a friend gave him one of their records, he thought "Those guys really had the blues sound." I remember asking if he traveled a lot; he said no, he didn't really work much outside of Chicago, he mentioned Gary [Indiana] or Michigan City, somewhere he had a regular gig . . . We walked around a bit, I was trying to make him feel welcome I guess, in my own small way. I walked him around Copley Square, showed him the church, pointed out where I went to school, stuff like that . . . [We] probably spent a couple hours altogether . . .

The impression Kazinoff got from Walter that day was markedly different from his behavior at the gig: "This was pretty late at night, the last set. He just got wild, he was jumping around on stage, tossing the microphone around. At one point he took his suit coat off, he was fumbling with his shirt—he just literally tore the sleeve off his shirt . . . and he just kept on playing with that one-sleeved shirt. He was pretty demented that night . . ." Kazinoff had seen Muddy and his band a year or so before at Club 47 and thought the shows were fantastic and totally together: "To see Walter, who I always thought was greater than Muddy, in the state he was in was extremely disillusioning for me, a dose of hard reality . . . there was definitely a different economic strata going on there . . ."

Peter Ivers, an avant-garde jazz harmonica player based in Boston, had his own opportunity to show Walter some of the local sights. Ivers later recalled to some friends that he had taken Walter on a walking tour and visited the Revolutionary War era war-ship, "Old Ironsides" (the USS Constitution), permanently anchored in Boston Harbor. As they walked around Boston Walter's crippled leg began to give him pain. The diminutive Ivers stood only about 4' 11"—an extremely short man—and Walter at times rested his hand on Ivers' shoulder to take some of the weight off his bad leg. Ivers remarked, "He [literally] used me as a cane," which was as much a bemused comment about his own stature as it was a sad one about the chronic pain in Walter's leg from extended walking.

The promoter who had brought Walter to Boston later told the story of Walter losing the cash payment from his gig by the side of the road outside of town, when he had his car pull over so he could urinate. Walter woke him at 2:00 AM to help search for it, instructing him to look for "a shiny bush" he'd wetted; they walked up and down the side of the highway, but it never turned up.

Walter returned to Chicago, feeling lower than when he left, and around this time another golden opportunity was missed. Koester's label Delmark Records had recently released Junior Wells' breakthrough LP *Hoodoo Man Blues*, and mainstream interest in blues in general and Junior in particular was at an all-time high. According to Bob Koester, a film crew from a TV program called "The Bell Telephone Hour" (a popular mid-'60s variety show) had made arrangements to shoot footage of Junior Wells performing at Pepper's Lounge on the South Side. While shooting there, Walter showed up, and Koester pointed him out to the producer: ". . . he is probably the greatest living blues harmonica player, and I think you should film him." However, the producer was reluctant to make last-minute changes, and the opportunity was lost. And so another chance at garnering some mainstream recognition and potentially tapping into the growing market for blues among young white fans slipped away.

On May 20th, the University of Chicago put on a blues festival in Mandell Hall, featuring Little Walter with a thrown-together band, along with performances by Otis Rush, Buddy Guy, Junior Wells, and J. B. Hutto (who included Big Walter Horton in his band). As usual Norman Dayron recorded the concert:

> The only time I saw him when he was completely surreal was at that concert. He was so intimidated, I think, by 2,000 white people applauding everything he did that something snapped in his mind and he thought he was in a different world, where all the standards were different. There's this concert in a beautiful hall, plush red velvet seats, you looked out and knew it wasn't a club . . . these were all U. of C. people, not just a bunch of guilty white liberals who didn't know anything about the music and would applaud anything an old black guy did . . . they were projecting unconditional love. . . .
>
> You could see him testing, he would play a terrible note on the harmonica, people would applaud . . . he was trying to figure out where they were coming from. In other words, it was clear they didn't understand the music, he was drunk out of his mind, could not get his shit together, couldn't sing in tune or in time with the band, he was just terrible. But he was laughing uncontrollably, he was having such a good time, like a kid in a toy store. That's why I said surreal, he was laughing like somebody on an acid trip, out of touch with reality . . . it was like a man exploring this surreal world where you could do no wrong, even though in his own mind he knew he wasn't playing anything solid . . . if he had any memories of it, he might say, "Oh yeah, I had a good time."

Photos shot that day by Ray Flerlage show Walter in apparent stoned ecstasy, making swooping, exaggerated gestures. There were four songs recorded, Walter backed by a trio that included Sam Lawhorn (then with Muddy's band) on guitar, taking long solos with the thin distorted tone currently in mode with psychedelic groups, and possibly Fred Below on drums. Walter sings two numbers; in "Going Down Slow" he sadly changes the lyric line from its usual prophesy to past tense in a comment on his own situation: "I know my health is failing, I've already gone down slow." The other vocal is an almost unrecognizable version of his own "You're So Fine." The instrumentals include a generic shuffle number and "Watermelon Man," both played with mushy harp tone and only ghostly remnants and brief hints of Walter's former sharp incisive riffs and darting rhythmic jumps. Dayron says, "I've never released these tapes and never will. Because it's morally wrong to put something like that out." Be that as it may, the tapes have been issued and reissued on a number of labels, mostly from Europe, over the years.

In June, Paul Butterfield was back in Chicago after weeks on the road for a successful psychedelic ballroom and club tour with his band. A reviewer for *Blues Unlimited* attended a local Muddy Water's club date, where Butterfield showed up to play: "Muddy was fine, the rest of the group were poor. Cotton was not interested as he had a sprained ankle, a bad eye, and was leaving that week to start his own group . . . Paul Butterfield took over from Cotton half-way and though he did well, he did too much, almost drowning out Muddy at times . . ." Muddy had recently fired several band members, and other personnel shifts were discussed. "I suggested to Muddy that he get Little Walter back and he said, 'Yeah, I might do that'—he meant it too." Perhaps at that moment he might have, and it wasn't the first or last time it would be mentioned, but ultimately nothing permanent came of it—although apparently the groundwork had been laid for a brief studio reunion of the former bandmates.

On the West Coast, guitarist Mike Bloomfield was proselytizing, telling ballroom bookers and anybody else who'd listen about the real heavy bluesmen like Muddy, Wolf, Cotton, Little Walter, and others, still alive and playing well back in Chicago. He urged bookers to hire them, and Bill Graham and others occasionally did, mixing blues and psychedelic acts on bills that found favor with the hippies, whose minds and tastes in music were expanding equally.

Despite the disastrous Boston trip, Walter got another chance to try to hook into the lucrative hippie concert scene when he was booked for a four-day weekend run in early August at a tiny psychedelic club on Fillmore Street in San Francisco called The Matrix. Additionally, there was a Sunday show put on by the Family Dog, a cooperative group of hippies who booked concerts in the Bay area in opposition to Bill Graham, at The Longshoreman's Hall, on a bill with Bo Diddley and the local group The Sons Of Adam.

Once again Walter showed up solo, without an expected backup band. He told Ron Polte, then manager of the group Quicksilver Messenger Service, that his advance money had been stolen by some agent, and that all he had was a roundtrip plane ticket and a three-night hotel room in North Beach. He suggested that he would have to do the gig solo, because he couldn't afford to pay a band. Rising to the bait, Polte volunteered the group's services gratis. The five-man group were popular in the ballrooms with their blues-tinged rock numbers, so it didn't appear to be a total mismatch like some of Walter's earlier debacles. Bassist David Freiberg didn't recall there being any real rehearsal, other than possibly a sound check at the small club with a capacity of around one hundred people.

Quicksilver guitarist Gary Duncan recalled:

. . . Walter heard me playing a Freddie King song, maybe "Hideaway," he recognized the song. Right before the set he says, "Why doncha go out there and play two or three of them Freddie King tunes?" So we go out, I play all the Freddie King I know, the announcer goes, "Ladies and gentlemen! From Chicago, the one and only Little Walter!" Walter comes out, he does "My Babe" and "Juke." Then he turns around to me and says "Play a couple more of them Freddie King tunes," and he leaves the stage. He did that every set, he'd come out, play the same two fucking songs, and tell me to play Freddie King tunes—and he'd sit back in the dressing room and drink gin. In those days, when black musicians would play for a white audience, they generally wouldn't do their show. They'd jive the white folks, know what I mean? It was okay, everybody cheered and screamed, he played fucking great. . . . I went in and said "Walter, why you drink so much gin?" He says, "My teeth, my teeth is hurting me." When I asked him where he got that big old scar on his head he said, "My old lady hit me with a wine bottle."

One night he asked me, "You got a little pote?" I said, "What?" He said, "You know [inhale sounds], pote." I said, "Oh, sure man." I took him out in the alley, had my car parked there—we got in, opened up the glove box, there was a half a kilo in there. He looked at it, didn't know what it was—"What's that?" I said "That's pot." He says, "That ain't pote . . . What's them little funny white things in there?" I said "That's the seeds." When he grasped how much quantity there actually was there he totally flipped out. Jumped out of the fucking car in a panic, man—"I'm gonna get arrested, goddamn, old lady gonna kill me!"—and he ran back in the club.

Walter came back onstage at the end of the show after Quicksilver closed it out, and asked the audience for a round of applause for the band, saying "Now can't these white boys play?" John Goddard, a young blues enthusiast, attended the show the first night, but was so disappointed in the quality of it that he did not bother to come again. He managed to click off some snapshots of a thoroughly inebriated Little Walter performing, dressed in a shiny sharkskin suit that contrasted sharply in one photo with the jeans and long hair of guitarist Duncan.

Goddard cornered Little Walter after the show for an autograph. He had brought a page torn from a magazine with photos of various bluemen: Muddy Water, Howlin' Wolf, and Little Walter. Walter was so drunk that he repeatedly tried to sign his name to some other bluesman's photo, not his own; he had to be stopped and redirected. Goddard was an acquaintance of Quicksilver guitarist John Cipollina, who told him that he had housed Little Walter for the duration of the Matrix date at his place in La Gaunitas. He remarked that Walter had stayed drunk the whole time he was there.

Freiberg said:

> We did take him—the Grateful Dead were staying at a camp out in Marin county, out in the woods, used to be a kid's camp [known as Rancho Olompali, near Novato, California]. They stayed there the whole summer, all the furniture was like half-sized—but it had a swimming pool so we spent a lot of time out there . . . somehow we brought Walter out. He got pretty loose, there was a jam, I think he had a pretty good time with Pigpen, he was the only other real drinker there, though it's pretty hazy . . .

By the second day of the engagement, Walter was becoming some kind of legend in the hippie community. But that didn't seem to help the attendance of his gig at the Longshoreman's Hall with Bo Diddley. The crowd was so small that the promoters canceled Bo's upcoming gig in nearby Oakland.

While in the Bay Area, Walter looked up his sister Lillian, who was living in Oakland; she'd only seen him four or five times over the years since she'd moved there. When Walter had traveled to California with his band, around 1954, the whole group stayed with Lillian and her husband Buddy for a couple of weeks. "I had a big house, they all stayed upstairs. They played all around in these little old small places over there, but they made good money." Lillian confirms that, unlike those early days, on his recent trips Walter traveled solo. "He didn't have nobody with him then, it got too expensive, he started hiring guys out of the union . . . they'd practice once, two, three hours and that was it." She recalled going to his last gig at a club out there, ". . . some hippie owned it or something . . . I told you I didn't know he could play guitar. He played that whole time with a guitar, up until about an hour. They said 'Blow the harp Walter, blow the harp!' So then he blowed the harp. . . ."

One night during this stay, the talk turned philosophical, and Walter asked Lillian a question that haunted him all his life: Why didn't his mother Beatrice come to look for him after he'd been taken away as a two-day old infant, not to see her again until he was eleven? Lillian tried to comfort him, saying "Because we couldn't *find* you, Walter!" They also talked about his ways with women, and Lillian again asked if he'd thought about marriage. Lillian said that Walter replied, "'Baby I ain't got time to be tied down' . . . I asked him, last time I saw him, 'Why don't we buy an apartment house, when you get tired of blowing that old harp, I'll get you a nice strong rocking chair, you can just rock away, draw your money and royalties?' He said, 'Aww baby, I don't like it over here.' I said 'What—it's not fast enough?' He said 'No, I don't want to do that.' He never wanted to live in California. . . ."

The talk turned darker when Lillian asked, "'. . . err, when you die, where you wanna go at? You wanna go back to Marksville?' He told me 'Noooo, I don't wanna go back there, I wanna be buried in Chicago. Chicago made me, that's where I want my remains to be at . . . I don't wanna go to Marksville, in that water and stuff . . . I don't wanna be buried in no ground where the maggots will eat at me . . .'" This was the last long conversation the siblings would ever have.

14 *mean old world*

Chicago/Europe/UK/Chicago:
Fall 1966–February 1968

In September 1966, business was steady in the jazz, rock, and soul fields, and the Chess brothers began moving into their new headquarters: a six-story building at 320 East 21st Street, a few blocks east of their old setup, purchased for just under a half-million dollars. The new studios were twice as large, and the facility would now include their own pressing plant, plus a penthouse with a barbershop and sauna built in—not that they ever had time to take advantage of the amenities.

Things were looking up at Chess, but the same could not be said for Walter. He was working a three-night weekend gig at a joint at Sawyer and Ogden on the West Side, ". . . an old winehead gig," according to Guitar Red. "That's the only signed gig we went to every weekend, that would keep him in wine money. He told me, 'When I went to going down, my boys quit me,' the boys that played with him, Tucker, Jimmie Lee, the rest of 'em." Red and Bob Woodfork soldiered on with Walter. Woodfork was another Arkansas native who'd settled in Chicago. After his army service in World War II, he began gigging with Otis Rush, and had done sideman work and sessions with people such as Jimmy Rogers, Howlin' Wolf, George Smith, and Sunnyland Slim.

Red said, ". . . in his last years he got to where he couldn't blow, he could only blow about two songs, he'd have to quit . . ." According to Red, part of the reason for his diminished capacities was a lung ailment:

> . . . he had a knot, he let me feel it. It rosed up in his back one night when he was blowing. He said he wasn't able to perform much no more . . . he'd start off numbers, they'd [other harp players] be around him, he'd give 'em the harp—"Bet you can't do that," fool 'em into playing . . . sometimes they'd say "Oh Walter, would you play 'Juke'?" He'd say, "You look at that joker there, that joker must be crazy" . . . he was insulting to people like that . . . he was ignorant, he'd walk in places order hamburgers, get 'em and walk out without paying, people do that in Chicago . . .

Red asked Walter about his limp, and was told that he'd been crippled when he was caught in bed with another man's wife and was forced to jump out a third-story window. When people would ask Walter what happened to all the money he'd made, he'd joke, "I turned it back to the rightful owner." Red drove Walter to and from gigs in Walter's increasingly dilapidated white 1960 Cadillac, since he'd lost his license again. Sometimes Walter just wanted to ride around aimlessly to kill time.

Red also repeated a story that has approached urban-legend status, with a number of people claiming they saw it happen at various times and locations. Red says he was working with Walter:

> . . . on the 1500 block of Roosevelt. That's where a guy walked into the tavern, he'd cut his old ladies head off, threw it up on the bar, says "Give her a drink and me too." He had the head in a paper bag, Walter said "Good God!" Guy was drunk, they called him Snuff . . . he fried his hair like the brothers do now, and parade down the street with his lips painted red. He was crazy . . . he had a sawed off shotgun I think . . . or what looked like a shotgun. Folks was runnin'.

Leonard Chess had been grooming his son Marshall to take over more responsibility at the company; Marshall started out by keeping things moving when Leonard or Phil went to the bathroom. ("There was always a Chess overlooking a session," Marshall says.) He was soon producing sessions. He had a younger generation's sensibilities, and perceived the Chess artists in new roles, reaching new markets. He thought there was an untapped potential in the hippie youth culture, and came up with the idea for the first Chess concept albums. The plan was to make over some of the older artists on the blues roster for the youth market, recording them with hard-rock backing featuring fuzz-tone guitars and other psychedelic musical effects. This eventually resulted in both Muddy and Wolf cutting hybrid psychedelic-blues albums that horrified purists but at the time outsold their deep-blues original forerunners.

As an extension of Marshall's plan, on Wednesday, January 4, 1967 a rather odd summit meeting took place at Chess's Ter-Mar (named for Phil and Leonard's sons Terry and Marshall) Studios: Bo Diddley, Muddy Waters, and Little Walter were booked for a joint session. Sidemen included Otis Spann and Buddy Guy, with Cookie Vee (Connie Redmond) from Bo's group on tambourine and backing vocals. Ralph Bass was listed as producer, while Phil and Marshall Chess were credited with "album supervision."

According to Marshall, ". . . the series I put out, *Super Blues*, that was to get money for the artists and for the company . . . it was about expanding them to that generation, they were designed and marketed. Those were specifically not for the black people in the least, one iota. It was all about spreading it, for their sake and ours." Bo Diddley had a different take on the project:

> I was responsible for the whole idea. I was in there for a session, said, "Let's do something different—call Muddy Waters and Little Walter—call 'em up before I come into Chicago and set it up with them. Let's see if we can't do something—all the other record companies are combining artists on albums—why is it Chess and Checker can't do it?" It took several weeks to happen, but it finally did. We sat down and talked about what to do . . . the three of us . . . we named the songs we was going to identify ourselves with. I said, "Let's jump to it," and we ran straight through it [suggesting that the songs were all done in single takes].

The idea was to approximate a loose jam session with lots of friendly jiving and a party atmosphere, but the results come off as rather forced good humor, and several numbers continue to plow on long after the interesting or original ideas have already been used up. Bo Diddley's tremolo guitar and Muddy's slide are an odd matchup, and Walter's harp is often lost in the mix. Walter's singing is tired, and only one of the cuts he led—"My Babe"—was included on the resulting album. (Versions of "Juke" and "Sad Hours" were eventually released on the 1992 CD reissue, while "Blues With A Feeling" remains on the shelf.)

"Juke," although taken at a rushed pace, provides an example of how Walter's harmonica style was changing. Probably equally influenced by both his increasingly obvious physical decline and the changes in music in general, his playing was becoming more rhythm-based, relying more on repeated short figures with fewer lengthy single-note excursions. The band here, like most of the bands he'd played with in recent years, makes little effort to interact with him; gone is the tight-as-a-drum ensemble playing of the original "Juke," replaced by the more orthodox "jamming over generic blues backing" style that had for the most part replaced the old style that Walter had helped to create. Walter begins "Juke" with its familiar ascending six-note phrase, and from then on improvises an entirely new number, which while far from the groundbreaking original, is not without some interesting moments as he struggles to flex his creative muscles.

The original "Sad Hours" was one of Walter's best slow, moody instrumentals, but between takes, someone in the studio suggests doing it here and adding a vocal. "'Sad Hours' is an instrumental," Walter says plaintively. "I don't give a damn what it is," comes the reply. "Put some words to it, make some words . . . if you can't, give it to Bo Diddley. . . ." Walter begrudgingly obliges, and quickly improvises some lyrics while the band tunes up. The track begins with Bo talking; by now Walter sounds like he's put the forced joviality aside and is genuinely incensed as he puts down Bo: "Every time I get ready to go to work, here you come. . . ." Walter gamely tries to sing a verse, but he has trouble holding pitch, so Bo and Muddy each take a verse while Cookie croons wordlessly in the background. It's clear that ad-libbing the lyrics was a bad idea to begin with, and the results speak for themselves.

When released, the album cover featured a cartoonish psychedelic painting, with even sillier liner notes on the back about "Diddleyman, Mighty Muddy and Super-Walter" helping out the president in Vietnam by playing their music until the Viet Cong ended the war and signed a treaty. The photos from the session on the back cover tell a different story. A rather defeated Walter looks at least a decade older than his thirty-six years, with graying hair and puffy swollen eyelids; in the foreground of one shot a tight-lipped, irritated-looking Phil Chess looms. As odd an item as it seems today, the album did in fact make some inroads and actually accomplish Marshall's goal to an extent. If nothing else, it made its fans appreciate real blues even more when they looked further into the Chess catalog.

A couple more tracks featuring Walter backed by Bo Diddley's band that have never been released were rumored to have been recorded at Bo's home studio around this time, but aural evidence suggests they may actually have come from this session, with Muddy and Spann laying out; both songs feature a female chorus and tambourine rattling sounding a lot like Cookie's contributions to the rest of the *Super Blues* session. "Feel So Bad" is based on the song of the same title Walter had attempted at his aborted session a year earlier; it's easy to imagine that there was a reason for this recurring theme. His vocal is hoarse, but on pitch for the most part, and with Bo's guitar providing solid rhythmic support, the outcome is much stronger than the earlier attempt. The more optimistic "Make It All Right" is an uptempo rocker; the chorus "Let's try to make it all right, try to make something out of life" is especially poignant considering his current circumstances. But it's probably not his song: someone in the background is heard prompting Walter on the lyrics before one of the verses. As with the rest of the *Super Blues* tracks, Walter plays strong harp on both numbers, but his raspy vocals are pained, and there's little question as to why these tracks were left on the shelf.

Later that month, Chess released another collection of Muddy's earlier singles, calling it *More Real Folk Blues* in another attempt to market it to younger white fans. Walter is heard in his prime on half of the album's twelve tracks, providing what may have been unwelcome comparisons that drove home how much his music had changed—and how much he had lost.

An April 1967 session found Muddy back in the studio with his then-current band. Some later discographers have attributed the harp on this session to Mojo Buford, but a number of harmonica aficionados have asserted that in fact it is Walter who is heard on the four-song session, albeit not anywhere near up to his usual form, even for the time. It's a testament to his gift that even at the nadir of his career, there are some of his trademark stylistic touches heard here that were still beyond the reach of Buford— or any of Muddy's other harp players—at that point. "It's All Over' is a slow blues featuring Muddy on slide guitar, with some subtly interwoven harp behind the vocal. "County Jail" was an old-style blues lament. On the last two tracks, the group was augmented by keyboard man Pinetop Perkins (who would later join the band full time) on organ. "Two Steps Forward" is built on a variant of the popular "Green Onions" theme. "Blind Man" is an uptempo jump blues. When the harp is audible, this song presents the strongest evidence of Walter's presence on the session. Although the phrasing is loose, Walter's unique way of toying with the beat, and adding interesting little off-the-beat accents, comes through.

A couple of months later, in June, Muddy returned to Chess for another session. Again, some discographers later credited the harp to others, but the aural evidence here is much stronger that it's actually Walter on "Find Yourself Another Fool" and "Kinfolk's Blues." The harp is acoustic and somewhat lost in the mix on both tunes, but it's sharper and cleaner than on Walter's other recent outings, and most harp buffs agree that the rhythmic twists and turns and unique phrasing could only belong to Little Walter.

Chicago's South and West Side blues scenes were definitely slowing down; there were fewer clubs booking blues regularly, and those that did were generally smaller, rougher, and less-successful places. Meanwhile Junior Wells was gaining recognition on the folk/rock cafe and ballroom circuit, successfully making a transition to white audiences, working places like Club 47 in Boston and the Avalon and Fillmore Ballrooms in San Francisco, sharing the bill with popular rock acts like The Doors, The

Jefferson Airplane, and The Grateful Dead. Wells had recently appeared at the Club 47 with The Aces, his and Walter's original backup band of Louis and David Myers with drummer Fred Below. Wells played solidly for the crowd of mostly white students, but got away with a fair amount of clowning in front of the indulgent, near-fawning audience. On a two-week coffeehouse gig in Toronto in May, Wells summed up for an interviewer the decline of the Chicago scene, noting, "Otis Rush still has very few jobs, Little Walter was doing nothing and Muddy's been sick."

People such as Willie Anderson, a former idolater and emulator who ". . . would've died for Walter" according to Billy Boy Arnold, now began to turn on him, showing up to scoff at him in the gritty dives where he now played. "Willie started challenging him on stage," Arnold related. "Go on his gigs, [say] 'You ain't shit, motherfucker, I'll blow you off the goddamn stage!' . . . See, when he looked up to him it was in awe. Children do that, they look up to you 'til they see some weakness, they figure 'You ain't who I thought you was', then they start scorning you. . . . That's the way he did Walter, challenging him on gigs. A few years earlier, he'd give up his right arm for Walter."

According to Honeyboy Edwards, Walter had started using hard drugs:

I remember once he played a good gig and went out and bought himself a big old white '56 Cadillac. He called me one day and said "Come meet me in Jewtown." I got in his car, he said, "Well, I've got a couple of suits in the back seat that I'm going to give you." Walter was always thinking about me. They was suits he'd performed in and he got new ones. He stopped at a tavern on 14th and Newberry and bought me a half pint of whiskey. That's when I found out he was using drugs. When I opened that bottle in the car I said "You want a drink?" and he said, "Man, I don't fool with stuff like that." I looked at him. He went around the corner, found this guy and the man handed Walter a little bag. At that time Walter was going with Memphis Slim's old lady, she lived in a house there in Jewtown. She would have a lot of people playing cards and gambling all night at her house, and Walter had his room there. We went there and Walter said, "Have a seat Honeyboy, sit down and drink your whiskey." And he cut out. Later I went to the bathroom and when I opened the door he was in there. I opened the door and he was standing there with a needle in his arm. He said, "What'd you come in here for?" That's the only way I found out he was using. He didn't want to tell me. We were real close friends and he didn't tell me he was using dope. I felt real bad about that.

Most others who were close to Walter have disputed this story; several expressed Walter's distaste for needles, and denied that he used hard drugs.

Charlie Musselwhite had recently recorded his first album and toured a bit himself, and when he came back to Chicago in 1967 he found Walter playing a club called The Red Onion:

It was a regular neighborhood type bar, nothing fancy about it at all. Little bitty bathroom, Formica topped tables, a pool table in front of the stage that they covered up during the gig. Walter would be standing on the floor, the band would be up on the stage . . . it was more like a jam session than anything. There'd be people sitting in, some lady in the audience might get up and sing a song—it was kinda like a party, a get together . . . there was a little talking back and forth with the audience, totally informal, like the music was just sort of a thing to bring people together, part of the neighborhood . . .

Sometimes Musselwhite would sit in: "He'd come over to me, he liked to kind of walk around with a long cord on the mike, he'd just shove it at me, like, 'Here, take this' . . . I'd blow, either he'd come back over or just get involved talking to somebody else and I would signal the band to end it, I'd feel kind of foolish." Charlie said Walter was a generous guy: "He'd buy me drinks a lot, he knew I was broke so he'd buy me a setup, which was like a little bowl of ice cubes with a cherry in it, usually buy me a pint and a Coke . . ." He also acted as his sponsor in other ways: "Sometimes he'd give me a ride home, or have somebody else give me a ride. One time we had a pretty big old fight in there, it had something to do with this lady I kinda liked and her old man showed up. I wanted to stay, and he thought it was a good idea I should leave. So he walked with me to the bus stop and made sure I got on the bus." Musselwhite thought that often when he'd seen him before, like at Hernando's Hideaway (with a guitar player called Big Bad Ben ". . . who had a 'doo that was about a foot tall") he was just going through the motions and seemed disinterested, but on this return trip, "This time he was like really playing, that was one of the best nights I remember seeing him . . ."

Walter never really gave Charlie any tips on playing, but sometimes dropped hints:

> Once at Rose & Kelly's Blue Lounge I saw Walter Horton playing, holding two harps back to back—he'd play one for awhile, then flip them over and play the other one. I knew the tune was in "A" and that one of Shakey's harps was a "D" but I couldn't figure out what the other harp was from listening to it. When he was through, I asked Shakey to show me what harps he was playing—the other harp was a "C." This is what got me to thinking about how many positions there might be . . . not long after this I saw Little Walter and told him I saw Shakey playing in "A" on a "C" harp. He said, "That's nothing, you can play in 'E' on a 'C' harp too!"

With the decreasing demand for harp players, some of them began picking up other instruments; both Carey Bell and Billy Boy Arnold also began jobbing as bass players. Arnold had worked with Johnny Young and toured with Musselwhite on bass. "In the '50s you couldn't get a gig without a harmonica in the band," Arnold said, "'Cause Walter and Muddy had made it so popular." With the changing times and tastes, gigs were catch as catch can. One time Arnold wound up as bass man in a band where Walter was also a jobbing sideman: "Muddy Waters Junior Band [with Smokey Smothers] had a gig at the Red Onion on 43rd, I was playing bass, Little Walter on harmonica, I forget who else . . . right around the corner from Muddy's house, I'm sure Muddy could hear us playing from his back porch. Walter asked me, 'Hey Billy, you ain't playing your harp no more?' I said 'Yeah, I'm still playing but I'm playing bass right now.' He looked so disappointed at that . . ."

With fall coming, it was time for the Seventh Annual American Folk Blues Festival tour in England and Europe. Once again, the German promoters Horst Lippman and Fritz Rau contracted Willie Dixon to book the musicians. As usual, the idea was to feature both the old and the new, with prewar solo artists such as Bukka White (a cousin of and inspiration to B. B. King) and the venerable Delta rediscoveries Skip James and Son House. The latter had been an early influence on Muddy's style and material, and had cut his first sides for Paramount a couple of months after Walter was born. Then there was the new: a group of more modern electric players put together to function as backup band, showcasing "the Chicago sound" while its various members took turns fronting the group. This year the band was comprised of singer Koko Taylor, Hound Dog Taylor, the raunchy slide guitarist from the Elmore James school, veteran drummer Odie Payne (taking a leave from his janitorial day gig at the post office), Little Walter on harp, and Dillard Crume of The Soul Stirrers and The Crume Brothers gospel groups, who had somehow been recruited to play electric bass. The two unrelated Taylors and Walter each took turns leading the band, and Crume served as the congenial master of ceremonies during the "modern blues" segment of the shows. Rounding out the revue that year were English favorites, the folk blues duo Sonny Terry & Brownie McGhee, making another return trip.

Again the question of Walter's passport came up. This time his sister Lillian filed a notarized affidavit of birth in the vital records office of Alameda County, California on September 21st, 1967, certifying that she was the sister of Marion Walter Jacobs. She listed his date of birth as May 1, 1930, the place as Alexandria, LA, and approximating their ages at the time of Walter's birth, listed his parents as Adam Jacobs (musician, 26 years old) and Beatrice Leviege (housewife, 25 years old), both born in Marksville. This did the trick and Walter was cleared to leave when the troupe flew to Europe, to begin the tour in Stockholm, Sweden on Friday, October 6th.

Walter had been told to leave his amp at home since the electrical voltages were different in Europe, so once again he was at a disadvantage, having to blow his harp acoustically through the standup P.A. microphone also used for vocals. On his trip to England in 1964 he'd been able to plug a harp mike into a guitar amp, or at least cup his harp to the vocal mike in an attempt to get his preferred amplified harp tone. But this time he was discouraged from even cupping the vocal mike. "Horst and them come talkin' 'bout, I'm too close to the mike. I said, 'I know how to operate the mike,' and the man who controlled it, going, 'But you're not supposed to take 'em off the stand' . . . I said, 'Aww . . . ,'" he recalled later. Not only did this mean he wouldn't be able to get his signature tonal and dynamic volume effects, it also meant it'd be difficult for the band to hear him, and for Walter to hear himself over the rest of the band. Factor in cheap sound systems and lousy hall acoustics where the band's sound would bounce off the back wall and come back a split second later, and the result was a real audio goulash, and a situation guaranteed to get Walter's goat.

The show opened with several numbers from Bukka White, then Walter was scheduled to play behind Hound Dog Taylor with the band for a couple, then do a few of his own; Son House closed out the first half of the show. After the intermission, Skip James led off, followed by Koko Taylor (backed by the full band), the show closing with Sonny and Brownie. The opening concert in Stockholm was broadcast on the radio, and the tape shows Walter striving to swing over the rather stilted backing on "Blues With A Feeling," with his harp too low in the mix. "Oh Baby" fares a little better, with the band a little more animated and the harp a bit more audible. Walter's numbers are well-received by the audience, so he encores with "My Babe," but is hampered by Taylor's fumbling guitar chording. Walter was also in the backing band for Koko Taylor's "I Wonder Why," but he's virtually buried in the mix. A review noted that his ". . .

Affidavit of Birth

PERSONAL and STATISTICAL PARTICULARS

Full name of child ..... marion walter Jacobs

Date of birth ..... May 1 1930

Place of birth ..... Alexanaria Lousiana

Sex of child ..... Male

Full name of father ..... Adam Jacobs

Residence at child's birth ..... General Delivery Markaville Lousiana

Age at child's birth ..... 26 Yrs.

Color or race ..... Negro

Birthplace ..... Markeville Lousiana

Occupation at child's birth ..... Musician

Full maiden name of mother ..... Beatrice Leviege

Residence at child's birth ..... Marksville Lousiana

Age at child's birth ..... 25 Yrs.

Color or race ..... Negro

Birthplace ..... Marksville Lousiana

Occupation at child's birth ..... House Wife

I hereby certify that I am the ..... Sister ..... of this child, who was born on the date above stated.

AFFIANT ..... Lillian Marshall

ADDRESS ..... 2140 - 9th ave Oakland Calif

Subscribed and sworn to before me

this ..... 27 ..... day of ..... Sept. 19 67

Theodore R. Williams

Theodore R. Williams Notary Public

THEODORE R. WILLIAMS, JR.
NOTARY PUBLIC
ALAMEDA COUNTY, CALIF.
My Commission Expires Sept, 28, 1968

In and for the .....

County of ..... Alameda

State of ..... California

Form AF22X-9 PICA, Oakland, Calif.

Figure 14.1 Birth Affidavit prepared for Walter's tour of England, 1967.

Figure 14.2 American Folk Blues Festival advertisement, *Melody Maker*, October 14, 1967.

harmonica and vocal pretty much got lost in the competition with the high volume of the electric guitars." Fighting jet lag, poor sound mixing, unsympathetic backing, and a live radio broadcast on the very first night, the mediocre show was a rather inauspicious opener for the tour.

On Wednesday the 11th, the troupe was photographed on arrival at the Copenhagen airport—Walter with a hat on and cigarette on his lips—all waving for the camera. The newspaper item noted that most of the artists, with an average age of 53, went straight to bed, and that the concert at the famous Tivoli Concert Hall was almost sold out. While in Copenhagen, the entire crew was ushered into a rather sterile TV studio for an abbreviated run-through of their set without an audience, which was filmed for Danish TV. The acoustic performers were given the bulk of the allotted time, with only two songs—one from Hound Dog and one from Koko—performed by the full band lineup, Walter providing some nice backing but not singing.

With the kinks beginning to be worked out, things sounded a bit better by the next show, in Helsinki, Finland on Thursday the 12th. Despite a broken amplifier that necessitated both bass and guitar being played through a single unit, the sound is improved. Hound Dog led off with an instrumental that was actually more of a duet with Walter, then did "Wild About You," an Elmore James number. Walter's harp was more audible this night, if a bit restrained. For his feature numbers, Walter kicked off with "You So Fine," giving it an expressive vocal. "Blues With A Feeling" fared a bit better, largely because the harp was loud enough to add some interest to the pedestrian backup. With a few shows now under their belts, "My Babe" was actually sort of driving, resulting in some prolonged applause. After the interval, the band backed Koko on three tunes. Walter jumps in prematurely and plays over Koko's intro to her second number, "What Kind Of Man Is This," but acquits himself well in the backing on it and her hit number, "Wang Dang Doodle."

The group's arrival in Amsterdam on Saturday the 14th was documented by a journalist who rode on the KLM shuttle bus with them from the airport to the hotel. He notes a disturbing premonition on Walter's part:

> Opposite on the arm of a chair, Little Walter. Walter is rather small, supple, especially in his face. His eyes are a bit wet all the time, they can look very sad and move all the time; skittish but very expressive grimaces are signs of his quick mood changes. Colleagues always say he's tough and he didn't seem to be doing too good, physically and mentally, in the last few years. But he hasn't dozed off, to the contrary he's very lively. Lively, nervous—and scared. He tells Belgian blues fiend George Adins, who accompanies the tour, that drummer Billie Stepney has died [on stage, during a set], and names recent others— J. B. Lenoir, Harold Burrage and Washboard Sam. [The recent obituary list also included harpist Jazz Gillum, Smiley Lewis, and Lucky Millinder in 1967.] Then he looks out the window, puffs his lips, abruptly turns his head and says, "I'm sacred. Man, I'm scared." And nobody doubts that.

Later at the hotel in the Wanningstraat section of Amsterdam, the journalist spots Walter sitting restlessly on a sofa, his hat and a bag of Hohner Marine Band harmonicas on his knees. Asked about Junior Wells:

> . . . He responds, "Oh, he was just like you, just a little boy, hanging 'round"— walking behind him all day long to learn the art. [Walter had] no good words for the imitators, Junior Wells, Jimmy Cotton, Shakey Jake, Snooky Pryor. There are good words for Walter Horton, who plays differently from Walter, and is himself. A big annoyance; it's impossible on this tour to play as he wants and is used to, with a hand microphone pressed against the harmonica . . . he makes a discontented waving gesture—"Man, I don't like it, it's not my style." A few moments later he leaves to buy a large bag of Chinese food at a restaurant.

On the bus heading to the concert in the Circus Theater, Den Hague, Walter falls asleep. When he's tapped on the shoulder, he reportedly springs awake, startled, fists raised. The concert follows a pork-chop dinner for all in a restaurant with a soccer game on TV. As for the concert, the journalist writes of Hound Dog and Walter's five-song set, "It does not reach the audience very well—when the band is warmed up, they have to go. Little Walter is average, but a far cry from the formidable harp blower he once was. He is standing a safe distance from the microphone, and it sounds rather tame." Another writeup called his performance uninspired and tiresome, and for anyone expecting the Walter heard on his hit records, it probably was. There was a second concert in Amsterdam at the Concert Hall at midnight: "Little Walter and Hound Dog Taylor have to share one microphone that they have to push each other around to gain control of. This leads to an interesting psychological duel (the aggressive sensuality of Walter against the grinning ignorance of The Dog) but it's a pity it happens in the fifteen minutes a year we could've heard a good blues group. . . .'"

The following day the revue appeared at the Kongress-Halle in Berlin, and the concert was recorded by tour promoters Lippman and Rau, with excerpts eventually issued on an album on their L&R label. Walter is heard behind Hound Dog on "Sky Is Crying," and featured on "You So Fine," then backing Koko on her two numbers. His vocal is somewhat lackluster, but his harp work is excellent. While his approach has been "dumbed down" to suit the times and the accompanists, his playing here is sharp, incisive, and inventive. Despite the disappointed press notices the tour is getting, the surviving recordings show that, overall, Walter is playing much better here than he did at the Mandell Hall show earlier that spring. His playing actually seems to be improving again, and it sounds like he's beginning to pull himself out of a slump.

On Tuesday, October 17th, the troupe is back in Holland to perform on a TV program, filmed at the new National Television building in Hilversum, a small town between Amsterdam and Utrecht, for station KRO. The forty-five minute program, directed by a Miss Tineke Roeffen, was shown on Dutch TV in November.

Several concerts on the tour were broadcast on radio. On one of them, probably from Montreaux, Switzerland, Walter is heard playing a swinging instrumental shuffle that sounds like it's based on "You're So Fine." The large crowd responds with polite applause. Trying to incite the crowd to a little more interaction, Walter yells "Yeah," the crowd yells "Yeah" back, so he does it again. "Let everybody say yeah!" he urges. "Let's get on the *ball* here! Now we gonna do one of our older recordings, title of the little thing is 'My Babe.'" Walter's harp is strong, his vocals a little less so—but this time the crowd responds with some fervor, yelling and whistling. On another show, Walter played a swinging new chromatic instrumental to a raucous response, the crowd's clapping and cheering building during a rousing last chorus, followed by a prolonged ovation. As the tour progressed, Walter was attempting to make the very best of an unsatisfactory musical arrangement, and along the way was recapturing at least some of the former glory—even if Hound Dog never did learn the chord changes to "My Babe."

After the show in Montreaux, there were a few days off before the next scheduled AFBF show. Walter and the rest of the Chicago contingent took this opportunity to do a couple of non-AFBF club gigs in Switzerland before heading to England to rejoin the rest of the troupe for a final week of concerts in the U.K., the last leg of the tour. On Sunday the 22nd, they played Leicester; Monday, Newcastle; Tuesday, Bristol; Wednesday, Birmingham; and closed the tour on Thursday the 26th at the Odeon in Hammersmith, as part of Jazz Expo 67. At the first U.K. show, the musicians were backstage when two proper English types in suits showed up, carrying rolled umbrellas and briefcases, and asking for Walter Jacobs. The musicians suspected this meant trouble, so no one answered them. The men left to find the promoter, Harold Davison.

As it turned out, Walter still owed back taxes from his previous tour there in 1964—and unless those fees were paid, they would garnish all the box-office receipts from tonight's show. Which of course meant there would be no show, because the other men wouldn't play without pay. Davison had no choice but to pay up, and the show went on. Hound Dog Taylor related another brush with trouble that Walter had, this time involving a "miscommunication" of sorts. Hound Dog recalled Walter attempting to charm the cleaning woman at one of the hotels where they'd stayed. "She didn't know what the devil he was trying to say, started screaming . . . the manager kicked us all out of the hotel," Taylor later said.

While in England, Walter relaxed with a drink and spoke to another journalist, who found him far from happy with his backup musicians, especially Hound Dog: "Them damn country coons. What's he doing with me? He ain't no use at all . . . damn southern coon! . . . Man, if you heard what I've been given to use, I'd been better with nothing. They disgusted me with it all—and how can I do what I want when that's how I'm fixed up? One time I done 'Juke,' they weren't listening, so I just done it again and again." The writer noted that Walter could still play like nobody else, and had proved it on numerous occasions when idly sitting around with a drink in one hand and a handy harp in the other. Walter also surprised fans by playing an entire club set on only one harp, playing it in three different keys, although ". . . this has been stated as impossible by several notable musicians" according to the writer. Another time, Walter was observed fixing a dilapidated old chromatic harp with a pocket screwdriver, and soon had it in playable condition.

As he took another long drink, Walter spoke condescendingly about Rice Miller: "I just don't know how he could take peoples' money . . . I mean to say, it was like thieving. There was *one* Sonny Boy and that's it, just one, and I don't mean that second one. Man, I'll never know how he could take peoples' money!" He continued ranting, ". . . just about everybody else took it from me, you know, all them other cats. But look, I set the patterns, see? Then they all listened and took it from me. You ask Muddy about that." From anyone else this would have been an idle boast, but in this case it was close to the truth. Confirming the rumors and speculation that had been heard recently (and possibly in light of his recent reuniting with Muddy in the studio), he added, "Muddy and me thinking 'bout working together a bit . . . but you know how it is, all sorts of things go on." Walter commented on the popularity of blues in the U.K. "I want to fix up some tour or something, get a group behind me with real musicians, then work clubs and things. I'd make it real big over here . . ."

While in the U.K., Walter was photographed onstage again by friend Val Wilmer, and backstage by Sylvia Pitcher, the photographer wife of Frank Weston, who'd promoted Walter's 1964 tour. She took a few quick shots of Walter posing against a wall; they show a tired-looking man with haunted eyes, and a decidedly distressed look on his face. His main woman Matty Rollins was certainly on his mind. They'd grown apart, and he was missing her, hard and deep, enough so as to reach out to her from overseas. "He went to London, England and he sent me a letter, to ask me to marry him. He had Koko Taylor write the letter for him, he could write, but not good enough for it to come here," Matty later said. ". . . I told him I wouldn't, until he got clean, I told him no," she said sadly. "I know he loved me . . . He used to tell me, 'When we get old, we gonna have a nice place and we gonna be together,' he bought me a beautiful bedroom suite . . ."

Son House was being heaped with praise and adulation, including receiving a standing ovation in Amsterdam and a large share of the press coverage. The final show at Hammersmith was no exception; again House was the main focus of the *Melody Maker* write-up. Walter was mentioned only as appearing ". . . somewhat uneasy in the foreground" for his three numbers. House also received glowing notices in *Blues Unlimited*, but in a review in the same issue, headlined "All Time Low," Mike Rowe was harsh. ". . . I stared at the back of two hairy heads that continually nuzzled each other. When they parted I could see the embarrassing antics onstage. Hound Dog hacking out songs which I can listen to any time by the real thing [meaning recordings of Elmore James] and the great Walter, bitter about the pathetic company he was in and proving it by drowning out Koko or turning his own act into a tasteless mockery . . . it was a pathetic spectacle." Rowe offered as a contributing factor ". . . an unfortunate element of backstage hostility, which might have accounted for some of the apathetic playing." Obviously some of the hostility was Walter's, who probably wasn't shy about letting his accompanists know what he thought of their work. Even so, it wasn't all unpleasantness, according to Rowe, who said, "It was good to talk to Walter again and laugh over happenings on his last trip."

Perhaps it was this show that Eric Clapton saw while working on the second Cream album, which inspired his later comments; he said, "Little Walter was a very, very powerful influence on me. There was something in his attitude that gave me access because he didn't seem to have much skill in any area, even the harmonica. It was very crude, but he had so much emotion put into that, it meant—ah, ah, this is roomy—there is somewhere I can go with this. I don't have to have fantastic facility if I channel everything I feel into this . . ." Later, Clapton would do an intense cover of Walter's version of "Key To The Highway."

The tour over, once again Walter returned to Chicago and his day-to-day scuffle, playing sporadic low-rent gigs in local taverns. Drummer Sam Lay was hustling gigs around town, putting together bands with various sidemen, sometimes using former "name" artists and bandleaders who had fallen on hard times. Sam led the bands, singing from behind the drums. He secured a regular one-night-a-week gig at the L&H Lounge on Madison and Kedzie, and sometimes he would hire Walter. Lay recalled, "I would call him on my jobs, he had to play with me to make ends meet—so did John Lee Hooker, Jimmy Reed, Eddie Taylor—all of 'em has been in my midst at one time or another. I was paying $17 a night, that was good money, more than I had got from him, I was getting $15 when I was working for him . . ."

One night when Lay's ever-shifting band consisted of Louis Myers and Eddie Taylor on guitars, Ernest Gatewood on bass, and Walter, Sam brought in his portable tape recorder with the idea of making an audition tape to get some more work. Thanks at least in part to the sympathetic accompaniment, the resulting recording catches Walter recapturing some of his old fire on three or four tunes, and is one of the best examples of the evolution in his harp style in the 1960s. His performance is sharp, focused, and creative, and while his style had changed since his early recordings, he clearly was still capable of occasional greatness. The jaw-dropping creative whirlwind of his early years is gone, but within almost every chorus there is still some unique twist or turn of a phrase or a melody that no other harp player had yet played, nor was likely to play before hearing Walter do it first; he was still making an effort to present something that was uniquely "Little Walter." On the surface, this music may not contain the beauty and freshness of his earlier masterpieces, but freed from comparisons to his past achievements, by any other standard his playing still contained enough originality and excitement to secure his place at the forefront of blues harmonica. The Little Walter style of old was gone, in its place a new spin on the music, still containing a high degree of inventiveness and occasional flashes of real brilliance.

The tape (most of which subsequently appeared on a bootleg LP) is primitively recorded, but it does capture the feel of a good, loose night of Chicago Blues performed by men who are comfortable with each other and their audience. Lay does three Muddy tunes and Walter's "My Babe," the latter inspiring a little good-natured repartee when Lay calls it out. "I'll take anybody's baby, skinny legs and all," Lay says, quoting from a current R&B hit by Joe Tex. "No, no, no, no . . ." Walter demurs. "I don't buy no bones—I ain't no cat!" At one point Sam good-naturedly chastises Walter for coming on stage with a drink in his hand; Walter jokes, "That's water! [laughing] I carries water!" Sam imitates the voice of his former employer Howlin' Wolf, who used to fine his band members to keep them in line; "I'm gonna have to charge you $10." Walter picks up the joke with his own imitation of Wolf's gravelly voice; "I'm gonna have to take you down to the union hall," he says, and laughs. Elsewhere Walter is heard between songs muttering into his harp mike, "Let me get to my 'Juke,'" and joking with both Sam and the audience. The tape ran out during a driving version of Muddy's slide classic "I Can't Be Satisfied"; it's too bad there's not more of it.

In addition to audio recordings, Lay was also documenting the scene with his home movie camera, getting color footage of many of his contemporaries in Chicago clubs. He even captured some silent footage of Walter, walking into a crowded club nattily dressed, collecting some money from the club owner, and then making a hasty exit. As he walks past Lay, he jokingly waves a wad of bills in front of Sam's camera.

Mark Kazinoff, who had bought lunch for Walter during his week in Boston in 1966, had moved to Chicago in the fall of 1967 to go to the University there, caught Walter on a good night around the same time. It was at ". . . one of those white clubs on the North side . . . I remember getting there just at the end of Walter's set, I don't even remember who was playing with him, which is a shame—I only got to hear three or four songs . . . compared to the Boston gig, it was happening, yeah! Like ten times as good . . ."

Around this time, Charlie Musselwhite encountered Walter again and found him down and out. Musselwhite remembers him:

> . . . talking about coming back from Europe, he said he had shopping bags full of money . . . he was a little bitter, he just seemed kinda pissed off . . . The last time I saw him, he was on a chair on the floor, in front of the band—at Big John's [a club in the Old Town area]. The band was playing and he was just sitting there, had his harp in one hand and his microphone in the other, staring at the floor. I walked up, pulled a chair over next to him, and I asked him how he was doing, if he was feeling okay. He was just like, "Nyahhh—I'm alright," he didn't want to talk. You could tell he was just—seemed confused.

Walter's constant drinking was obviously taking its toll.

Walter's sister Marguerite heard from him on Thanksgiving Day, when he called out to California and found her at their sister Sylvia's. She'd left Chicago for the West Coast that month without letting him know she was going. Walter was still pining for his lost lover Matty, who'd been friendly with Marguerite, and he thought his sister might be able to help:

> . . . He fell in love with Matty. He told me it hurt so bad. He said "Baby, talk to her for me." I said, "No, brother Walter, I'm not calling her." He said, "I love her, you can make it right." I said, "No, you have to do it." I didn't tell him I was leaving—he said, "You hurt me too, you disappointed me, why did you do me like that?" And I started crying, Sylvia said [to Walter], "Oh no, she's crying about [something else]." He said, "Put her back on the phone," and his last words to me, "I love you." He said that all the time.

Early in 1968, blues fan Bill Lindemann persuaded Walter to sit for an interview, with Louis Myers also sitting in. He showed up carrying a reel-to-reel tape machine, and recorded about an hour of conversation. He probably brought along a couple of six packs for lubrication, considering the number of cans heard being opened on the interview tape. Louis was voluble and reminded Walter of stories and events; Walter was amiable but terse, responding more to Myers than to his interviewer. Lindemann asked wide-ranging questions about Walter's history, influences, and recording sessions, and wound up with the most in-depth interview Walter ever gave.

Lindemann mentions that he'd like to see the two on ". . . a really big television show where everyone can see them." Having done numerous TV appearances in Europe but never in his home country, Walter is a bit cynical; "Funny ain't it? I think they fixed over here for TV shows." Louis adds, "They ain't gonna bother with cats like us." Walter continues, "You know when they get him? . . . Man, a good man that can play, they wait till the man get maybe fifty, sixty years old, he walloped then . . . and they use him for a gimmick, then he ain't good for nothing . . ." One gets the impression that Walter is bitterly resigned to his current status. He's critical of the current state of blues music and most of the people playing it; his only fond reminiscences seem to come from days far in his past, when he was on the road with his original band, or running around Chicago with a pocketful of money and no worries. As for his future, he seems sadly unwilling or unable to think or talk about it, and doesn't reveal any plans or hopes.

While Lindemann probed deeper and longer than any other interviewer, there are still a million questions unasked and unanswered that remain for today's fans to shake their heads over. Lindemann held onto the interview tape for a few years until it was first transcribed and edited by Bruce Iglauer for publication in the seventh issue of the growing American blues magazine, *Living Blues*, in Winter 1971–72. The introduction noted that, at the time of the interview, Walter was working only occasionally, and then mostly as a sideman; during the interview Walter also refers to his recent sideman work with Sam Lay.

The few gigs that Walter was getting as a leader were strictly pickup affairs. Drummer Robert Plunkett, who'd worked with Elmore James and Rice Miller in their waning years, served the same role with Walter:

When he started going down, he couldn't hold a top band. He had to come and get some of the little guys, and I was his pick. We got to be real close, I worked with him lots. As good as he could blow, he was hard to follow. Tricky you know . . . plus he was mean, real mean. Badass temper, wanted to fight and would fight. Walter wanna whoop you and make you play like he wants you to play. Little guy was strong too—plus he would keep a pistol . . . Ernie [Gatewood] played bass for Walter then and I played drums.

Walter's St. Louis buddy DJ Gabriel Hearns recalls:

The blues was sliding, he was seeing his career going to hell. Muddy Waters and John Lee Hooker had luck that Walter didn't have, they were picked up by the white promoters. I'll tell you something, if it weren't for white people there'd be no blues today. Black people are ashamed of the blues . . . He begun to drink a little heavy—I never saw him get staggering drunk, though I'm told he did around Chicago. He seemed to hold his liquor pretty good . . . but they found out—if he'd get a little high, women go in his pocket, try to take his money. As his popularity began to wane he'd take jobs that he'd turn his nose up at before—he'd take a job if they give him $50–75, just like Sonny Boy Williamson.

Walter had been staying off and on with Matty at her apartment at 8125 S. Vernon, in a nice middleclass neighborhood. Although she'd declined his marriage proposal, she was still hoping to work things out. She'd accepted his wandering ways, long absences, late nights, and drinking more readily early in their relationship, but as time went by she hoped that Walter would eventually settle down. He told her that he truly loved her, and she knew that she loved him. After several attempts to jolt him to his senses, in early February she finally laid down the law: she told him to take his things and not to come back until he decided he was ready to settle down once and for all. She hoped for the best, and fully intended to take him back if he showed any indication of changing his ways.

As was his custom, Walter ended up at another woman's apartment, although by most indications romance wasn't part of the deal this time. Having someone to cook a hot meal, do his laundry, and make sure he had a decent place to crash after a gig—and *not* try to tell him how to live his life—were more likely the key factors in his choice to stay with Armilee Thompson's friend Katherine, at her apartment at 209 E. 54th Street. Walter had known her for a while, both through Armilee, and because Katherine had been involved with Robert Junior Lockwood before he moved to Cleveland in the early '60s.

On the night of February 14th, Lay received a call from Walter around 11:30 PM or so:

I'm so used to Walter calling, trying to get a dollar or two from me to get him some of that Wild Irish Rose. I had to go buy it for him, go out and get it, bring it back to him wherever he was. Anyway, he told me to come across town there. I say why? He say he got into it with a fella, a fella hit him over the head. I said who? He said "My old lady's brother," said his name was Odell. I say what he hit you with? He say "He hit me with his fist—I laid that knife in his side, too," that's what he told me. He said it was 'cause Odell claimed that Walter had taken his sister's watch and pawned it. They got into it, and he hit Walter with his hand. Walter was talking about having a real bad headache. His old lady had dialed the phone for him. He laid down across the bed, but he wanted to call me first, she dialed the call and handed him the phone. He told me he'd like me to come over there, 'cause he knew I had a gun. Everybody know the reputation I got, I've carried two weapons nearly all my life. [But] I didn't have no car, and I wouldn't have went anyway, to be honest about it. 'Cause me and Walter wasn't on the best of terms . . . but I would talk to him. I said maybe tomorrow I could come over. I'll tell you his exact words to me: "Get some more niggers together and y'all come over and we'll go get that nigger. . . ," or something like that. I said, "Yeah, okay," and we hung up the phone.

Sam didn't give this conversation another thought.

A few hours later, in the early hours of Thursday, February 15th, there was another call to Sam's house—not from Walter this time, but about him. Howlin' Wolf's wife Lillie Burnett was calling to tell Sam to wake up and turn on the radio, quickly, to station WOPA.:

I turned it on, I said 'Yeah, that's Walter, what about it?' Lillie, on the phone, said "Walter's dead!" I said, "That can't be, I just talked to him a couple hours ago!" The song ends, the DJ says something like, "That was the very late Walter Jacobs" . . . I said "Whaaat?" The phone rang again, it was Bob [Woodfork]. I said what happened? He said, "I don't know, all I know is he's gone"—he broke down and started crying, somebody took the phone from him and hung it up. Apparently what had happened was [Walter's] old lady came into the room a little later [after we'd talked] and found him laying across the bed, dead cold.

The word spread quickly as each person who heard the news passed it on. Muddy called Walter's baby sister Sylvia. She recalls:

He said, "Baby, you gonna have to come tomorrow morning—your brother's gone." I said, "What? How'd it happen?" He said "Baby, I don't know nothing, all I know is this woman say he had a headache and when she went in there the next morning he was dead." I said, "Where is my brother?" He said he was taken to Provident Hospital, then they put him in the next place, a little dump. I said, "My brother's body in a dump? I'm coming, claim his body, get him out of there!"

Armilee Thompson also got a phone call from her friend Katherine early on Wednesday morning to tell her that Walter had passed:

Katherine said that Walter was up in a tavern on 55th and Garfield, went around there to get a beer or something. Him and some guys was in the back, in the alley gambling, shooting craps . . . she said Walter and this guy had got into it, and the guy hit him in the head with an iron pipe. Walter went on to the house where he was staying, with Katherine, and 'fore day that morning she heard a noise, that he had rolled out of bed. She called an ambulance, and from what I understand, it was a blood clot that caused his death.

Though they hadn't seen a lot of each other lately, she was stunned by the news. "I was sad, naturally I cried."

The last conversation Marguerite had with her brother was the Thanksgiving Day phone call a couple of months earlier. At the time of Walter's death, Marguerite and her children had moved in temporarily with Lillian in Oakland, while she continued to look for a place of her own. It seemed like she'd been having some strange premoni-

STATE OF ILLINOIS } ss. DAVID D. ORR. County Clerk
County of Cook,

I, DAVID D. ORR, County Clerk of the County of Cook, in the State aforesaid, and Keeper of the Records and Files of said County, do hereby certify that the attached is a true and correct copy of the original Record on file, all of which appears from the reports and files in my office.

IN WITNESS WHEREOF, I have hereunto set my hand and affixed the Seal of the County of Cook, at my office in the City of Chicago, in said County.

David D. Orr
County Clerk

STATE OF ILLINOIS

CORONER'S CERTIFICATE OF DEATH

STATE FILE NUMBER C 605676

| REGISTRATION DISTRICT NO. | | | | | |
| REGISTERED NUMBER | | | | | |

| DECEASED—NAME FIRST | MIDDLE | LAST | SEX | DATE OF DEATH (MONTH, DAY, YEAR) |
| 1. MARION | WALTER | JACOBS | 2. MALE | 3. FEB. 15 1968 |

RACE WHITE, NEGRO, AMERICAN INDIAN, ETC. (SPECIFY)	AGE—LAST BIRTHDAY (YRS.)	UNDER 1 YEAR	UNDER 1 DAY	DATE OF BIRTH (MONTH, DAY, YEAR)	PLACE OF DEATH	COUNTY
		MOS. DAYS	HOURS MIN.			
4. NEGRO	5a. 36	5b.	5c.	6. May 2 1931	7a. COOK	

| CITY, TOWN, TWP. OR ROAD DISTRICT NUMBER | INSIDE CITY (YES/NO) | HOSPITAL OR OTHER INSTITUTION—NAME | IF NOT IN EITHER, GIVE STREET AND NUMBER. |
| 7b. CHICAGO | 7c. YES | 7d. DOA PROVIDENT | |

| BIRTHPLACE (STATE OR FOREIGN COUNTRY) | CITIZEN OF WHAT COUNTRY | MARRIED, NEVER MARRIED, WIDOWED, DIVORCED (SPECIFY) | NAME OF SURVIVING SPOUSE (IF WIFE, GIVE MAIDEN NAME) |
| 8. Marksville, La. | 9. USA | 10. Never Married | 11. None |

| SOCIAL SECURITY NUMBER | USUAL OCCUPATION | KIND OF BUSINESS OR INDUSTRY | U.S. WAR VETERAN (YES/NO) | WAR OR DATES OF SERVICE |
| 12. 435 26 3469 | 13a. Musician | 13b. Self Employed | 13c. No | 13d. None |

| RESIDENCE STATE | COUNTY | CITY, TOWN, TWP. OR ROAD DISTRICT NO. | INSIDE CITY (YES/NO) | STREET AND NUMBER |
| 14a. Illinois | 14b. Cook | 14c. Chicago | 14d. Yes | 14e. 8125 So. Vernon Ave |

| FATHER—NAME FIRST | MIDDLE | LAST | MOTHER—MAIDEN NAME FIRST | MIDDLE | LAST |
| 15. Adams | | Jacobs | 16. Beatrice | | Leviege |

| INFORMANT'S SIGNATURE | RELATIONSHIP | MAILING ADDRESS (STREET AND NO. OR R. F. D. CITY OR TOWN, STATE, ZIP) |
| 17a. Andrew Williams | 17b. Sister | 17c. 4852 So. Prairie Ave |

PART I. DEATH WAS CAUSED BY:	(ENTER ONLY ONE CAUSE PER LINE FOR 18I. 19I. AND 20I.)	APPROXIMATE INTERVAL BETWEEN ONSET AND DEATH
18. IMMEDIATE CAUSE (a) CORONARY THROMBOSIS		Unknown
CONDITIONS, IF ANY, WHICH GAVE RISE TO IMMEDIATE CAUSE (b) DUE TO, OR AS A CONSEQUENCE OF		
STATING THE UNDERLYING CAUSE LAST (c) DUE TO, OR AS A CONSEQUENCE OF		

| PART II. OTHER SIGNIFICANT CONDITIONS: CONDITIONS CONTRIBUTING TO DEATH BUT NOT RELATED TO CAUSE GIVEN IN PART I. | AUTOPSY (YES/NO) | |
| 19. | 19a. NO | 19b. |

ACCIDENT, SUICIDE, OR HOMICIDE OR UNDETERMINED (SPECIFY)	DATE OF INJURY (MONTH, DAY, YEAR)	HOUR	HOW INJURY OCCURRED (ENTER NATURE OF INJURY IN PART I OR PART II OF ITEM 18)
20a.	20b.	20c. M.	20d.
INJURY AT WORK (YES/NO)	PLACE OF INJURY AT HOME, FARM, STREET FACTORY, OFFICE BUILDING, ETC. (SPECIFY)	LOCATION (STREET AND NO. OR R. F. D., CITY OR TOWN, STATE, ZIP)	
20e.	20f.	20g.	

I CERTIFY THAT IN MY OPINION BASED UPON MY INVESTIGATION AND OR THE INQUISITION THIS DEATH OCCURRED ON THE DATE, AT THE PLACE AND DUE TO THE CAUSE(S) STATED, AND THAT	THE DECEDENT WAS PRONOUNCED DEAD ON	AT
	MONTH DAY YEAR	
CORONER'S SIGNATURE	21b. 2 - 15 -68	21c. 5:20 P M.
22a. Andrew J. Toman M.D.	DATE SIGNED (MONTH, DAY, YEAR)	
	22b. 2-15-68	
CORONER'S PHYSICIAN'S SIGNATURE	DATE SIGNED (MONTH, DAY, YEAR)	
23a. Wm. Mcnabola	23b. 2-15-68	

| BURIAL, CREMATION, REMOVAL (SPECIFY) | CEMETERY OR CREMATORY—NAME | LOCATION CITY OR TOWN | STATE | DATE (MONTH, DAY, YEAR) |
| 24a. Burial | 24b. St. Mary's | 24c. Evergreen | Illinois | 24d. 2-22-68 |

| FUNERAL HOME NAME | STREET AND NUMBER OR A F.O. | CITY OR TOWN | STATE | ZIP |
| 25a. METROPOLITAN | 4445 South Parkway | Chicago | Illinois | 60653 |

| FUNERAL DIRECTOR'S SIGNATURE | FUNERAL DIRECTOR'S ILLINOIS LICENSE NUMBER |
| 25b. | 25c. 3786 |

| LOCAL REGISTRAR'S SIGNATURE | DATE REC'D BY LOCAL REGISTRAR |
| 26a. Samuel L. Andelman M.D. | 26b. FEB 19 1968 |

VS 2025 (1968) ILLINOIS DEPARTMENT OF PUBLIC HEALTH — BUREAU OF STATISTICS (BASED ON 1968 U.S. STANDARD CERTIFICATE)

Figure 14.3 Little Walter's Death Certificate.

tions: "First, my daughter broke her foot." She wasn't comfortable at Lillian's, and told her, "It looked like I see smoke on the floor and smoke ahead of me—I don't know if this is a warning or not. When I look down, it's not there . . . I was standing in Lillian's kitchen, my kids were outside, I heard a harsh sound, [car] hit the brakes and I heard this loud sound—I dropped one of her antique bowls, broke it—I said, 'My kids!' One got hit by the car . . . that was a week before Brother Walter died.

"I knew Walter was dead before Lillian told me. That morning, 3:00 AM, I was sleeping on the couch, she came out of the bedroom and said Muddy had just called. I started screaming, I started running, I said 'Please don't tell me! Don't tell me!' I don't remember riding on the train, I don't remember going to Chicago . . ." When Marguerite arrived, she was still in a state of shock, and says she found that Walter's body was at Biggs and Biggs Funeral Home, where a mortician told the family, "I hustle bodies." Marguerite went to where Walter had died, ". . . This elderly woman's house, Katherine. My brother used to wear a cross, he never took it off his neck. She had the cross, somebody else had his rings. Leonard asked me did I want them? I said no . . . she kept telling me, 'I didn't do nothing to him, it was Chuck—whoever Chuck was— he had a fight with Chuck . . .'"

Other items of Walter's had already disappeared as well, including his amp; Marguerite recalled:

> I think this big tall woman named Lilly Mae that says she was his wife sold it—or kept it. She was in love with my brother—she was about 6'7", and her breasts would kill one of us—big feet, big hands, big everything. My brother never had any sexual dealings with her, she used to just give him money, she was a whore—B. She tore up all his pictures up in the room where he stayed . . . she got that amp and his Cadillac, too . . .

At the funeral home, the family felt the embalmer had done a bad job: Walter's lips were too big and his color too dark, a sensitive matter since Walter was particularly proud of his lighter Creole skin tone. Lillian said:

> . . . they put some wax on him, I said, "My brother's not black, why you put all that black stuff? He's not black, why you want to make him black?" So he said, "Well sorry ma'am, we didn't know how he looked, he's been dead a week or ten days . . . we got to put something on to lighten him up or darken him up." I said, "Well you make him look right . . . you see the way I look, the color I am? This is the color, me and him the same color." So they made him the color he was.

After protests were made, the body was moved to the prestigious South Side Metropolitan Funeral home, where Walter's early hero John Lee "Sonny Boy" Williamson had been laid out twenty years earlier.

Armilee's daughter Marion had just begun working on learning to play the acoustic guitar Walter had bought her; he'd shown her a few chords. Then she got the news as well: "I was in fifth grade and didn't know how to really take it. I got to school real early, there was no one to talk to, I went in the classroom and wrote on the chalkboard over and over, 'My daddy is dead,' 'My daddy is dead . . .'" Her favorite nun came in, looked at the board and said, "'Well, I don't have to ask you what's wrong . . .'" Marion said she went to the funeral at Metropolitan with Armilee:

The thing I never will forget is so many women was there, like "Oh my husband, my husband" . . . B. B. King was there, Muddy Waters, the big stars were there . . . In front of his casket they had a little kneeler, where you kneel down to pray. I turned to my mom and said, "Mom, all of these people here, but I wanna pray for my daddy . . ." She said, "Baby, if that's what you wanna do, you do it, don't you worry about what nobody else has to say or anything!" I went up there, kneeled in front of that casket and I prayed. It hurted me so bad . . . even today I go to the cemetery and put flowers on his grave, I just feel still a part of him. . . .

As people walked up to the open casket, someone laid a rose beside his head, while others took a last, parting photograph as they stood there. A photograph of Walter in the open coffin, from the collection of the late bluesman Sonny Lane, shows a sad figure: Walter lying there with swollen, puffy jowls, dressed in a dark suit. One can clearly see Walter's prized Masonic tiepin neatly perched on his tie.

The death certificate was signed by Coroner's Physician William Monabola on Wednesday, February 15th, and gave the pronounced time of death as 5:26 PM on that day. "Immediate cause" of death was listed as "coronary thrombosis"—a blood clot in the heart—suggesting that whatever injuries he had sustained in the fight were not outwardly obvious. Despite his young age and the suddenness of his death, there was no mention of foul play, no notation of any external injuries, and no police report was made, reinforcing the suggestion that Walter died from a relatively minor blow that aggravated a previous injury. There was no autopsy. Sylvia gave the information for the death certificate, listing his birthdate incorrectly as May 2, 1931, and his age as 36. His parents were identified as Adam Jacobs and Beatrice Leviegs [sic]. She also provided the 8125 Vernon address for him—the location of Matty's apartment—and reported that Walter was never married and not a war veteran. Burial was to take place on February 22nd at St. Mary's Catholic cemetery in Evergreen Park, Illinois, just outside the Chicago city limits.

News of Walter's death made the papers a week later. The Wednesday, February 21st issue of the *Chicago Defender* managed to garble several basic facts:

BLUES STARS RITES SET THURSDAY A requiem mass will be offered tomorrow at 10 AM for blues star Little Walter in Our Lady of Sorrows Roman Catholic Church, 3121 W. Jackson Blvd., the *Defender* learned. Born Marion Walter Jackson, the Chess recording star lived at 5509 S. Indiana Ave. His body was found in the apartment of a friend at 209 E. 54th St. He had died of unknown or natural causes, police said. At the time of his death, Mr. Jackson was the guitarist in blues star Muddy Waters band. However, the harmonica was his favorite instrument. The artist was best known for his tunes "Juke," "My Babe" and "Blues With A Feeling." Visitation will be held tonight at the Metropolitan Funeral Home, 4445 South Parkway from 9–10 PM.

The *Chicago Sun Times* item of the same date at least got his name right: RITES SET FOR BLUES MAN LITTLE WALTER JACOBS, 38. They also added that he ". . . was known for amplifying the harmonica for unusual effects . . . he started his own band shortly after leaving Waters in the 1950s and played until shortly before his death . . . he made a number of recordings reflecting the electronic pop-rock sound. He is survived by the widow Lillie, and four sisters, Mrs. Sylvia Williams, Mrs. Margaret Byes, Mrs. Lula Blackmore and Mrs. Lillian Marshall."

Things were tumultuous at the wake. Sam Lay said, "There was a helluva fight in the back of the funeral home, in the back of the audience. I don't know who it was but I had my camera, I snapped some pictures, then put my camera down and went to try to help separate—I still don't know who was fighting—I was just going back to help break it up." Walter's sister Marguerite was probably the culprit; still in a state of shock and distress, she was lashing out at those she thought were responsible. She said, "I knew the potentials of my brother, they [Chess] helped destroy him. Muddy had a lot to do with that—I tore Muddy Water' face up in the funeral hall. I beat him with my fists. I scratched him and everything—I went into total shock. I just took my hand and went down as hard as I could. . . ."

For her part, Sylvia says she ". . . did all the preparation, paid all the bills . . . I buried him in a mahogany coffin." Probably figuring the family wouldn't get back to Chicago to visit the site much, she paid for a plain, inexpensive burial plot at St. Mary's Cemetery, just a few yards from busy Pulaski Rd., just inside the cemetery's fence. There were two services; the one at Metropolitan was ". . . packed, people standing outside . . . Muddy was there, I think Bo Diddley, Pinetop Perkins, Sammy Lay, Jimmy Reed. . . ." Though it had been several years since Walter had released a record, his early contributions to the success of his old record label were not forgotten:

> Leonard Chess was very helpful. After my brother was dead and buried, before I got ready to come back home, Muddy said he wanted to see me. When I went down to see Mr. Chess, he says, "Well, I'm so sorry about your brother—what did you spend?" I said, "Why is this your concern?" He said, "I just want to know." I reached in my pocket and every bill that I had paid, he wrote out a check in my name, gave it back to me, told me good luck, that he would be in contact with us.

Slowly the world took notice. In England the music paper *Melody Maker* ran a story covering several columns with a photo. The Swedish blues magazine *Jefferson* reported his death and reflected on his recent tour there: "One always hopes that a man will die happily, and content. But Walter died without being able to prove that he was still the great master, while Sonny Boy II, who Walter all along looked upon as an imitator, had made Europe's blues enthusiasts lay at his feet—and had a chance to enjoy enormous success in the autumn of his days."

According to Buddy Guy, Walter died on the verge of making a comeback; Chess was considering giving Walter one more recording shot:

> . . . Just before Little Walter died we had rehearsed some beautiful stuff with Fred Below on drums . . . We never did make it to the studio and I often think about that, because Leonard Chess had set up the studio for me and Walter, but Walter was really ill . . . he lived a tough life, used to like to gamble in the alley, drink, play cards and dice, so the session never did take place, because I was in San Francisco when he died.

As the news spread and the story was passed on, the details mutated, changing it seemed with each telling. It wasn't long before lesser-known musicians began telling their own versions of what happened, and in many cases including themselves as active participants. The mythmaking process had already begun.

When Big Guitar Red was asked about the fatal night he replied:

> . . . I was with him. Walter ain't had no gig 'cause he couldn't hold a gig 'cause he couldn't blow . . . he'd go around sitting in . . . we went out on 68th and Halsted I think it was, somewhere along there . . . this tall light-skinned guy had a band, I didn't know him, but we'd seen him around. Walter made fun of the fellow blowing harmonica. Him and the guy had a rumble, the guy hit him in the head with the harp, right in the place, they broke it up. But nobody think it was a big thing. . . . So we went home, I took him home, he'd lost his license plates and everything, he couldn't drive. Next morning I called his old lady over there . . . she found him dead in the bed with a blood clot in the head, that's what she told me . . . he died like that.

Red didn't go to the wake. Red recalled, "You remember a guy called Slim Willis? Walter told Slim Willis, 'If I die, I hope I die in my sleep'—and sure enough, he did." Bartender/harpist Otis Hunt had his own tale:

> Just before he got killed, I met him right over here on Kedzie. You know that a few years earlier he got shot in the foot. His foot swelled up from that and he couldn't wear no good shoe. He said "Yeah, damn. These feets has wore the hell out of me." He said, "I'm gonna leave it up to you. I taught you to blow and there ain't no more left for me." I said, "I don't like to hear you talk like that." He said, "I'm leaving it up to you. Now fuck it!" He gave me his phone number, said, "Anytime you want me, I'll be at this number." That was a tavern on 55th. So I didn't call him—and that's where he took those guys out what drinked with him, and went to his girlfriend's room. They bust his head open and killed him. Robbed him, $35 he had on him.

Junior Wells's version agreed at least somewhat with what Katherine had told Armilee:

> We were still hanging out together . . . over here on 43rd and Lake Park at a place over there [probably The Red Onion]. And then we always used to be down at Theresa's and everything, so Walter was over there like they do, shooting dice on the street. He's shooting dice and a man throwed the dice and hit Walter in the butt with 'em and went to reach and get the money and Walter picked up the money. The man asked Walter for the money and Walter wouldn't give him the money and he took a hammer and hit Walter in the head with it. And nobody thought anything about it. You know, 'cause he didn't even knock him down or nothing like that, it didn't sound like it was that hard of a lick. And he went on home and told his old lady to give him something, 'cause he said "I got a bad headache." So she gave him something for his headache, and the next morning she woke up, he was dead. See, she didn't know that he had a concussion that was bleeding and he hemorrhaged to death. And that was it.

In Honeyboy Edwards' account, Walter was going with a ". . . no-good woman who had four or five kids, she lived on 54th and Indiana." She was married but separated, and according to Honeyboy, Walter would show up there every month when she got her welfare check; "She'd give Little Walter $150 to put in his pocket." Walter would drive off with her money, and she wouldn't even buy shoes for the kids. One day she got her check, the husband came by, and so did Walter. "He had been drinking and Walter was full of dope, full of cocaine . . . they got to fighting and tussling out there, hitting each other and this guy had a blackjack . . . he took that blackjack and knocked Walter out. Walter was unconscious. They took him to Michael Reese hospital and he never gained consciousness, never come back no more. When I went to see him he was out, he didn't know nothing . . . after a few days he died . . ."

Bill Warren was a veteran drummer who in the '50s held down a seven-nights-a-week gig with his band at Theresa's for eighteen months, and in the '60s worked with Buddy Guy and Junior Wells. According to Warren, he was playing on a gig with Walter the night he died, ". . . at The Red Onion . . . when I started playing with him he wasn't playing any really big gigs then, he was kinda cooling out." Though his memory was dim, he thought Poor Bob Woodfork may have been the bass player that night; "We used to play with Walter . . ." By his recollection the fatal beating took place between sets, but not at the club, which could correlate with Walter's propensity for disappearing and sometimes stopping into another joint while on a break from his own gig:

> We were on a break at the time, when that happened. When we came back and got started to playing, he was messed up then . . . we was all coming in, different cats, when they said that had happened . . . they say Walter got beat up . . . I don't think he completed the gig . . . just one of those things, like he got into it that night and so he got hit with a jack handle and it killed him . . .

According to guitarist Joe Carter, who'd known Walter since they were both playing regularly at the 708 Club in the early '50s, Walter had been gambling with a group of men in the basement of an apartment building, and that when a dispute broke out, Walter pulled a knife. His antagonist picked up a big piece of a broken masonry planter and hit Walter in the head with it, causing the fatal injury. Big Walter Horton reportedly later said that Walter had gotten in a fight in the street, fell and hit his head on the curb, and "dust came out."

Aspiring drummer and fan Chuck Herron frequently followed Walter around, and remembered him from gigs at the Red Onion as well:

> Little Walter was a loner. He might finish a gig, then go hop over to another couple clubs before he went home. Walter was always sharp even when he had that slight limp from the gunshot wound. He still carried himself well. But he did let himself go right before the end. The night he got killed I remember he finished up at one club and then went off to some other club. I think Walter was living around 35th and Lasalle in some two-flat. But you didn't really know where he was going when he said he was going home. He had a lot of girlfriends and he went where he wanted to go.

Those words could serve as his epitaph; "He went where he wanted to go"— regardless of the consequences. Along the way he left behind a total of just over fifteen hours of recorded music, which has forever altered the shape and vocabulary of his instrument. He began as a precociously tough and headstrong youngster on the streets, became a world-famous musical innovator, but never really left the mean streets behind.

He had hit records and played at some of the top venues both here and abroad, made money by the trunkfull, and threw it away. He went from sleeping on pool tables, to driving brand new Cadillacs, to working corner bars for pocket change. He charmed some with his spontaneous generosity and drove others away with his secretive arrogance. Along the way he attracted—loved—and left women too numerous to count, made and lost countless friends, and eventually succumbed to the self-destruction that goes hand-in-hand with severe alcoholism. He was undeniably a musical genius of rare gifts, evidenced by the fact that his innovations are still awe-inspiring today, over thirty years after his death and close to a half-century after his most prolific period. He is unquestionably the most influential blues harmonica player ever to pick up the instrument, an artist who has often been imitated but never duplicated; indeed, some have said that the magnitude of his achievements simply cannot be improved upon. Like many artists of his social and cultural background, he never reaped the rewards he earned, either financially or emotionally. And, he never seemed really comfortable in this world, and carried himself through it restlessly, as if haunted by something unknown: "He went where he wanted to go."

epilogue

1968–Present

To an extraordinary degree, Little Walter's music was a direct reflection, even an amplification, of his own personality. At times angry and even violent, sometimes surprisingly tender, but restless and constantly moving—it seems that the most personal and direct expression of his essence is found in his music. And for all his faults, it's the music that reaches out across the generations and over barriers in a way that he could never have imagined.

What was it that drove Walter's relentless creativity with the harmonica? It's been said that "Every note he played meant something," and obviously a part of this meaning came from an uncanny ability to infuse all of his playing with the elements of melody, harmony, rhythm, and "swing." While it's not uncommon for skilled harmonica players to exhibit these traits, it's rare for all of them to be brought together simultaneously, even more so to be united with such a high level of improvisational creativity, and rarer still to achieve such consistently excellent results in the process.

The standard modus operandi for virtually all of Walter's contemporaries in the blues harmonica field was to develop or appropriate a handful of licks that worked musically, and once "perfected," use them as the basis of one's playing forevermore. Walter's entire approach was based not on settling for what he'd already found that worked, but constantly seeking new and different things that could *also* work, and the level at which he succeeded in this is astounding. His best work is like perfectly arranged tone poems, made all the more impressive by the fact that much of it was improvised on the fly.

But there's little evidence that Walter romanticized his art in the name of artistry. While he was well aware and justly proud of his unique achievements and influence, he apparently viewed the uniqueness of his work primarily as a commodity to be traded upon rather than any sort of lasting, artistic creation. Walter learned fairly early on that individuality and having something that no one else possessed was a key to success in his business, and so he worked tirelessly to get—and keep—a step ahead of the competition. Once he'd realized that goal, he worked constantly at creating something new and different, something that would keep the competition playing a game of catch-up, knowing that by the time they did—*if* they did—he'd have already moved on to something even newer. Having discovered his formula for success—which in reality was the *absence* of a rigid formula or pattern—he seldom looked back. He steadfastly moved forward, knowing that to be satisfied with his achievements, to settle into a pattern, was to allow himself to recede back into the pack occupied by his contemporaries. Once he'd tasted the fruits of success, he had no interest in being just another harmonica player. So it appears that his artistic motivation was in fact pure, but not purely artistic; it was the unadulterated pursuit of material and financial success. And considering his more-than-humble origins and the milieu in which he existed, there is no lack of nobility in this quest. Little Walter discovered a vein of gold inside himself, and mined it for all it was worth.

So what went wrong? According to Dave Myers, Walter was ill-prepared for the fame and relative fortune his talent brought him:

> Walter wasn't ready for his record, he had never did anything like that before. He wasn't ready for that, he wouldn't have been this type person. It hurt him; Walter wanted to play like always, but when it came down to business and responsibilities, Walter wasn't ready. It carried him too fast, he couldn't catch up. He became very dominating—with himself. . . . Walter kept goofing, Louis wanted to just go on and quit. I understood him, I never told him once not to . . . It wasn't that he wasn't a nice guy, we had a lot of good times—just, Walter wasn't a business man, he was the type guy you couldn't tell him [anything]. What he did, he took advantage of himself as being himself, you see? . . . He wouldn't listen to us like he should. We could've had a family type thing, swap our ideas around, get a very [good] understanding. He didn't rely on us no kind of way—he just did what he wanted, no matter who it hurt.

The unraveling of Little Walter's career coincided with changes in music that touched all of his contemporaries as well. Unprepared for fame, he was even less prepared to forsake it. His talent had taken him places he couldn't have imagined when he got his first twenty-five cent harp as a boy, but now his talent wasn't enough, wasn't bringing him the same rewards anymore. Maybe when he saw how fleeting the fame and fortune was, he lost respect for his own gift—and for himself. And once he began his prolonged downward spiral, circumstances and his own choices seemed to conspire to bring it to its inevitable conclusion.

By the time of this writing, many of the principal players in Walter's story are dead and gone. Muddy Waters was the reigning patriarch of Chicago blues when he succumbed to cancer at home in suburban Chicago in April of 1983. He'd spent much of the previous decade touring the world with a band of mostly younger players. In late 1967 he hired his first white sideman, harpist Paul Oscher, after James Cotton left the band. In subsequent years he employed guitarist Bob Margolin and harpman Jerry Portnoy, a Walter disciple—stating simply that they were the best men for the job. Muddy's 1969 concept album *Fathers and Sons* featured his longtime partner Otis Spann along with Paul Butterfield and Mike Bloomfield revisiting some of his old standards, and was a successful entry into the crossover market. Bloomfield died of a drug overdose on February 15, 1981, coincidentally the 13th anniversary of Walter's death. Butterfield met a similar fate a few short years later.

Of Walter's original recording and touring band, The Jukes, a/k/a The Aces, ironically only the oldest member, Dave Myers, survived to be interviewed for this book, although he did not live to see it published. He died in September of 2001. His brother Louis Myers passed in September of 1994 after a series of strokes, and drummer Freddie Below died from a heart attack in August of 1988. Guitarist Luther Tucker relocated to the San Francisco area, where he died of heart problems in June of 1993.

Jimmy Rogers passed away in December of 1997 after coming out of self-imposed musical retirement in 1970; he'd supported his family through the '60s running a clothing store and a cab business. Rogers enjoyed a relatively successful second music career until his death. Barely a month later, in January 1998, Junior Wells died of lymphoma; he too had enjoyed a successful later career on the blues festival circuit. The harp player who some feel was Walter's only serious rival in Chicago, Big Walter Horton, had a moderate level of success as a band leader in the '60s and '70s, but never seemed comfortable in the spotlight, preferring the sideman's role. After a long, prolific, and frustratingly inconsistent career, he died of heart failure in 1982.

Several of the up-and-coming Windy City harpmen from Walter's time are still active. After supporting himself outside of music for years, Billy Boy Arnold has enjoyed a career resurgence in the last decade, and is still alive and well, and playing better than ever, as is James Cotton. Cotton's voice has eroded from the wear-and-tear of many years on the road, but he still sometimes plays with the force of yore. Another veteran from those days still actively recording and touring is Walter's expressway racing buddy, Carey Bell (who claimed to have ended up with Walter's amp after his death, and used it on stage until it was stolen a few years later).

Maxwell Street veterans still active include Snooky Pryor, healthy and blowing strong in his late seventies. Guitarist Jimmie Lee Robinson recently went on an eighty-one day fast/hunger strike to protest the planned demolition of what little remains of the rich-in-history Maxwell Street market area. He lost some 40 pounds. These days Robinson performs mainly as a solo singer/guitarist, and says he is still visited in dreams by Walter. Freddie Robinson enjoyed a relatively successful career as a sideman and also had several releases under his own name in the 60s and 70s. He later changed his name to Abu Talib and now resides on the West Coast. Like his "Robinson" namesake and predecessor in Walter's band, he also makes occasional appearances as a solo singer/guitarist. Robert Lockwood Jr., well into his eighties, continues to play and record, and is revered more for his connections to Robert Johnson and the prewar blues era than for his work with Walter. Bob Margolin, who'd toured with Lockwood in late 1998, mentioned a backstage conversation: "... He said something that just broke my heart—about how Walter in the mid-sixties had really lost his shit and wasn't playing good, was all fucked up. Robert said, 'That's when I left his band—but if I knew he was gonna get that bad I woulda stayed with him and tried to help him.'" In his 1997 autobiography, Honeyboy Edwards wrote about his pal, "... that kind of friendship will never be no more for me. The closest one I was to was Little Walter. I miss that boy." He devoted an entire chapter of his book to Walter, giving it the title "He Didn't Know How Good He Was."

In 1998, Walter's longtime lover Matty Rollins sadly recalled their lost opportunities for a life together:

> ... He gave me his mother's picture. A little before he died, he called me one night and told me to bring his mother's picture to him. I told him "I'm afraid to come out this late at night Walter. I'll get it to you sometime ... ," but I never did ... He loved me, I know he did, and I loved him ... I hate it that he died so young ... whiskey was the cause of it, I think ... now that I have time to think about it, I never would've quit him—I didn't quit him, I thought about letting him alone for awhile, [maybe] he would act better ...

As is usually the case, death was a great marketing tool. Shortly after Walter's death, Chess Records compiled and released an album of his early singles, appropriately titled *Hate To See You Go*. Before long, Hit Sound, a small southern label, issued a single, "A Tribute To Little Walter" by Junior Wells, a reworking of "It Hurts Me Too." (Just a few years earlier Junior had released his "Tribute To Sonny Boy Williamson" after Rice Miller's death.) Another Muddy Waters harp alumnus, George "Harmonica" Smith, who had sometimes billed himself as Little Walter Junior, weighed in with a tribute as well. In a three-day session at the Los Angeles studios of World-Pacific Records in early October of '68, Smith recorded with Muddy's band and cut a ten-song tribute album. Titles ranged from "My Babe" to "Juke." Pete Welding coproduced this album, and wrote in the notes of the intention ". . . to acknowledg[e] . . . the profound vitalizing influence [Little Walter] exerted and continues to exert on modern blues." (A few years later Welding would bluntly state in the notes to a Little Walter collection, "Little Walter was one of the very greatest, most exciting and original interpreters the blues has ever seen.")

Smith also cut a single for the tiny Carolyn label called "Blowing The Blues." As the band comps behind him he declares, "Yes, everybody talks about ol' Sonny Boy Williamson. They even talk about the great Little Walter. But I, George Smith, are left to carry this harmonica blues business on ... now you can talk about ME, because I'm going to blow some blues." And he did, carrying the torch as one of the blues harp greats until his death from heart problems in October of 1983.

Some other kinds of business were being carried on as well. The question of Walter's estate started with confusion, and has gotten thornier over the years. After the funeral, his sister Lillian went over to the Chess offices:

> I said, "What about some of the money you owe him?" He went to show me some kind of papers, what he had scratched all over it, wasn't nothing there. He said "He don't have no money coming, 'cause he owes me." I said, "Show me a contract or a receipt where you let him have some money"—he didn't show me either of those. Finally he said, "Who must I send these checks to? How many are you all?" I said, "Me and my brother had the same father, my sisters we have the same mother but not the same father. But I want to make sure, I want the money to be divided in fourths." When I got back to Oakland, he sent a check for $400. I called and asked where was the rest of my brother's money? He said, "I told you to go down, cash the check, and don't ask no questions." I said "No, I went to the bank and they told me I could not cash this check unless I had his will probated." He say, "Oh, you don't have to do that." I said "Maybe that's the way you do business, I'm not doing that."

Lillian eventually hired a couple of lawyers, and about a year after Walter died some royalty money started coming. According to Waver Humphries, one of the larger checks was sent to her first (maybe Leonard recalled the dinner she attended with Walter), and she forwarded it on to Lillian.

Early in 1969 the Chess brothers sold their company to the GRT Corporation for a reported $6.5 million, plus 20,000 shares of GRT stock. Phil, Leonard, and Marshall all had separate employment contracts and continued to work at the company until Leonard's death in October 1969. Phil left not long after, and by mid-1970 Marshall quit. The last Chess had left the building.

Armilee Thompson made an attempt to see if there were any death benefits that she and her daughter might be entitled to collect from the Musicians Union. She furnished a birth certificate for her daughter that identified Walter as Marion's father, and a note in the union files listed Armilee as a "former wife." However there was no death benefit available, since Walter's union membership had lapsed long before—he'd last paid dues in 1966. Later Armilee contacted the Social Security office, and in September of 1975 17-year-old Marion Jacobs began receiving Walter's Social Security survivor's benefits of $121.50 a month—payments which were made until November 1977, shortly after her 20th birthday.

A month earlier, GRT had closed their record operation, and the Chess labels were bought by New Jersey based All-Platinum Records. When the Chess building was sold, the new owners were said to have destroyed an inventory of some 250,000 records with chain-saws, hauling them out in dumpsters. As the Chess master tapes changed hands several times through the 1970s and 1980s, various compilations and collections of Little Walter's work continued to be issued, both on legitimate releases and on questionably licensed pseudo-bootlegs. Included among these were many of the previously unreleased tracks and leftovers from his earlier sessions, until today almost every note he ever recorded while with the Chess brothers has now seen the light of day.

In the wake of Walter's death, a school of young white harp players who were closely studying his style began slowly emerging and making names for themselves. In Chicago there was Jerry Portnoy, who had his own roots on Maxwell Street; his father had owned a carpet store there in the 1940s. In the early '70s Portnoy moved into Little Walter's former seat in Muddy's band. On the West Coast were Rick Estrin, who later formed the popular blues band Little Charlie and The Night Cats ("The Night Cats" had been the name listed as Walter's backing band on the labels of his first Checker singles), and Kim Wilson, a powerful singer and harp player who founded the popular blues and rock act The Fabulous Thunderbirds. Californian Rod Piazza had entered the sweepstakes even earlier, initially influenced by Paul Butterfield, but later recording several note-for-note re-creations of Walter's songs. Each of these players has in turn spread Walter's influence even wider, to yet another generation of harp fanatics.

The scope of Walter's influence was felt outside of the blues world as well. The dean of country harp players, Charlie McCoy, recorded a cover of "Juke" on his 1968 debut LP, and later did a harp instrumental titled "Tribute To Little Walter" on his 1975 album *Harpin' the Blues*. In the song's spoken intro, McCoy confesses his debt: "The best blues harp player I ever heard was Little Walter. He was the king of the blues harp. I guess I stole more licks from him than any man alive. Nobody ever really played the blues as good as Walter, but a whole lot of us tried." When Elvis Presley made his return to performing in Las Vegas the fall of 1969, the set list for his debut gigs included Walter's "My Babe."

In July of 1979, Walter's former friend and sometime stand-in Willie Anderson cut the album *Swinging the Blues* for a small Chicago label, backed by several of Walter's old sidemen, including Robert Jr. Lockwood, Fred Below, and Jimmie Lee Robinson. Though only "Everything Gonna Be Alright" was credited to Walter, the album bore his unmistakable stamp. There were several instrumentals in the Walter mode, including a cover of one of Walter's favorite jazz numbers, "Lester Leaps In." Although a bit rougher sounding, Anderson recreated much of Walter's later style intact.

In the autumn of 1991, blues musician, producer (and author) Scott Dirks and harp player Eomot Rasun discovered that Walter's grave had not been marked with a headstone, and set about rectifying the matter. A small ceremony was held on February 15, 1992, the 24th anniversary of Walter's death, at the gravesite in St. Mary's Cemetery. Afterwards there was a Little Walter tribute and jam session at a local club that was attended by many of those who'd been close to Walter over the years, including Louis and Dave Myers, Big Smokey Smothers, Jimmie Lee Robinson, Honeyboy Edwards, Sam Lay, harpist Golden "Big" Wheeler, Walter's sister Lillian Marshall, and others.

On December 30, 1996, Armilee Williams' daughter Marion Jacobs Diaz filed a petition in probate court, claiming she was Walter Jacobs' only living child (there was mention of one other child of Armilee's and Walter's who had previously died), attaching her birth certificate, baptism records, and Social Security forms as proof of her parentage. Diaz (her married name) had been working as a 911 operator in the police department. One day her sergeant was playing some jazz CDs in his office, and Marion mentioned that her father was the blues singer, Little Walter. The sergeant asked why she was even working there, with such a well-known and presumably well-off father. Marion had been unaware of any continuing interest in or sales of Walter's music, so coworkers began bringing in books and CDs for her to check out—and only then did she realize that there was an active market. She contacted the Bar Association, got the name of a lawyer, and went ahead with proving her claim. On March 10, 1997 the circuit court declared her Walter's "true heir," and administrator of his estate.

Walter's sisters all reacted with disbelief: how could Walter possibly have had a child they knew nothing about? Marguerite mentioned Walter's comments about "shooting blanks," and added, "Where was she when he died? Why wasn't she at the funeral? That's mighty strange, as close as my brother and I was that I never seen that baby." Younger sister Sylvia said:

> My uncle [Sam Leviege] stated that my brother had contracted venereal disease, that he had told my uncle he could not have no children . . . and he also had the mumps . . . When Leonard [first] starting giving us the royalties, he said, "Now, your brother never had no children, never been married . . ." If he'd had children, Leonard Chess who was taking care of all his business, he would've at least known something! . . . If that's his daughter, sure, I'd want her to have it—but I don't believe she is. He would've brought her around.

Consequently, on July 16, 1997, Sylvia (Glascock) Williams filed a petition to revoke Diaz's heirship and replace her with the four sisters. After various other petitions in opposition, amendments, and other legal forms were filed, on December 15, 1997 the case went before a judge. Among the evidence presented for Walter's alleged paternity was a photograph of him holding a four-month-old Marion. (Sylvia denies that it's Walter in the photo.) Another photo of Walter performing in a club wearing an eye-catching checkered suit was inscribed on the back, in shaky handwriting that appears to be Walter's: "to my wife form [sic] Mairon [sic] Jacobs /Love to Irma All ways." Armilee (who is also known as Irma) dated the photo as from 1963. Several friends of Armilee's testified that they'd heard Walter saying things like "That's my baby" and told of him holding, hugging, and kissing her. On December 18th the court denied Sylvia's petition to amend the heirship.

On January 16, 1998, Sylvia filed a petition to reconsider, citing new evidence in the form of an affidavit from Matty Rollins, who stated she had lived continuously with Walter for twenty years and that "the deceased never mentioned having a child," although no such affidavit was attached. Sylvia also said that only DNA testing would be conclusive, and offered to pay for exhumation and testing of Walter's remains. Marion was agreeable to a DNA test, but the court refused to consider it, and after more legal maneuvering, on March 31, 1999 the Appellate Court upheld the previous rulings, declaring Diaz as true heir. Among the reasons given were that proper documents weren't filed at the proper times by Sylvia, and now it was too late in the process. Therefore, because the court deemed that it had acted properly, the appeal was denied. On April 7, 1999 the law firm of Jay B. Ross & Associates in Chicago issued a press release proclaiming, "True heir of Little Walter established!" It briefly outlined the ruling, and stated that "The estate is valued in the millions of dollars." Sylvia is still hoping to find a lawyer to help her reopen the case.

Of course, the memorabilia market has kicked in. On the internet auction site eBay, an autographed 8 x 10 Shaw Agency publicity photo of Walter, with a neat and some-what suspect "autograph," recently sold for over $1,100. A near-mint copy of Walter's first 78 RPM single on the Ora-Nelle label brought $999, and his other small label records regularly fetch in the hundreds of dollars. Amplifiers similar in type to those Walter was thought to have used sell for upwards of $1,000 to collectors, and old "bullet"-shaped microphones like the ones he favored in the 1950s are highly prized by harmonica players.

Over the years, the search for film or video footage of Walter performing has taken on the aspect of a Grail quest, fueled by the knowledge that he was known to have done a handful of televised performances on overseas tours. (Oddly, there is no evidence that he ever appeared on TV or film in the U.S., even though almost all of his contemporaries did at some point.) Unfortunately it seems that precious little of the European footage still exists; a few years back the BBC was reported to have dumped the only copies of much of their old archival material, which would have included a few of Walter's TV appearances. A similar story is told regarding his TV appearances in Germany. All that has ever been found to date is a rarely seen snippet shot in Copenhagen during the October 1967 American Folk Blues Festival tour. It shows Walter in an accompanying role, backing Hound Dog Taylor on the Elmore James-styled "Wild About You," and Koko Taylor on "Wang Dang Doodle." (Recently, bootleg copies of the tape have been offered for sale on eBay.) The hunt continues.

Meanwhile, in Boston, harp player and filmmaker Mike Fritz has been sporadically working on a documentary of Walter's life for over ten years; he's filmed interviews with many of the principles in the story, but the project seems to have stalled due to lack of funding.

Nick Gravenites, partner with Paul Butterfield in a folk duo in the early '60s, summed up many of the major contradictions in Walter's character:

> [Walter] was like a God-given natural . . . Music was everything to him. One of the big differences between most of the black and the white blues players, the black players have a pretty limited perspective—it's drinking, and playing, and chasing girls . . . it's that traveling bluesman life, you know. A lot of the white guys don't have that tradition; they have something totally different . . . It was like they had maybe other choices, but a lot of these blacks guys didn't have much choice you know, they'd go on down to makin' music—they'd start makin' money in the hat, and they knew a good thing when they saw it you know, and they stayed with it to the end. . . . People would say, "Walter's in town!" And they still use that, you know, when someone hits the scene you know, and they're partyin' like mad, chasing after women, and drugs, and going crazy and all . . . they still use that, say, "Hey, Walter's in town," 'cause that's what he used to do, used to party all the time . . . he was a show-off. He loved to spread the money around, and party around and showoff, look good in his clothes, and he was "The King." He left Muddy's band and made a big success for himself. Many times that's the hardest thing for a blues musi- cian to do is to leave a good thing, go out on their own. That's real hard for people. It's real hard to leave that steady niche, but Walter was a big hit. He was a big hit with Muddy, and he had the nerve to go out on his own and become a big hit that way. So he was different from a lot of those guys who tend to just make the money and go on to the next gig. He had some ambition. I don't know, I can't think of too many people having anything bad to say about Walter.

Even Hound Dog Taylor, who'd been the victim of some of Walter's wrath during their tour together through Europe, readily praised him, stating in no uncertain terms that Walter was without peer. When asked to name the best harp player he'd ever heard, Hound Dog—who had heard them all—replied, "Little Walter, that's it, and that's all of it brother. One thing now, people say you can't take it with you, well he took it with him!"

Walter is a frequent topic of discussion on an internet discussion group, the "harp-list," where his technique has been dissected in minute detail. One still-recurring "thread" began in 1996 when a player noted that in the original recording of "Juke" there were several beats missing from the second chorus—that Walter had jumped time. In a detailed two-page breakdown and analysis of the recording, harmonica specialist Winslow Yerxa agreed, and also suggested that, contrary to popular belief, Walter played no tongue-blocked octaves in the piece, and that the few notes that sounded that way had probably been the result of amplifier distortion. This topic has resurfaced periodically and sparked some hot debates, which eventually ran to over thirty pages of printouts. Experts such as Jerry Portnoy and Kim Wilson were quoted, but few par- ticipants changed their opinions along the way, and no definitive conclusions were reached—and so the debate continues.

It's amazing the far-reaching implications a single take of a 2:47 tune cut almost a half century earlier by a 22-year-old can have. But it was originated by the man who pioneered the dialect that all blues harp players now must study in order to begin speaking the language of "Blues Harp." Today, Walter's legacy lives on—every time a blues harpist hits the power switch on his amp to play a gig. He's become part of the fabric of blues.

He lives in the memory of friends as well. His one-time companion Waver Humphries is still haunted by her memories: "... he often comes to me in dreams, trying to tell me something. When he does, before he can, I just see him fade away...."

Little Walter
chronological recordings

COMPILED BY TONY GLOVER

This work varies from previous discographies in the area of later Muddy Waters and Jimmy Rogers sessions. In the absence of new hard documentation, special weight was given to the considered opinions of harp players familiar with the stylistic habits of Junior Wells, Walter Horton, and James Cotton, as well as Little Walter. In the case of disputed sessions, aural evidence took priority.

The first column lists the known master numbers, assigned by the record company when a title was deemed ready for release. Most of the earlier Chess/Checker recording sessions took place at Universal Studios in Chicago, at 111 West Ontario Street, on the near North Side. Guitarist Dave Myers said *all* sessions he was on were at Universal, although a few are not so designated. In mid-1954, Chess opened new offices at 4750 South Cottage Grove, and began doing some recording at a small two-track studio there. In mid-1957, Chess began using their new studios at 2120 S. Michigan Avenue (Sheldon Studios, called Ter-Mar Studios by 1967) and later around the corner at 320 E. 21st Street. All along, they had continued recording at Universal as well, the studios were sometimes used concurrently, although a general rule of thumb could be that all master numbers with a "U" prefix come from Universal sessions. However, not all Universal sessions have the "U" listing. Caveat emptor. Although the master numbers help with determining chronology, they are not infallible. What are we to make of the sudden appearance of masters in the 4300 series, when previous records were in the 7400 range? According to conversations and interviews with the Chess brothers, they had an idea at one point of "presenting the music by category; jump blues would be 2000, all harp, 3000 etc. . . ." Although this was abandoned, the use of 4300 and 4400 series may have been an attempt to set apart titles that were hopefully more in the R&B/R&R crossover field.

The title column, when possible, lists the take numbers. False starts are indicated as "fs."

The third column lists the initial 78/45 RPM single releases, with "UNIS" designating those tracks not released as such during Walter's lifetime. Prior to his death, he could be heard on four LP's: *Best of Little Walter* (a 1958 compilation of hit singles cut through 1955) and with Muddy Waters on some tracks of *Best of Muddy Waters* (1958), *Real Folk Blues* (Jan. 1966), and *More Real Folk Blues* (Jan. 1967). The latter three were also compilations of prior singles.

The last column lists the most readily obtainable, in most cases in-print (as of this writing), sources where each track can be found. (For the myriad of compilation and reissue albums where each title also appears see previous discographies.) "Tape" indicates a private collectors source, not generally available. Dotted lines are used to separate individual dates/sessions.

Abbreviations

V-vocal; hca- harmonica; g-guitar; b-bass; el-b-electric bass; d-drums; p-piano; mrcs-marracas mdn-mandolin

Reference Sources

- Personnel listings from *Blues Records 1943–1970*, amended and updated with additional research by Scott Dirks.
- The work of Mary Katherine Aldin, Scott Dirks, Leslie Fancourt, Ward Gaines, Mike Leadbitter, Pete Lee, Paul Pelletier, Fred Rothwell, Neil Slaven, and Phil Wight.
- Miscellaneous vinyl and CD issues and reissues, as well as correspondence and conversations with annotators and compilers.

Thanks to Scott Dirks for collaborative insights, research and suggestions. Without his help this would be nowhere near as thorough, wide or deep. Thanks to Cyd Nadler for typing, re-typing, re-re-typing, and layout formatting. Not to mention general patience with an obsessive quest. Thanks to everyone else who faxed, xeroxed, emailed or made dubs available . . . your efforts are appreciated.

The Recordings

OTHUM BROWN   1947   Chicago, IL
V/g, with LW-hca, Jimmy Rogers-g (?)

711A	ORA NELLE BLUES (#1)	UNIS	CB47
711A	ORA NELLE BLUES (#2)	Chance 1116	"

LITTLE WALTER   1947
V/hca with Brown-g, Rogers-g (?)

711B	I JUST KEEP LOVING HER(#1)	UNIS	CB47
711B	I JUST KEEP LOVING HER(#2)	Chance 1116	"

JIMMY ROGERS   1947
V/g with LW-hca

?	LITTLE STORE BLUES (#1)	OraNelle/UNIS	CB47
?	LITTLE STORE BLUES (#2)	"	"

SUNNYLAND SLIM/(LITTLE WALTER)   1948
P with LW-V/hca, Muddy Waters-g, Leroy Foster-d

A/B	BLUE BABY	TempoTone 1002	DIBM
	I WANT MY BABY	"	"

JIMMY ROGERS   1949
V/g with LW-hca, Sunnyland Slim-p, Waters-g, Big Crawford-b

1218-2	LUDELLA	Regal/UNIS	ERB

LITTLE WALTER TRIO   1/50
V/hca with Waters-g, Rogers (?)-g, Foster-d

H511	JUST KEEP LOVING HER	Pkwy 502	BWoLW

BABY FACE LEROY TRIO   1/50
V/d with LW-hca, Waters-g, Rogers * (?)-g

H512	BOLL WEEVIL*	Pkwy 104	BWoLW
H513/14	ROLLING & TUMBLING pt I & II	Pkwy 501	"
H515	RED HEADED WOMAN*	Pkwy 104	"

LITTLE WALTER TRIO   1/50
V/g with Waters-g, Foster-d

H517	MOONSHINE BLUES	Pkwy 502	BWoLW
R1356	MUSKADINE BLUES	Reg 3296	"
R1357	BAD ACTING WOMAN	Reg 3296	"

MUDDY WATERS   8/50
V/g with LW-hca, Crawford-b

U7261	YOU'RE GONNA NEED MY HELP	Chess 1434	RS:GA
U7262	SAD LETTER	"	"
U7263	EARLY MORNING BLUES	Chess 1490	"
U7264	APPEALING BLUES	Chess 1468	"

JIMMY ROGERS TRIO   8/15/50—Tuesday
V/g with LW-hca, Crawford-b

U7269	THAT'S ALRIGHT	Chess 1435	JRCCR
U7270	LUDELLA (alt)	UNIS	"
U7270	LUDELLA	Chess 1435	"

MUDDY WATERS   10/23/50—Monday
V/g with LW-hca, Crawford-b

| U7275 | LOUISIANA BLUES | Chess 1441 | RS:GA |
| U7276 | EVANS SHUFFLE | " | " |

JIMMY ROGERS   10/23/50
V/g with LW-hca, Waters-g, Crawford-b

| U7277 | GOING AWAY BABY | Chess 1442 | JRCCR |
| U7278 | TODAY TODAY BLUES | " | " |

JOHNNY SHINES   10/23/50
V/g with LW-hca, Rogers-g, Crawford-b

| U7279 | JOLIET BLUES | Chess 1443 | DDM |
| U7280 | SO GLAD I FOUND YOU | " | " |

MUDDY WATERS   1/23/51
V/g with LW-hca, Crawford-b

U7304	LONG DISTANCE CALL	Chess 1452	RS:GA
U7305	TOO YOUNG TO KNOW	"	"
U7306	HONEY BEE (LW-gtr)	Chess 1468	"
U7307	HOWLING WOLF	UNIS	"

EDDIE WARE   1/23/51
V/p with LW-g, Eddie Chamblee-ts (voc on 7314), Crawford-b, Elga Edmonds (AKA Elgin Evans)-d

U7311	JEALOUS WOMAN	Chess 1507	?
U7312	WANDERING LOVER	Chess 1461	CBP
U7313	I FOUND OUT	UNIS	"
U7314	LIMA BEANS	Chess 1461	"
U7315	RUMBA DUST	UNIS	"

MUDDY WATERS   7/11/51—Wednesday
V/g with LW-hca, (Rogers-g on 7360?) Leonard Chess-bass d

U7357	COUNTRY BOY (1ST electric)	Chess 1509	RS:GA
U7358	SHE MOVES ME	Chess 1490	"
U7359	MY FAULT	Chess 1480	"
U7360	STILL A FOOL (LW-gtr)	"	"

JIMMY ROGERS   7/11/51
V/g with LW-hca, Eddie Ware-p, Willie Dixon-b, Edmonds-d

U7361	MONEY MARBLES & CHALK (LW-gtr)	Chess 1476	JRCCR
U7362	HARD WORKING MAN (")	UNIS	"
U7363	CHANCE TO LOVE	Chess 1476	"
U7364	MY LITTLE MACHINE	UNIS	"

MUDDY WATERS   12/29/51
V/g with LW-hca, Rogers-g, Edmonds-d (omitted, *)

U7413	THEY CALL ME MUDDY WATERS	UNIS	RS:GA
U7414	ALL NIGHT LONG (alt)	"	"
U7414	ALL NIGHT LONG (alt)*	"	"
U7414	ALL NIGHT LONG	Chess 1509	"
U7415	STUFF YOU GOTTA WATCH	UNIS	"
U7416	LONESOME DAY	"	"

FLOYD JONES   12/29/51
V/g with LW-hca, Rogers-g, Willie Coven-d

U7417	OVERSEAS	UNIS	BV6
U7418	PLAYHOUSE	"	GEN3
F1006	DARK ROAD	Chess 1498	"
F1007	BIG WORLD	"	"

LITTLE WALTER   5/12/52
V/hca with Waters/Rogers-gs, Edmonds-d

U7437	JUKE (#2)	Ckr 758	BoLW
U7437	JUKE (#4-alt)	UNIS	BWF
U7438	CAN'T HOLD OUT MUCH LONGER (#2) (alt)	UNIS	BWF
U7438	CAN'T HOLD OUT MUCH LONGER (#6)	Ckr 758	BoLW

MUDDY WATERS   5/12/52
V/g with LW-hca, Rogers-g, Edmonds-d

U7439	PLEASE HAVE MERCY (#5)	Chess 1514	RS:GA

MEMPHIS MINNIE   7/11/52
V/g with LW-hca, Ernest Lawlars -g, ?-d

C1025	CONJOUR MAN	UNIS	CBOX
C1026	LAKE MICHIGAN	"	BV6
C1027	ME AND MY CHAUFFEUR	UNIS	CS
C1027	ME & MY CHAUFFEUR	Ckr 771	GEN1

ROCKY FULLER   c above session, 1952?
V/g with LW-hca

?	FUNERAL HEARSE AT MY DOOR	UNIS	BV6

LITTLE WALTER   10/52
Hca/v with Louis Myers-g, David Myers-g, Fred Below-d

1050	BLUE MIDNIGHT (alt)	UNIS	BWF
1050	BLUE MIDNIGHT	Ckr 955	HTSYG
1051	BOOGIE	UNIS	ELW
1052	MEAN OLD WORLD	Ckr 764	BoLW
1053	SAD HOURS	"	"

LITTLE WALTER   1/53
as above, but add Crawford-b

U4318	FAST BOOGIE (#6-last verse)	UNIS	Tape
U4318	FAST BOOGIE (#7-last verse)	"	"
U4318	FAST BOOGIE (#8-Incomplete)	"	"
U4318	FAST BOOGIE (#11)	"	BWF
U4318	FAST BOOGIE (#12)	"	CBOX
U4318	FAST BOOGIE (?-Incomplete)	"	Tape
U4318	FAST BOOGIE (#13)	"	"
U4319	DON'T NEED NO HORSE	"	ELW
U4320	DRIFTING (#1)	"	Tape
U4320	DRIFTING (#2)	"	BWF

LITTLE WALTER   3/53
V/hca with Louis/David Myers-gs, (Henry Gray-p on 4345) Dixon-b, Below-d

U4343	DON'T HAVE TO HUNT NO MORE	Ckr 767	RDBX5
U4344	CRAZY LEGS	Ckr 986	CTB
U4345	TONIGHT WITH A FOOL	Ckr 767	BWF
U4348	OFF THE WALL (alt)	UNIS	RDBX5
U4348	OFF THE WALL	Ckr 770	BoLW
U4349	TELL ME MAMA	"	"

JOHN BRIM   3/53
V/g with LW-hca, Louis/David Myers-g's, Below-d

U4350	RATTLESNAKE	Ckr 769	WMS
U4351	IT WAS A DREAM	"	CBG

MUDDY WATERS   **5/4/53**
V/g with LW-hca, Rogers-g, Edmonds-d

U7501	BABY PLEASE DON'T GO (alt)	UNIS	MBOX
U7501	TURN THE LAMP DOWN LOW	Chess 1542	RDBX3
U7502	LOVING MAN	Chess 1585 CBG	

JIMMY ROGERS   **5/4/53**
V/g with LW-hca, Waters-g, Dixon-b, prob. Edmonds-d

U7503	LEFT ME WITH A BROKEN HEART	Chess 1543	JRCCR
U7504	ACT LIKE YOU LOVE ME (alt)	UNIS	"
U7504	ACT LIKE YOU LOVE ME (#3)	Chess 1543	"

JOHN BRIM   **5/4/53**
V/g with LW-hca, Eddie Taylor-g, Edmonds-d

| U7505 | LIFETIME BABY | UNIS | GEN3 |
| U7506 | ICE CREAM MAN | " | WMS |

LITTLE WALTER   **7/23/53**
V/hca with David Myers/Jimmy Rogers-gs, Dixon-b, Below-d

U4394	QUARTER TO TWELVE	Ckr 780	CTB
U4397	THAT'S IT	UNIS	BWF
U4398	BLUES WITH A FEELING (alt)	"	BWF
U4398	BLUES WITH A FEELING	Ckr 780	BoLW
U4399	LAST BOOGIE	UNIS	BWF
U4400	TOO LATE	Ckr 825	ELW
U4401	FAST BOOGIE	UNIS	"
U4402	LIGHTS OUT	Ckr 786	CTB
U4403	FAST LARGE ONE	UNIS	ELW
U4404	YOU'RE SO FINE	Ckr 786	BoLW
?	MY KIND OF BABY	UNIS	BWF

MUDDY WATERS   **9/24/53**
V/g with LW-hca, Otis Spann-p, Rogers-g, Edmonds-d

| U7551 | BLOW WIND BLOW | Chess 1550 | MBOX |
| U7552 | MAD LOVE (I WANT YOU TO LOVE ME) | " | RS |

MUDDY WATERS   **1/7/54**
V/g with LW-hca, Spann-p, Rogers-g, Edmonds-d

U7589	I'M YOUR HOOCHIE COOCHIE MAN(alt)	UNIS	RDBX3
U7589	I'M YOUR HOOCHIE COOCHIE MAN (#16)	Chess 1560	MWHB
U7590	SHE'S SO PRETTY (#5)	"	OMM

JIMMY ROGERS   **1/7/54**
V/g with LW-hca, Henry Gray or Johnny Jones-p, Waters-g, Dixon-b, Odie Payne-d

| U7591 | BLUES ALL DAY LONG (#13) | Chess 1616 | JRCCR |
| U7592 | CHICAGO BOUND (#3) | Chess 1574 | " |

LITTLE WALTER   **2/22/54**
V/hca with Dave Myers/Robert Lockwood-gs, Dixon-b, Below-d

7603	COME BACK BABY	UNIS	BWF
7604	ROCKER	Ckr 793	CTB
7605	I LOVE YOU SO (OH BABY)	UNIS	BWF
7608	OH BABY	Ckr 793	HTSYG

MUDDY WATERS   **4/13/54**
V/g with LW-hca, Spann-p, Rogers-g, Edmonds-d

| U7630 | JUST MAKE LOVE TO ME | Chess 1571 | MWHB |
| U7631 | OH YEAH | " | OMM |

JIMMY ROGERS   **4/13/54**
V/g with LW-hca, Spann-p, Waters-g, Edmonds-d

| U7632 | SLOPPY DRUNK | Chess 1574 | JRCCR |

THE CORONETS   5/22/54
(Vcl grp with LW -hca, rest as below?)

| 7651 | COBELLA | UNIS LRDB2 | |
| 7652 | BEGGING & PLEADING | " | " |

LITTLE WALTER
V/hca with David Myers/Lockwood-gs, Spann-p, Dixon-b, Below-d

7653	I GOT TO FIND MY BABY (alt)	UNIS	CBOX
7653	I GOT TO FIND MY BABY	Ckr 1013	HTSYG
7654	BIG LEG MAMA (Peach Tree)	UNIS	BWF

LITTLE WALTER   7/1/54
V/hca, with David Myers/Lockwood-gs, Dixon-b, Below-d

| U7669 | MERCY BABE (MY BABE) | UNIS | BWF |
| U7670 | LAST NIGHT (alt) | " | ELW |

LITTLE WALTER   7/14/54
(as above, sub Tucker for Myers?)

| U7673 | YOU BETTER WATCH YOURSELF | Ckr 799 | BoLW |
| U7674 | BLUE LIGHT | " | " |

MUDDY WATERS   9/1/54
V/g with LW-hca, Spann-p, Rogers-g, Dixon-b, Below-d

U7697	I'M READY	Chess 1579	MWHB
U7698	SMOKESTACK LIGHTNING	UNIS	MBOX
U7699	I DON'T KNOW WHY	Chess 1579	OMM

MUDDY WATERS   c 10/54
(as above)

| U7746 | I'M A NATURAL BORN LOVER | Chess 1585 | R&U |
| U7747 | OOH WEE | Chess 1724 | RDBX3 |

LITTLE WALTER   10/5/54
V/hca with Lockwood/Luther Tucker-gs, Dixon-b, Below-d

U4416	LAST NIGHT	Ckr 805	BoLW
U4417	MELLOW DOWN EASY	"	HTSYG
U4418	INSTRUMENTAL	UNIS	RDBX5

LITTLE WALTER   1/25/55
V/hca- with Lockwood-gs, Dixon-b, Below-d

| 7776 | THUNDERBIRD | Ckr 811 | BWF |
| 7777 | MY BABE | " | BoLW |

MUDDY WATERS   2/3/55
V with LW-hca, Spann-p, Rogers-g, Dixon-b, Clay-d

U7783	THIS PAIN	UNIS	RDBX3
U7784	YOUNG FASHIONED WAYS	Chess 1602	MBOX
U7785	I WANT TO BE LOVED	UNIS	MW-A
U7785	I WANT TO BE LOVED	Chess 1596	OMM
U7797	MY EYES	"	RS

JIMMY ROGERS   2/3/55
V/g with LW-hca, Spann-p, Dixon-b, Clay-d

| 7800 | YOU'RE THE ONE | UNIS | JRCCR |

LITTLE WALTER   4/28/55
V/hca with Bo Diddley, Luther Tucker-gs (Lockwood replaces Diddley on 7828), Dixon-b, Below-d

U7888	I HATE TO SEE YOU GO (COME BACK BABY)	Ckr 825	BWF
	(note: released version omits last verse, fading at 2:17)		
U7827	ROLLER COASTER	Ckr 817	HTSYG
U7828	I GOT TO GO	"	CTB

BO DIDDLEY   **5/10/55**
V/g with LW-hca, Jerome Green-mrcs, Dixon-b, Clifton James-d

| U7836 | DIDDLEY DADDY | Ckr 819 | BDHB |

LITTLE WALTER   **7/14/55**
V/hca with Lockwood/Tucker-gs, Dixon-b, Below-d

U7874	LITTLE GIRL	UNIS	ELW
U7875	CRAZY FOR MY BABY	Ckr 986 BWF	
U7876	CAN'T STOP LOVING YOU	UNIS	"

MUDDY WATERS   **11/55**
V with LW-hca, Spann-p, Rogers-g, Dixon-b, Clay-d

U7937	I GOT TO FIND MY BABY	Chess 1644	OMM
U7938	SUGAR SWEET	Chess 1612	TNM
U7939	TROUBLE NO MORE	"	MBOX
U7940	CLOUDS IN MY HEART	Chess 1724	RDBX3
	(note: Cotton has claimed to play on this session)		

LITTLE WALTER   **12/55**
V/hca with Lockwood/Tucker-gs, Dixon-b, Below-d

U7966	ONE MORE CHANCE WITH YOU	Ckr 838	CTB
U7967	WHO	Ckr 833	BWF
U7968	BOOM BOOM OUT GO THE LIGHTS	Ckr 867	ELW
U7969	IT AIN'T RIGHT	Ckr 833	CTB

JIMMY ROGERS   **12/55**
V/g with LW-hca, Lockwood-g, Dixon-b, Below-d

| 7970 | YOU'RE THE ONE | Chess 1616 | JRCCR |

MUDDY WATERS   **1/56**
V with LW-hca, Spann-p, Pat Hare?/Hubert Sumlin-gs, Dixon-b, Below-d

| 8012 | 40 DAYS & 40 NIGHTS | Chess 1620 | MBOX |
| 8013 | ALL ABOARD (w/ JamesCotton-2nd hca) | " | TNM |

LITTLE WALTER   **3/9/56**
Hca with Lockwood/Tucker-gs, Dixon-b, Below-d

| 8068 | FLYING SAUCER | Ckr 838 | BWF |

JOHN BRIM   **4/5/56**
V/g with LW-hca, Lockwood-g, Dixon-b, Below-d

| 8080 | BE CAREFUL | Chess 1624 | WMS |
| 8081 | YOU GOT ME WHERE YOU WANT ME | " | " |

MUDDY WATERS   **7/56**
V with LW-hca, Spann-p, Hare?/Sumlin-gs, Dixon-b, Payne-d

8147	JUST TO BE WITH YOU	Chess 1644	MBOX
8148	DON'T GO NO FARTHER	Chess 1630	"
8149	DIAMONDS AT YOUR FEET	"	"

LITTLE WALTER   **7/27/56**
V/hca with Tucker/Lockwood (*)-gs, Dixon-b, Below-d

8191	IT'S TOO LATE BROTHER	Ckr 852	ELW
8192	TEENAGE BEAT (1st acoustic)	Ckr 845	BWF
8193	TAKE ME BACK *	Ckr 852	HTSYG
8194	JUST A FEELING *	Ckr 845	BoLW2

MUDDY WATERS   **12/1/56**
V with LW-hca, Spann-p, Hare/Sumlin-gs, Dixon-b, S P Leary or Clay-d

8388	LIVE THE LIFE I LOVE	Chess 1680	MBOX
8389	ROCK ME	Chess 1652	"
8392	LOOK WHAT YOU'VE DONE	Chess 1758	"
8393	GOT MY MOJO WORKING	Chess 1652	"

LITTLE WALTER 3/5/57
V/hca with Lockwood -g,/Tucker-g on 8434 & 36, el-b on 8433 & 35, Below-d

8433	NOBODY BUT YOU	Ckr 859	HTSYG
8434	TEMPERATURE (alt)	UNIS	RDBX5
8435	SHAKE DANCER	Ckr 1071	BWF
8436	EVERYBODY NEEDS SOMEBODY	Ckr 859	HTSYG

(note: flip side of Ckr 1071 is Digging My Potatoes by Washboard Sam, c 5–53)

OTIS RUSH c 3–57
V/g with LW-hca, Harold Ashby-ts, Lafayette Leake-p, Jody Williams-g, Dixon-b, Payne-d

C1008	GROANING THE BLUES (#1)	UNIS	OR&BG
C1008	GROANING THE BLUES (#2)	UNIS	"
C1008	GROANING THE BLUES (#3)	Cobra 5010	TCR
C1009	IF YOU WERE MINE	"	"

OTIS RUSH c 6–57
V/g with LW-hca, Harold Ashby-ts, Lafayette Leake-p, Jody Williams-g, Dixon-b, Payne-d

| C1018 | LOVE THAT WOMAN | Cobra 5015 | TCR |
| C1019 | JUMP SISTER BESSIE | " | " |

LITTLE WALTER 6/20/57
V/hca, with Tucker/Jimmie Lee Robinson-g's, Dixon-b, Below-d

8525	TEMPERATURE (#6)	UNIS	BWF
8525	TEMPERATURE (#30)	UNIS	RDBX5
8525	TEMPERATURE (#35–38)	UNIS	"
8525	TEMPERATURE (#24)	Ckr 867	CTB
8526	AH'W BABY (alt)	UNIS	BWF
8526	AH'W BABY	Ckr 945	ELW
8527	I'VE HAD MY FUN (alt)	UNIS	"
8527	I'VE HAD MY FUN	Ckr 945	HTSYG

JIMMY ROGERS 9/18/57
V/g with LW-hca, Spann-p, poss. Tucker-g, Dixon-b, Clay-d

8597	WHAT HAVE I DONE (alt)	UNIS	JRCCR
8597	WHAT HAVE I DONE	Chess 1687	"
8598	MY BABY DON'T LOVE ME (alt)	UNIS	"
8598	MY BABY DON'T LOVE ME	UNIS	"
8599	TRACE OF YOU (alt)	UNIS	"
8599	TRACE OF YOU	Chess 1687	"

LITTLE WALTER 1/58
V/hca with Tucker/Jimmie Lee Robinson-gs, Leake-p/or, Dixon-b, Odie Payne-d

| 8644 | THE TODDLE | Ckr 890 | CTB |
| 8645 | CONFESSING THE BLUES | " | " |

MUDDY WATERS 8/58
V with LW-hca, Spann-p, Hare/Tucker-gs, Dixon-b, Hunter-d

8979	SHE'S 19 YEARS OLD (#1)	Chess 1704	MBOX
8980	CLOSE TO YOU (#2)	"	"
9140	WALKING THROUGH THE PARK (#2)	Chess 1718	"

LITTLE WALTER 8/58
V/hca with Waters/Tucker-gs, Dixon-b, Clay-d

8981	KEY TO THE HIGHWAY (#2)	Ckr 904	HTSYG
9141	WALKING ON	UNIS	ELW
8982	ROCK BOTTOM (#9) (alt—w/chromatic)	UNIS	BWF
8982	ROCK BOTTOM (#10)	Ckr 904	CTB

MUDDY WATERS 1/59
V with LW-hca, Spann-p, Tucker/Hare-gs, Andrew Stephens-b, Clay-d

9193	BLUES BEFORE SUNRISE	UNIS	MBOX
9194	MEAN MISTREATER	Chess 1718	RDBX3
9195	CRAWLIN' KINGSNAKE (alt)	UNIS	OMM
9195	CRAWLIN' KINGSNAKE	"	TCMW

LITTLE WALTER   1/59
V/hca with Spann-p, Tucker-g, Stephens-b, Hunter-d

9196	YOU GONNA BE SORRY (SOMEDAY) (alt)	UNIS ELW	
9196	YOU GONNA BE SORRY (SOMEDAY) (#6)	"	BWF

LITTLE WALTER   2/25/59
V/hca with Tucker/ Fred Robinson-gs, Dixon-b, Hunter-d

9243	BABY	UNIS BWF	
9244	MY BABY'S SWEETER (#10) (alt)	"	"
9244	MY BABY'S SWEETER (#11)	Ckr 919	HTSYG
9245	CRAZY MIXED UP WORLD (#3)(alt)	UNIS	BWF
9245	CRAZY MIXED UP WORLD (#6)	Ckr 919	CTB
9246	WORRIED LIFE	UNIS	ELW
9246	WORRIED LIFE (alt)	"	BWF

LITTLE WALTER   7/21/59
V/hca with Spann-p, Tucker/Freddie Robinson-gs, Dixon-b, Billy Stepney-d

9619	EVERYTHING GONNA BE ALRIGHT (#1)	UNIS RDBX5	
9619	EVERYTHING GONNA BE ALRIGHT (inc)	"	BWF
9619	EVERYTHING GONNA BE ALRIGHT (alt)	"	RDBX5
9619	EVERYTHING GONNA BE ALRIGHT	Ckr 930	ELW
9620	MEAN OLD FRISCO (# 1/2)	UNIS	RDBX5
9620	MEAN OLD FRISCO (alt)	"	BWF
9620	MEAN OLD FRISCO	Ckr 1117	CTB
9621	BACK TRACK	Ckr 930	ELW

LITTLE WALTER   8/12/59
V/hca with Tucker/ Freddie Robinson-gs, Hunter-d

9654	ONE OF THESE MORNINGS	UNIS BWF	
9655	BLUE & LONESOME (alt)	"	"
9655	BLUE & LONESOME	Ckr 1117	HTSYG

JIMMY ROGERS   11/59
V/g with LW-hca, Spann-p, Tucker/Fred Robinson-gs, Dixon-b, Hunter-d

9808	YOU DON'T KNOW (alt)	UNIS	JRCCR
9808	YOU DON'T KNOW	"	"
9809	CAN'T KEEP FROM WORRYING (alt)	"	"
9809	CAN'T KEEP FROM WORRYING	"	"

LITTLE WALTER   11/59
V/hca, with Spann-p, Tucker-g, Fred Robinson-b, Hunter-d

9810	ME & PINEY BROWN	Ckr 938	BWF
9811	BREAK IT UP	"	"

LITTLE WALTER   12/59
V/hca with Tucker/prob. Fred Robinson-gs, Dixon-b, Hunter-d

9889	GOING DOWN SLOW	UNIS	BWF
9891	YOU'RE SWEET	"	"

MUDDY WATERS   4/23/60
V/g with LW-hca, Spann-p, Rogers-g, Stephens-b, Clay-d

10030	WOMAN WANTED (#1/2-fs)	UNIS	RDBX3
10030	WOMAN WANTED (#3-alt)	"	"
10030	WOMAN WANTED (#4/5-fs)	"	"
10030	WOMAN WANTED (#6/7-breakdown)	"	"
10030	WOMAN WANTED (#8-alt)	"	"
10030	WOMAN WANTED	Chess 1774	"
10031	READ WAY BACK (#1/6-fs)	UNIS	"
10031	READ WAY BACK (#7-alt)	"	"
10031	READ WAY BACK (#9-alt)	"	"
10031	READ WAY BACK (#10-track)	"	"
10031	READ WAY BACK	Chess 1752	"
10032	I'M YOUR DOCTOR	"	"
10033	DEEP DOWN IN MY HEART	UNIS	"

LITTLE WALTER   **12/60**
V/hca with Spann-p, Tucker/Fred Robinson-gs, Dixon-b, Hunter-d

10593	I DON'T PLAY	Ckr 968	ELW
10594	AS LONG AS I HAVE YOU	"	HTSYG
10595	YOU DON'T KNOW	UNIS	BWF
10596	JUST YOUR FOOL	Ckr 1013	ELW

LITTLE WALTER   **2/5/63**
V/hca with Jarret Gibson/Donald Hankins-sax, Billy Emerson-or*, Buddy Guy-g, Jack Meyers-b, Duncan-d

U12168	UP THE LINE	Ckr 1043	CTB
U12169	I'M A BUSINESS MAN *	Ckr 1081	BWF
U12170	DEAD PRESIDENTS *	"	ELW
U12171	SOUTHERN FEELING *	Ckr 1043	"

BLUES CONCERT AT U OF CHICAGO   **5/9/64**
JOHNNY YOUNG
V/mdn with LW-hca, Jimmy Walker-pno

?	BABY YOU DON'T HAVE TO GO	Testament CD 6011	DHH
	BUMBLE BEE	Testament CD 6004	MB

ROBERT NIGHTHAWK
V/g with LW-hca, Johnny Young-g or *-mdn

?	KANSAS CITY	Testament CD 5010	RN&HS
?	SWEET LITTLE WOMAN	Testament CD 6011	DHH
?	THAT'S ALL RIGHT	Testament CD 6009	DHS
?	EVERYTHING GONNA BE ALRIGHT*	"	"
?	ANNA LEE	"	"

JOHNNY YOUNG   **c 1964**
V/mdn with LW-hca, Jimmy Walker-p

?	I'M LEAVING YOU BABY	Testament CD 5003	JY&F
?	YOU MADE ME FEEL SO GOOD	"	"
?	FORTY FOUR BLUES	"	"
?	HEAR THAT WHISTLE BLOW	Milestone LP 3002	
?	CRAWLING KING SNAKE	Testament CD 6004 MB	

SHEL SILVERSTEIN   **10/2/65**
——— **"I'M SO GOOD I DON'T HAVE TO BRAG"** Cadet LP 4052
V/g with LW-hca (overdubbed at later date), Malcom Hale-g, Robert Matthews-b, Charles Walton-d
reissued as: **"CROUCHING ON THE OUTSIDE"**   Janus LP 2JLS 8052

	(Live at Mother Blues)		
14230	PLASTIC	"	
14231	THE UGLIEST MAN IN TOWN	"	
14235	I ONCE KNEW A WOMAN	"	
14248	I CAN'T TOUCH THE SUN	"	

LITTLE WALTER   **2/66**
V/hca with J T Brown-ts, Lee Jackson-g, Junior Pettis-b, George Cook-d

14573	BACK IN THE ALLEY	UNIS	LRDB3
14574	I FEEL SO BAD (#1)	"	"
14575	I FEEL SO BAD (#2)	"	"
14576	CHICKEN SHACK	"	BWF
	"	"	

UNIVERSITY OF CHICAGO FOLK FEST   **May 20, 1966**
    ("LIVE IN THE WINDY CITY")   Columbia River CD CRG 120009
V/hca with Sam Lawhorn-g, unknw b & d

———	GOING DOWN SLOW		
———	WALTER'S BLUES	"	
———	LOVING YOU ALL THE TIME (YOU SO FINE)	"	
———	BLUE MOOD (WATERMELON MAN)	"	

'SUPER BLUES' 1/4/67
MUDDY WATERS/LITTLE WALTER/BO DIDDLEY MCA CD 9168
with Spann-p, Buddy Guy-g, Sonny Wimberley-b, Frank Kirkland-d

15498	MY BABE	"	
15500	I'M A MAN	"	
15502	WHO DO YOU LOVE	"	
15503	JUKE	"	
15505	LONG DISTANCE CALL	"	
15506	BO DIDDLEY	"	
15507	I JUST WANT TO MAKE LOVE	"	
15525	YOU DON'T LOVE ME	"	
15526	YOU CAN'T JUDGE A BOOK	"	
15527	SAD HOURS	"	

LITTLE WALTER (probably from above session)
V/hca with Bo Diddley-g, ??-b, ??-d

?	FEEL SO BAD	UNIS	Tape
?	MAKE IT ALRIGHT	"	"

MUDDY WATERS c April 1967
V, g (*) with prob LW-hca, PeeWee Madison, Sam Lawhorn-gs, Otis Spann-p, Sonny Wimberley- bs, Willie Smith-dms, Pinetop Perkins-or (+)

15655	ITS ALL OVER *	UNIS	TCMMW
15656	COUNTY JAIL	"	"
15657	TWO STEPS FORWARD +	"	"
15658	BLIND MAN +	"	"

MUDDY WATERS c June 1967
V with prob LW-hca, Spann-p, Pee Wee Madison, Sam Lawhorn-gs, Ernest Johnson-b, Willie Smith??-d

15840	FIND YOURSELF ANOTHER FOOL	UNIS	TCMMW
15841	KINFOLK'S BLUES	"	"

AMERICAN FOLK BLUES FESTIVAL 1967
LW-hca with Hound Dog Taylor-g, Dillard Crume-b, Odie Payne-d, Koko Taylor-V

Stockholm Sweden 10/6/67 — — — Tape

	OH BABY	Little Walter	
	I WONDER WHY	Koko Taylor	

Helsinki Finland 10/12/67 – Thursday — — — Tape

	SCUFFLIN'	Houndog/Walter	
	WILD ABOUT YOU	Houndog Taylor	
	BLUES WITH A FEELING	Little Walter	
	MY BABE "		

West Berlin 10/15/67—Sunday

——	THE SKY IS CRYING	Hound Dog Taylor	Optimism CD 2070
——	YOU'RE SO FINE	Little Walter	"
——	WANG DANG DOODLE	KoKo Taylor	
——	WHAT KIND OF MAN IS THIS	"	

Koln, Germany 10/16 (?)/67—Monday

	SLOW INSTRUMENTAL	Houndog/Walter	Tape
	SHAKE YOUR MONEY MAKER	Houndog Taylor	"

Unkown locations on AFBF tour October 1967

	CHROMATIC INSTRUMENTAL	Little Walter	Tape
	YOU SO FINE (instrumental)	"	"
	WALTER'S JUMP	"	"
	MEAN OLD WORLD	"	"

SAM LAY DEMO winter 1967–68
V/d with LW-hca, Louis Myers/Eddie Taylor-gs, Ernest Johnson-b

——	TROUBLE NO MORE	L&H Lounge	Demo Tape
——	19 YEARS OLD	"	"
——	MY BABE	"	"
——	CAN'T BE SATISFIED (inc)		

SOURCE ABBREVIATION GUIDE

BDHB	Bo Diddley His Best	Chess CD 9373
BoLW	Best Of Little Walter	Chess CD 9192
BoLW2	Best Of Little Walter Vol 2	Chess CD 9292
BV6	Blues Volume 6	Chess CD 9330
BWF	Blues With A Feeling	Chess CD 2–9357
BWoLW	Blues World of Little Walter	Delmark CD 648
CBOX	Chess Blues Box	Chess CD 4–9340
CB47	Chicago Boogie 1947	Pvine CD 1888
CBG	Chess Blues Guitar Chess	CD 2–9393
CBP	Chicago Blues Piano-ology	Pvine LP 6022
CS	The Chess Story 1947–75	MCA 380 596-2
CTB	Confessing The Blues	Chess CD 9366
DIBM	Devil Is A Busy Man (Sunnyland Slim)	Official 6043
DDM	Drop Down Mama	Chess CD 93002
DHH	Down Home Harp	Testament CD 6011
DHS	Down Home Slide	Testament CD 6009
ELW	Essential Little Walter	Chess CD 2–9342
ERB	Early Rhythm & Blues 1949	Biograph CD 124
GEN1	Genesis Box Set 1	Eng Chess 6641047
GEN3	Genesis Box Set 3	Eng Chess 6641174
HTSYG	Hate To See You Go	Chess CD 9321
JRCCR	Jimmy Rogers Complete Chess Recordings	Chess CD2–9372
JY&F	Johnny Young and Friends	Testament CD 5010
LITWC	Live In The Windy City (Rush/LW)	Col River CD 120009
LRDB2	LeRoi De Blues Vol II	————
LRDB3	LeRoi De Blues Vol III	————
MB	Mandolin Blues	Testament CD 6004
MBOX	Muddy Waters Chess Box	Chess CD 3–80002
MRFB	More Real Folk Blues	Chess CD 9278
MWHB	Muddy Waters His Best 1947–55	Chess CD 9370
OMM	One More Mile (Muddy Waters)	Chess CD 2–9348
OR&BG	Otis Rush/Buddy Guy	Flyright LP 594
RDBX5	Little Walter Box	Charley Red Box 3
RDBX3	Muddy Waters Box	Charley Red Box 5
RN&HS	Robert Nighthawk & Houston Stackhouse	Testament CD 5010
RS	Rolling Stone	Chess LP 8202
RS:GA	Rolling Stone: Golden Anniversary	Chess CD 301–2
R&U	Rare & Unissued	Chess CD 9180
TCMMW	They Call Me Muddy Waters	Chess CD 9299
TNM	Trouble No More	Chess CD 9291
TCR	The Classic Recordings—(Otis Rush)	Charly LP 1107
WMS	Whose Muddy Shoes—(Brim/James)	Chess CD 9114

sources and notes

Unpublished Interviews and Correspondence

Billy Boy Arnold, interview by Scott Dirks, July 30, 1998; Latelle Barton, interview by Tony Glover, December 7, 2000; Pierre G. T. Beauregard IV, conversation with Ward Gaines, February 2001; Carey Bell, interview by Ward Gaines, March 21, 1998; Elvin Bishop, interview by Tony Glover, October 3, 1997; Rosa (Jacobs) Brown, interviewed by Tony Glover February 10, 1999; Joe Lee Bush, interview by Ward Gaines, December 7, 1997; Paul Butterfield, conversations with Tony Glover, c. 1963; Joe Carter, conversation with Scott Dirks, c. 1991; Marshall Chess, interview by Ward Gaines, October 7, 1998; Francis Clay, interview by Ward Gaines, October 7, 1997; James Cotton, unpublished interview by Robert Gordon, 1998; Norman Dayron, interview by Ward Gaines, December 16, 1996; James DeShay, interview by Michelle DeShay and Ward Gaines, August 1998; Gary Duncan, interview by Ward Gaines, September 1997; Honeyboy Edwards, interviews by Scott Dirks October 2, 1999 and Ward Gaines, June 28, 1997; David Freiberg, interview by Ward Gaines, September 1997; Fred Glaser, interview by Tony Glover, August 30, 1998; John Goddard, correspondence with Ward Gaines, February 1, 2001; Nick Gravenites, interview by Ward Gaines, October 1, 1997; Bernie Hayes, interview by Ward Gaines, September 5, 2000; Bob Hall, correspondence with Scott Dirks, November 1999; Gabriel Hearns, interview with Ward Gaines, October 7, 2000; Waver (Glascock) Humphries, interview and correspondence with Tony Glover, March 1999, February 2000, and March 2000; Little Walter [Jacobs] and Louis Myers, interview by Bill Lindemann, early 1968, unedited transcript by Scott Dirks; Breton Littlehales, correspondence with Ward Gaines, February 1, 2001; Mark Kazinoff, interview by Ward Gaines, June 14, 1999; Bob Koester, interview by Scott Dirks, February 19, 1999; Sam Lay, interviews by Tony Glover October 9, 1997 and Scott Dirks April 17, 1998; Samuel R. Leveige, interviewed by Tony Glover April 25, 2000; Jim Lombardi, interview by Ward Gaines, November 16, 1998; Bob Margolin, interview by Tony Glover, May 10, 2000; Lillian (Jacobs) Marshall, interviewed by Scott Dirks, April 29, 1992; John "Pops" McFarlane, interview by Tony Glover, November 14, 1999; Charles Musselwhite, interview by Tony Glover, December 19, 1997; Dave Myers, interviews by Bill Greensmith, October 1995, Robert Gordon, Spring 1998, and Scott Dirks, October 6, 2000; Paul Oliver, unpublished interview by Robert Gordon, n.d.; Ron Polte, interview by Ward Gaines, September 24, 1997; Mark Power, interview by Ward Gaines, June 14, 1999; Big Guitar Red, interview by Ward Gaines, April 22, 1998; Freddie Robinson (aka Abu Talib), interview by Scott Dirks, August 20, 2000; Jimmie Lee Robinson, interviews by Scott Dirks March & May 1998, August 10, 2000; Mattie Rollins, interview by Scott Dirks, August 28, 1998; Bobby Rush, interview by Karen Hanson, 1998; Jessie Mae Sampson, interview by Tony Glover January 24, 2000; Paul Shapiro, interview by Ward Gaines, April 1, 1999; Hugh Smith, interview by Ward Gaines, March 23, 1999; Luther Tucker, unpublished interview by Bob Corritore, 1983; Marguerite (Glascock) Wallace, interview by Scott Dirks July 31, 1998; Bill

Warren, interview by Scott Dirks, April 10, 1998; Frank Weston, interview by Ward Gaines, April 28, 1999; Armilee Thompson Williams, interview by Scott Dirks, June 21, 2000; Jody Williams, interview by Scott Dirks, October 17, 2000; Sylvia (Glascock) Williams. interview by Tony Glover January 23, 2000; Val Wilmer, interview by Ward Gaines, March 12, 1999.

Session transcripts are from session tapes from the MCA/Universal Music Group vaults.

Notes
All quotes are from authors' interviews, except as noted below. The text page number for each note is given in bold.

Chapter 1: Night Train
2: "There was a four corner road." Tisserand (1998), p. 41.

2: "using French words within." Spitzer (1979), pp. 2–3.

2: "a person of French." Grau (1989), p. iv.

2: "The farm of Louis Leveige on Duprines Road": Residents then didn't know the lane was named, but the road was well-populated by members of the Leveige clan. The next two dwellings listed were home to Louis' brother Sidney and his father Philogene, a cousin lived a couple of doors the other way. In fact, present-day maps now show the town even has a Leveige Street.

6: "I just liked the sound of it." Wilmer (1964).

10: "It was with a guy called Toopsie.": Marguerite may be thinking of another Jordan tune. The riff that later became "Night Train" was a Duke Ellington composition, and not released until 1947 on Musicraft. It was Part Two of "Happy Go Lucky Local," itself part of a southern suite of Ellington's. It was first titled "Night Train" on a November 1951 recording by Jimmy Forrest, an Ellington alumnus. Wynonie Harris with Lucky Millender's orchestra had a vocal version some six months later, and it was a hit again for Earl Bostic in 1957. Perhaps the tune might have been Jordan's instrumental "Saxa-Woogie." Recorded in April 1941, the timing would be about right.

Chapter 2: Good Evenin' Everybody
16: "There was more [musicians] in Helena." Guida and Black (1977), p. 19.

16: "It seems that there was music everywhere." Harvey (1986), p. 25.

18: "down to Helena Crossing . . ." Harvey (1986), p. 26.

19: "Honeyboy Edwards used to come." Dunas (1999), p. 85.

20: "All the whiskey I could drink." O'Neal and Greensmith (1973), p. 12.

20: "Just a kid." Hoffman (1995), p. 18.

21: "I went looking for Little Walter," Edwards (1997), p. 147.

21: "During the wartime." Edwards (1970), p. 21.

Chapter 3: Wonder Harmonica King
24: "Big Walter would tell him." O'Neal and Greenfield, p. 20.

24: "I heard a harp player" and following quotes from Honeyboy Edwards, Edwards (1997), pp. 148–50.

26: "Lord I'm talkin about the wagon": "Maxwell Street Blues" by Papa Charlie Jackson, Paramount 12320, September 1925, transcribed by Guido van Rijn, 15 April 1998 from The Papa Charlie Jackson Home page (www.openair.org/maxwell/papaj.html).

27: "built out of pasteboard boxes." Moon (1999), p. 36.

28: "On the stands were dumped." Motley (1950), p. 91.

28: "I'd heard about Jewtown." Berkow (1977), p. 426.

30: "They'd have a stack of cards." O'Neal (1974), p. 31.

31: "At night we'd have." O'Brien (1983), p. 11.

31: "Maybe this Sunday." Brisbin (1996), p. 34.

32: "suburban places." Titon (1969), p. 9.

33: "Kind of sloppy." O'Neal, Wisner & Nelson (1995), p. 14.

35: "I was talking to Muddy." Voce (1972), p. 6.

Chapter 4: I Just Keep Loving Her

37: "I slept in a little bedroom." Berkow (1977), p. 103.

38: "After I start singing." Jones (1964b), p. 8.

39: "Jewtown was Sonny Boy's . . ." Townsend and Greensmith (1999), pp. 91–2.

39: "We'd go from one club to the other." Rowe (1974), p. 14.

39: "He had a record shop." O'Brien (1983), pp. 11–12.

42: "That's when him and Johnny Young." Brisbin (1996), p. 36.

42: "Walter vanished off the scene." O'Neal and Greensmith (1973), p. 13.

44: "We'd go on over." O'Neal and Greensmith (1973), p. 13.

44: "We started playing for him." O'Neal (1980), p. 55.

45: "The only problem." O'Neal and Greensmith (1973), p. 13.

45: "Little Walter was a good little hustler." Rooney (1971), p. 112.

47: "We kept that Mississippi sound," Welding (1964), pp. 19–20.

48: "On the harp, well, I heard them all." Jones (1964b), p. 8.

48: "Sonny Boy used to go by Sunnyland's." Brisbin (1998), p. 32.

Chapter 5: Ebony Boogie

54: "No, I don't want you." Rowe (1977), p. 6.

54: Junior's older sister. O'Neal (1995), p. 18.

55: "I went out there and started." Ulrey (1992), p. 9.

56: "Memphis Minnie, Tampa Red and Memphis Slim." White (mid-'70s).

57: "You would find him acting." Palmer (1981), pp. 162–63.

58: "That was a lot of fun." O'Neal and Greensmith (1973), p. 12.

60: "I'd be out there playing." Rowe (1974).

60: "I had a heck of a time." O'Neal and van Singel (1985), p. 33.

60: "we had to try to." White (mid-'70s).

61: "Muddy got himself in pretty." Rowe (1975), p. 75.

65: "Walter was so great." Margolin (1995), p. 13.

66: "My drummer couldn't." Palmer (1981), pp. 164–65.

67: "was where comedians." Pruter (1996), p. 237.

67: "really a beautiful." Rowe (1977), p. 10.

69: "All he [Chess] wanted to do was just." O'Brien (1984), p. 8.

Chapter 6: "Juke"

75: "Snooky had this thing." O'Neal and Greensmith (1973), p. 15.

75: ". . . it was a good thing." O'Neal (1995), p. 16.

76: "Walter knew about two, three verses." Townsley (1994), p. 25.

77: "Blues has always been." Golkin (1989), p. 29.

79: Jimmy Rogers later suggested. Brisbin (1997b), p. 25.

79: "I thought you brought it witcha." Palmer (1981), p. 211.

79: In Wells's version. O'Neal (1995), p. 16.

79: "Hey Walter." Townsley (1994), p. 26.

80: "that ended that . . ." Plumpp & Ulrey (1992), pp. 34–35.

80: "Drove around and put placards up." Edwards (1997), p. 156.

81: "He was sleeping on crap tables . . ." O'Neal (1974), p. 31.

81: "When Little Walter quit me." Margolin (1995), p. 15.

81: "Well, after Little Walter." O'Neal and Van Singel (1985), p. 36.

81: "After Little Walter." Rooney (1971), p. 122.

82: "If a harmonica player." Walters, Garman and Matthews (1974), p. 18.

87: "Fresh out." Lieser (1973), p. 29.

87: "He come over there in the daytime." Brisbin (1997a), p. 30.

87: "He had just went to the Apollo." Rowe (1977), p. 10.

Chapter 7: Diamonds and Cadillac Cars

94: ". . . Fess, the professor." Greensmith (1976), p. 11.

94: "They have a different." O'Neal and Van Singel (1978), p. 22.

95: "We was whipping it on 'em strong." Greensmith (1976), p. 11.

96: "He loved that corn." Nelson (1994), p. 10.

99: According to Brim. Cushing (c. 1990s)

105: Albert Ayler anecdotes. Wilmer (1977), pp. 97–98.

110: "Every time he said four or five." Nicholson (1998), p. 30.

112: "I said, 'Man you.'" Greensmith (1976), p. 11.

112: "Me and Snooky and Moody." O'Brien (1984), p. 9.

Chapter 8: You Gonna Miss Me When I'm Gone

115: "Louis, he stayed with Walter." Moon (1998), p. 40.

115: "I was like a father." Hoffmann (1995), p. 26.

122: "Don't rehearse." Margolin (1995), p. 13.

125: ". . . going door to door." Smothers (1978), p 18.

125: ". . . We all used to play." Birnbaum (2000), p. 206.

125: "I'd been knowing him." O'Neal and Van Singel (1985), p. 35.

125: "He was the best harp." Rowe (1975), p. 147.

127: "Chess was a funny guy." Dixon (1989), p. 193.

130: "That was when he recorded." Arentson (1994), p. 40.

131: "Muddy couldn't play." Brisbin (1997), p. 24.

Chapter 9: Roller Coaster

134: ". . . people would come up." Field (1993), p. 14.

135: "I made 'Last Night'." Leadbitter (1971), p. 21–2.

136: "He was on the bandstand." Brisbin (1997a), p. 33.

140: "We couldn't find Tucker." Hoffman (1995), p. 26.

141: "I had been trying." Dixon (1989), p. 88.

142: "I went in and listened." Lee and Nelson (1992), pp. 36–7.

144: "Leonard kept telling Bo." Aldin (1994), p. 26.

145: "They went round to Bo's house." Rowe and Greensmith (1978), p. 21.

147: "Bo started to play." Rowe and Greensmith (1978), p. 21.

148: "'If that was me." Rowe and Greensmith (1978), p. 21.

150: ". . . it's a new." Lerner (1955).

152: "Well, I'll tell you one thing." Rowe and Greensmith (1978), p. 21.

152: "this is Chicago" Gravenities (1996), p. 15.

152: "He was used to hearing." Greensmith (1976), p. 9.

Chapter 10: I've Had My Fun

162: "You can't say that Walter." Cohodas (2000), p. 127.

162: Honeyboy Edwards and his wife. Edwards (1997), p. 194.

172: "Me and [harp player] Raful Neal." Darwen (1989), p. 23.

172: "I got some gigs here." Brisbin (1993b), p. 27.

172: ". . . beat them out of . . ." Moon (1966), p. 30.

174: "Walter just took it." Moon (1996), p. 30.

176: "I've got a daughter." Fifth Division Appellate Court Order, case #1–98–0766, March 31, 1999.

Chapter 11: Crazy Mixed Up World

178: "Him and his woman." Hoffman (1995), p. 26.

183: "A harmonica player . . ." O'Neal and Greensmith (1973), p. 19.

184: "We used to go by Muddy's." Dahl (1999), p. 53.

188: "His best work." Dahl (1999), p. 53.

192: "Walter had a thing going." Dahl (1999), p. 53.

192: "That killed his spirit." Dahl (1999), p. 53.

197: "When Little Walter wasn't." Semler (1991), p. 7.

200: "Shit, you know I." DeKoster (1992), p. 21.

200: "There was a place." Greensmith (1995), p. 7.

Chapter 12: I Ain't Broke, I'm Badly Bent

203: In the fall of 1959, Demetre and Chauvard (1995), pp. 126–8.

204: "Walter was equally an innovator." Demtre (1991), pp. 6–7.

212: "I had Little Walter on harp." Oliver (1965), p. 151.

215: "My first trip on the road." Darwen (1990), p. 5.

222: "Sonny Boy, he blow Walter." Greensmith (1976), p. 10.

222: Chuck Herron was an aspiring drummer. Paulus (1998), p. 11–12.

223: "'Course his leg was broke." Brisbin (1993a), p. 12.

Chapter 13: Back in the Alley

226: ". . . a spine chilling." Broven (1963), p. 15.

226: ". . . told us that Little Walter." Leadbitter (1963).

227: "My favorite blues singer." Welding (1964).

227: "Chuck Berry, me, Little Walter." Ward (1983), p. 25.

228: One afternoon Walter stopped photographer Ray Flerlage. Flerlage (2000), p. 9.

228: "... despite some good tunes." Kent (1964), p. 8.

229: "I want you to come down here." O'Neal (1995), p. 21.

230: "I was in the booth singing." Guy and Wilcock (1993), p. 58.

231: "... although he has featured." Jones (1964a), n.p.

231: "Memphis didn't tell me." Jones (1964b), p. 8.

231: "We got drunk together." Wilmer (1989), p. 316.

231: "There are some good musicians." Wilmer (1964), p. 316.

232: "When I met him." Broven (1964a), p. 7.

232: "... the proceedings were informal." Jones (1984), p. 11.

233: "The evening declined." Radcliffe (1964), p. 10.

233: "... really awful." Broven (1964b), p. 7.

236: "... with unnerving instinct." Harper (2000), p. 71.

236: "... did not even begin." Radcliffe (1964), p. 10.

237: "Eventually a grey Ford." McLagen (2000), p. 40–2.

238: "He was great at." Brunning (1986), p. 173.

239: "The first time I saw Little Walter." Leadbitter (1968).

239: "Man, after all one time." O'Brien (1977), p. 16.

240: "his playing was incoherent." Tillman (1969b), p. 14.

243: "Johnny Pepper opened." Dahl (2000), p. 30.

Chapter 14: Mean Old World

252: "I was responsible." Dwyer (1970), p. 11.

255: "Otis Rush still has." Metheral (1967), p. 11.

255: "I remember once he." Edwards (1997), p. 194.

259: "harmonica and vocal." Stenbeck (1968), p. 15.

261: "Little Walter and Hound Dog." Van Voss (1968), p. 7.

262: "She didn't know what the devil." O'Neal and Cuniff (1970–71), p. 4.

262: "Them damn country." Tillman (1969a), p. 11.

263: "... I stared at the back." Rowe (1967), p. 20.

263: "Little Walter was a very." Scorsese (1995).

271: "One always hopes." Sturesson (1968), p. 40.

271: "... Just before Little Walter." Burke, Briggs, and Atherton (1990).

272: "Just before he got killed." Brisbin (1997a), p. 33.

272: "We were still hanging out." O'Neal (1995), p. 20.

272: "... no-good woman." Edwards (1997), pp. 194–5.

273: "Little Walter was a loner." Paulus (1998), p. 12.

Epilogue

280: On March 10, 1997. Fifth Division Appellate Court Records, No. 1–98–0766.
"Little Walter, that's it." Race (1972), p. 8.

bibliography

Aldin, Mary Katherine (1994). "I Had No Intention of Stopping—Billy Boy Arnold." *Living Blues* 113, February.

Arentson, Robert M. (1994). "Sure I Have A Dream—Eddie Burks." *Living Blues* 117, October.

Berkow, Ira (1977). *Maxwell Street: Survival in a Bazaar*. New York: Doubleday.

Bird, Christiane (1994). *The Jazz and Blues Lover's Guide to the US*, 2nd ed. New York: Grove Press.

Birnbaum, Larry (2000). "Jody Williams." In *Rollin' and Tumblin': The Postwar Blues Guitarists*, ed. by Jas Obrecht. San Francisco: Backbeat Books.

Brisbin, John Anthony (1993a). "Willie Kent: Learn to Follow . . . and Then to Lead." *Living Blues* 108, April.

——— (1993b). "Lovie Lee." *Living Blues 110*, August.

——— (1996). "Being Regular With The People—Uncle Johnny Williams." *Living Blues* 127, June.

——— (1997a). "Sleepy Otis Hunt." *Living Blues* 134, July.

——— (1997b). "Jimmy Rogers." *Living Blues* 135, September.

——— (1998 Spring). "Snooky Prior's Harp Is Definitely Unplugged." *King Biscuit Times*, 8(2).

Broven, John (1964a). "Blues With a Feeling." *Blues Unlimited*, October.

——— (1964b). "Little Walter at Brighton." *Blues Unlimited*, October.

——— (1963). "New Little Walter Single." *Blues Unlimited* 4, August.

Brown, Ron, Liner Notes to *GASPARD/LACHNEY/J.BERTRAND CD* (Yazoo 2042).

Brunning, Bob (1986). *Blues: The British Connection*. Poole, U.K.: Blanford.

Burke, Tony, Keith Briggs, and Mike Atherton (1990). "Buddy's Second Coming." *Blues & Rhythm*, September.

Cohodas, Nadine (2000). *Spinning Blues Into Gold: The Chess brothers and the legendary Chess Records*. New York: St Martin's Press.

Cushing, Steve (c. 1990s). "John Brim." Radio interview.

Dahl, Bill (1999). "Abu Talib interview." *Living Blues*, March.

——— (2000). "The Soulful Saxophone of Gene 'Daddy G' Barge." *Living Blues* 151, May–June.

Darwen, Norman (1989). "Up In Chicago," *Blues & Rhythm*, May.

——— (1990). "We Gotta Learn You How to Chop that Thing Up." *Blues & Rhythm*, August.

DeKoster, Jim (1992). "Waterloo Blues—Louis McTizic." *Living Blues* 105, September/October.

Demetre, Jacques (1991). "Memories of Little Walter." *Soul Bag* 123, Summer (Original in French; trans. Ward Gaines).

Demetre, Jacques and Marcel Chauvard (1995). *Land of the Blues*. Paris: Clarb Publishers.

Dixon, Willie, with Down Snowden (1989). *I Am the Blues*. New York: Da Capo.

Dunas, Jeff (1999). *State of the Blues*. New York: Aperture Press.

Dwyer, Bill. (1970). "Interview with Bo Diddley." *Blues Unlimited* 72.

Edwards, David Honeyboy (1970). "*Living Blues* Interview." *Living Blues* 4, Winter.

——— (1997). *The World Don't Owe Me Nothing: The Life and Times of Delta Bluesman Honeyboy Edwards*. Chicago, IL: Chicago Review Press.

Field, Kim (1993). *Harmonicas, Harps and Heavy Breathers*. New York: Simon & Schuster.

Flerlage, Ray (2000). *Chicago Blues*. Toronto: ECW Press.

Golkin, Pete (1989). "Blacks, Whites & Blues." *Living Blues* 88, September/October.

Grau, Shirley Ann (1989). "Introduction." In George Washington Cable, *Old Creole Days*. New York: Signet Classics.

Gravenities, Nick (1996) "Bad Talking Bluesman." *Blues Revue* No. 21, Feb/Mar.

Greensmith, Bill (1976). "Just Whaling—Louis Myers." *Blues Unlimited*, January.

——— (1979). "Cotton in Your Ear." *Blues Unlimited*, July.

——— (1995). "Little Cooper." *Blues & Rhythm*, April.

Guida, Louis and William Black (1977). "Cedell Davis Interview." *Living Blues* 32, May–June.

Guy, Buddy, and Donald Wilcock (1993). *Damn Right, I've Got the Blues*. San Francisco: Woodford Books.

Harper, Colin (2000). "Light and Shade." *Mojo*, July.

Harvey, Hank (1986). "Growing Up With The Blues." *Living Blues* 71, Summer.

Hoffman, Larry (1995). "Robert Lockwood Jr." *Living Blues* 121, June.

Jones, Max (1964a). "Little Walter: The Man Who Sparked a Revolution." *Melody Maker*, September 12.

——— (1964b). "Britain Takes Little Walter By Surprise." *Melody Maker*, September 26.

——— (1984). "All Night Long." *Melody Maker*, September 26.

Kent, Don (1964). "Blues At Chicago University." *Blues Unlimited* 13, July.

Leadbitter, Mike (1963). "Joe Williams Comments." *Blues Unlimited*, December.

——— (1965). "Little Walter." *Blues Unlimited*, January.

——— (1968). "Letter to the Editor." *Blues Unlimited*, April.

——— (1971). *Nothing But the Blues*. London: Hanover Books.

Lee, Peter and David Nelson (1992). "Right Off the Cottonfield—Willie Foster." *Living Blues* 106, November/December.

Lerner, Leonard (1955). "Rock and Roll Revue Does That At State." *Boston Daily Globe*, May 21.

Lieser, Willie (1973). "Down In The Alley." *Blues Unlimited* 100, April.

Margolin, Bob (1995). "Can't Be Satisfied." *Blues Review*, December.

McLagen, Ian (2000). *All the Rage*. New York: Billboard.

Metheral, Merv (1967). "Blues News Canada." *Blues Unlimited*, May.

Moon, D. Thomas (1999). "Riding the Reefers and the Rods." *Living Blues*, May.

——— (1966). "The Lonely Traveler—Jimmie Lee Robinson." *Blues Revue*, April.

——— (1998). "Somebody Has to Live It First—Dave Myers." *Living Blues* 142, November.

Motley, Willard (1950). *Knock on Any Door*. New York: Signet.

Nelson, David (1994). "I Got to Sing the Blues—Jerry McCain." *Living Blues* 113, February.

Nicholson, Bob (1998). "Willie Foster." *Juke Blues* 40, Spring.

O'Brien, Justin (1977). "Lee Jackson: All Around Man." *Living Blues* 34, September/October.

——— (1983). "The Dark Road Of Floyd Jones." *Living Blues* 58, Winter.

——— (1984). "The Dark Road Of Floyd Jones, Pt. 2." *Living Blues* 59, Spring.

Oliver, Paul (1965). *Conversation with the Blues*. New York: Horizon Press.

O'Neal, Jim (1974). Houston Stackhouse interview. *Living Blues* 17, Summer.

——— (1980). "Blue Smitty: Chicago Blues Part 2." *Living Blues* 45/46, Spring.

——— (1995). "Junior Wells." *Living Blues* 119, February.

O'Neal, Jim and Bill Greensmith (1973). "Jimmy Rogers." *Living Blues* 14, Autumn.

O'Neal, Jim and Amy van Singel (1985). "Muddy Waters interview." *Living Blues* 64, March/April.

——— (1978). "Eddie Boyd interview, Pt. 2." *Living Blues* 36, January/February.

O'Neal, Jim and R. T. Cuniff (1970–71). "Hound Dog Taylor." *Living Blues* 1(4).

O'Neal, Jim, Steve Wisner, and David Nelson (1995). "I Started the Big Noise Around Chicago." *Living Blues* 123, September.

Palmer, Robert (1981). *Deep Blues*. New York: Viking.

Paulus, George (1998). "Late Hours with Little Walter." *Blues & Rhythm*, October.

Plumpp, Sterling and Lois Ulrey (1992). "Louis Myers." *Magic Blues* 4.

Pruter, Robert (1996). *Doo Wop: The Chicago Scene*. Champaign, IL: University of Illinois Press.

Race, Wes (1972) "Hound Dog Taylor." *Blues Unlimited* 94, September.

Radcliffe, Charles (1964). "Little Walter on Tour." *Blues Unlimited*, November.

Rooney, James (1971). *Bossmen*. New York: Dial Press.

Rowe, Mike (1967). "All Time Low." *Blues Unlimited* 48, December.

——— (1974). Liner notes. *Genesis, Volume Three: Sweet Home Chicago*. Chess UK 6641174.

——— (1975). *Chicago Breakdown*. New York: Drake Publishers.

——— (1977). "I Was Really Dedicated—Billy Boy Arnold, Part II." *Living Blues* No. 35, November/December.

Rowe, Mike and Bill Greensmith (1978). "I Was Really Dedicated, Part III—Billy Boy Arnold" *Living Blues* 36, January/February.

Scorsese, Martin (1995). *Nothing But The Blues*. Video. From the PBS series, "In The Spotlight." New York: Thirteen/WNET & Cappa Productions Inc., in association with Reprise Records.

Semler, Derrick (1991). "J. D. Nicholson and the West Coast Blues." *Blues and Rhythm*, September.

Smothers, Otis "Big Smokey" (1978). *Living Blues* 37, Apr/May.

Spitzer, Nick (1979). "Zodico: Louisiana's Black Creole Music" *Sing Out!* 27(6).

Stenbeck, Lennart (1968). *Orkesterjournalen* #11, Spring.

Sturesson, Mats (1968). "Blues Legends—Little Walter." *Jefferson* 58, Spring. Original in Swedish; trans. by Robert Palinic.

Tillman, Keith (1969a). "Little Walter: A Reminiscence." *Blues Unlimited*, April.

——— (1969b). "Bringing It to Jerome." *Blues Unlimited* 63, June.

Tisserand, Michael (1998). *The Kingdom of Zydeco*. New York: Arcade Publishing.

Titon, Jeff (1969). "Calling All Cows." *Blues Unlimited*, April.

Townsend, Henry and Bill Greensmith (1999). *A Blues Life*. Champaign: University of Illinois Press.

Townsley, Tom (1994). "Jimmy Rogers/Dave Myers." *Blues Revue*, Fall.

Ulrey, Lois (1992). "Interview with Junior Wells." *Magic Blues* #4.

Van Voss, A. J. Heerma (1968). "Blueszangers In De Rijndelta." *Jazz Wereld*, January. Trans. by Bert van Oortmarssen.

Voce, Frank (1972). Jimmy Rogers, interview, *Blues Unlimited*, September.

Walters, David, Lawrence Garman, and John Matthews (1974). "Jimmy Rogers." *Blues Unlimited*, December.

Ward, Ed (1983). *Michael Bloomfield: The Rise and Fall of an American Guitar Hero*. New York: Cherry Lane.

Waterhouse, Jon and David Nelson (1992). "Cash McCall interview." *Living Blues* 103, May/June.

Way, Bert (1997). "Maxwell Street Beat," Preserve Maxwell Street website (http://www.openair.org/maxwell/pway.html), July 27th.

Welding, Pete. "Muddy Waters—Last King Of The South Side?" *Downbeat*, Oct. 8.

———— (1964). "Interview with John Lee Hooker." *Nothing But the Blues*, edited by Mike Leadbitter. London: Hanover Books.

White, Ray Wilding (mid-'70s). "Interview with Jimmy Rogers." Radio broadcast, WFMT-FM,
Chicago.

Wilmer, Val (1964). "Little Walter Blows In." *Jazzbeat*, Oct.

———— (1977). *As Serious As Your Life*. London: Allison & Busby.

———— (1989). *Mama Said There'd Be Days Like This: My Life in the Jazz World*. London: Women's
Press.

index

the authors

Tony Glover has been a professional musician and writer since 1962. He is the author of a best-selling guide to playing the blues harmonica, in continuous print for over four decades. He has performed in a legendary blues trio with "Spider" John Koerner and Dave Ray off and on since the 1960s. He lives in St. Paul, Minnesota.

Scott Dirks has written for blues magazines, hosted blues radio, produced blues recordings, and performed in blues bands over the last twenty years. He lives outside of Chicago, Illinois.

Ward Gaines is a graphic designer, art restorer, and professional musician, and is a noted writer and researcher on the blues. He lives in Washington, D.C.